'One of the best books I've seen on the financial crisis. It is engagingly written and stands out for its precision and exceptional analytical depth.'
Jean-Claude Trichet, President, European Central Bank

'An important German economist has written a sharply perceptive, hard-hitting book about the deep origins of the crisis in institutional and even cultural laxity. Seeing events in the US from abroad provides Hans-Werner Sinn with a perspective worthy of Jonathan Swift. Even where I agreed with him, I learned something. In the places where I disagreed, I was forced to think things out anew. Try it.'
Robert Solow, Professor of Economics, MIT and Nobel Laureate in Economics

'Once again Hans-Werner Sinn has shown how much can be learned by combining simple but rigorous economics with a mastery of the facts. Nowhere else can you find such a clearly reasoned and comprehensive analysis of the global financial crisis and what to do about it.'
Peter Howitt, Professor of Economics, Brown University

'I strongly recommend this book to anyone concerned as it will become a bible in the field of money and banking in a highly integrated global economy. It analyses comprehensively and meticulously the recent (and still non-ending) financial upheaval that engulfed the world, and finds that fundamental causes of the upheaval lie in failure in properly regulating limited liability and irresponsible securitizations (that were based on the assumption of stochastically independent risks), all of which induced rational investors to take socially excessive risks. To establish a stable world finance system, the author proposes various unique regulatory reforms mainly aimed at strengthening the principle of liability. Well-organized presentations and clear expositions make the book accessible to a wide audience, despite its highly sophisticated contents.'
Hirofumi Shibata, Professor of Finance, Osaka University

'An excellent and balanced explanation of the emergence of a highly lever-aged international financial system and its downfall.'
Assar Lindbeck, Professor of the Institute for International Economic Studies, University of Stockholm and Former Member of the Nobel Committee

'This book is as gripping as a thriller and provides meticulous analysis instead of moralizing appeals. Recommended for everyone who wishes to understand the financial crisis and its consequences.'

Clemens Fuest, Professor of Economics, Oxford University and Chairman of the German Finance Ministry Advisory Committee

'Fascinating reading, convincing arguments, clear presentation—exactly what you would expect from Hans-Werner Sinn.'

Otmar Issing, Professor of Economics, Würzburg University and former Chief Economist, European Central Bank

'Today's competing policy orthodoxies tend to treat the state and the market as alternative instruments for organizing economic life. But in the German liberal tradition, which has served that country so well for six decades, they are more often viewed as working together: the state creates and maintains an institutional framework within which the market then functions, either well or badly. This conception provides the unobtrusive but systematic basis of Hans-Werner Sinn's entertaining and provocative book. Even—perhaps particularly—those who do not fully share it should pay careful attention to his diagnoses of what has lately been ailing the international financial system, and to his prescriptions for its future.'

David Laidler, Professor of Economics, University of Western Ontario

'In this book Professor Sinn thinks hard about what caused the recent financial crisis and what to do about it. Highly recommended for readers who are similarly prepared to think hard about the causes of the crisis and the future of the financial system.'

Barry Eichengreen, Professor of Economics, University of California, Berkeley

'Professor Sinn's book, *Casino Capitalism*, ranks undoubtedly among the most thoughtful, best researched, and complete of all books written on the crisis. The book is addressed to the normal interested reader while explaining some of the most complex financial products and transactions that contributed to the global crisis. Sinn proves again his deep and subtle expertise in global financial economics, which has contributed to his ranking among the most reputable economists of our times.'

Andre Horovitz, Investment Banker

'Sinn's book is argumentative, against the overly simplistic explanations of the financial crisis—but also against those who do not draw any conclusions from it. I have read many books on the financial crisis. Sinn's book belongs amongst the two, three best ones.'
Bernd Ziesemer, Chief Editor, Handelsblatt

'Hans-Werner Sinn's *Casino Capitalism* has shaped the discussion of the financial crisis in Germany like nearly no other book. It is a must-read.'
Nikolaus Piper, Correspondent of Süddeutsche Zeitung and author of Die Große Rezession

'*Casino Capitalism* is a brilliant, factually rich analysis of the 2008 crisis and its possible consequences. It is a highly enjoyable read: warmly recommended not only for economists!'
Reint Gropp, Professor of Economics, Business School Oestrich-Winkel

'Even if I do not subscribe to some of Hans-Werner Sinn's labour market or social policy diagnoses, *Casino Capitalism* has convinced me of his high competence to explain the financial crisis in its entirety. He exposes the public finger-pointing, namely at individual misconduct, as a half-truth, uncovering in detail the systemic failures of the global financial system and convincingly substantiating how the state is not the saviour but itself part of the crisis. Reading the book impressed and inspired me deeply.'
Friedhelm Hengsbach, Professor of Christian Sciences and Economics and Social Ethics, Graduate School of Philosophy and Theology Sankt Georgen

'Hans-Werner Sinn's book still provides the best analysis of the crisis. It should be read in particular by those responsible for the regulatory framework and for regulating markets and institutions, but also by the so-called experts in the media and in courts of justice.'
Albrecht Schmidt, Former CEO of HVB (HypoVereinsbank)

'There are bad and good books on the financial crisis. And there is Hans-Werner Sinn's book, by far the best book on the subject—a book one wishes to have written oneself.'
Wolfgang Wiegard, Professor of Economics and Member of the German Council of Economic Advisors

'Hans-Werner Sinn has given us a convincing and unique analysis of how the US housing and banking crises of 2006–2007 led to the Black Friday stock market collapse of October 2008, and then to the 'Great Recession' from which we are now recovering. Sinn describes how artificial incentives for excess risk-taking (due to limited liability and encouraged by lax regulation and expected public sector rescue) resulted in catastrophically risky housing and banking decisions. He explains how the systemic collective failure in these sectors then infected the world economy. While Sinn's analysis will not be universally accepted, his arguments will have to be addressed by all serious discussions of the causes of, and cures for, this sad outcome.'

Robert Haveman, Professor of Economics, University of Wisconsin and former Editor of the American Economic Review

'The Great Recession may have subsided, but it has left us with many scars and, one may hope, many lessons. In his wide-ranging book, *Casino Capitalism*, Hans-Werner Sinn discusses how the limited liability corporation, once viewed as 'the greatest single discovery of modern times,' engendered a family of mutant offspring that nearly brought down the world financial system. Sinn's lucid description of the financial crisis, its antecedents and its aftermath provides a clear picture of what happened and sets the stage for the book's final chapter, a careful evaluation of a range of potential reforms.'

Alan Auerbach, Professor of Public Finance, University of California, Berkeley

'The book provides a most welcome contribution to the analysis and debate about the causes and consequences of the financial crisis, and about the policy prescriptions on how to get out of it. The book is well-written and contains a wealth of information. It is extremely insightful and benefits from having a—sometimes controversial—point of view. I could not put it down once I started to read it.'

Xavier Vives, Professor of Economics and Finance, IESE Business School, Barcelona and Former President of European Economic Association

'I started reading this book with the anticipation that I could not learn much new on the financial crisis. How wrong I was! The book has the suspense of a thriller and the inevitable outcome of a Greek tragedy. Given the bizarre incentives that guided financial operators, all the actors in the tragedy behaved rationally, while the music kept playing. Unfortunately their actions were leading to a disaster and there was no invisible hand capable of leading to a different outcome. Readers will appreciate the careful description of events and especially the European interpretation of some peculiarly American legal institutions. This book should be considered a must in the fast-growing literature on the financial crisis.'

Vito Tanzi, Professor of Economics and Former Head of the Fiscal Affairs Department, IMF

'The complexities, esoteric terminology, and minute-by-minute dramas of the financial crisis make it hard to grasp the fundamental economic forces that created it, and so also hard to know how to prevent the next one. In this book, Hans-Werner Sinn once again uses his unparalleled ability to isolate the basic economic principles that underlie difficult problems to do exactly that—and his penchant for the telling phrase to make his analysis as readable as it is persuasive. The result is an account of the crisis that is informative, deeply insightful and more than a little scary. Some of his recommendations for reform will be controversial. Policy makers, as usual, will do well to consider them all carefully.'

Michael Keen, Professor of Economics and Head of the Fiscal Affairs Department, IMF

CASINO CAPITALISM

CASINO
CAPITALISM

HOW THE FINANCIAL CRISIS CAME ABOUT
AND WHAT NEEDS TO BE DONE NOW

HANS-WERNER SINN

OXFORD
UNIVERSITY PRESS

OXFORD

UNIVERSITY PRESS

Great Clarendon Street, Oxford OX2 6DP

Oxford University Press is a department of the University of Oxford.
It furthers the University's objective of excellence in research, scholarship,
and education by publishing worldwide in

Oxford New York

Auckland Cape Town Dar es Salaam Hong Kong Karachi
Kuala Lumpur Madrid Melbourne Mexico City Nairobi
New Delhi Shanghai Taipei Toronto

With offices in

Argentina Austria Brazil Chile Czech Republic France Greece
Guatemala Hungary Italy Japan Poland Portugal Singapore
South Korea Switzerland Thailand Turkey Ukraine Vietnam

Oxford is a registered trade mark of Oxford University Press
in the UK and in certain other countries

Published in the United States
by Oxford University Press Inc., New York

© Hans-Werner Sinn 2010

The moral rights of the author have been asserted
Database right Oxford University Press (maker)

First published 2010

British Library Cataloguing in Publication Data
Data available

Library of Congress Cataloging in Publication Data
Data available

Typeset by SPI Publisher Services, Pondicherry, India
Printed in Great Britain
on acid-free paper by
Clays Ltd., St Ives Plc

ISBN 978–0–19–958827–5

1 3 5 7 9 10 8 6 4 2

When the night is darkest, dawn is nearest.

PREFACE

In 2008 and 2009 the world economy was caught up in the first true recession since the Second World War. The world financial system nearly collapsed, and only with gigantic rescue measures have governments been able to prevent the worst and stabilize the world. The crisis left deep wounds. It will take the world years to recover.

The private American mortgage securitization market, which had driven the US economy for many years, disappeared and so did the trust that a market economy needs for its financial contracts. In view of exploding US sovereign debt, China, the world's largest capital exporter, is now even shunning US government bonds and is turning to investments in Africa instead. A number of smaller countries like Iceland, Greece or Hungary are at the brink of insolvency, while others like Ireland, Spain, Portugal or Italy are seriously endangered. With brutal force international capital markets are realigning to find a new equilibrium: the business models of quite a number of countries, not only the USA, have to be readjusted or even reinvented. As unemployment and government debt are rising in most Western countries, scepticism about the capitalist system is spreading among the peoples of the world. No one knows where all of this will end.

People who have lost their homes, their jobs, and their money are frustrated and angry. They are looking for those to blame for the crisis. The media is spotlighting facets of the banking crisis by reporting on personal failures, greed, and examples of abysmal human character. Representatives of churches are also entering the debate with their own judgements, all the way to the moral abhorrence of interest-taking. One is almost reminded of the debates in the Middle Ages that led to the canonical prohibition of usury under Pope Innocent III.

Economists, in contrast, do not look at the problems in terms of individual failures, but rather in the light of systemic errors that must be rectified. If thousands or even millions of people behave erroneously, and if this collective erroneous behaviour results in a crisis, even the most interesting stories about individual wrong behaviour cannot yield any true insight. A target rate of return of 25 per cent for a bank may indeed be too high. The problem, however, is not primarily the lacking morals of the actors but the wrong incentives, generated by the legal concept of limited liability, combined with excessively lax regulation. Because banks are allowed to run their business on a minimum of equity, they should not be blamed for gambling with their customers' money in the international financial markets.

That people are greedy is deplorable but can hardly be changed. Greed is not limited to bank executives and managers. It is also seen in the faces of lottery players and many ordinary savers. Of course, whoever breaks the law out of greed must be punished. Bank executives who were guilty of breaking the law must be called to account for their deeds just like the banks' investment consultants who failed to tell their customers about the risks involved. But looking for individual guilt does not help explain the crisis nor does it help define new rules for the financial system that would protect the world against a repetition of the crisis.

A country's welfare is the result of the combined effects of individual human decisions that are essentially explained by the institutional rules of the game as represented by laws and decrees. These rules of the game must be analysed if the systemic errors are to be found and recommendations for a new organization of the economy are to be made.

This is not a question of the capitalist system as such, as some people think. One should not throw out the baby with the bathwater, for compared to the economic chaos and the dictatorship of the socialist systems even the financial crisis and its effects are relatively minor problems. Also, futile experiments of history have shown that there is no 'Third Way' between socialism and a market economy. A market economy is built on the principle of private property and free exchange, notwithstanding the fruitful role of governments within a market framework. If this principle is not respected, inefficiency, poverty, and despotism will result.

The crisis is a crisis of the American financial system that mutated into the 'by-product of a casino', to use a Keynesian term,[1] and has also found more and more imitators in Europe. It is the result of the inability of the international community of states to create a uniform regulatory system for banks and other financial institutions that would channel the self-interest of the actors in such ways as to unfold as beneficially and productively as may be expected from a market economy. This book endeavours to contribute to knowledge and understanding, and to help create a better and more stable financial system.

H.-W.S.

Munich, February 2010

[1] J. M. Keynes, *The General Theory of Employment, Interest and Money* (Macmillan and Cambridge University Press, Cambridge, 1936), 142.

ACKNOWLEDGEMENTS

This is the first English edition of my book *Kasino-Kapitalismus*. The first German edition was published in May 2009 with Econ, and the third edition is on its way. I thank Oxford University Press and its referees for their careful work and their suggestions, which have improved the book.

Writing a book like this is like trying to hit a fast-moving target, as things are changing so fast. For the English edition the book has been entirely updated twice, and new information has been included. Moreover, I changed the perspective from that of a German reader to that of international readers. I am grateful to Heidi Sherman for providing me with a first translation of the German version, on which I could build. Heidi Sherman, Paul Kremmel, and, in particular, Julio Saavedra looked through any subsequent changes, helping to polish my English. Edwin Pritchard carefully edited this book. I thank my colleague Ray Rees, who also teaches at the University of Munich, for carefully reading and correcting an earlier version of this manuscript.

In many interviews, several newspaper articles, and discussion rounds I had already developed some of the arguments of the book before the first German edition was published. I also gave several lectures on the topic, for example at the Barcelona Business School in November 2008, before the EU Committee of the Regions in Brussels in the same month, at the University of Munich (LMU) in December 2008, at the University of Bergen in January 2009 (Agnar Sandmo Lectures), at the Augsburg Chamber of Trade and Industry in February 2009, at the CESifo International Spring Conference in Berlin, as well as the University of Western Ontario, McGill University, and the University of Waterloo in Canada in March 2009. These presentations prompted many useful reactions that helped me sharpen my awareness of the problems. The presentation of my thoughts on this topic in the crammed auditorium at LMU was one of my most memorable experiences. The intense concentration in the lecture hall recalled the atmosphere of my student days in 1968. Only, I had now traded places. (This lecture may be viewed at www.cesifo.de.) It is emotional experiences like this that led me to write the first version of this book during the winter of 2008/9.

I was able to learn from the insights of a number of colleagues who also dealt with the topic and with whom I was able to discuss the events. Thanks are extended, in particular, to Olivier Blanchard (Munich Lecture in November 2008), Uto Baader (lecture at the Ifo Institute in December 2008), Bernd Rudolph (lecture at the Protestant Church of Gauting in January 2009), and Martin Hellwig (lecture at the Ifo Institute in February 2009). In addition, I was able to benefit from various Ifo reports developed under the leadership of Kai Carstensen, discussions in the Scientific Advisory Council to the German Ministry of Economics, and a report of the European Advisory Group at CESifo (EEAG) of February 2009, in which I myself had participated. I want to thank the other colleagues of the EEAG: Giancarlo Corsetti, Michael P. Devereux, Luigi Guiso, John Hassler, Tim Jenkinson, Gilles Saint-Paul, Jan-Egbert Sturm, and Xavier Vives for lively and enlightening discussions. My thanks also go to the late Pentti Kouri, a recent member of the EEAG team, economist, and investor, who shared with me some background information on the events, in particular the role of AIG. Discussions or written exchanges with various experts, all of whom had also dealt extensively with the crisis, were extremely useful too. I want to mention Alan Auerbach, Dirk Auerbach, Uto Baader, Axel Bertuch-Samuels, Knut Borchardt, Oswald Braun, Markus Ernst, Rolf Friedhofen, Erich Gluch, Fernando González, Charles Goodhard, Alexander Groß, Peter Hampe, Hans-Olaf Henkel, André Horovitz, Otmar Issing, John Kay, Martin Knocinski, Christian Koth, David Laidler, Lothar Mayer, Jürgen Mayser, Wernhard Möschel, Wolfgang Nierhaus, Pär Nyman, Günther Picker, Alexander Plenk, Richard Portes, Josef Schosser, Richard Schröder, Robert Solow, Peter Sørensen, Wolfgang Sprißler, Konrad Stahl, Christian Thimann, Mark Thoma, Jean-Claude Trichet, Kurt Viermetz, Wolfgang Wiegard, Theodor Weimer, Thorsten Weinelt, and Martin Wolf. Albrecht Schmidt and my wife Gerlinde read the first German manuscript and made many useful suggestions at the time.

Wolfgang Meister and Johannes Mayr of the Ifo Institute were of great help in collecting facts and data and serving as discussion partners. They helped me in preparing both the German and English editions. Max von Ehrlich, Darko Jus, and Beatrice Scheubel put together the chronology. Christoph Zeiner produced the graphs for the English edition. Barbara Hebele helped manage the production process. All of the persons mentioned deserve my gratitude for their excellent work. They are, of course, absolved of any remaining errors or the political statements in the book.

CONTENTS

LIST OF FIGURES

LIST OF TABLES

CHAPTER 1

The World in Crisis

A near meltdown

The Ifo Institute has monitored the economy for more than sixty years and has never observed a crisis as severe as the one that hit the world economy in 2008 and 2009. North America, Western Europe, Japan, Latin America, and the countries of the former Soviet Union were all in recession. The recession was accompanied by a financial crisis, the likes of which the world has not seen since the Great Depression. In the course of 2008, more than 100 American and British financial institutions disappeared or were nationalized in part or entirely. In Iceland all the banks were nationalized, and for all practical purposes, the country is bankrupt. Ireland, Hungary, and Greece have payment difficulties, and many think that Great Britain and Italy will also face serious difficulties. And many East European countries within and outside the EU are in trouble. At the time of giving this text a final polish, in January 2010, the recession has ended, but this may only be a temporary relief, as the banking crisis is still far from being overcome and a public debt crisis is looming.

10 October 2008 will enter history as a new Black Friday, because on this day a week ended in which stock prices fell worldwide by 18.2 per cent, a magnitude of decline that had not been observed for generations. Such a price collapse within one week had not even been experienced in 1929. At that time the Dow Jones Industrial Index fell by 10.1 per cent from the beginning of the week until 'Black Thursday', 24 October 1929.

Of course, the history of stock markets has known several Black Fridays. The term originated in England where, after the bankruptcy of the bank Overend, Gurney and Co. Ltd. on Friday, 11 May 1866, there were panicky sales of stocks with corresponding price slumps. And, on Friday, 9 May 1873, stock prices dropped sharply on the Viennese stock exchange, marking the beginning of the Panic of 1873.[1] The price collapse on the Berlin stock exchange on 13 May 1927 may also be traced to a Black Friday.[2]

Three days after the new Black Friday, on Monday, 13 October 2008, the world financial system would have experienced a meltdown if on the preceding Saturday at their Washington meeting the governments of the G7 countries had not developed guidelines for a rescue strategy and if, in addition, the heads of state and government of the EU had not agreed on joint action in Paris on the very next day. There would have been bank runs, stampedes on bank accounts, that would have made the banks insolvent within a few days.

No bank has the money on hand that it shows in its accounts. As is well known, banks lend much more money than they have by crediting the accounts of their customers. For example, in the euro area, before the crisis (2007) each euro of real money issued by the central bank was matched by 3.6 euros of fictional book money that existed only virtually in the banks' computers. This is legal, but works only if customers do not all try to withdraw their money at the same time.

The markedly increased cash withdrawals and gold purchases in the week before the new Black Friday had already given a warning signal of a possible run on accounts. On 10 October itself and the following Monday, banks ran as many transports to supply their branches with cash as they normally do in two months. In Austria, the run by East European customers was so strong that several bank branches had to be closed temporarily.

Limited financial crises are frequent historical events. Recall the inter-national debt crisis of the early 1980s, when many developing countries

---

[1] On this Black Friday the fall of stock prices averaged 94%, from 180 guilders to 10 guilders. Cf. Deutsches Historisches Museum, *1870–1914 Gründerkrach und Gründerkrise*, online at www.dhm.de, accessed on 20 March 2009.

[2] In the three months after the Black Friday of 1927 stock prices lost about 22%. See S. Schmid, 'Deutschlands erster Schwarzer Freitag', manuscript, Bayerischer Rundfunk, online at www.br-online.de, accessed on 20 March 2009.

became insolvent; the Savings & Loan crisis of the early 1990s, when the American savings and loan institutions had to be provided with $500 billion; the Asian crisis of 1997 and 1998, during which many banks of the Asian Tiger countries became insolvent; or the Argentine economic crisis of 1999 to 2002, when the country suffered a deep recession with a decline in GDP of more than 18 per cent.[3] But none of these financial crises was of a magnitude of the worst-case scenario financial crisis that the world is presently facing.

During the Great Depression, which began in 1929, the financial sector also suffered a serious crisis that peaked in America in 1932 or 1933. The crisis of the financial sector occurred in the wake of the crisis in the real economy, however, and did not occupy centre stage as is the case today.[4] More important at the time was the crisis of the international monetary system, which entailed a substantial risk potential. The stock market crash of October 1929 by itself had a rather limited effect on the real economy.

During the Great Depression the real economy shrank dramatically. US GDP dropped by 29 per cent from 1929 to 1933, and German GDP, which collapsed somewhat earlier, fell by 16 per cent from 1928 to 1932, if the GDP statistics of the time are to be trusted.[5] From June 1929 to June 1932, world industrial output fell by one-third, and both US and German industrial output fell by about 50 per cent.[6] In the course of this development the unemployment rate surged to 25 per cent in the USA and to about 30 per cent in Germany.[7] In America, about 5,000 banks had gone bankrupt by

---

[3] For an excellent overview of previous crises see C. M. Reinhart and K. S. Rogoff, *This Time is Different: Eight Centuries of Financial Folly* (Princeton University Press, Princeton, 2009).

[4] See B. Bernanke and H. James, 'The Gold Standard, Deflation, and Financial Crisis in the Great Depression: An International Comparison', in R. G. Hubbard (ed.), *Financial Markets and Financial Crises* (University of Chicago Press, Chicago, 1991), 33–68; B. Eichengreen and P. Temin, 'Counterfactual Histories of the Great Depression', in T. Balderston (ed.), *The World Economy and National Economies in the Interwar Slump* (Palgrave Macmillan, London, 2002), 211–22.

[5] Cf. A. Maddison, *The World Economy: Historical Statistics* (OECD, Paris, 2003). The figures relate to the comparison of peaks and troughs.

[6] B. Eichengreen and K. H. O'Rourke, 'A Tale of Two Depressions', *VOX*, 1 September 2009 www.voxeu.org.

[7] T. Watkins, *The Depression of the 1930s and its Origins,* http://www.sjsu.edu/faculty/watkins/dep1929.htm; D. Petzina, 'Arbeitslosigkeit in der Weimarer Republik', in W. Abelshauser (ed.),

1932, a dramatic figure even if the banks were much smaller than today. Despondency and panic abounded, and politicians struggled with finding the right recipes for overcoming the crisis.

Because Germany's fragile democracy (the Weimar Republic) collapsed during the crisis, the Great Depression eventually turned into a catastrophe for Western civilization. The confidence of the German people, already shattered by the lost war, the hyperinflation of 1923, and the huge reparation burden stipulated in the Treaty of Versailles, increased its willingness to accept radical political solutions. Nazis and Communists competed, using similar arguments, for the favour of the masses. Lacking understanding of the economic relationships, they looked for scapegoats, for those supposedly guilty of causing the collapse, and believed they recognized them, among others, in the bankers of the time, the manifest representatives of financial capitalism.[8] But they failed to see the true system errors, the errors in the incentive structures and rules of the world economy that induced millions of people to adopt behaviour that helped to precipitate the crisis. The failure of the moderate politicians who were still in power to find a way out of the systemic crisis of the market economy was the breeding ground for the growth of National Socialism culminating in Hitler's seizure of power in 1933, with all the consequences the world had to suffer thereafter.

History will not repeat itself, at least not in the same part of the world. Today Germany is a democratically stable country, immune to radical solutions and firmly embedded in the European Union. And governments have learnt from the mistakes made in the Great Depression. All over the world, rescue packages for banks have been put together, amounting to about $7 trillion, in order to prevent further bank failures (see Chapter 9). The measures have already had positive effects and this will continue. Money in the banks is safe now, and because everybody knows this, there will be no bank runs. This does not mean, however, that the banking crisis

---

Die Weimarer Republik als Wohlfahrtsstaat: Zum Verhältnis von Wirtschafts- und Sozialpolitik in der Industriegesellschaft (Vierteljahrschrift für Sozial- und Wirtschaftsgeschichte, Supplement 81, Stuttgart, 1987).

[8] The criticism at the time had an anti-Semitic undertone. See C. Striefler, *Kampf um die Macht: Kommunisten und Nationalsozialisten am Ende der Weimarer Republik* (Ullstein/Propyläen, Frankfurt am Main, 1993).

is over. The danger of a credit crunch still exists for reasons that will be explained later (in Chapter 8). And there is the possibility of a double-dip recession of the Western countries, even though President Obama's Keynesian stimulus package of $787 billion (around 540 billion euros[9]), the Chinese programme of 4 trillion yuan (around 400 billion euros or $585 billion), and the EU programme of 200 billion euros ($290 billion) have prevented the worst and brought the US recession to an end in summer 2009.[10]

Recession or depression?

The abrupt turnaround in the economy and in the minds of the people that took place in 2008 is breathtaking. Right before the collapse the countries engaged in world trade still brimmed with optimism. After the stock market crash of 2000 and the attack on the World Trade Center on 11 September 2001, the mood became depressed, and the world suffered a three-year stagnation. But this was followed by a four-year expansion phase which, at growth rates of around 5 per cent p.a. of the international economy, dwarfed anything experienced in past decades. Europe participated in this growth for three of the four years. As Figure 1.1 shows, one must go back to 1970 to find a similarly dynamic growth phase. But now this phase has definitively ended. In 2008 world growth may only have amounted to a good 3 per cent, and for 2009 the International Monetary Fund (IMF) assessed a negative growth rate of −0.8 per cent. That is, as Figure 1.1 shows, the lowest growth rate in the post-war period and is even lower than the last trough in 1982, when the oil crisis caused a recession. The speed of the collapse also exceeds all historic dimensions. The hitherto

[9] Currency conversions in this book that refer to the present and near future are made on the basis of exchange rates of December 2009. Currency conversions concerning historical periods are made using the average exchange rates over those periods.

[10] See Congressional Budget Office (CBO), HR 1, *American Recovery and Reinvestment Act of 2009*, online at www.cbo.gov; European Commission, *Comprehensive Recovery Program of the Commission for Growth and Employment to Stimulate Demand and Rebuild Confidence in the European Economy*, online at www.europe.eu; and Global Insight, *State Council Signals Resolve with 4 Trillion Yuan Stimulus Package for China*, online at www.globalinsight.com, accessed on 16 February 2009.

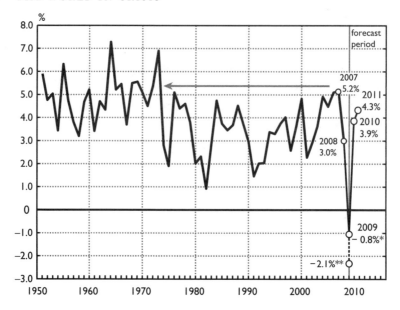

Fig. 1.1 World economic growth 1951–2011

*IMF forecast on the basis of purchasing power parities.

**IMF forecast on the basis of exchange rates.

Source: International Monetary Fund, *World Economic Outlook Database*, October 2009, International Monetary Fund, *Economic Outlook Update*, 26 January 2010.

sharpest decline of the international economic growth rate occurred between 1973 and 1975. At that time the growth rate fell from 6.9 per cent to 1.9 per cent in the course of two years. The decline thus amounted to 5 percentage points. In the present crisis the world has experienced a decline from +5.2 per cent to −0.8 per cent in two years, corresponding to 6 percentage points.[11]

In this context one should note how the International Monetary Fund arrives at its worldwide growth rate: it does not use exchange rates as country weights for calculating the aggregate growth rate, as is normally done, but purchasing power parities.[12] Purchasing power parities are

---

[11] International Monetary Fund, *World Economic Outlook Update: A Policy-Driven, Multi-speed Recovery*, 26 January 2010.

[12] Purchasing power parities are fictitious exchange rates, determined such that when moving from one country to another, life appears equally expensive. Since, as any tourist knows, services are cheaper in economically backward countries than in developed countries, actual exchange rates assign less weight to the former countries than do purchasing power parities.

exchange rates calculated so as to make well-defined market baskets equally expensive in the countries under comparison. In this way, the less developed but faster growing newly industrializing countries receive bigger weights than if actual exchange rates were used, thus increasing the calculated growth rate. Aggregating the growth rates of the individual countries in the usual way yields a growth rate for the world economy that is lower by more than one percentage point, that is a rate of −2.1 per cent instead of only −0.8 per cent, as represented by the lowest point of Figure 1.1.

The IMF now expects the world economy to grow by 3.9 per cent in 2010. That would point to the crisis having been overcome. The forecast for 2011 is also in this order of magnitude, attributable in particular to the emerging economies' brisk performance. Whether the Western countries affected by the financial crisis, above all the USA, return to economic vigour is another question altogether.

All countries have been affected by the recession, but to different degrees. Trade-dependent countries like Germany, Japan, or Russia were among those most severely hit. Figure 1.2 gives an overview of the most recent IMF growth estimates for the G-20 countries for 2009. The figure shows that Russia, Mexico, Turkey, Japan, and Germany suffered most, all with downturns of 5 per cent or more. The domestic product of the USA, where the crisis began, shrank by 2.4 per cent, and that of the EU by an estimated 4.0 per cent. China and India were only affected to the extent that their growth rates, which had been 9.0 per cent and 7.3 per cent respectively in 2008, declined to 8.7 per cent and 5.6 per cent.

The growth figures, as alarming as they are, do not fully reflect the drama that some industries faced during the current depression, since they refer to GDP, and GDP includes many activities that are financed with government money and hence are more immune to market shocks. By depicting the order inflows of US and EU manufacturing firms, Figure 1.3 shows how the more market-oriented business sectors were affected. The figure shows that within one year, from March 2008 to March 2009, these order inflows plummeted by 27 per cent in the USA and by 30 per cent in the EU from April 2008 to April 2009. These were by far the largest reductions in order inflows in the post-war period. The sharpest previous decline in the USA was 20 per cent from June 2000 to

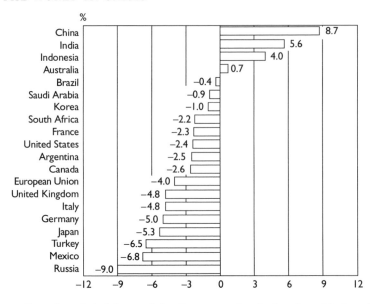

Fig. 1.2 Growth and shrinkage of the G-20 countries during the crisis (2009)

Sources: International Monetary Fund, *World Economic Outlook Database*, October 2009, International Monetary Fund, *World Economic Outlook Update*, 26 January 2010; Statistisches Bundesamt, *Germany Experiencing Serious Recession in 2009*, Press release No. 012 / 2010-01-13; National Bureau of Statistics of China, *National Economy: Recovery and Posing in the Good Direction in 2009*, Press release of 21 January 2010; Bureau of Economic Analysis, *Gross Domestic Product: Fourth Quarter 2009 (Advance Estimate)*, News Release of 29 January 2010.

June 2001, and in Europe (old EU), the hitherto sharpest decline was 10 per cent from December 2000 to December 2001.[13]

A good overview of the detailed development of the crisis over time is given by the Ifo Business Climate Indicator, which, based on a monthly survey of 7,000 German manufacturing firms, is Europe's most important business cycle indicator, according to Reuters.[14] Although the indicator is generated in Germany, it accurately depicts the development of the world economy as a whole, as Germany is the world's largest exporter of merchandise.[15]

---

[13] US Census Bureau, http://www.census.gov/cgi-bin/briefroom/BriefRm, and Eurostat, http://epp.eurostat.ec.europa.eu/portal/page/portal/statistics/search_database, accessed on 26 October 2009.

[14] See Reuters, *Poll: Eurostat Improved, but Can do Better, Economists Say*, 31 January 2005. The Ifo Institute surveys about 7,000 company units monthly regarding their assessment of their current situation and their expectations for the coming six months. From the mean of the two assessments, the Ifo Institute derives the Business Climate Index.

[15] During the crisis, Germany may have handed this position over to China, however.

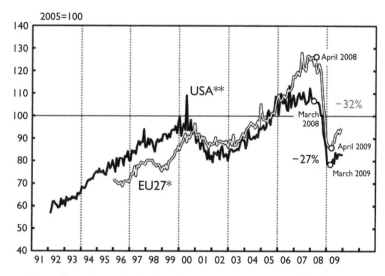

Fig. 1.3 Manufacturing order inflows (current prices, seasonally adjusted)

* Manufacturing, new orders, total.

** Manufacturing, new orders, durable goods, total.

Source: Eurostat, Euroindicators, *Industry, Commerce and Services*, Database; US Census Bureau, Business & Industry, Economic Indicators, *Manufacturer's Shipments, Inventories and Orders*, Historic Time Series; Ifo Institute calculations.

The German manufacturing sector exports the lion's share of its output to other countries and thus quickly comes to feel worldwide trends in economic activity. Figure 1.4 shows the so-called Business-Cycle Clock based on the indicator. The vertical axis measures the expectations for the next six months, and the horizontal axis the assessments of the current situation (or to be precise: the respective percentage differences between optimists and pessimists).

One can see that the world economy boomed from mid-2005 until April 2008 and began to decline thereafter. In August 2008, before the crisis came to a head, a substantial fraction of the way into recession had already been covered. The firms' expectations then were already as bad as after the attack on the World Trade Center. In subsequent months current assessments and expectations continued to deteriorate.

After the US Department of Treasury had announced on 10 September 2008 that it did not intend to save the investment bank Lehman Brothers and following the final collapse of the bank on 15 September 2008, credit transactions among banks came to a halt. That was the starting point of the most acute phase of the financial crisis and the acceleration of the crisis of

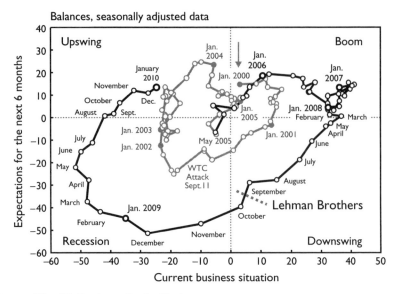

Fig. 1.4 The Ifo Business-Cycle Clock

Notes: Manufacturing industry including food and beverages.

The vertical axis shows the expectations and the horizontal axis the assessment of the current situation, each as the difference between the percentage of positive and the percentage of negative responses of the panel. Axis crossings indicate values of zero. The area above the horizontal line shows a majority of positive expectations, and the area below shows a majority of negative expectations. Correspondingly, to the right of the vertical line a majority assesses its business situation as good and to the left of it as poor. Over the business cycle the economy moves clockwise through the diagram. In a recession, current situation and expectations are poor, and the survey responses are shown as points in the lower left-hand quadrant. If a recovery is ahead, the situation is still bad, but the expectations are already positive; the point moves into the upper left-hand quadrant. Then the current situation follows the expectations and also turns positive, implying a movement to the right into the upper right-hand quadrant, which is the boom area. In a recession the opposite happens. Initially the expectations deteriorate, to be followed by the current assessments. The movement is through the right-hand quadrant to the lower left-hand quadrant.

Source: Ifo Business Survey.

the real economy. In November 2008 the Ifo Indicator entered recession territory, and from December the current situation and expectations were markedly worse than after the attack on the World Trade Center. While expectations barely improved, the current situation continued to worsen until May 2009.

Both assessments of the current situation and expectations as bad as these had never before been observed. Only during the recessions of 1975 and 1982 in the wake of the two oil crises of 1973 and 1979 had the current situation been assessed as equally bad. But at that time the expectations in the manufacturing industry were less pessimistic. Disquieting in the current recession was above all the speed at which the assessments of the current situation deteriorated. The downward movement was faster than the Ifo Institute had ever observed in the forty years for which the survey time series exist.

As of January 2010, at the time of finalizing this manuscript, it was not fully clear how the journey would continue, but widespread hope prevailed that the worst was over. As Figure 1.4 shows, expectations in the Ifo Business-Cycle Clock had brightened considerably and even the assessments of the current situation had improved. Furthermore, the rise in stock prices (see Figure 2.6), good news from China, and various other business indicators suggested an end to the recession. For example, the Ifo World Economic Indicator, based on a poll of expert opinions in ninety countries, rose in the second, third, and fourth quarters of 2009, reaching a level comparable to the situation between 11 September 2001 and the beginning of the Iraq War in 2003. In view of the good news, the IMF in July revised its world growth forecast for 2010 from 1.9 per cent to 2.5 per cent, in October to 3.1 per cent, and in January 2010 to 3.9 per cent as mentioned above (see Figure 1.1).

However, the good news is relative. In the Ifo Business-Cycle Clock, the improved expectations up to August 2008 had only meant that the majority of pessimists had diminished, not that there was a majority of optimists. Only from October 2009 was there a slight majority of optimists. And, more importantly, by the beginning of 2010 the vast majority of firms still felt their business situation was poor, even a bit worse than after 11 September 2001.

In light of the unresolved financial crisis, many observers fear that the current upswing will be short-lived and will be followed by a further slump of the world economy. A tightening of the worldwide credit squeeze as further bad loans, regulatory deficiencies, and bankruptcies are detected, as will be discussed in Chapter 8, is feeding fears that the world will experience a double-dip recession in the coming years. Another reason for such a development could be that governments will not be able to continue their counter-cyclical Keynesian policies in 2011 and beyond because their public debt cannot be further expanded. In 2010, most European countries are violating the EU's Stability and Growth Pact, the USA is heading towards a debt–GDP ratio of 100 per cent, and Japan is moving towards one of 200 per cent, both extremely alarming figures (see Chapter 10). Moreover, in Europe at least, firms may not be able to stem the tide forever and maintain current

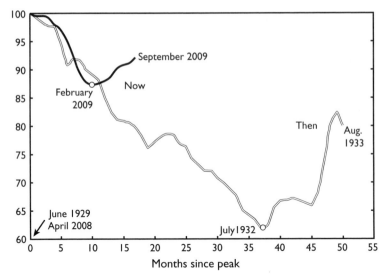

Fig. 1.5 World industrial output, Great Depression, and current recession

Note: The two curves show the development of world industrial output during the Great Depression and the current recession, from the respective output peaks (April 2008, June 1929).

Source: M. Almunia, A. Bénétrix, B. Eichengreen, K. H. O'Rourke and G. Rua, 'From Great Depression to Great Credit Crisis: Similarities, Differences and Lessons', NBER Working Paper, No. 15524, 2009.

employment levels in order to avoid high statutory lay-off costs and keep on board the skilled workers they have trained. When their losses have depleted their equity stocks, a continuation of this strategy may be unfeasible. Many firms may cease operations after a year or two, then unemployment figures would rise and consumption would plummet, with the risk of another downward spiral of economic activity.

Barry Eichengreen and Kevin O'Rourke have argued that the current recession could, in fact, be the beginning of a long-lasting depression, because many economic indicators are developing in a similar way to those in the Great Depression that began in 1929.[16] The most striking similarity concerns the decline of industrial output, as demonstrated in Figure 1.5. The figure shows the decline of world industrial output in the months following June 1929 and April 2008, the two months in which output had peaked before the respective crises. Industrial output declined at roughly the same pace during the first ten months of the crisis, 11 per cent then and 12 per cent

---

[16] B. Eichengreen and K. H. O'Rourke, 'A Tale of Two Depressions', op. cit.

now, until February 2009. Since then, however, industrial output has been rising again, which nourishes the hope that the parallels between the Great Depression and the current crisis will be limited to the initial downswing.

Other indicators in the current recession showed an even worse development than in the Great Depression. For example, in the first thirteen months of the current recession, the volume of world trade declined by 21 per cent, while it declined by 'only' 10 per cent in the first fourteen months of the Great Depression.[17] Again, however, it is unclear what the future development will be, and there is every hope that because of the massive government interventions, the present recession will have paralleled the Great Depression only in the initial phase.

The downturn phase of the Great Depression lasted more than three years. World industrial output declined by 38 per cent in thirty-seven months, and world trade shrank by 31 per cent in thirty-eight months. It is frightening to imagine what our future would have been had the Western governments not intervened with massive Keynesian policies.

Lags

At the time of writing, shortly after the collapse of the world economy, there is a remarkable difference in the perception of the crisis in various countries due to different labour market reactions. Unemployment rates reflect the state of the economy perceived by the population much more than business indicators or the growth rates published by statistical offices. While in Anglo-American countries the population is feeling much pain from the crisis, the populations of countries in the heart of Europe like Germany, Austria, or, to some extent, even Poland are hardly affected. People read about the crisis in newspapers and books like this, but wonder where it is and when it will come. The reality of crowded shops and full bank accounts does not fit the sinister stories of the economists.

This difference in perception results partly from different degrees of welfare protection and partly from a lag between the American and the European business cycles. Indeed, in recent years the cyclical turnaround

[17] Eichengreen and O'Rourke, 'A Tale of Two Depressions', op. cit.

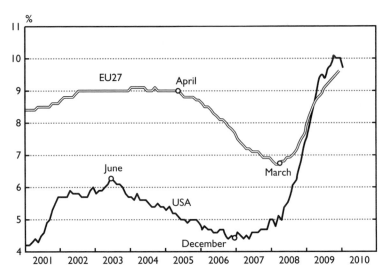

Fig. 1.6 Unemployment rates in the USA and the EU

Source: Eurostat, Euroindicators, Labour market, Database, US Bureau of Labor Statistics, Databases & Tables, Unemployment, accessed on 29 January 2010.

always started in the USA and then spread to the rest of the world via a change in American imports and financial contagion effects.

The lag is clearly evident in Figure 1.6, which compares the unemployment rates of the USA and the EU in the last boom and the recent recession. While US unemployment peaked first in June 2003 during the Iraq War and declined from the second half of that year, EU unemployment declined from April 2005, twenty-two months later. And whereas (seasonally adjusted) US unemployment had reached its minimum around December 2006, where it stayed until May 2007, EU unemployment had reached its minimum in March 2008, indicating a lag of fifteen months. Even if the levelling off in US unemployment as shown in Figure 1.6 does signal that the country's labour market may indeed have turned the corner in winter 2009/2010, Europe will probably have to wait more than a year until it experiences similar relief.

As Figure 1.7 shows, the lag is even bigger for some European countries. While in France unemployment began to increase after May 2008 and in the UK after April 2008, it took Poland until October 2008 and Germany until December 2008 to reach the turning point. Only Spanish unemployment moved synchronically, starting to rise after May 2007. In autumn 2009

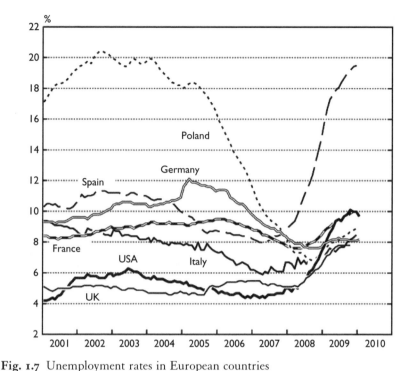

Fig. 1.7 Unemployment rates in European countries

Source: Eurostat, Euroindicators, Labour market, Database, US Bureau of Labor Statistics, Databases, accessed on 29 January 2010.

Spanish unemployment was heading towards a record level of 20 per cent. All other EU countries followed the Spanish development with a delay. Hungary came after July 2007; Luxembourg after September 2007; Italy and Latvia after November 2007; Lithuania after December 2007; Ireland after January 2008; Estonia after March 2008; Sweden after April 2008; Belgium, Portugal, and Finland after May 2008; Denmark and Austria after June 2008; Greece, Malta, Romania, Slovenia, and Cyprus after September 2008; the Czech Republic and Slovakia after October 2008; and Bulgaria and the Netherlands after November 2008.

Germany, Europe's biggest economy, came last in this sequence. It followed the USA with a lag of twenty-one months in the upswing and twenty-three months in the downswing. At the end of 2008 the German unemployment rate had reached the lowest level in sixteen years, while the American unemployment rate had reached its highest level in sixteen years. Germany's relatively good performance at that time was mostly due to the effects of *Agenda 2010*, the labour market reform programme introduced by the Schröder government in 2003, but it also resulted from the cyclical lag. As the reader may recall, German policy-makers had been rather reluctant to put together a stimulus programme in autumn 2008, thus annoying the Americans and other Europeans.[18] The excellent performance of the German labour market at that time may be an explanation for this reluctance. The feeling of urgent distress which a finance minister needs to have in order to sacrifice his consolidation goals had not reached Germany in the winter of 2008/9. Surprisingly, the distress had not even reached the German public by the end of 2009, and even the forecasts at that time predicted only a very modest increase in unemployment during 2010. In addition to Chancellor Schröder's reforms, this was probably due to Germany's short-term work subsidy programme that allows firms to cut work hours and compensates the employees for about 70 per cent of the wage loss.

Shock producers and shock absorbers

The crisis began in America and spread from there to the world, leading to an unprecedented contraction of world trade. American imports, the world's largest, collapsed first. From January 2008 to January 2009 they fell by 27 per cent, which is way outside the normal scope even for economic slowdowns.[19] The collapse of US imports was like an earthquake whose shock waves spread from the epicentre in the USA to the entire world.

The effects of the bursting bubble were then mitigated through extensive worldwide bank rescue packages of $7.3 trillion and discretionary Keynesian measures in the order of $1.4 trillion (Chapter 9). However, the stabilizing effects were not only the result of discretionary policy measures, but also, and in many countries primarily, the result of the built-in flexibility of the national tax expenditure systems. When GDP declines, tax revenue

---

[18] French President Sarkozy remarked: 'Germany ponders, France acts', see 'Zweifel an Merkels Führungsstärke', *Badische Zeitung*, 9 December 2008, online at http://www.badische-zeitung.de/nachrichten/deutschland/zweifel-an-merkels-fuehrungsstaerke–8906515.html. See also P. Krugman, 'The German Problem', *New York Times*, 10 December 2008; P. Krugman, 'The Economic Consequences of Herr Steinbrueck', *New York Times*, 11 December 2008.

[19] US Bureau of Economic Analysis, press release of 13 March 2009.

drops while most government expenditure, including transfers and salaries of government employees, remains stable. Some government expenditure, notably unemployment benefits, even increases in the crisis. Thus, the budget deficit of the government automatically becomes larger, stimulating the economy. One of the major differences between the Great Depression and the current crisis is that today government shares in GDP are much bigger than they were in 1929 and so the automatic stabilizers of the tax expenditure systems are much stronger. For example, in 2008 the US government's share in GDP was 34.1 per cent while it was only 9.5 per cent in 1929,[20] and in Germany the government's share in net national income (NNI) now is 50.3 per cent while it was 24.8 per cent in 1929.[21]

The origins of the crisis, natural lags, discretionary policy measures, and automatic stabilizers created shocks and shock absorbing reactions throughout the world. Figure 1.8 depicts the shock producers and shock absorbers by way of showing the changes in the country-specific trade balances from the second quarter of 2008 to the second quarter of 2009 for a number of selected countries. Nearly everywhere in the world exports and imports fell during the crisis, but typically these quantities did not fall by equal amounts. Countries whose imports fell more than exports reduced their net demand of goods from the rest of the world. They were shock producers or shock amplifiers. And countries whose exports fell more than imports were shock absorbers, as their net demand for goods from the rest of the world was increased.

Obviously, the USA has been by far the world's largest shock producer in this crisis. Its annualized imports shrank by $424 billion more than its exports. Somewhat surprisingly, Spain, South Korea, the UK, and France were also in the category of shock producers or shock amplifiers. The shock absorbers on the other hand were Germany, Russia, and China. Their exports all shrank more than their imports—by $160 billion, $108 billion,

---

[20] Total expenditure less capital transfer payments and less net purchases of non-produced assets, see US Bureau of Economic Analysis, *National Income and Product Accounts Tables*, table 3.1.

[21] See Federal Statistical Office, *Special Series 18*, Series 1.4, 2008 (Wiesbaden, 2009), table 2.1.2 and table 3.4.3.2, and A. Behnisch, T. Büttner, and D. Stegarescu, *Public Sector Centralization and Productivity Growth: Reviewing the German Experience*, Discussion Paper No. 02-03, Centre for European Economic Research (Mannheim, 2001).

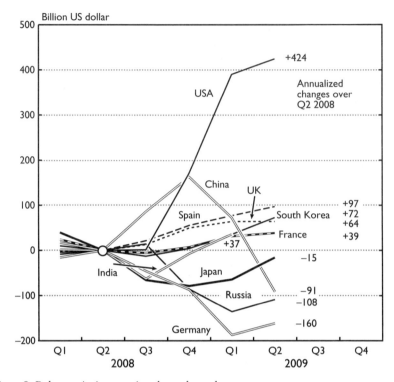

Fig. 1.8 Balances in international goods trade

Note: Annualized and seasonally adjusted quarterly figures.

Source: Reuters EcoWin Pro database, Ifo Institute calculations.

and $91 billion, respectively. (With smaller values Canada, Norway, and the Netherlands, which are not shown in the graph, are also in the group of shock absorbers.) The two extremes of the spectrum are marked by the USA and Germany. While the USA was the biggest shock producer in this crisis, Germany obviously was the world's biggest shock absorber.

Germany's role as a shock absorber may be explained by the fact that the German economy is still surprisingly stable internally. The huge German welfare state has many allocative disadvantages in the long run, but in a crisis it has a cushioning effect. Forty-two per cent of adult Germans live on government transfers including state pensions, and the government pays short-term work insurance for up to twenty-four months to employers who keep their employees on the payroll working short-time during the crisis. Moreover, Germany has had no housing bubble, and its mortgage system is particularly safe and stable. The world has benefited from this stability.

A remarkable development is shown by China. Although the country was indeed negatively affected due to its close trade links with the USA (one-fifth of Chinese exports but only one-fifteenth of German exports go to the USA), it was initially able to further increase its trade surplus, which had already been the largest in the world before the crisis. From the last quarter of 2007 until the last quarter of 2008, China's imports declined by an annualized total of $150 billion more than its exports, which themselves actually increased by 5 per cent. However, thereafter the trend reversed itself and over these four quarters its overall trade balance deteriorated by $91 billion, making China a member of the group of shock absorbers. Remarkably, in the first two quarters of 2009, the country became the world champion merchandise exporter, overtaking Germany, which hitherto had held this title and whose exports in terms of US dollars declined by 33 per cent relative to the first two quarters of 2008.[22] When the dust of this crisis has settled and a clearer picture of what has happened emerges, it may well turn out that China is the big winner of the crisis.

[22] Reuters EcoWin Pro database, accessed on 16 September 2009.

CHAPTER 2

Life on Credit

America has been living beyond its means

The financial crisis has micro- and macroeconomic aspects. It can be understood from the point of view of the individual decision-makers in the relevant markets or from the perspective of the overall economy. To gain an overview, let us begin with a bird's eye view as reflected in the national accounts.

The most important macroeconomic aspect is illustrated in Figure 2.1. It presents the development of the savings rate of American households since 1929. The savings rate shows the share of disposable income (gross income after taxes and social security contributions are deducted) not consumed by private households but saved. The figure shows that the savings rate increased from about 5 per cent to 10 per cent in the period from the Great Depression to about 1970, with a peak of about 25 per cent during the Second World War. The savings rate then remained in the neighbourhood of 10 per cent until about 1980. After 1980, it followed a declining trend for about a quarter of a century, and finally approached zero in the period from 2005 to 2008, with an average rate of 0.9 per cent and only 0.4 per cent in 2005, as reported in the statistics of the time. In comparison: the savings rate of eurozone households averaged 8.7 per cent from 2005 to 2008.[1]

Interestingly enough, however, the US Bureau of Economic Analysis changed its classifications and further details of its accounting system in

[1] Eurostat, Database, *Economy and Finance*, Annual Sector Accounts, accessed on 11 January 2010.

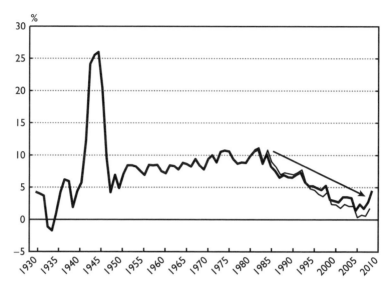

Fig. 2.1 The savings rate of American private households (1929–2009)

Note: The thin line shows the US savings rate before the data revision of July 2009.

Source: US Bureau of Economic Analysis, *National Income and Product Accounts Tables*, table 2.1, Personal Income and its Disposition.

July 2009, with the effect of retroactively pushing these numbers a bit further away from the zero line. The revision increased the average savings rate for the period 2005–8 from 0.9 per cent to 2.0 per cent and the 2005 savings rate from 0.4 per cent to 1.4 per cent. The bold line in the figure shows the savings rate after and the thin line before the revision. Only in 2009, in the midst of the crisis, do we see a substantial increase in the savings rate towards 5 per cent according to the new definitions.[2]

During the twenty or so years preceding the crisis, Americans obviously enjoyed life and neglected to provide for their future. And note that these numbers are averages. Since wealthier Americans also saved in this phase, poorer Americans must have spent more than their disposable income. They lived beyond their means, paying for part of their consumption out of borrowed money. As we shall see below, they largely borrowed against their homes.

[2] See US Bureau of Economic Analysis, *National Income and Product Accounts Tables*, table 2.1.

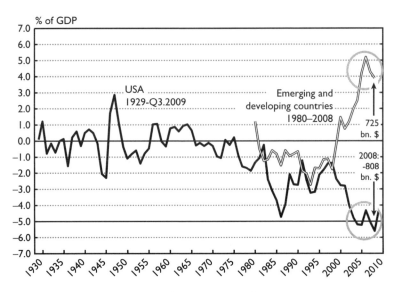

Fig. 2.2 Net capital exports (+) and imports (−) relative to GDP

Note: USA: difference between net saving and net domestic investment as percentage of GDP, 2009: average of first quarter to third quarter. Emerging and developing countries: aggregated current account balance as percentage of aggregated GDP. The 20 most important emerging and developing countries as defined by the IMF include China, Brazil, Russia, India, Mexico, Turkey, Indonesia, Poland, Saudi Arabia, Islamic Republic of Iran, South Africa, Argentina, Thailand, Venezuela, Colombia, Malaysia, United Arab Emirates, Romania, Nigeria, and Chile. The US curve covers the period until the 3rd quarter of 2009. The lowest point of the black curve refers to the year 2008.

Source: US Bureau of Economic Analysis, *National Income and Product Accounts, Tables*, table 1.1.5, Gross Domestic Product, and table 5.1, Saving and Investment; International Monetary Fund, *World Economic Outlook Database*, October 2009, by country groups, balance of payments, current account balance.

When private households fail to save, the government continues to incur debt and firms also try to finance part of their investments by borrowing, then only one source of financing remains: capital imports from abroad. Indeed, Americans relied heavily on this source, as Figure 2.2, showing US capital imports as a percentage of gross domestic product (GDP), indicates. It is evident that capital exports became negative from about 1980, that is, turning into capital imports, and that these capital imports have followed a rising trend.

Capital imports are the mirror image of a current account deficit, ignoring the negligible changes in stocks of foreign currency. A current account deficit is the excess of imported goods and services over the corresponding exports, net of transfers of gifts from foreigners. If a country is a net importer of goods and services, it must sell an appropriate amount of assets. The outflow of these assets from America is called capital imports by Americans or, analogously, capital exports by the rest of the world. As this outflow consists of about two-thirds of pure financial claims instead of direct investment or equities, one can also say that Americans were living on credit.[3]

In recent years the US capital import and the matching current account deficit amounted to as much as 5 per cent of GDP, in 2008 even 5.6 per cent. There has not been a period with similarly high net capital imports since 1929. Even in 1986, when the Plaza Agreement of the big industrial countries and the large US current account deficit pushed the dollar into depreciation, capital imports relative to GDP amounted only to 4 per cent. In the years before the crisis the US current account and thus capital imports broke all historical records. Those who are still not impressed by the percentage need only look at the absolute number. In 2008, American net capital imports amounted to the truly gigantic sum of $808 billion.

The financiers of the world capital markets

US capital imports were financed by those countries that, due to their export surpluses, were net capital exporters. While it is impossible to earmark capital and trace the precise flow from one country to another, the aggregate statistics nevertheless reveal interesting comparisons. One such comparison in shown by the upper curve in Figure 2.2, which refers to the aggregate of all emerging and developing countries. These countries had imported capital during the 1980s and 1990s, but their capital imports declined after the early 1990s, turning into capital exports after 2000, mirroring the US curve. In 2008, when the crisis emerged, net capital exports of the emerging and developing countries amounted to 3.9 per cent of their GDP or $725 billion in absolute terms, which was roughly the size of US capital imports, the $808 billion mentioned above. In the period 2005 to 2008 the average annual net capital exports of the emerging and developing countries amounted to $624 billion, and the average annual net capital imports of the USA was $746 billion.

---

[3] US Flow-of-Funds Statistics for the end of the 3rd quarter of 2009 show a stock of $15.072 trillion for the financial investment in the USA by the rest of the world. Direct investment including company assets accounts for only 32.8% of this. See Federal Reserve, *Flow of Funds Accounts of the United States,* table L.107, online at http://www.federalreserve. gov/releases/z1/Current/z1.pdf, accessed on 12 January 2010.

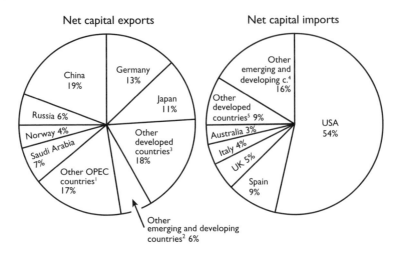

Fig. 2.3 Breakdown of net capital exports and imports in 2005–2008

Notes: Net capital exports including net gifts to foreigners and net capital imports, including net gifts received from abroad (current account balances).

1. Kuwait (3.3%), United Arab Emirates (2.1%), Nigeria (1.9%), Algeria (1.9%), Venezuela (1.8%), Libya (1.7%) etc.
2. Malaysia (1.8%), Azerbaijan (0.5%), Brunei Darussalam (0.4%), Trinidad and Tobago (0.4%), Indonesia (0.4%) etc.
3. Netherlands (3.8%), Switzerland (2.6%), Sweden (2.2%), Singapore (2.1%), Taiwan (1.6%) etc.
4. Turkey (2.4%), Romania (1.3%), South Africa (1.2%), Poland (1.1%), India (1.0%) etc.
5. Greece (2.6%), France (2.0%), Portugal (1.6%), Ireland (0.8%), New Zealand (0.7%) etc.

Source: International Monetary Fund, *World Economic Outlook Database*, October 2009.

Amongst the group of emerging and developing countries, China contributed the largest part to net capital (and goods) exports. This is shown in Figure 2.3, which provides the net capital exports and imports of all countries in the period 2005–8. Obviously, the USA absorbed more than half of the world's net capital exports, and China contributed a fifth of these exports; $303 billion per year on average. Other emerging and developing countries contributed 35 per cent to net capital exports and yet another group of emerging and developing countries accounted for about 16 per cent of all net capital imports. In summary, all emerging and developing countries except China provided net capital exports of $321 billion per year and, including China, the $624 billion mentioned above.

The fact that the developing and emerging countries exported nearly as much capital as the USA imported is a surprising aspect of globalization. A rich country like America, which is well endowed with capital, should have exported capital to the less developed part of the world, not vice versa. First, the emerging and developing countries should be able to offer a higher rate of return to capital, as capital is scarce there and wages are correspondingly low. Second, it would make sense for these countries to have tried to smooth consumption over time by borrowing abroad against their anticipated higher future incomes. However, both arguments fail to explain what happened. Measured against the predictions of economic theory, capital flowed in the wrong direction. It was as if the Rhine was flowing from the North Sea to Switzerland.

The puzzle can, however, be explained to a large extent by petrodollars recycling from the oil exporting countries, which are included in the group of developing and emerging countries. Because oil exporters have only limited possibilities to invest their sales revenue at home and also do not wish to consume everything immediately, they have to export large parts of this revenue as capital to other countries. As is shown in Figure 2.3, the aggregate net capital exports of all major oil exporting countries, including Russia, Saudi Arabia, and Norway, in the four years under consideration, was 33 per cent of total net capital exports or $516 billion per year.

Aside from the petrodollars, the main explanation is that on both sides of the table non-market forces were at work. Thus, the Chinese central bank would not allow the exchange rate of the yuan to vary freely against the dollar, but instead manipulated it in such a way that its own currency was always undervalued, leading to high export surpluses of goods and services and thus also of capital. And the citizens of the USA established a good life for themselves by borrowing heavily against their real estate; the prices were inflated artificially by deficiencies in the US legal system, as will be explained in this book. Evidently, both practices were a perfect match. They fed on and reinforced each other.

In addition to the USA, Spain and the UK also stood out as big capital importers, absorbing 9 per cent and 5 per cent of world capital exports, respectively. As shown in Figure 2.10, both countries, like the USA, experienced a housing boom accompanied by a strong economic boom that attracted substantial capital resources from all over the world.

In addition to the developing and emerging countries, Japan and Germany were also big capital exporters. Together with China these latter two countries contributed more capital than the USA needed. The huge capital exports of Germany and Japan were due to their extremely low internal investment rates. Little of their domestic savings was invested at home, the lion's share went abroad as capital exports. In the OECD statistics both countries have been competing for years with Switzerland for the lowest net investment rate among the thirty industrialized countries. Germany, at a net investment rate of 3.2 per cent in 2005–7, stood below Japan, at 3.7 per cent, and Switzerland, at 4.7 per cent, occupying the very end of the international comparative range.[4] In these three years, Germany had on average aggregate annual savings of 220 billion euros, of which it used only 65 billion euros for domestic net investment, sending 155 billion euros ($201 billion) abroad.[5]

Germany's low investment rate is an implication of the country's excessively high wages for unskilled labour. Due to massive government interventions in terms of high replacement incomes, the country has had a very high implicit minimum wage, making it a leader in terms of the unemployment of the poorly skilled among the countries in the West.[6] This minimum wage has driven capital from the labour-intensive sectors to the skill- and capital-intensive export sectors as well as to other countries. The result was both an excessively high value added in exports and an excessively high capital export or, what is the same, an excessively high current account surplus, accompanied by unemployment and low growth.[7] Germany and the rest of the world would have done better if Germany had lived with a more widely spread

[4] See OECD, *OECD National Accounts Statistics*, Annual National Accounts, table 1, Gross Domestic Product: Expenditure Approach, and table 4, Disposable Income, Saving and Net lending/Net borrowing, online at www.oecd.org, accessed on 11 November 2009. At the time of writing, the 2008 investment data for Switzerland and Japan were not yet available. Germany in 2008 had a net investment rate of 5.1% which probably again was the lowest of all OECD countries. See Federal Statistical Office, *Special Series 18*, Series 1.2 (Wiesbaden, 2009), 2nd quarter 2009, table 1.2 and table 1.5.

[5] According to the Federal Statistical Office, *Special Series 18*, Series 1.2 (Wiesbaden, 2009), 2nd quarter 2009, table 1.5, savings amounted to 659 billion euros in 2005–7 and net investment to 195 billion euros. From this it follows that capital exports were 464 billion euros. Converted at the annual exchange rate (1 euro = $1.2441 in 2005, 1 euro = $1.2556 in 2006, 1 euro = $1.3705 in 2007; see Deutsche Bundesbank, *Statistisches Beiheft zum Monatsbericht 5, Devisenkursstatistik*, January 2009).

[6] See OECD, *OECD Employment Outlook 2009* (Paris, 2009), Statistical Annex, table D.

[7] The high wages for the unskilled implied a reduction in the price of skill- and capital-intensive goods relative to the labour-intensive goods that turned into a price decline relative to

wage distribution, and hence stronger internal sectors, and if its domestic firms had taken the funds and themselves put to work the machines produced by Germany's investment goods industries instead of allowing them to be shipped abroad. The UK and the USA had a point when they blamed Germany at the G-20 Summit in Pittsburgh in September 2009 for having contributed to the imbalances of the world (although their argument that Germany needs higher consumption is flawed).

Notwithstanding all these idiosyncratic explanations of capital flows, the huge capital imports of the USA dwarf all other aspects of the world capital market. Year after year Americans sold hundreds of billions of new securities to the world. In 2008, US net capital imports, accumulated since 1970, amounted to $7.7 trillion, which happens to be similar in magnitude to the value of American housing lost since the crash ($8 trillion, see Figure 2.8 below).[8] American net capital imports were so gigantic as to throw the international capital markets into substantial disarray. As will be shown later on, US capital imports have been due less to the strength of the USA as an investment location than to the innovativeness of its financial system; or rather to the tricks used by American bankers to make the savers of the world empty their pockets.

Ben Bernanke, the American central bank chairman, still held in 2007 that US capital imports signalled the solidity of the American capital market, which was said to be so attractive due to its 'depth, liquidity, and legal safeguards' that investors from all over the world carried their funds to America in order to participate in the dynamism of that country. America, he said, had accepted the 'savings glut' of the world, thereby helping other countries.[9] However, representing the issue in this way came close to propaganda attributable to the attempt to fend off a potential crisis.

---

other countries via a real devaluation (i.e. less than average inflation). Cf. H.-W. Sinn, *Can Germany be Saved? The Malaise of the World's First Welfare State* (MIT Press, Cambridge, Mass., 2007); H.-W. Sinn, 'The Pathological Export Boom and the Bazaar Effect: How to Solve the German Puzzle', *World Economy*, 29 (2006), 1157–75; H.-W. Sinn, *Die Basar-Ökonomie. Deutschland: Exportweltmeister oder Schlusslicht?* (Econ, Berlin, 2005).

[8] See US Bureau of Economic Analysis, *National Income and Product Account Tables*, table 5.1. Saving and Investment, and table 1.1.5. Gross Domestic Product.

[9] Cf. B. Bernanke, *Global Imbalances: Recent Developments and Prospects*, Bundesbank Lecture, Berlin, 11 September 2007 (http://www.federalreserve.gov/newsevents/speech/

Just the opposite was true. Because Americans had stopped saving, the country had to find financing abroad by selling more and more securities. It became ever more difficult, however, to find buyers, as the portfolios of the international investors were increasingly being flooded by American securities and moving into disequilibrium. Financial investors normally seek to diversify their portfolios in order to limit their risks. The continuous American supply of securities undermined this effort. Foreign investors' reluctance to keep the game going grew from year to year. As a result, Americans had to accept ever lower prices and promise ever higher yields in order to overcome this reluctance.

The value of an American asset in the hands of an international investor whose home currency is not the dollar consists of the product of two prices: the price of the asset in terms of dollars and the price of the dollar in terms of the other currency, that is, the exchange rate. At least one of these prices had to fall to be able to find buyers for US assets who would be willing to finance the US current account deficit. Had the savings glut theory been true, there should have been an excess demand for American assets and at least one of these two prices would have had to have gone up in the years preceding the crisis. But the opposite was true. As will be shown in the next two sections, both sharply declined.

Depreciation of the dollar

The price decline during the years before the crisis was manifest primarily in the exchange rate of the dollar, shown in Figure 2.4. But let us first adopt a somewhat longer perspective before we turn to the events before the crisis. The diagram starts with 1963, when the Bretton Woods System of fixed exchange rates still existed.[10] At that time the price of the dollar was 4 deutschmarks. (Before the 1961 revaluation of the deutschmark, it had even

bernanke20070911a.htm), where he said: 'These external imbalances are to a significant extent a market phenomenon and, in the case of the US deficit, reflect the attractiveness of both the US economy and the depth, liquidity, and legal safeguards associated with its capital markets.'

[10] See Deutsche Bundesbank, *Die Deutsche Bundesbank, Aufgabenfelder, Rechtlicher Rahmen, Geschichte* (Frankfurt am Main, 2006).

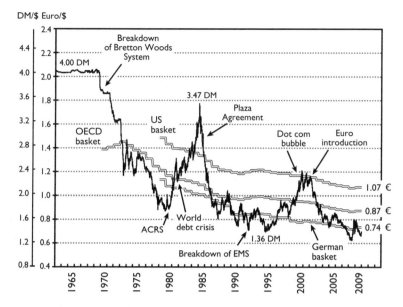

Fig. 2.4 Exchange rate of the dollar compared to its purchasing power parities (daily rates from 1 January 1963 to 31 December 2009)

Note: The three parallel curves represent purchasing power parities for the US market basket, the OECD market basket, and the German market basket. Purchasing power parities are 'natural' exchange rates that equalize the prices of well-defined market baskets in the countries under consideration. The natural price of a currency appears high if using the market basket of that country, but low if using the market basket of another country, because the relative prices of the countries are different, and more of the cheaper goods are purchased in each country.

Sources: OECD, *Purchasing Power Parities for Private Consumption*; Federal Statistical Office, *Internationaler Vergleich der Verbraucherpreise*; Federal Statistical Office, *Statistisches Jahrbuch für das Ausland*; Deutsche Bundesbank, *Devisenkursstatistik*; Ifo Institute estimates.

been 4.20 deutschmarks.) On the left-hand side, the diagram shows the price of the dollar in deutschmarks as well as in euros, the two values being determined at the official exchange rate between deutschmark and euro at the 1999 currency conversion. It can be seen that the dollar has declined over the course of decades from the heights it had reached during the Bretton Woods System.

To be sure, there were two intermediate rallies, the first one in the early 1980s and the second one on the eve of the physical introduction of the euro, but in view of the chronic deficit in the US current account the dollar tended to remain weak. The first intermediate rally began when President Reagan introduced the Accelerated Cost Recovery System (ACRS), massively stimulating investment via new depreciation rules, pushing up interest rates, and the demand for dollars in the years after 1981.[11] The rally was reinforced by the world debt crisis beginning in 1982, which itself could have been triggered by Reagan's reforms. The second rally started when the introduction of the euro was announced and Eastern Europeans changed from the then transaction currency deutschmark to the dollar, because they feared exchange losses, and tax dodgers tried to escape official conversion of their money so as to hide their wealth.[12]

In interpreting the diagram caution is needed, as the high inflation rate in the USA also played a role. This is shown by the three parallel curves for three different purchasing power parities. Purchasing power parity is a calculated exchange rate that equalizes the prices of a well-defined market basket in the countries under consideration. If we use the American market basket, which contains a lot of gasoline, homes, and hamburgers, the dollar looks expensive, although the purchase of this market basket compared to the same basket in Europe would not put anyone off. Correspondingly, the American purchasing power parity is presented by the uppermost of the three parallel curves in the diagram. The middle curve shows the purchasing power parity on the basis of the OECD market basket, representing average international consumption habits. The lowest curve reflects the purchasing power parity of the German market basket containing, among others, wine, cheese, long vacations, things that Americans buy less frequently because they are so expensive at home. Purchasing the German market basket in America requires deeper pockets unless the dollar is correspondingly cheap. Purchasing power parities define a natural range of dispersion for the actual exchange rate, because a deviation of this rate would cause purchases of goods and currencies in one or the other direction that would bring the exchange rate back to the dispersion range. If the dollar is very cheap, many Europeans exchange euros for dollars in order to buy American goods and thereby drive up the exchange rate of the dollar. If the dollar is very expensive, many Americans

[11] H.-W. Sinn, 'Die Bedeutung des Accelerated Cost Recovery System für den internationalen Kapitalverkehr', *Kyklos*, 37 (1984), 542–76; H.-W. Sinn, 'Why Taxes Matter: A Comment on Reagan's Tax Reforms and the US Trade Deficit', *Economic Policy*, 1 (1985), 239–50.

[12] H.-W. Sinn and F. Westermann, 'The Euro, Eastern Europe, and Black Markets: The Currency Hypothesis', in P. de Grauwe (ed.), *Exchange Rate Economics: Where Do We Stand?* (MIT Press, Cambridge, Mass., 2005), 207–38.

exchange dollars for euros in order to buy goods in Europe. This drives up the euro and consequently drives down the dollar.

Since countries have different rates of inflation, purchasing power parities change over time. America has always had a higher inflation rate than the core countries of Europe. This devalued the dollar according to all three definitions of purchasing power parities, which is reflected in the declining movement of the corresponding curves. And it is evident that the actual exchange rate of the dollar essentially tended to follow the purchasing power parities. It is remarkable, however, that during past decades the dollar was also weak compared to the range of purchasing power parities. Even in the years after the introduction of the euro, after the temporary special effects in favour of the dollar had disappeared, the dollar weakened substantially and slid again below the German purchasing power parity until the beginning of 2008, when the American housing crisis was already widely known. Compared to the purchasing power parities, the dollar was again as cheap as after the crisis of the European Monetary System in 1992. The reader may remember that at that time the European Monetary System, developed by French President Valéry Giscard d'Estaing and German Chancellor Helmut Schmidt, had collapsed because the deutschmark had become subject to a high appreciation pressure as a consequence of German unification.

On closer inspection, it becomes clear that the dollar temporarily strengthened again in the second half of 2008 and the first half of 2009. In view of the crisis of the American economy the slight strengthening was surprising at first glance. It was probably due to the breakdown of the American interbank trade. American companies and banks, which had incurred debt through short-term revolving credits in their own currency in order to finance long-term investment, faced liquidity problems, because these credits failed. Subsequently they tried to obtain the credits in Europe, where the credit crunch was somewhat less severe. The euros they acquired were changed into dollars, thereby again driving up the dollar exchange rate. What happened may also be described in terms of an increased demand for US liquidity. The collapse of the interbank market, which began in America, dramatically increased American liquidity preference, that is, the demand for dollar cash, to such an extent that all other assets being sold by investors, including stocks of euro cash, became cheaper relative to the dollar.[13] This was only a temporary though important effect that disappeared once the interbank market stabilized again after banks regained confidence in the second half of 2009.

From time to time the undervaluation of the dollar may again be interrupted for speculative reasons. A tendency toward undervaluation will be necessary, however, as long as the current account remains as massively in deficit as it is today, as this is a sign that American money and American securities will be in excess supply on world capital markets. Only when the current account normalizes or declining asset prices take over the adjustment pressure will the dollar exchange rate be able to return to normal. Over time, a normalization of the current account is indeed to be expected, as a cheap dollar lowers not only the foreign price of American securities but also that of American goods, thereby permitting American exports to rise again. Moreover, in America imported goods will become more expensive, causing Americans to buy fewer of them.

The process of normalization will take some time, however. A deficit which was built up over forty years can hardly be eliminated in just four years. To accomplish this, the American economy must be restructured to create new export capacities, a feat that will take some time.

Stock price collapse

Not only has the value of the dollar fallen dramatically since 2000, but so have the prices of American stocks in terms of dollars. This is shown in Figure 2.5, which presents the price–earnings ratio in a long time series from 1881 to the end of 2008.

---

[13] According to the so-called currency hypothesis, the exchange rate between two currencies is determined by the relative demand for stocks of cash and demand deposits (M1) rather than the demands for interest-bearing assets as such. According to this hypothesis, an increase in US liquidity demand relative to European liquidity demand had to revalue the dollar, and this would even be true with sterilizing interventions of the central banks aiming at stabilizing short-term interest rates. Cf. Sinn and Westermann, 'The Euro, Eastern Europe, and Black Markets', op. cit. The explanation that the dollar was driven up by the increase in US liquidity demand due to the breakdown of the interbanking market and the prediction that it would decline again when this market recovers was made before the event. See the first German edition of this book published in April 2009: H.-W. Sinn, *Kasino-Kapitalismus*, 1st edn. (Econ, Berlin, 2009), 41.

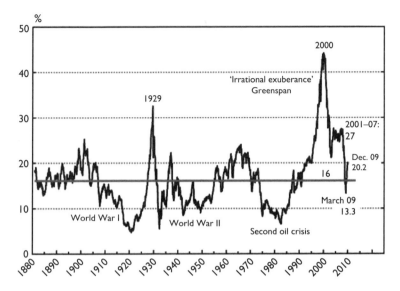

Fig. 2.5 The price–earnings ratio of the stocks in the Standard & Poor's 500 index (January 1881–December 2009)

Source: Robert Shiller Online Data (http://www.econ.yale.edu/~shiller/data/ie_data.xls, accessed on 18 January 2010); US Bureau of Labor Statistics; Ifo Institute calculations.

It is interesting to use this time series to retrace the history of the world economy. In the First World War stock prices fell. In the 1920s they rose again, peaking temporarily in the autumn of 1929 and then falling into a bottomless pit. Those were the times of the hitherto worst crisis in the world economy, as reported in Chapter 1. During the Second World War stock prices were still rather low, rising in the post-war period until the middle of the 1960s. The period from the Vietnam War to the second oil price shock was then characterized again by a decline in stock prices. Thereafter a development began that is directly related to today's crisis of the world economy. Stock prices rose astronomically until August 2000. As early as 1996 Alan Greenspan, chairman of the Federal Reserve, had already conjured up the risk of 'irrational exuberance' in the run-up to the crisis.[14] In 2000 the stock price bubble burst. After the attack on the World Trade Center on 11 September 2001, followed directly by the invasion of Afghanistan and in the spring of 2003 by the Iraq War, stock prices seemed to lose their

---

[14] Cf. A. Greenspan, *The Challenge of Central Banking in a Democratic Society*, address, American Enterprise Institute, Washington, 5 December 1996.

footing. Yet, at that time, they fell only to an intermediate level. The price–earnings ratio of 27 in 2007 was, measured against its long-term average of 16, still extremely high. Not until the autumn of 2008 did stock prices slide in a dramatic way from this intermediate level, as described in Chapter 1 in the context of Black Friday on 10 October 2008. By March 2009 the price–earnings ratio had fallen to 13, and in the consecutive months it climbed again when the signs of an end of the recession became stronger. By the end of 2009 it had reached a value of 20. This value is, as shown in the diagram, above the long-term average.

The collapse of US stock prices seems to corroborate the hypothesis that an excess supply of American securities on world markets depressed their prices. However, as Figure 2.6 shows, the stock prices of the German DAX and the Euro Stoxx also declined roughly in parallel to the American stocks. By itself, this points to other explanations that also apply to many countries. Thus, one possible explanation is that stocks were pushed up worldwide by exaggerated promises of yields and that a correction was therefore unavoidable. Another is the already mentioned increase in the demand for liquidity accompanied by investors' sharply rising risk aversion. But these, too, are superficial explanations that fail to penetrate to the core of the events.

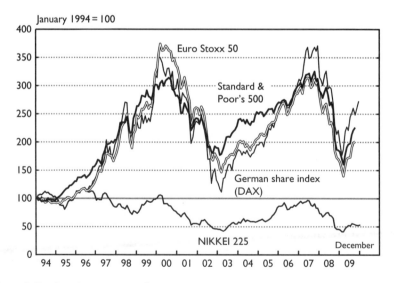

Fig. 2.6 Stock prices compared

Source: Deutsche Börse, Dow Jones and Company, Bank of Japan.

Savings glut or glut of toxic assets?

A better understanding of the events can be gained by looking at the stocks of American financial institutions and here especially at the collateralized debt obligations (CDOs) they issued, whose prices are shown in Figure 2.7. CDOs are the often-cited securities collateralized by real estate, the owners of which have lost a great deal of money in the crisis. CDOs are securitized claims against a chain of further claims, at the end of which we usually find American housing loans, credit card loans, and car leasing contracts. These securitized claims are traded among banks in various tranches of credit-worthiness and reach different prices depending on their risk class.

The tranches of creditworthiness may be explained by a kind of cascading construction of the CDOs that Chapter 7 will deal with in detail. When homeowners pay back their mortgages, the claims of the highest tranche (senior tranche or AAA tranche) are fully met first, then the claims of the middle tranche (mezzanine tranche) are serviced, and finally, if there is any

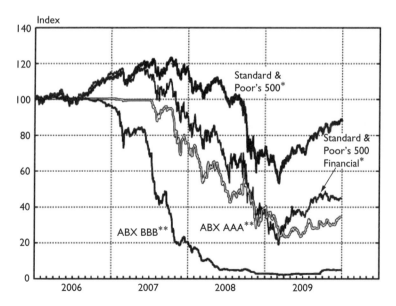

Fig. 2.7 Various investments compared

* Standard & Poor's stock indices for companies or financial institutions.
** Indices of the prices of mortgage-based CDOs of the category AAA and BBB.
Source: Standard & Poor's, Markit Group, Ifo Institute calculations.

money left because all borrowers are still solvent, the claims of the worst tranche (equity tranche or BBB tranche) are met.

As the figure shows by means of the two lower curves, the prices of the CDO tranches have successively dropped in recent years and have lost ground relative to the stock prices. As early as the beginning of 2007, the price of the worst CDO tranche (ABX BBB) started to fall and collapsed in the course of the year. In 2009, the market price of these assets amounted to only 5 per cent of that at mid-2006. People holding such assets lost almost everything. Significantly later, around the middle of 2007, the AAA-rated CDO trance (ABX AAA) followed. People who had bought these assets were told by the rating agencies that they were as safe as government bonds, and yet their values fell to about 30 per cent of their face value and will probably never recover, due to the institutional deficiencies that in the meantime have been detected in their construction.

The shares of the financial institutions (Standard & Poor's Financial), which had risen with the general trend until the summer of 2007, eroded correspondingly, as the banks had these CDOs on their accounts and had to write them down in accordance with their price decline, thereby reducing their equity. By early 2009, the stock prices of the financial institutions had fallen to a level of only about 30 per cent of their 2006 average or to about one-quarter of their peak price in the first half of 2007.

All of this was the markets' reaction to the supply of increasingly suspect American securities that, as has become clear in the course of the crisis, will never be serviced as promised, because the claims they represent are not well founded and cannot be enforced, if necessary, with legal procedures due to the complexity and opaqueness of their construction. World financial markets are not suffering from a 'savings glut', as Fed Governor Bernanke claimed, but from a glut of American toxic assets. The next few chapters of this book will clarify this in detail and explain why the savings glut theory might have to be replaced with an institutional deficiency theory of what caused the events.

The housing crisis

It was primarily the falling creditworthiness of the claims rather than the mere overcrowding of portfolios that was responsible for all this, as is illustrated by Figure 2.8. The figure shows the development of house prices,

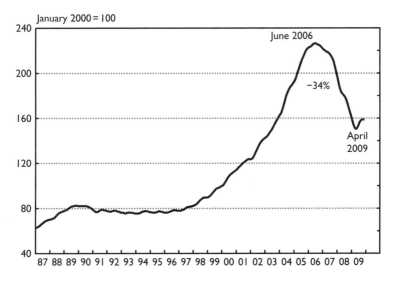

January 2000 = 100

Fig. 2.8 US house prices (Case-Shiller Index, January 1987–November 2009)

Source: Standard and Poor's, S&P/Case-Shiller Home Price Indices, accessed 26 January 2010.

more precisely the Case-Shiller Index that covers the sale prices of one-family homes in ten metropolitan areas. As shown, the prices of these homes rose rapidly from the second half of the 1990s to the first half of 2006. The rate of price increase in the ten-year period from 1996 to 2006 amounted to 190 per cent, corresponding to an annual average of 11.2 per cent. As this increase by far exceeded the growth rate of the economy, the term 'housing bubble', which is usually used for it, is entirely appropriate.

The ever-inflating bubble was an essential driver of American consumption that for many years increased faster than disposable income. The long-term downward trend of the savings rate of private households shown in Figure 2.1 reflects the excessive growth of consumption. The savings rate is, after all, that part of disposable household income that is not consumed. If the savings rate declines, consumption grows correspondingly faster than disposable income. Americans neglected to save because they thought they would be protected in old age by the steady increase in home prices. Furthermore they also frequently took advantage of borrowing more and more against their homes. The rising home prices are therefore also the deeper reason for the increasing US current account deficit, that is the surplus of goods received from abroad over those exported, that was paid for with debt certificates and various assets (Figure 2.2).

Bubbles have to burst some time. The American bubble did so in June 2006. At that time prices peaked. After that they fell at an unprecedented speed. During the two years and ten months from the peak of house prices in June 2006 to April 2009, the price decline was 34 per cent. This corresponds to a loss in the value of American housing of about $8 trillion.[15] A nuclear bomb exploded in the middle of the USA, whose shock waves were felt throughout the world.

Falling house prices resulted in many homeowners becoming overly indebted, making the orderly servicing of their mortgages and the CDOs based on them more and more unlikely. This is what, in the final analysis, lies behind the collapse of the tranches depicted in the previous diagram.

Although it was primarily the American financial institutions that suffered from the gigantic loan losses, in the end the whole world was affected. As shown in Figures 2.2 and 2.3, due to their export surpluses China, Germany, Japan, and a number of smaller emerging and developing countries were the major financiers of the world capital markets in recent years. It might be assumed therefore that these countries were hit especially hard by the losses of the American securities. However, because of their negative experience during the Asian crisis at the end of the 1990s, China and Japan had essentially bought US government bonds and eschewed CDOs.[16] Things were different in Germany, where all the large banks, especially the banks of the federal states (*Landesbanken*), participated in buying American securities. As Germany is one of the three big capital exporters of the world and, in contrast to China and Japan, had no reservations against these securities, a substantial part of the toxic US securities may have ended up here. Also affected, however, are the banks of many other capital exporting countries and even of countries that are not net exporters of capital, like

---

[15] At the end of the second quarter of 2006 the stock of housing assets amounted to $23,712 billion. Applying the percentage decline from Figure 2.8 (34%) yields a loss of $7,955 billion. See Federal Reserve Board, *Flow of Funds Accounts*, http://www.federalreserve.gov/releases/z1/Current/, accessed on 22 September 2009. Please note that the loss of wealth due to the bursting of the housing bubble cannot be calculated from the change in the value of the housing stock shown in the statistics, because in the meantime there was new residential construction.

[16] K. Viermetz, *Globale Finanzmarktkrise: Entwicklung, Verlauf, Reaktionen*, Bridging the Gap Conference, Munich, 28 November 2008.

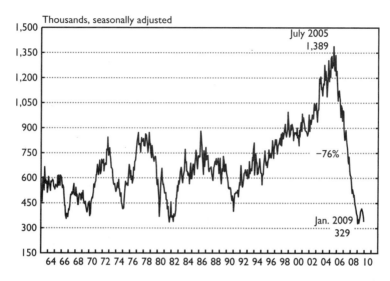

Fig. 2.9 Start-up home sales in the USA (January 1963–December 2009)

Source: US Census Bureau, *Economic Indicators, New Home Sales*, online at www.census.gov, accessed on 27 January 2010.

Ireland and Great Britain, as they specialized in investment banking, allocating substantial funds to seemingly high-interest CDOs.

The collapse of house prices not only shocked the financial sector, but the real sector of the economy as well. The most direct effect of falling house prices was on building activity. When prices fell below construction costs, it no longer paid to build new houses. Figure 2.9 shows the dramatic declines in the sales of newly built one-family homes in the USA. From its peak in July 2005 until January 2009 sales volume sank by 76 per cent; the volume of new home construction fell by a similar amount (79 per cent).[17] In January 2009, home sales were at their lowest level since the beginning of the survey of sales data in 1963, although in the meantime the American population had grown from 200 to 300 million people.

The collapse of new home construction resulted in unemployment in the construction industry and in the building materials industry. In parallel the construction industry reduced its investments and bought less construction equipment and fewer services from other industries, causing unemployment to

[17] See US Census Bureau, *Economic Indicators, Housing Starts*, online at www.census.gov, accessed on 12 January 2010.

rise there as well. The affected workers reduced their consumption with the result that the consumer goods industries, which supplied the affected workers, faced less demand and also laid off people. This was true for domestic goods as well as for imports. A negative multiplier was generated that initially affected the American economy and then successively spread to the world at large. Finally, all countries participating in international trade felt the downswing.

Consumption was also slowed down by other effects. Just as homeowners and stockholders had increased their consumption when they became richer, they cut back when the value of their homes declined. Many feared for their retirement provisions and tried to save more to make up the losses. Others had to limit their consumption because banks no longer extended expiring mortgage loans when home prices fell. In any case, consumption shrank, triggering negative multiplier effects for the world economy, whose consequences on the business cycle were already described in Chapter 1. The slowdown emanating from America was so enormous because America is an economic giant and because the lion's share of its wealth is invested in real estate. The bursting of the house price bubble triggered the chain reaction in the rest of the world that caused the first true worldwide recession after the Second World War.

In America and Europe stock prices collapsed, as was shown in Figures 2.5 and 2.6. In the capitals of the developing countries banks faced trouble, and economic growth weakened. In Dubai cranes stopped moving as they did in Astana, the capital of Kazakhstan. There is not a single region in the world that managed to escape the crisis. There were even temporary mass lay-offs in China.

In Europe it was especially Spain, Ireland, and Great Britain that were hit by the crisis, countries in which housing bubbles had developed in recent years. House prices declined from their respective peaks by 16 per cent in Spain until the second quarter in 2009, 31 per cent in Ireland until December 2009, and 17 per cent in Great Britain until April 2009. While France was also hit, albeit to a lesser extent, Germany and Italy were not affected, because they did not have a building boom. Figure 2.10 provides an overview of the real estate prices of these countries. For Spain, where the price decline was also substantial, the statistics unfortunately do not go back very far, but far enough to see the bubble bursting.[18] As the figure shows, Ireland's housing prices declined most.

---

[18] On the methodological details and the data see Instituto Nacional de Estadística (http://www.ine.es).

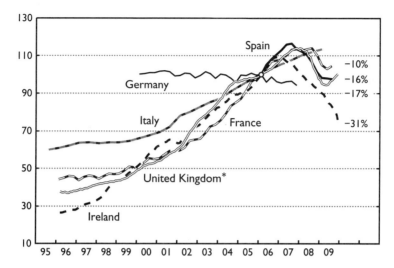

Fig. 2.10 Real estate prices in Europe

* England and Wales.

Note: The percentages on the right show the price declines between the respective maxima and minima of the curves.

Sources: The Economic and Social Research Institute (ESRI), *House Price Index*; Land Registry, *House Price Index Report*; Instituto Nacional de Estadística, Database: Construction and housing—Housing price index; Federal Statistical Office; Banca d'Italia, *Statistical Appendix: Economic Bulletin*, no. 53, July 2009.

Towards the end of 2009 there were still no signs of moderation of the precipitous downward trend. It is no wonder that Ireland suffered the biggest decline in GDP (about 7.5 per cent) of all Western European countries in 2009.

The reason for the collapse of the real estate markets outside the USA is primarily the contagion effects that unfold via expected growth rates. Housing prices depend very much on expected changes in rents, which in turn are determined by economic growth. Even small changes in the expected growth rate of rents can induce huge changes in housing values.[19] Spain and Great Britain had growth rates since the middle of the 1990s that were way above the Western European average, and correspondingly high housing prices that now, at a more realistic assessment, seem no longer warranted.

[19] According to the present value formula for perpetuities the house price equals the ratio of the rent to the difference between interest and nominal growth rate. For example, an annual rent of 20,000 euros, an interest rate of 8%, and a growth rate of 3% yields a house price of 400,000 euros. A growth rate of 4% would yield a house price of 500,000 euros, and a growth rate of 2% would yield a home price of 333,333 euros.

The contagion effects, which have spread to the entire world by means of the real estate and financial sector of the economy, have meanwhile resulted in massive wealth losses everywhere that far exceed the direct losses of the American homeowners. Thus, as Olivier Blanchard, the chief economist of the International Monetary Fund, reported at the Munich Lectures in November 2008, the IMF estimated the stock price losses in all markets in the period from July 2007 to November 2008 at $26.4 trillion.[20] And the Asian Development ment Bank even estimated that the worldwide loss of wealth for all assets combined was about $50 trillion in 2008,[21] which is nearly as much as the gross national product of the entire world ($60.9 trillion or 41.4 trillion euros in 2008).[22] In contrast, the direct loss incurred for the asset-backed securities of lowest quality, as represented by the lowest curve in Figure 2.7, only totalled $210 billion,[23] and the value loss of all credit claims already in the balance sheets by 31 January 2010, as shown in Chapter 8 (Figure 8.1), amounted to about $1.7 trillion. The losses in value of all assets of the world thus totalled 240 times the losses of the worst-rated CDOs, 29 times the losses in value of credit claims, and six times the losses of American residential real estate properties. The American housing crisis has unhinged the world financial system and triggered an immense destruction, historically unparalleled in this form.

Was monetary policy to blame?

The obvious question is: how did the crisis arise? Some economists see the essential problems in the area of monetary policy. Thus, Alan Greenspan, the former chairman of the Federal Reserve, is accused of having facilitated the collapse of house prices as well as of security prices by his extremely easy monetary policy in the aftermath of the attack on the World Trade Center. By setting interest rates so low, he is said to have driven stock prices to the

[20] O. Blanchard, *The Crisis: Basic Mechanisms, and Appropriate Policies*, Munich Lecture, CES, University of Munich, 18 November 2008, published in *CESifo Forum* 10, no. 1 (2009), 3–14.

[21] See Asian Development Bank, *Global Financial Turmoil and Emerging Market Economies: Major Contagion and a Shocking Loss of Wealth?*, online at http://www.adb.org.

[22] See International Monetary Fund, *World Economic Database*, April 2009, online at: http://www.imf.org/external/, accessed on 23 September 2009; converted into euros at the average annual exchange rate (1 euro = US $1.4708), see Deutsche Bundesbank, *Devisenkursstatistik*, July 2009.

[23] See International Monetary Fund, *Global Financial Stability Report*, October 2008, table 1.1.

heights from which they had dropped in the period from 2006 to 2008.[24] Conversely, he is also frequently accused of having caused the crisis by excessively fast increases in interest rates.[25] What are the facts?

As shown in Figure 2.11, the Federal Reserve did indeed set interest rates very low compared to the European Central Bank. The interest rate on banks' short-term refinancing transactions at the Federal Reserve, which peaked at 6.5 per cent in 2000, had already fallen to 1.75 per cent at the end of 2001 and then even declined to 1 per cent by the summer of 2003, until then the lowest interest rate in American history. This low interest rate effectively contributed to economic recovery and helped pull America out of the recession a good one-and-a-half years ahead of continental Europe. It also encouraged people to invest their own money or borrowed funds in homes and stocks.

It would be inadvisable to denounce this policy out of hand. As sentiment was extremely depressed after the attack on the World Trade Center and the economy was in the doldrums, most commentators lauded Greenspan at the time for his courageous interest rate policy. Leftist European economists even recommended the European central bank to follow suit and criticized it for not being willing to implement a similarly easy interest rate policy.[26]

---

[24] See e.g. R. Ahrend, B. Cournède, and R. Price, 'Monetary Policy, Market Excesses and Financial Turmoil', *OECD Economics Department Working Papers*, no. 597 (2008). With the words 'With low interest rates Greenspan has triggered the credit flood', Joseph Stiglitz also joins Greenspan's critics: see 'Nobelpreisträger: "Greenspan und Bush schuld an Finanzkrise"', *Die Presse*, 27 April 2008, online at http://diepresse.com/home/wirtschaft/finanzkrise/379928/index.do?from=simarchiv.

[25] See L. Knappmann, 'Greenspans explosives Erbe', *manager-magazin*, 3 February 2006, online at http://www.manager-magazin.de/geld/artikel/0,2828,398801,00.html.

[26] Cf. e.g. H. Flassbeck, 'Falsche Prognosen—falsche Politik' ('Wrong Forecasts—Wrong Policies'), *Handelsblatt*, 28 August 2001: 'Es ist ... Amerika, das in der Finanzpolitik auf Expansionskurs gegangen ist, während Europa mit "ruhiger Hand" die Krise verschärft. Es ist die amerikanische Geldpolitik, die handelt, während die europäische abwartet.' ('It is America ... that has followed an expansionary fiscal policy while Europe is aggravating the crisis with a "steady hand". It is American monetary policy that acts, while the European one waits.'); H. Flassbeck, 'Jobless Growth ohne Growth?', *Financial Times Deutschland*, 25 March 2004: 'In Europa tut die Zentralbank im dritten Jahr der Stagnation nichts, um die Zinsen wenigstens auf amerikanisches Niveau herunter zu bringen.' ('In Europe the central bank has done nothing, in the third year of stagnation, to reduce interest rates at least to the American level.')

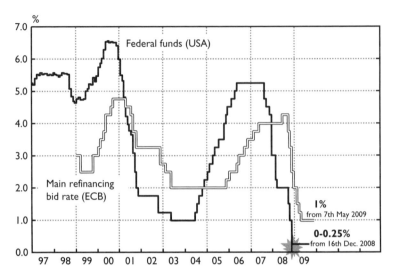

Fig. 2.11 Interest rate policy in the USA and Europe

Source: European Central Bank, Federal Reserve Board.

At the time, Greenspan faced a conflict between the necessity of preventing the housing bubble and the desire not to let stock prices drop precipitously. A look at Figures 2.5 and 2.6 shows that he did a rather good job. Contrary to a frequently heard assertion, no new bubble formed on the stock markets after the collapse of 2000. Although stock prices of US corporations rose again after the attack on the World Trade Center in 2001, they rose more slowly than profits. The price–earnings ratio of the 500 most important US corporations (as covered by 'Standard & Poor's 500' stock index) fell during the years before 2007 to a level of about 27.

To be fair, the accusation must refer to the stock price bubble of 2000 and its development up to this point, not to monetary policy in the last decade. Instead of only talking about 'irrational exuberance' during the bubble formation in the 1990s, Greenspan could have raised interest rates much more in order to brake the stock price boom in time. At that time he definitely made mistakes. But it is far-fetched to attribute the stock price collapse in 2008 to monetary policy in the 1990s.

It is however correct to say that the current crisis was triggered by the rising interest rates from the second half of 2004, for which Greenspan, who relinquished his job to his successor Bernanke in January 2006, must share the

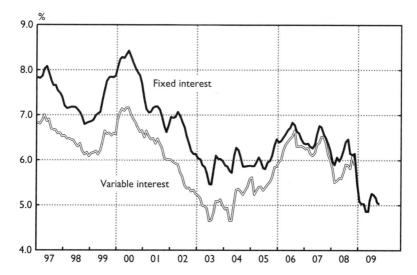

Fig. 2.12 Mortgage rates (January 1997–November 2009)

Source: Federal Housing Finance Board (http://www.fhfa.gov, data accessed on 12 January 2010).

responsibility. However, interest rates at the start of the housing crisis, in the summer of 2006, were, despite the preceding increases, far lower than during the last economic boom, the peak phase of the dot-com companies in 2000.

Mortgage rates, too, which are held to be primarily responsible for the bursting of the housing bubble by some economists, did not climb to an exorbitant level, as shown in Figure 2.12. They did rise, but at their peak they were between 6.5 per cent and 7 per cent before the house prices crashed, and thus considerably below their peak in 2000.

When the economy booms, the central bank must raise interest rates in order to prevent overheating and be ready to cut interest rates to cushion the next downswing. Thus the Federal Reserve cannot be accused of having triggered the crisis with its interest rate increases. The structural factors of the banking and housing crisis had to become manifest at some point. What triggers a crisis is not the underlying reason for an undesirable development, just as the heavy load of a truck is not to blame for the collapse of a rickety bridge.

The following chapters will disclose the true reasons for the crisis and indicate what corrective policy measures should be applied.

CHAPTER 3

Bank Failures

Record number of failures

The negative effects of the American housing crisis on the construction industry, private consumption, and investment soon unleashed their full force in the so-called real economy. They were bad enough for the world economy. The international eruptions, however, took on a new dimension through the banking crisis that was triggered by the housing crisis. The banking crisis reinforced the downward trend of the real economy and drove the world into its first true recession after the Second World War.

Banks hold credit claims and own securities and equity. If credit claims must be written off and if the market prices of the securities and stock holdings drop because debtors become insolvent or profits dwindle, then the little equity capital that banks have shrinks more than proportionally. Banks go bankrupt or are at least substantially weakened, so that they are no longer able to maintain their loans to private business. The cut-back of loans reduces business investment and hurts the construction and capital goods industries. As these industries lay off people, consumption declines and finally the international economy is hit a second time.

The banking crisis started in August 2007, when interbank transactions broke down temporarily and could only be revived by massive central bank interventions. This was preceded by a drastic change in the valuation of mortgage-backed securities that had been issued on the American market: the American rating agencies lowered the rating of these securities in part by several credit standing grades. The downgrading by the agencies, which in itself was the consequence of the collapse of house prices in America that had already been going on for one year (see Figure 2.8), shook the confidence in the creditworthiness of the mortgage-backed securities. Substantial losses in market value were experienced in all valuation categories or tranches, as was already shown in Figure 2.7. The devaluation also fed the general suspicion that banks may collapse. This suspicion undermined the confidence in the creditworthiness of market partners, so that banks stopped lending to each other. In the autumn of 2007, the crisis, which many people did not notice during their summer holiday, seemed to be over, and more confidence spread again among the banks and their customers. Confidence did not last long, however. When at the end of the year the balance sheets were prepared, it turned out that many banks had become excessively indebted, which forced them to take legal steps or at least made refinancing more difficult. A great many banks collapsed.

2008 will go down in history as a year of bank failures, since well over 100 banks disappeared worldwide that year through bankruptcy and acquisition or were nationalized at the last minute. These included twenty-seven US banks insured by the FDIC (Federal Deposit Insurance Corporation) that went bankrupt because they were not considered systemically relevant and were therefore not bailed out by the government. In 2007 only three such banks had gone bankrupt. And 2009 was probably even worse, as in the USA alone another 140 FDIC member banks declared bankruptcy.[1] Table 3.1 provides an overview of the developments, which is by no means complete and covers only a selection of the dramatic events during the crisis. A more detailed but still incomplete chronology of the financial crisis is contained in the appendix to this book.

It began in late summer 2007 with the British bank Northern Rock. Because of a relatively low level of deposits, Northern Rock had to rely on refinancing on the financial markets. When bottlenecks developed in the interbank market as a consequence of the US mortgage crisis, the bank experienced difficulties because other banks called in their loans. When rumour of this news spread, worried depositors began to clean out their accounts. Figure 3.1 shows customers queuing up at a branch of the bank to

[1] Federal Deposit Insurance Corporation, *Failed Bank List*, online at www.fdic.gov/bank/individual/failed/banklist.html, accessed on 18 January 2010.

Table 3.1 Chronology of the banking crisis in 2008

24 Jan	Norlarco Credit Union acquired by Public Service Credit Union (USA)
25 Jan	Douglass National Bank acquired by Liberty Bank and Trust Company (USA)
17 Feb	**Northern Rock nationalised (UK)**
7 Mar	Hume Bank acquired by Security Bank (USA)
17 Mar	**Bear Stearns acquired by JP Morgan Chase & Co. (USA)**
1 Apr	**Sachsen LB acquired by LBBW (Germany)**
3 May	St. Luke Baptist Federal Credit Union bankrupt (USA)
9 May	ANB Financial acquired by Pulaski Bank and Trust Company (USA)
12 May	Father Burke Federal Credit Union bankrupt (USA)
30 May	First Integrity Bank acquired by First International Bank and Trust (USA)
7 Jun	Catholic Building Society acquired by Chelsea Building Society (UK)
1 Jul	Countrywide Financial acquired by Bank of America (USA)
1 Jul	Cal State 9 Credit Union bankrupt (USA)
1 Jul	Sterlent Credit Union bankrupt (USA)
11 Jul	**IndyMae nationalised (USA)**
14 Jul	Alliance and Leicester acquired by Banco Santander (UK, Spain)
16 Jul	Meriden F.A. Federal Credit Union bankrupt (USA)
25 Jul	First National Bank of Nevada acquired by Mutual of Omaha Bank (USA)
28 Jul	New London Security Federal Credit Union bankrupt (USA)
1 Aug	First Priority Bank acquired by SunTrust Bank (USA)
8 Aug	Port Trust Federal Credit Union acquired by CPM Federal Credit Union (USA)
21 Aug	**IKB acquired by Lone Star (Germany, USA)**
22 Aug	The Columbian Bank and Trust Conpany acquired by Citizens Bank and Trust (USA)
26 Aug	Roskilde Bank acquired by Danmarks Nationalbank (Denmark)
5 Sep	Silver State Bank acquired by Nevada State Bank (USA)
8 Sep	**Fannie Mae and Freddie Mac nationalised (USA)**
8 Sep	Derbyshire Building Society acquired by Nationwide Building Society (UK)
8 Sep	Cheshire Building Society acquired by Nationwide Building Society (UK)
15 Sep	**Lehman Brothers bankrupt (USA)**
15 Sep	**Merrill Lynch acquired by Bank of America (USA)**
17 Sep	**AIG nationalised (USA)**
17 Sep	**HBOS acquired by Lloyds TSB (UK)**
17 Sep	Interfaith Federal Credit Union bankrupt (USA)
19 Sep	AmeriBank acquired by Pioneer Community Bank (USA)

Table 3.1 (Continued)

22 Sep	**Goldman Sachs and Morgan Stanley become regular commercial banks (USA)**
26 Sep	**Washington Mutual acquired by JP Morgan Chase & Co. (USA)**
29 Sep	Integrity Bank acquired by Regions Bank (USA)
29 Sep	Kaiperm Federal Credit Union acquired by Alliant Credit Union (USA)
29 Sep	**Fortis rescued by the state (Belgium, Luxembourg, Netherlands)**
29 Sep	**Bradford & Bingley nationalised (UK)**
29 Sep	**Hypo Real Estate rescued by the state (Germany)**
29 Sep	**Wachovia acquired by Wells Fargo (USA)**
30 Sep	**Dexia rescued by the state (Belgium, France, Luxembourg)**
30 Sep	Irish government provides a 400-billion-euro guarantee to six Irish banks
2 Oct	Greece declares deposit guarantee
3 Oct	TEXDOT-WF Credit Union acquired by Postel Family Credit Union (USA)
6 Oct	N&W Poca Division Federal Credit Union bankrupt (USA)
7 Oct	**Landsbanki nationalised (Iceland)**
8 Oct	Kaupthing Singer & Friedlander nationalised (Iceland, UK)
8 Oct	Heritable Bank acquired by ING Direct (Iceland, UK)
8 Oct	Kaupthing EDGE acquired by ING Direct (Iceland, UK)
8 Oct	**Glitnir nationalised (Iceland)**
9 Oct	**Kaupthing Bank nationalised (Iceland)**
9 Oct	Bank West acquired by Commonwealth Bank of Australia (Australia)
9 Oct	Icesave nationalised (Iceland, UK)
10 Oct	Main Street Bank acquired by Monroe Bank and Trust (USA)
10 Oct	Meridian Bank acquired by National Bank (USA)
10 Oct	Yamato Seimei Hoken bankrupt (Japan)
11 Oct	G7 meeting in Washington agrees on global rescue plan
12 Oct	European countries meet in Paris and agree on concerted plan of action
13 Oct	**Royal Bank of Scotland, HBOS and Lloyds nationalised (UK)**
13 Oct	Sovereign Bank acquired by Banco Santander (USA, Spain)
16 Oct	**The state of Iceland becomes insolvent**
16 Oct	**Hungary threatened by bankrupcy, ECB makes €5 billion in assistance available**
17 Oct	**Constantia Privatbank acquired by five banks (Austria)**
22 Oct	Barnsley Building Society acquired by Yorkshire Building Society (UK)
24 Oct	Commerce Bancorp acquired by Toronto-Dominion Bank (USA, Canada)

(cont.)

Table 3.1 (Continued)

24 Oct	National City Bank acquired by PNC Financial Services (USA)
24 Oct	Alpha Bank and Trust acquired by Stearns Bank (USA)
31 Oct	Freedom Bank acquired by Fifth Third Bank (USA)
3 Nov	Commerzbank makes use of German government's rescue package
3 Nov	Kommunalkredit Austria nationalised (Austria)
4 Nov	Scarborough Building Society acquired by Skipton Building Society (UK)
7 Nov	Franklin Bank acquired by Prosperity Bank (USA)
7 Nov	Security Pacific Bank acquired by Pacific Western Bank (USA)
8 Nov	Parex Bank nationalised (Latvia)
9 Nov	Franklin Bank bankrupt (USA)
21 Nov	The Community Bank bankrupt (USA)
21 Nov	Downey Savings and Loan Association bankrupt (USA)
21 Nov	PFF Bank and Trust bankrupt (USA)
21 Nov	Downey Savings and Loan acquired by U.S. Bank (USA)
21 Nov	PFF Bank and Trust acquired by U.S. Bank (USA)
21 Nov	The Community Bank acquired by Bank of Essex (USA)
1 Dec	London Scottish Bank nationalised (UK)
5 Dec	West Hartford Credit Union bankrupt (USA)
5 Dec	First Georgia Community Bank acquired by United Bank (USA)
12 Dec	Haven Trust Bank acquired by BB&T Company (USA)
12 Dec	Sanderson State Bank acquired by The Pecos County State Bank (USA)

withdraw their funds. This happened as early as 14 September 2007.[2] Cash outflows in turn forced the bank to look for even more credit, aggravating the difficulties. Thus the queues became longer and longer, and insolvency threatened. At first the Bank of England refused to help so as not to set a precedent. After all, bankruptcies are part of the normal course of business. The Bank of England could not withstand the political pressure, however. Thus, in the end the government helped out with funds of its own, and Alistair Darling, the Treasury Secretary, announced the nationalization of the bank on 17 February 2008. Based on an emergency law, selling of Northern Rock stocks was suspended on 18 February 2008, and on the same day the distinguished crisis manager and former chief executive of Lloyd's of London, Ron Sandler, was appointed chairman of Northern Rock.[3]

---

[2] See H. Wallop, 'Northern Rock Customers Withdraw £1bn', *Telegraph*, 16 September 2007, www.telegraph.co.uk, accessed on 18 February 2009.

[3] See Northern Rock, *Provisional Northern Rock Restructuring Plan*, Executive Summary, March 2008, online at www.northernrock.co.uk, accessed on 23 January 2009.

London, September 2007

Fig. 3.1 Bank run on Northern Rock

Next to encounter difficulties was the US investment bank Bear Stearns. It specialized in investing in risky corporate bonds and the mortgage trade. Bear Stearns stumbled over two hedge funds it had founded that were deeply involved in the trade of subprime US mortgages. In March it was announced that it was to be sold to JPMorgan Chase & Co. at the last minute to avoid imminent bankruptcy. In 2007 Bear Stearns was the fifth largest US investment bank, with a balance sheet of $400 billion and a staff of 14,000.[4]

The German Landesbanken

The banks of the German federal states (*Landesbanken*), which carry out about a fifth of the German banking business and had combined total assets of 2.06 trillion euros in 2007, were among the first victims of the banking crisis in Europe.[5] They had purchased a large volume of securities issued by American

---

[4] See Bear Stearns, *Annual Report 2007*, online at www.sec.gov, and Fortune500, *Annual Ranking of America's Largest Corporations 2007*, online at www.money.cnn.com, accessed on 19 February 2009.

[5] In addition to the banks of the federal states there are local public banks, the Sparkassen, which account for about 30% of the overall banking market in Germany.

investment banks that had become distressed due to the bursting of the US housing bubble. They typically had conducted huge transactions via their Irish special purpose vehicles (SPV), which they had founded for this purpose. Often these vehicles or firms were organized as conduits, as non-profit foundations with little equity. The special purpose vehicle raised short-term loans in the Eurobond market and invested them long-term in American securities. This seemed to be an excellent business, as short-term loans up to a maturity of three months were available at interest rates of only 1.5 per cent, while the American securities promised a yield of about 7 per cent. Thus the interest margin amounted to 5.5 per cent. This business worked very well as long as the special purpose vehicles were held to be reliable partners, which initially seemed warranted due to the guarantees of the sponsor companies in Germany. In the course of the devaluation of the mortgage-backed securities, many of which were held by the special purpose vehicles, the customers lost confidence, however, and replacing the short-term loans became difficult. The sponsor banks could have done the deal on their own accounts, but they profited from the low taxes in Ireland and the circumstance that they did not have to carry the transactions of the special purpose vehicles on their books and hence did not have to hold equity against them. By maintaining a shadow banking system they were able to do deals that far exceeded their own capacities. In the end this caused them enormous trouble.

The first victim was the bank of the federal state of Saxony (Sachsen LB), a mid-sized bank with a balance sheet of 68 billion euros. It had to be rescued with huge guarantees from the Association of Savings Banks (17.3 billion euros) and the state of Saxony (2.75 billion euros) before it was taken over by the Landesbank of Baden-Württemberg (LBBW). The next victim was the Landesbank of North-Rhine Westphalia (WestLB). The bank had to accept valuation losses amounting to 1.3 billion euros in the accounting year 2007. During the same period, the Landesbank of Hesse (Helaba) was forced to make write-downs and valuation adjustments in the amount of 300 million euros that were followed by another 224 million euros in the first half of 2008.[6]

---

[6] See WestLB Group, *Annual Report 2007*, online at www.westlb.de, as well as Helaba, *Annual Report 2007* and *Half-Year Financial Report 2008*, online at www.helaba.de, accessed on 23 January 2009.

Especially hard hit was the Landesbank of Bavaria (BayernLB). Via its special purpose vehicles it had become heavily involved in the US housing market. By the end of 2009, the bank had received state equity support in the order of 10 billion euros and state guarantees of 19.8 billion euros.[7]

In total, the Landesbanken had received 18 billion euros in state equity and 106 billion euros in state guarantees by the end of 2009. If the largely state-owned Deutsche Industriebank (IKB) is added, which was sold to the private equity company Lone Star on 21 August 2008, the latter two amounts increase to 19 billion euros and 125 billion euros, respectively ($28 billion and $183 billion). (See also Chapters 8 and 9.)

One reason for the substantial losses of the German Landesbanken may be that, as a result of a decision of the European Commission, they had lost the protection of the public liability guarantee from 2005 on. Because the liability guarantee had offered direct repayment claims against the German federal states to the creditors of the public banks, the public banks had been able in the past to refinance on very favourable terms. However, contrary to what the government expected, this advantage was not really transferred to industry in Germany, as the Landesbanken invested their funds internationally. As a result they earned high profits, of which they reinvested a larger fraction than is normal for private banks. Rapid balance sheet growth was the consequence.[8] This business model collapsed as a result of the EU Commission's decision of 2001 to abolish the state guarantee by 2005. The rating agencies reclassified the banks, and the market then forced them to offer their creditors higher interest rates, wiping out their profit margins. The EU had attempted to mitigate the consequences of its decisions by installing a grandfathering clause, according to which credit claims established before the deadline would continue to be protected for another ten years. However, as the grandfathering clause was announced as early as 2001, four years before the deadline, it gave banks the incentive to speed up

---

[7] See Bavarian State Chancellery, press release of 28 November 2008, Seehofer and Zeil: 'Umfassendes Hilfsprogramm für die BayernLB zur Stärkung der Kapitalbasis und zur Zukunftssicherung notwendig/Absolute Transparenz der Hilfen durch eigenes Haushaltskapitel', online at www.bayern.de, accessed on 23 January 2009, and BayernLB Group, *Financial Report 2008*, online at www.bayernlb.de, accessed on 25 September 2009.

[8] See H.-W. Sinn, *The German State Banks: Global Players in the International Financial Markets* (Edward Elgar, Cheltenham, UK, and Northampton, Mass., 1999).

their business and raise huge amounts of credit so as to expand their investment business to the limits before the door was closed, knowing that the government would stand in for any potential losses. As was confirmed by the guarantees and support payments that they were given in 2008, the banks had made their decisions on the basis of rational expectations.[9]

The next victims

The list of victims of the financial crisis is long. In the USA it hit the American housing financier IndyMac. IndyMac was one of the biggest US mortgage banks. In 2007 it had a balance sheet of $33 billion and 7,200 employees. Its main business strategy was to originate and securitize subprime loans (mostly Alt-A) on a large scale. This resulted in a rapid growth and high concentration of risky assets mainly in residential real estate markets in California and Florida. It had given an especially high volume of mortgages to customers with low creditworthiness, reacting to the incentives the government had set with its Community Reinvestment Act (see Chapter 5). But since it was 'too big to fail', it was taken over by the US government.

In Germany, the state-owned KfW sold its majority holdings in IKB to the American private equity company Lone Star in August.[10] IKB, with a 2007 balance sheet of 53 billion euros, had already faced difficulties in 2007 due to risky investments in the American housing market.[11] As a part of the rescue operations, KfW had increased its shareholdings step by step to 90.8 per cent by August 2008, but in the end bankruptcy seemed near and so IKB was sold for a scrap value of just 137 million euros.[12]

The financial crisis assumed dramatic dimensions in September 2008, after the summer vacation, at a time of the year when most of the financial

---

[9] See H.-W. Sinn, 'The German State Banks: Creative Destruction', *Ifo Viewpoint*, no. 93, www.cesifo.de, published in German as 'Großer Scherbenhaufen', *Wirtschaftswoche*, 18, 28 April 2008.

[10] Whereas an investment bank has numerous tasks, an investment company confines itself to fund management.

[11] See IKB, *9-Monats-Zwischenmitteilung zum 31. Dezember 2007*, online at www.ikb.de, accessed on 29 September 2009.

[12] See IKB, *Kapitalerhöhung der IKB: Finales Zeichnungsvolumen*, press release of 19 August 2008, online at www.IKB.de, accessed on 26 January 2009.

and stock market crises happen. At first the international public was shocked to hear that the American mortgage financiers Fannie Mae and Freddie Mac had to be nationalized. Fannie Mae (Federal National Mortgage Association, FNMA) and Freddie Mac (Federal Home Loan Mortgage Corporation, FHLMC) are the two largest mortgage banks worldwide. They have operated since 1968 and are organized as Government-Sponsored Enterprises (GSE). According to their special legal status, they pursued business objectives in the public interest but were privately owned. Because they were able to resort to credit lines of the American Treasury in case of liquidity problems, they received first-class ratings by the rating agencies and were thus able to refinance at lower interest rates than private competitor banks. They ran into difficulties because, in line with their mandate, they had bought a large volume of mortgages that were no longer serviced by the homeowners. At year-end 2007 the portfolio of private housing loans managed by Fannie Mae and Freddie Mac had reached a combined volume of about $5 trillion. The two banks thus guaranteed close to half of all private US mortgages, totalling $11.8 trillion. Due to rapidly increasing defaults, especially in the area of subprime mortgages, Fannie Mae and Freddie Mac reported a total loss in 2007 of about $5.2 billion.[13]

Lehman Brothers and the collapse of interbank operations

Then Lehman Brothers went bankrupt. Lehman Brothers, one of the world's largest investment banks, had been founded by German immigrants more than 150 years ago.[14] It had been regarded as one of the most profitable banks, had total assets of $504 billion in 2006, and a market value of $54 billion. In 2006 and 2007 it achieved a return on equity of 33 per cent and 27 per cent, respectively.[15] In Europe the bank was particularly well known

[13] See Fannie Mae or Freddie Mac, *Annual Report 2007*, online at www.fanniemae.com or www.freddiemac.com, accessed on 23 January 2009.

[14] The founders were the Lehman brothers who had immigrated from Rimpar in Franconia. See R. Flade, *Die Lehmanns und die Rimparer Juden: Zur Dauerausstellung im Rathaus Rimpar* (Königshausen & Neumann, Würzburg, 1996); 'Der Vorfahre aus Unterfranken', *Süddeutsche Zeitung*, 21/22 February 2008, p. 25.

[15] See Lehman Brothers, *Annual Report 2006* and *Annual Report 2007*.

for offering certificates in the form of bets on certain price developments on the stock markets.[16]

The financial community had erroneously assumed that Lehman Brothers was also 'too big to fail' and would therefore be rescued by the government. When Treasury Secretary Henry Paulson, former CEO of Lehman's competitor Goldman Sachs, declared on 10 September 2009 that he would not rescue Lehman Brothers, panic spread and the bank filed for bankruptcy five days later. But not only Lehman Brothers collapsed, the interbank market as such broke down, because an event that hitherto had been considered impossible had become possible. The banks feared that they would not get back the funds they had lent to other banks. After all, it was not known which assets the other banks had on their books, and whether they were robust enough to survive the banking crisis. The long-smouldering crisis became a large-scale fire, because the trust on which financial markets are built had disappeared.

Banks make a living from credit transfers. Some specialize in collecting funds from savers, the others in lending it to firms. Interbank operations ensure that the two functions match. In addition, banks conduct maturity transformation. They borrow funds short term at low interest rates and lend them longer term at high interest rates. That, too, is an important economic function that ensures that long-term real investment can be undertaken even when savers want to lend their money only short term. All of this stopped when interbank operations broke down. Banks that had funds were left sitting on them, and banks that needed funds to lend and invest could not get any. The separation between commercial and investment banks that characterizes the US financial system proved to offer no advantage in this crisis, because it grants such a preponderant role to the transfer of savings through the capital market. Chapter 11 will discuss this in more detail, pointing to the particular role of the Glass–Steagall Act (1933 –1999) that had enforced this separation.

To the extent interbank operations with loans continued despite the loss of trust, the creditors demanded enormously high interest rates because they feared they would not be able to recover their funds. Figure 3.2 presents the interest mark-up that banks must offer compared to the German state,

---

[16] According to the Schutzgemeinschaft für Kapitalanleger (Investor Protection Association) there are 400,000 different types of certificates in Germany of various issuers with a total volume of 140 billion euros. See 'Dummes deutsches Geld', *Süddeutsche Zeitung*, 8 April 2008, p. 28.

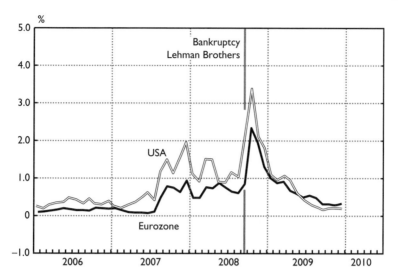

Fig. 3.2 Risk premium on the interbank market

Note: The time series presented here describe the differences between the London three-month interest rate in dollar or euro interbank operations (London Interbank Offered Rate, Libor) and the interest rate of German treasury bills (Bubills) of the same maturity. Daily data were converted to monthly averages.

Source: British Bankers Association, *BBA Libor*, online at www.bba.org.uk, Federal Reserve Board, *Selected Interest Rates*—H.15, Treasury bills (secondary market) and Reuters.

which traditionally can borrow at the most favourable conditions in Europe, if they want to get funds from other banks. The interest mark-up is a measure of creditors' fears of not getting their money back because the debtors become insolvent before repaying the loans. As shown above, the interest mark-up surged immensely after the bankruptcy of Lehman Brothers on 15 September, destroying the interest rate margins on relending the funds to private business and thus making lending unattractive. When the worst of the crisis was over, the risk premiums gradually fell again, and at the time of writing they had largely disappeared.

In many cases, savings banks, and other banks that collect households' savings, were not willing to lend funds even at high interest rates, as they distrusted the very people who were willing to accept even unfavourable credit terms.[17] Quantity restrictions resulted and created disequilibrium

---

[17] This is the core of the theoretical explanation of the credit constraint by J. Stiglitz and A. Weiss, 'Credit Rationing in Markets with Imperfect Information', *American Economic Review*, 71 (1981), 393–410.

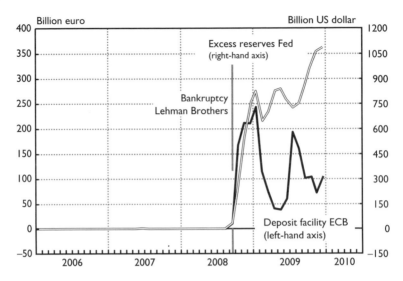

Fig. 3.3 Banks' excess deposits at central banks

Note: Deposit facilities are interest-bearing deposits of banks in the euro area on a daily basis at the European Central Bank. Excess reserves are banks' deposits at the European Central Bank (without time limitation) above and beyond their legal minimum reserves. The ratio of minimum reserves is 10% of the minimum reserve base in the USA, 2% in the euro area. (In general, demand deposits of a bank are defined as their minimum reserve base. The ECB asks for a positive reserve ratio for daily deposits, deposits with an agreed term or an agreed term of up to two years and securities with an original maturity of also up to two years. The Fed limits minimum reserve obligations to so-called transaction accounts (cheque deposits) and further adds the stock of cash of the financial institutions to the minimum reserve base.) In the euro area, minimum reserves bear interest. In the USA this has only been the case for minimum and excess reserves since October 2008. Daily data (ECB) and weekly data (Fed) were converted to monthly averages.

Source: European Central Bank (ECB), Statistics, *Monetary Operations*, Minimum reserves and liquidity; Federal Reserve Board (Fed), *Money Stock and Reserve Balances*, H.3 Aggregate Reserves of Depository Institutions and the Monetary Base.

between the demand and supply of credit that could no longer be eliminated by interest rate changes. Credit circulation came to a halt, and stocks of liquid funds accumulated, which economists call 'money hoarding' or 'growing liquidity preference'. As a consequence, a lack of demand developed in the real economy, in consumption and investment. Although the central banks tried to counter this by making available hundreds of billions of dollars and euros in additional liquidity, they could not fill the credit gaps.

The de facto collapse of interbank operations from liquidity hoarding is shown in Figure 3.3 by means of the volume of excess deposits that commercial banks held with the central banks. Normally, banks invest funds they do not need in the short term overnight at another bank that is in need of funds. In this way, the entire banking system generates a maximum of credit volume and interest earnings on the basis of the available money supply. As banks no longer trusted one another in the crisis, those that received savings deposited the accumulating funds at the central bank, and the others, which needed funds to lend, borrowed them there. Credit transactions were passed, as it were, through the central banks, which gave the funds lent a kind of repayment guarantee.

The volume of these short-term deposits at the central bank is shown in Figure 3.3. As can be seen, this volume also surged dramatically at the same time interest spreads widened after the demise of Lehman Brothers. Interestingly enough, these funds had not disappeared a year after the crisis, even though channelling the short-term credit operations through the central banks is costly, as the central banks pay lower interest than they charge. (The difference for lending and deposit facilities is about 1.5 percentage points in Europe and about 0.25 percentage points in the USA.) This indicates that there was still some tension in the market and that confidence and trust had not returned to their full extent.

The collapse of Lehman Brothers on 15 September 2008 was not the fundamental reason but rather the trigger of the present financial crisis that almost resulted in the collapse of the entire banking system of the Western world. In its wake, at least another fifty-three banks had gone under or had been nationalized by the end of the year.[18]

And still more victims

On the day that Lehman Brothers collapsed, Merrill Lynch, the third biggest US investment bank, with a 2007 balance sheet of $1.02 trillion, was acquired by Bank of America.[19] Merrill Lynch rose to prominence on the strength of its brokerage network, often referred to as the 'thundering herd'. The acquisition of residential and commercial mortgage related companies, such as the major subprime lender First Franklin, led to the creation of a mortgage assembly line that allowed Merrill Lynch to generate in-house

---

[18] See Table 3.1.

[19] Merrill Lynch, *Annual Report 2007*, online at www.ml.com, accessed on 28 September 2009.

mortgages that it could package into CDOs and sell to investors. Significant losses were attributed to the drop in value of its large and unhedged mortgage portfolio in the form of CDOs.

Two days later the American International Group (AIG), the world's biggest credit insurer, was nationalized because the collapse of this insurance company would have necessitated the worldwide write-down of ailing credit claims amounting to some $452 billion.[20] This would have triggered a barely controllable flood of bankruptcies. The government took 79 per cent of the shares, because with 80 per cent or more the bank's debt would have had to be included in the official government debt figure. AIG is an insurance company, founded in Shanghai, that had relocated its headquarters to New York in 1939. Its main business was the sale of flexibly designed credit default swaps (CDS) that it pioneered and offered to the whole world.[21]

Among the policyholders were 100,000 small firms, municipalities, pension funds, and corporations, primarily also the big banks of this world. Their supposed advantage was that, as an insurance company, AIG could utilize a gap in regulation that allowed it to carry out its transactions without backing them with corresponding equity holdings. But this was the very thing that caused its collapse.[22] In the fourth quarter of 2008, which was after its nationalization, AIG reported the biggest loss that until then any corporation worldwide had incurred in such a short period of time, and its loss of almost $100 billion for the entire year 2008 was also beyond any historical scope.[23]

AIG is of vital importance for the financial system of the entire world, as the reinsurance bought from AIG has enabled many banks to satisfy the regulatory minimum equity requirements of their countries. A bankruptcy of that company would immediately have forced many investment banks of the countries that adopted the Basel system for bank regulation to underlay

---

[20] AIG, *Annual Report 2007*, online at www.aig.com, accessed on 23 January 2009.

[21] Credit default swaps were invented by JPMorgan Chase & Co., but AIG developed them on a large scale.

[22] N. Piper, 'Das gefährlichste Unternehmen der Welt', *Süddeutsche Zeitung*, 7/8 March 2009, p. 34.

[23] 'AIG vor größtem Verlust der Wirtschaftsgeschichte', *Die Welt*, 25 February 2009, p. 12; 'AIG-Disaster reißt Börsen mit', *Handelsblatt*, 3 March 2009, p. 1.

their assets with much more equity capital. Given the widespread dearth of equity capital, this would have threatened many banks with the withdrawal of their licence or, at least, forced them to cut back massively on their loans to the real economy, with the effect of increasing the risk of a credit crunch. Furthermore, the banks insured by AIG would have run into serious difficulties if AIG had been unable to meet its payment obligations in the midst of the crisis. The Deutsche Bank alone, for instance, received insurance payments from AIG to the tune of $11.8 billion in 2009, which, considering the bank's own $30.7 billion equity capital, is not exactly insignificant. If the US government had not rescued AIG, Deutsche Bank would have probably gone bankrupt. The shock waves sent through the financial system would have been even higher than after the collapse of Lehman Brothers. So there was no alternative for the US government to nationalizing AIG and financing the losses with taxpayer money.

Even though AIG was rescued, further dramatic events took place. On the day of the decision to nationalize AIG, it was announced that the Halifax Bank of Scotland (HBOS) would be acquired by the British bank Lloyds (TSB). Another five days later Goldman Sachs and Morgan Stanley, the two remaining US investment banks, relinquished their formal status of investment bank and declared themselves regular banks. They did this although it meant complying with the regulation of the Federal Reserve and limiting their leverage ratio (see Chapter 7). As investment banks they had enjoyed great freedom of action and had not been regulated. Now they submitted to regulation in order to replace the diminishing credits from other banks by savings deposits of their own, to enjoy the protection of the Federal Deposit Insurance Corporation (FDIC) and, above all, to have access to the cheap credit the Federal Reserve was providing to commercial banks.

Then the floodgates opened. Washington Mutual, the biggest US savings institution, with a balance sheet of $328 billion in 2007, was sold to JPMorgan Chase & Co.[24] The acquisitions of various companies since 1990 had made Washington Mutual the third largest mortgage lender and one of the top ten credit card companies in the United States. Kerry Killinger, the former

---

[24] Washington Mutual, *Annual Report 2007*, online at www.sec.com, accessed on 28 September 2009.

CEO, wanted to make Washington Mutual the 'Wal-Mart of Banking' by focusing on lower- and middle-class consumers who other banks deemed too risky.[25]

In Belgium the Fortis Bank was rescued with state funds. Fortis, with a balance sheet of 871 billion euros and 62,000 employees in 2007, was one of the biggest banks of the Benelux countries.[26] Together with the Royal Bank of Scotland and Banco Santander it had formed a consortium that announced in October 2007 the acquisition of ABN-AMRO for 71 billion euros, the largest-ever bank takeover in history. To finance its part of the purchase, about 24 billion euros, Fortis tried to raise additional capital. Due to worries about upcoming future write-offs on ABN-AMRO, Fortis could raise the capital only by granting a discount of 25 per cent; its share price dropped rapidly. The bank ran into liquidity problems in September 2008 when bankruptcy rumours caused large withdrawals by business customers. On one day, Friday, 26 September, 20 billion euros were withdrawn, with an additional withdrawal of 30 billion euros expected for the following Monday.[27] Fortis was partially nationalized and split up on 29 September among the Netherlands, Belgium, and Luxembourg, who invested a total of 11.2 billion euros in the bank.[28]

In the UK the Bradford & Bingley bank was nationalized. Bradford & Bingley was one of the biggest mortgage lenders in the UK, with total assets of £62.9 billion ($126.7 billion) in 2007.[29] Apart from mainstream mortgages, the bank provided loans to individuals who wanted to invest in UK property, a programme called a *buy-to-let strategy*. In the course of the financial crisis and the credit crunch on the interbank market, the bank ran into liquidity problems. In June 2008, it launched a £400 million rights issue, which was not well subscribed by shareholders, leaving much of the issue with underwriters. As the share price dropped dramatically, the bank was nationalized

[25] 'Saying Yes, WaMu Built Empire on Shaky Loans', *New York Times*, 27 December 2008, online at www.nytimes.com, accessed on 28 September 2009.

[26] Fortis, *Annual Report 2007*, 5.

[27] *Fortis-klanten haalden op een dag 20 miljard weg*, online at www.zibb.nl, accessed 18 January 2010.

[28] Fortis, *Annual Report 2008*, 11.

[29] Bradford & Bingley, *Annual Report 2007*, online at www.bbg.co.uk, accessed on 29 September 2009.

by the British government on 29 September 2008 and split into two parts. The mortgage book remained with the now nationalized Bradford & Bingley plc, and the deposits and branch network went to the Spanish bank Grupo Santander.[30]

In Germany, Hypo Real Estate (HRE) was close to bankruptcy and could only be rescued temporarily by state and private credit lines in the amount of 50 billion euros and government guarantees of 52 billion euros.[31] Hypo Real Estate, Europe's biggest issuer of mortgage bonds and, with assets of 400 billion euros, of a similar size as Lehman Brothers, was not created until 2003 when it was spun off by HypoVereinsbank with part of the latter's real estate portfolio.[32] Since HRE had been given a risk cushion by HypoVereinsbank, it could initially float along quite comfortably on the waves of the cyclical upswing. Its stock price rose from 11 to 55 euros. But in 2007 HRE acquired the Depfa Bank, located in Ireland, and a short while afterwards assumed responsibility for this bank. In previous years Depfa had made money by refinancing long-term government credits with short-term loans, just like Sachsen LB Europe and the other German public banks. This business model, which functions as long as short-term funds are cheaper than long-term capital, failed when the money market collapsed with the Lehman bankruptcy. In June 2009, Hypo Real Estate was nationalized, the state acquiring an ownership share of 90 per cent with the aim of squeezing out the remaining shareholders. Without the nationalization, the European system of housing finance would probably have collapsed.

In the USA, the big Wachovia bank tumbled. With a balance sheet of $783 billion and 122,000 employees, Wachovia was the fourth biggest US bank.[33] In 2006, Wachovia acquired the mortgage bank Golden West

---

[30] Bradford & Bingley, *Annual Report& Accounts 2008;* HM Treasury, *Bradford & Bingley plc*, press release 97/08, 29 September 2008; HM Treasury, *Government Guarantee Arrangements: Bradford & Bingley plc*, press release 98/08, 29 September 2008.

[31] Hypo Real Estate Group, press releases of 12 November 2008, 9 December 2008, 20 January 2009, and 11 February 2009, online at www.hyporealestate.com, accessed on 18 February 2009.

[32] See Hypo Real Estate Group, *Annual Report 2007*, online at www.hyporealestate.com, accessed on 18 February 2009.

[33] See Wachovia, *Annual Report 2007*, online at www.wachovia.com, accessed on 29 September 2009.

Financial with a portfolio of about $122 billion, mainly risky loans, such as adjustable rate mortgages. In the course of the subprime crisis, Wachovia experienced heavy losses in its loan portfolios. On 26 September, the shares lost one-third of their value and businesses and institutional depositors withdrew money from their accounts in order to lower their balances below the $100,000 insured by the FDIC, an event known in banking circles as a 'silent run'. Wachovia lost $5 billion in deposits that day. Although this was only 1 per cent of the bank's total deposits, Wachovia ran into serious trouble. On 29 September 2008, the bank was taken over by Wells Fargo. Next to Citigroup (see below), Wachovia totalled up the biggest write-off losses of all banks in the financial crisis. For the period from July 2007 to October 2009 they were estimated at $101.9 billion (see Chapter 8), one-third more than the bank's equity capital.

In Belgium the Bank Dexia Group had to be supported by government guarantees and financial aid by Belgium, France, and Luxembourg to a total amount of 6.4 billion euros. Dexia was a Belgian-French financial institution that specialized in the public finance business. The Dexia Group was founded as a dual-listed company. In 1999 the Belgian entity took over the French entity to form a single company headquartered in Brussels. The bank had become shaky because of a billion-euro credit to Depfa, the special purpose bank maintained by Hypo Real Estate in Ireland, which itself had refinancing problems.[34]

Not only were banks pushed to the edge of bankruptcy, but also entire countries. Landsbanki, Glitnir, und Kaupthing Bank, the three largest Icelandic banks, with a joint balance sheet of $174 billion in 2007, more than eight times the GDP of Iceland, ran into difficulties because they were no longer able to refinance long-term loans with short-term credits.[35] Between 7 and 9 October they were acquired by the Icelandic state. This event actually triggered the worldwide stock market crash that same week which, as was mentioned in Chapter 1, was stronger than in the worst weeks of 1929. The large extent of the financial gap of the nationalized institutes meant that neither the Icelandic state nor the 320,000 inhabitants of Iceland

[34] Press release of 5 October 2008, online at www.dexia.com/e/news/press-release

[35] Kaupthing Bank, Glitnir, and Landsbanki, *Annual Report 2007*, online at www. kaupthing.com, www.reuters.com, and www.landsbanki.is, accessed on 29 September 2009.

were able to provide the missing funds. On 16 October the nationalized Glitnir Bank failed to repay a bond of 750 million euros, de facto announcing Iceland's insolvency.

Foreigners had also invested money in Icelandic banks. British individuals, companies, and municipalities had deposits in the order of 5 billion euros[36] and German banks may even have held claims against Icelandic banks in the order of 20 billion euros. To ensure that its institutions and individuals would get their money back, the British government temporarily froze the funds at British branches of the Icelandic banks by resorting to an anti-terror law enacted after the Al-Qaeda attacks on the World Trade Center.[37]

Iceland is a small country with a population not larger than that of many European cities. Much more ominous for world financial markets were the difficulties facing Hungary in October 2008 because of its collapsing banks. Due to the large deficits in its current account and government budget, the market for government bonds threatened to dry up in addition. As a consequence, in a short period of time the country's currency, the forint, lost more than 20 per cent of its value against the euro. The Hungarian central bank reacted by raising the key interest rate by 300 percentage points, and the European Central Bank provided a loan of five billion euros. A consortium consisting of the IMF, the World Bank, and the European Union provided additional financing amounting to 26.2 billion euros.[38]

And Hungary was no exception. Ireland, once known as the Celtic Tiger, was the first state of the euro area to declare an official recession in September 2008. The Irish banking system faced major challenges in financing their day-to-day operations due to the turbulences on the world's interbank markets and the bursting of the Irish property bubble in 2008, which led to a massive decline in Irish property values. To ensure the stability of its financial system,

---

[36] Reuters, *Britain, Iceland Make Progress on Icesave Deposits*, 11 October 2008, online at www.reuters.com/article/idUSLB53875520081011, accessed on 22 January 2010.

[37] The Anti-terrorism, Crime and Security Act was passed by the British parliament on 19 November 2001 in reaction to the attacks on the World Trade Center. Among other things it contains the right to freeze deposits of persons who execute or plan transactions that have negative consequences for the country.

[38] International Monetary Fund, *Review of Recent Crisis Programs*, 2009, www.imf.org, accessed on 19 January 2010.

the Irish government reacted by launching a state guarantee for deposits and liabilities of the six Irish-owned banks worth 400 billion euros, more than twice Ireland's annual GDP. The government guarantee was followed by the nationalization of the Anglo Irish Bank in January 2009 and the recapitalization of the Allied Irish Bank as well as the Bank of Ireland with an equity injection of 3.5 billion euros each.[39]

The situation in Greece initially did not seem too bad, and many people thought the crisis would bypass the country. After all, the country's banks did not evidence any particular exposure to toxic US assets. However, as will be explained in Chapter 10, Greece, due to its exceptionally large government debt, unsound public finances, and dubious accounting practices, ran into severe problems in winter 2009/2010, coming to the brink of insolvency.

Nationalization as a last resort

Let us return to the chronology. On Saturday, 11 October 2008, representatives of the G-8 countries met in Washington and on the following day the twenty-seven EU countries met in Paris to agree on a comprehensive rescue operation. The agreement was to prevent any further bankruptcy of a systemically relevant bank. To realize this goal, guarantees were to be provided, shaky credit claims to be purchased, and equity aid to be made available. As has already been mentioned, together the countries of this world set up rescue packages for their financial systems of nearly $8 trillion (see Chapter 9).

This agreement was implemented with special vigour by the British, the state becoming partial owner of the already-mentioned banks Lloyds TBS and HBOS as well as the Royal Bank of Scotland (RBS), which was one of the biggest European banks, with assets of £1.9 trillion or 2.6 trillion euros in 2007.[40] In April 2008, the bank announced the largest share issue in British company history to raise £12 billion in new capital to offset huge write-downs

[39] Anglo Irish Bank, *Annual Report & Accounts 2008*, 2 and irishtimes.com, *Government Statement on Recapitalisation*, 11 February 2009, online at www.irishtimes.com, accessed on 19 January 2009.

[40] See Royal Bank of Scotland, *Annual Report 2007*, online at www.rbs.com, accessed on 23 January 2009.

on bad assets and to shore up its reserves after the purchase of ABN AMRO. As the share issue failed to secure more than minimal take-up, the British government increased its share to 58 per cent in October 2008, injecting a total of £37 billion ($63 billion) into the UK banking system. In April 2009 the government converted the preference shares of RBS that it had acquired to ordinary shares in order to increase the state's holding in the bank from 58 per cent to 70 per cent.[41]

In the USA, too, the state helped the big banks by providing equity. On 14 October, Treasury Secretary Paulsen called together the chief executives of Bank of America, Wells Fargo, Citigroup, JPMorgan Chase & Co., Goldman Sachs, Morgan Stanley, Bank of New York Mellon Corp., and State Street Corp. and forced them to accept state equity under the Capital Purchase Program (CPP), making the United States of America a co-owner. Creating a large variety of rescue programmes, the state supported about 600 banks and injected $332.5 billion in capital into its private banks, including AIG, up to the end of 2009. This represented, on the basis of the aggregate American banking system's capital at that time, a 15% state ownership in the private banking system, excluding Government-Sponsored Enterprises like Fannie Mae or Freddie Mac.[42] Including the Government-Sponsored Enterprises, the state equity injections during the crisis rose to $445.1 billion or 19 per cent of the total equity stock of the US banking system including AIG.[43] Chapter 9 will delve into this issue in detail.

Exceptionally large support was given to Citigroup, with a balance sheet of $2.2 trillion in 2007, the world's biggest bank.[44] At a sum of $123.9 billion by

---

[41] Reuters, *RBS Says UK Government Stake to Rise to 70 Percent*, online at www.reuters. com/article/idUSTRE5361ZX20090407, accessed on 19 January 2010.

[42] See U.S. Department of the Treasury, *TARP Transactions Report*, online at www. financialstability.gov, accessed on 25 January 2010. The aggregate amount of equity of the US banking system (excluding GSEs) by the end of third quarter 2009 including AIG was $2,266 billion. Including AIG and GSEs the amount was $2,331 billion. See Board of Governors of the Federal Reserve System, *Flow of Funds Accounts of the United States*, Flows and Outstandings Third Quarter 2009, tables L.109, L.114, L.124 and L.129, and American International Group, Inc., *Financial Supplement* Third Quarter 2009, 9.

[43] See Freddie Mac, *Third Quarter 2009 Financial Results Supplement*, 4, and Fannie Mae, *2009 Third Quarter Results*, 9.

[44] Citigroup, *Annual Report 2007*, online at www.citigroup.com, accessed on 30 September 2009; Citigroup, *Citi Issuance of $25 Billion of Perpetual Preferred Stock and Warrant to U.S. Treasury as Part of TARP Capital Purchase Program*, press release of 31 October 2008; *Citi*

1 February 2010, Citigroup had accumulated the biggest write-off losses of all private banks during the crisis (see Figure 8.1).[45] The state gave Citigroup $52 billion and assumed ownership of 34 per cent of its preferred shares.[46]

Additionally, the US Department of the Treasury, along with the FDIC and the Federal Reserve, guaranteed a $600 billion portfolio of assets through the TARP programme for all banks.

Once the recession ended and the stock market started to recover, private banks were able to repay substantial parts of the government equity they had received. As will be spelled out in Chapter 9, on 31 December 2009, the overall amount of state funds, net of the repayments, made available during the crisis to the private banking system, including AIG and the Government-Sponsored Enterprises, was $283.2 billion. Thus, during the crisis, the government had acquired around 12% of the aggregate equity of the American banking system.

The stock market also helped the banks raise additional equity to satisfy the government's demand to enhance their equity base during this period. They raised the $70 billion in additional private equity capital that government-run stress tests had shown to be necessary for an orderly conduct of business (see Chapter 9 for details). Only a bank belonging to General Motors, GMAC, failed to raise the required equity in private markets. It received $3.8 billion via the Automotive Industry Financing Program. This sum is included in the aggregate figures mentioned above.

In spite of the rescue packages many smaller banks went under that were not regarded as systemically relevant. Some of them are listed toward the end of Table 3.1. Remarkable is the fate of the Constantia Bank of Austria. This little private bank had a capital ratio of 16 per cent and actually was in good health. Yet the rumour arose and then spread like wildfire that the bank was insolvent. Similar to the British Northern Rock, with which the bank failures began, a bank run started. Within a single day, the bank had to

Issuance of $20 Billion of Perpetual Preferred Stock and Warrants to U.S. Treasury as Part of TARP Program Term Sheet, press release of 31 December 2008; *Citi Issuance of $7 Billion of Perpetual Preferred Stock*, press release of 16 January 2009, online at www.citigroup.com, accessed on 5 October 2009.

[45] Bloomberg list, accessed 1 February 2010.

[46] Bloomberg, *Citigroup 34% Stake Sale Discussed at US Treasury*, online at Bloomberg.com, accessed on 30 September 2009.

declare insolvency, and within hours was taken over by a consortium of big Austrian banks that bought the bank for one euro. The rescue package of the Austrian state, which in principle was available for this bank, could not be activated in time to prevent this fate: it was still in the legislative process and could therefore not be implemented to ensure the payments.

All of this is unlikely to be the end of myriad problems that financial sectors of the world must deal with, because new problems are in sight, including further write-offs of toxic assets, credit card and leasing risks, bankruptcies among the banks' clients in the real economy, dynamic changes in risk weights in the Basel system, defaults on CDS contracts, and, most importantly, problems with rapidly increasing government debts. Chapters 8, 9, and 10 will deal with these topics in detail.

CHAPTER 4

Why Wall Street Became
a Gambling Casino

Blind gambling instinct?

The title of this book 'Casino Capitalism' reflects the feelings evoked in many people by the events on the financial markets. The losses piled up in the financial crisis and the speculative business models that have been revealed are beyond anything conceivable and indeed suggest a comparison between the world of finance and a gambling casino. If within the span of one year more than 100 banks collapse or are partially nationalized and 60 per cent of all major US investment banks disappear because they were no longer able to shoulder the risks incurred, something must have gone very wrong.

But what was it precisely that pushed the financial world near the abyss? Was it psychological idiosyncrasies of the type observable in gambling casinos or lottery players? Was it a blind gambling instinct that pushed the banks into ruin? Or was it something else?

The answer is multifaceted: it was a gambling instinct, but not a blind one like that seen in gambling casinos. People who gamble in a casino must expect losses on average and in the long run. Although it is possible for winnings to exceed the stakes, the longer one gambles the more certain it becomes that one will not get back one's stakes. A private casino offers games with a negative mathematical probability to win, which is exactly the reason why casinos are good business. Even the state frequently participates in this business by means of licences and taxes. In roulette, one loses on average one-thirty-seventh or 2.7 per cent of one's stake, as there are thirty-seven numbers in the game, one of which belongs to the casino. The lottery is also a gamble whose attractiveness may only be explained by a blind gambling instinct, as the expected values of the payoffs are often 50 per cent below the stakes.[1]

On Wall Street things were different. Wall Street banks took part in a gamble that in itself had a positive probability of winning, a gamble in which the payoff, on average, is not below but above the stakes. After all, today's losses were accompanied by extremely high profits for many years. The speculation of the investment banks, which is at the heart of the events, was based on a rational business model that may have similarities to gambling but differs from it as it promises huge private profits in the long run at the expense of society. This does not make things any better but shows where the problems lie.

The basic principle that is responsible for the huge profits of the investment banks, of all banks even, is the legal institution of limited liability, as limited liability permits earning profits from mere risk-taking by privatizing profits and socializing losses. To understand this phenomenon, we should first take a look at the history of limited liability.

Limited liability as capitalism's secret of success

Whereas the beginnings of companies with limited liability may be traced back to Arabic and Byzantine commercial customs, even to Babylonia,[2] this type of company truly blossomed in medieval Italy in the form of the so-called *commenda*.[3] A *commenda* defined the legal relationship between

---

[1] M. Adams and T. Tolkemitt, 'Das staatliche Lotterieunwesen: Eine wirtschaftswissenschaftliche und rechtspolitische Analyse des Deutschen Toto-Lotto-Blocks', *Zeitschrift für Rechtspolitik,* 11 (2001), 511–18. See also *Focus*, 29 (2005), 134.

[2] H. Hattenhauer, *Europäische Rechtsgeschichte* (C. F. Müller, Heidelberg, 1999), 268 f., and C. S. Lobingier, 'The Natural History of the Private Artificial Person: A Comparative Study in Corporate Origins', *Tulane Law Review*, 13 (1938–9), 41 n., here p. 56.

[3] For a detailed overview of the historical origins of the *commenda* and the role of limited liability in maritime law see M. Weber, *Die Geschichte der Handelsgesellschaften im Mittelalter* (Ferdinand Enke, Stuttgart, 1889), English translation: *The History of Commercial Partnerships in the Middle Ages* (Roman and Littlefield, Lanham, 2003).

an investor (*commendator*), a managing partner (*commendatarius*), and the outside world and may be seen as the origin of the modern corporation. The *Kommanditgesellschaft* (limited commercial partnership), a popular German legal form of business organization, directly dates from it. Similarly the *kommanditnoje tovarishchestvo* in Russia, the *usaldusühing* in Estonia, or the *komanditní společnost* in the Czech Republic relate more or less directly to this company form. The basic idea of a *commenda* consisted in dividing profits according to the capital shares and labour input and, in any case, investors were liable to the outside creditors with their investment only but not with their private assets.[4] In the twelfth century, the *commenda* was of decisive importance in the economic growth of the north Italian cities of Genoa, Florence, Pisa, and Venice. Risk consolidation among the partners, combined with the limitation of liability to the outside, allowed the lucrative but dangerous sea voyages of the Italian merchants to North Africa and the Near East that made Venice at the time the richest city in the world.[5]

Today, the most important form of a company with limited liability is the joint stock corporation. It originated in the Netherlands. Considered as the first stock corporation is the Verenigde Oost-Indische Compagnie, VOC (United East India Company, usually called Dutch East India Company in English), founded in 1602.[6] The Dutch East India Company organized large parts of seagoing trade, by means of which the Dutch became wealthy in the seventeenth and eighteenth centuries. Like the Italian *commenda*, the Dutch East India Company had two types of owners, the simple partners (*participanten*), who only invested money, and the managing partners (*bewindhebbers*). But the special characteristic of the Dutch East India

---

[4] G. Lastig, *Die Accomendatio: Die Grundform der heutigen Kommanditgesellschaften in ihrer Gestaltung vom XIII. bis XIX. Jahrhundert und benachbarte Rechtsinstitute* (Verlag der Buchhandlung des Waisenhauses, Halle, 1907), 129, and A. Renaud, *Das Recht der Kommanditgesellschaften* (Tauchnitz, Leipzig, 1881), 9. See also J. Meyer, *Haftungsbeschränkung im Recht der Handelsgesellschaften* (Springer, Berlin, 2000), 50–1.

[5] See also H.-W. Sinn, 'Gedanken zur volkswirtschaftlichen Bedeutung des Versicherungswesens', *Zeitschrift für die gesamte Versicherungswissenschaft*, 77 (1988), 1–27.

[6] A predecessor was the Muscovy Company, chartered in England in 1555, which organized the trade of the British Crown with Moscow. However, it did not have tradable stocks, organized only a few sea voyages, and did not find any imitators. See W. B. Truitt, *The Corporation* (Greenwood Press, Westport, Conn., 2006), 3.

Company was that even the managing partners were only liable up to the amount of their investment and that there was no direct liability of partners and shareholders beyond corporate assets.[7] The company expanded its capital base in 1616 by issuing stocks, whose owners' liability also only extended to their investment. These were the first stocks in the world. The limitation of liability, combined with the possibility to collect capital from many small investors, was the model of success to which the Netherlands owed its rise to one of the most important merchant nations of the world.[8] The model also showed weaknesses, however, reminiscent of the current crisis of the financial system. After the Dutch East India Company had been crippled by excessive dividend payments, it went bankrupt in 1798. At the time, the acronym VOC was translated as 'vergann onder corruptie': passed away under corruption.

The British East India Company also followed the Dutch example. It was founded in 1600 under the patronage of Queen Elizabeth and acquired great wealth for the Crown and for England under Sir Francis Drake. However, it did not adopt an organizational form comparable to the Dutch model until 1613 and then also issued stocks, whose owners were only liable up to their investment. Although the East India Company acquired immense wealth for England, it developed into a state within a state with a private army of finally 260,000 men that was twice the size of that of the Crown. Having been put under state supervision in 1773, it was deprived of its economic functions in 1833 and formally dissolved in 1873.[9]

Following these historical beginnings, legal foundations for stock corporations were laid in many countries in the nineteenth century. For example, on 9 November 1843, the first stock corporation law came into being in Prussia. It introduced the form of legal person, regulated the issuance of stock, and allowed for the limitation of liability to the invested capital.[10]

---

[7] J. De Vries and A. Van-der-Woude, *The First Modern Economy: Success, Failure and Perseverance of the Dutch Economy, 1500–1815* (Cambridge University Press, Cambridge, 1997), 385; Truitt, *The Corporation*, 3–4.

[8] See J. Huizinga, *The Autumn of the Middle Ages* (University of Chicago Press, Chicago, 1996).

[9] Truitt, *The Corporation*, 5.

[10] See T. Baums, *Gesetz über die Aktiengesellschaften für die Königlich Preussischen Staaten: Vom 9. November 1843; Text und Materialien* (Scientia Verlag, Aalen, 1981), 216.

Among the initial great successes of the new joint stock corporation law was the construction of the railroad network in Germany, since only the issuance of railroad stocks permitted the collection of the immense funds necessary for the construction of the railway system. Later companies like Siemens, AEG, Telefunken, or Daimler were able, thanks to the stock corporation law, to achieve international reputations. Half a century after the introduction of the stock corporation law, on 20 April 1892, the legal form of GmbH, the limited liability company, was instituted that also granted small firms with a small number of owners the privilege of the limitation of liability. It proved to become the main driver of the development of efficient German small and medium-sized businesses.

Great Britain created the first legal basis for the establishment and registration of stock corporations with the Joint Stock Companies Act of 1844. It did not include a general limitation of liability for the stockholders. Nevertheless, a few years later, the Limited Liability Act of 1855 and the Joint Stock Companies Act of 1856 implemented the limitation of liability, as the interest in stock companies had remained small due to the direct liability of partners and shareholders beyond corporate assets. The Companies Act of 1862 also extended the possibility of limited liability to companies that were not organized as stock corporations.[11]

In the USA, corporations developed step by step at the state level in the late eighteenth and early nineteenth centuries. The New England states initially held on to the principle of unlimited liability.[12] The state of New York, however, permitted limited liability as early as 1811, New Hampshire in 1816, and Connecticut in 1818. Massachusetts followed in 1830.[13] Regardless of the legal rules, limited liability agreed by private law was a regular component of the corporation as early as the eighteenth

---

[11] B. D. Hunt, *The Development of the Business Corporation in England, 1800–1867* (Harvard University Press, Cambridge, Mass., 1936).

[12] For example, the first general establishment law of Massachusetts of 1808 only knew unlimited liability: the privilege of limited liability was only granted as an individual concession in exceptional cases. On the development of corporations and limited liability in the USA cf. A. Bruns, *Haftungsbeschränkung und Mindesthaftung* (Mohr Siebeck, Tübingen, 2003), 86 n.

[13] K. F. Forbes, 'Limited Liability and the Development of the Business Corporation', *Journal of Law, Economics, and Organization*, 2 (1986), 163–77, here 172.

century; it was indeed the true reason for the establishment of corporations.[14] The courts also increasingly treated limited liability as normal for corporations, unless the opposite had been agreed.[15] Later, toward the end of the nineteenth century, another legal form developed in the USA that also granted the possibility of limited liability to smaller, unincorporated firms, comparable to the German GmbH.[16]

While banks in Germany could make use of the limited liability provisions from the outset just like other firms in the real economy, in Anglo-Saxon countries such provisions were made available much later. In the United Kingdom, limited liability for banking corporations was allowed only in 1879, after the liquidation of the Glasgow Bank in 1878 had imposed high additional reserve liabilities on its shareholders.[17] In the USA, shareholders had to endure double liability (and in Colorado even triple liability) until well into the twentieth century. They not only had to cover losses with their bank's own equity, but, if that did not suffice, resort to their private wealth as well, which of course would require the issuance of registered shares in the first place. In the worst case, they had to tap their other sources of wealth for the same amount as their share of stock in the bank in order to meet the bank's creditors' claims. The double liability common during the nineteenth century in the Commonwealth countries still existed at the end of

---

[14] 'Limited liability was recognized as an attribute of an incorporated company, almost invariably without specific mention; indeed it was a principal object desired through incorporation.' J. S. Davis, *Essays in the Earlier History of American Corporations*, no. 4, 'Eighteenth Century Business Corporations in the United States' (Harvard University Press, Cambridge, Mass., 1917), 317.

[15] J. D. Cox, T. L. Hazen, and F. H. O'Neal, *Corporations* (Aspen Law & Business, New York, 1997), 30.

[16] In the states of Pennsylvania, Virginia, New Jersey, Michigan, and Ohio the 'Limited Partnership Association', a predecessor of the 'Limited Liability Company' (LLC), was created toward the end of the 19th century, an organizational form that closely resembles the German GmbH. But it took until the 1990s before all US states adopted the LLC laws. See A. Bruns, *Haftungsbeschränkung und Mindesthaftung*, 86 n.

[17] Starting in 1826, banks in Great Britain were allowed to establish themselves as corporations with unlimited liability of the registered stockholders. An effective limitation of the risk to the shareholders resulted in 1879 through the possibility of issuing registered transferable shares of stock. See C. R. Hickson and J. D. Turner, 'Shareholder Liability Regimes in Nineteenth-Century English Banking: The Impact upon the Market for Shares', *European Review of Economic History*, 7 (2003), 99–125.

the 1920s in thirty-five US states. It was not until 1933 and 1935 that a federal law granted the banks the option of limiting their liability to the corresponding shareholders' equity, and only in 1953 was the current legal basis established in the USA, when the option was turned into a rule.[18]

These historical developments were the basis of the capitalist system as we know it today. It allowed the corporation to collect money from many small investors that was needed by big companies. And the corporation needed limited liability and the protection of private wealth to convince the small stockholders to participate.

The limited liability corporation is the key success model of capitalism. It alone allowed the tremendous accumulation of capital that was the pre-requisite for industrialization and economic well-being of the Western world and still is. In a speech delivered in 1911, Nicholas Murray Butler, President of Columbia University, explained the reasons for America's economic success: 'I weigh my words when I say that in my judgment the limited liability corporation is the greatest single discovery of modern times... Even steam and electricity are far less important than the limited liability corporation, and they would be reduced to comparative impotence without it.'[19]

Undercapitalized investment banks

The dynamics of the capitalistic system, to which the standard of living of the Western world is owed, goes hand in hand with the corporation and limited liability. As such, limited liability is a necessary and beneficial legal concept.

However, the privilege of limited liability was expanded so much by the US investment banks, and not only by them, that in the end they were hardly liable at all because they worked only with minimal stocks of equity. Investment banks, until well into the 1970s, were all organized as partnerships, and as such offered their market partners the unlimited

---

[18] See N. C. Quigley, 'Shareholder Liability Regimes in Banking', in P. Newman, M. Milgate, and J. Eatwell (eds.), *The New Palgrave Dictionary of Money and Finance* (MacMillan Press, London, 1992), 441–2. See also A. Leijonhufvud, *A Modest Proposal*, unpublished text, UCLA and University of Trento 2010. Leijonhufvud pleads for reintroducing double liability for the managers' stock options.

[19] Cited after S. M. Bainbridge, 'Abolishing Veil Piercing', *Journal of Corporation Law*, 26 (2001), 479–535, here 479.

Table 4.1 Equity asset ratios and returns on equity of the five big US investment banks in 2006

	Equity asset ratio (%)	Return on equity before tax (%)	Return on equity after tax (%)
Bear Stearns	3.5	25.9	16.9
Goldman Sachs	4.3	40.7	26.7
Lehman Brothers	3.8	30.8	20.9
Merrill Lynch	4.6	25.1	18.2
Morgan Stanley	3.2	25.7	21.1

Notes: According to somewhat stricter European rules, all equity asset ratios would have been even lower than reported in the table. For example, American accounting law allows balance sheet abridgement in case of mutually interlaced claims among financial institutions, which is not possible in Europe. Cf. Chapter 7. Equity asset ratio: ratio of equity to total balance sheet volume. Return on equity: ratio of profits to equity (including retained earnings).

Sources: Individual annual reports.

private liability of their owners. But they evolved eventually into corporations in order to limit their liability to their equity capital. Goldman Sachs, today the world's largest investment bank, took this step only in 1999. In addition, investment banks expanded their business volume so much in relation to their equity capital that the liability ultimately shrank to a merely symbolic residue. Table 4.1 presents the equity asset ratios of the five big American investment banks in 2006, before the financial crisis erupted. These ratios ranged from only 3 per cent to about 4.5 per cent. In view of the mostly very risky transactions of the investment banks, this is very little as it means that business volume was leveraged by a factor of 22 to 33 of what would have been possible if only equity had been lent. Although this enormous leverage ensures high returns on equity, it also generates enormously high risks, initially for the bank itself, then for its creditors, and finally for the taxpayers, who must pay for the rescue packages in the end.

Some may presume that investment banks were so undercapitalized because stockholders did not have more money at their disposal. That this presumption is incorrect is shown in Table 4.1. Accordingly, in good times, the investment banks' returns on equity amounted to 25 per cent and more. Goldman Sachs had a return on equity of more than 40 per cent. Even after-tax returns still averaged 21 per cent in 2006. At such a return, equity doubles in less than four years if profits are retained. Had the banks forgone dividends for a few years without expanding their business volume, enough equity would have been available to cope with any crisis.

The reason for the low equity asset ratios was not the poverty of the investors but their ambition to get paid out as much money in dividends as possible in order to shelter it from risk. It was important to leave the smallest possible amount of capital in the bank, as whatever remained there could be lost in turbulent times. And when the collapse was near, the slogan was: 'Time to bail out.' It was symptomatic that the investment bank Bear Stearns paid out dividends in the amount of 76 per cent of book profits in 2007, shortly before its bankruptcy.

Mark to market

The distribution of profits was facilitated by the accounting rules of the International Financial Reporting Standard (IFRS). According to IFRS, the principle of 'mark to market' and its variant 'fair value' applied. Accordingly, the assets of banks and other companies must always be carried on the balance sheet at their current market price, actual or hypothetical, even if nothing was sold. Thus, in the phase of general stock price increases (see Figure 2.5), high profits had to be reported. And although business was no longer good, correspondingly high dividends, financed by debt, were distributed to the stockholders. To the outside world, this behaviour was explained as the principle of 'shareholder value', that is, the creation of value for the stockholders, although it simply reflected the effort to safeguard the profits achieved and not leave them to the vagaries of the banking business.

Such a development would not have been possible under continental European accounting rules, as the 'lowest-value principle', anchored there for reasons of creditor protection, demands values for the balance sheet based on historical purchase prices of the assets or market values, whichever is the lower of the two. According to this principle, in times of rising stock prices, unrealized profits would not have shown up in the balance sheet, but rather, saved from stockholders' access, would have formed a buffer for bad times as hidden or 'silent' reserves. Unfortunately, all big financial institutions worldwide use the IFRS today, which contributed substantially to the increasing undercapitalization of the banks, in turn adding to their susceptibility to crises.

Undercapitalization was not only caused by the distribution of dividends but often also by the fact that banks allowed borrowed funds to increase faster than the equity that rose due to retained earnings. The banks pursued the objective of strengthening the effect of leverage on the return on equity. This effect, too, was facilitated by the close to market valuation of the assets, as in times of rising stock prices the banks borrowed more because they had become richer on paper, and finished with a reduced equity asset ratio when stock prices normalized again.[20] Whether the banks' undercapitalization was created in this way or by increased dividend distributions, it agreed in any case with the wishes of the stockholders, who demanded from their CEOs a reduction of the equity asset ratio to a level that just sufficed for the normal course of business. The undercapitalization that politicians condemn today was simply part of the investment banks' business model.

Undercapitalization made investment banks susceptible to crises and implied that in critical times they had too little equity to buffer against losses. If a business volume of 100 units of money is only backed up by three to four-and-a-half units of equity, it can easily happen that in times of crises the losses eat up the equity and lead to bankruptcy. This is the real cause of the collapse of American investment banks.

Investment bankers as soldiers of fortune: the role of the Bloos Rule

Even worse was the fact that the low level of equity combined with limited liability induced the stockholders to demand ever riskier business models in order to increase their profits. It goes without saying that nobody is interested in losses. But if there is a chance to increase profits in good times at the expense of incurring losses in bad times, which because of limited liability one must bear only in part, the risk becomes more attractive. If some of the losses are borne by the creditors, who do not get their money back or get it from the state that acts as the rescuer, it pays to take the risk. Even if risky investment strategies fail to be more profitable on average than safe strategies, they still benefit the stockholders because upward deviations are

---

[20] This effect resulted in a strong pro-cyclicality of the system of accounting. See Chapter 7, section on Basel II, as well as the references given there.

privatized as profits and downward deviations are socialized as losses of the creditors or the taxpayers. The greater the dispersion of the profit distribution, that is, the higher the possible profits and losses, the bigger will be that part of the distribution that is cut off by limited liability and the higher the expectation of company profits. I have referred to the artificial risk preference, which is created in this way, as the *Bloos Rule*, others called the phenomenon *gambling for resurrection*.[21] The Bloos Rule is the microeconomic core of the financial crisis, and it explains the difference from gambling, where the average private gain is always negative. Chapter 8 (see especially Table 8.1) will shed some light on the empirical validity of the rule insofar as it demonstrates that during the crisis many important financial institutions, such as Citigroup, Wachovia, Washington Mutual, Fannie Mae, Freddie Mac, Merrill Lynch, or UBS, indeed incurred losses far exceeding their equity capital.

---

[21] According to the English saying 'It's like getting blood out of a stone' (=Bloos), cf. H.-W. Sinn, *Ökonomische Entscheidungen bei Ungewißheit* (Mohr Siebeck, Tübingen, 1980), esp. 172–92 (Dissertation, accepted by University of Mannheim in 1977, English edition: *Economic Decisions under Uncertainty* (North-Holland, Amsterdam, 1983), esp. 163–82) and H.-W. Sinn, 'Kinked Utility and the Demand for Human Wealth and Liability Insurance', *European Economic Review*, 17 (1982), 149–62. At the time, this theory was developed within an abstract risk-theoretic framework (expected utility theory and $\mu - \sigma$ theory) and applied to the insurance market, currency speculation, and a number of other examples, where limited liability imposes various kinds of lower bounds on an agent's wealth level. Later the term 'gamble for resurrection' was used to describe the phenomenon. See M. Dewatripont and J. Tirole, 'Efficient Governance Structure: Implications for Banking Regulation', in C. Mayer and X. Vives (eds.), *Capital Markets and Financial Intermediation* (Cambridge University Press, Cambridge, 1993), 12–35, and M. Dewatripont and J. Tirole, *Prudential Regulation of Banks* (MIT Press, Cambridge, Mass., 1994), 97 and 113. For early contributions using the same incentive mechanism, though not the term, see J. Stiglitz and A. Weiss, 'Credit Rationing in Markets with Incomplete Information', *American Economic Review*, 71 (1981), 393–410; G. J. Benston, M. Carhill, and B. Olasov, 'The Failure and Survival of Thrifts: Evidence from the Southeast', in R. G. Hubbard (ed.), *Financial Markets and Financial Crises* (NBER Books, National Bureau of Economic Research, Cambridge, Mass., 1991), 305–84. Later the theory was further developed in a model with banking and regulatory competition. See H.-W. Sinn, *The New Systems Competition*, Yrjö-Jahnsson Lectures (Blackwell, Oxford, 2003), chapter 7, 150–77: 'Limited Liability, Risk-Taking and the Competition of Bank Regulators'. For the history of economic thought on the artificial increase in risk-taking because of limited liability, see M. Hellwig, foreword to H.-W. Sinn, *Risk Taking, Limited Liability, and the Banking Crisis* (Selected Reprints, Ifo Institute, Munich, 2009). On the

A key example that is helpful in understanding this book and which is not atypical for the banking business may explain why it pays for a banker to behave like a soldier of fortune. Imagine a bank with assets of 100 units of money has backed these assets with 5 units of equity and 95 units of debt. The bond rate is 5 per cent, and at this interest rate the bank is able to issue securities, that is, to borrow for one year. Assume that the bank has the choice between two business models, a safe one and a risky one, both consisting of investments running for periods of one year. Using the safe business model, the bank can invest the available funds at 5 per cent. Using the risky model, it can invest the funds at 6 per cent but must expect to lose the invested funds at a probability of 1 per cent due to borrower insolvency. In other words, with the risky business model, on average, the invested money will be lost in one of 100 years and will generate a rate of return of 6 per cent in 99 of these hundred years.

If the bank chooses the safe business model, it does not make a profit on the borrowed and reinvested funds, but achieves the market return of 5 per cent on its equity. That is very little and too little to run a bank. Interesting business models look different.

Let us therefore look at the risky strategy. It is presented in Figure 4.1. At first glance the risky business model does not seem to improve things, as on average a return on investment of only 5 per cent is achieved. If, at a probability of 99 per cent, a return of 6 per cent is achieved and at a probability of 1 per cent a return of minus 100 per cent, the average return is also just 5 per cent.[22] Why invest at all, if one cannot get a higher return on average than with the safe strategy but must bear the risk?

The answer is that the return the bank earns on its investment is not the same as the return on equity. Return on equity is much higher, as the bank can pocket the risk mark-up of a one percentage point higher rate of interest in the normal case, whereas it can pass on most of the losses to others in case

general importance of the principle of liability in business decisions, see W. Eucken, *Grund-sätze der Wirtschaftspolitik*, 1st edn. (Francke und Mohr, Bern, 1952), here cited according to the 7th edn. (Mohr Siebeck, Tübingen, 2004), 279–85.

[22] That is the bankers' rule of thumb. Precisely calculated, the expected (average) rate of return is 4.94%: at a probability of 99% the value of the assets rises to 106 at the end of the period and at a probability of 1% it is zero, implying an expected value of the assets of 104.94% at the end of the period.

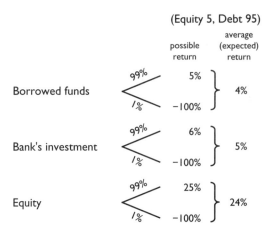

Fig. 4.1 The bank's calculation

of catastrophe. The share of its equity in the loss of 100, which happens with a probability of 1 per cent, is only 5 units.

In case of success, that is, at a probability of 99 per cent, the assets of the bank increase from 100 to 106, and its debt rises, due to the 5 per cent interest rate, from 95 to 99.75. The difference between 106 and 99.75 is earned by the bank. Its equity thus increases from the initial 5 to 6.25 units, implying a rate of return of 25 per cent. This number reminds us of the 25 per cent that has frequently been defined by bankers and analysts as the target rate.[23] So much for the normal case, when everything goes well.

At a probability of 1 per cent, the bank does not get its money back and goes bankrupt. In this case, its return on equity amounts to minus 100 per cent.

If success and failure are combined, the expected average return of 25 per cent declines to 24 per cent, which is still an amazing figure.[24]

---

[23] For example, the CEO of Deutsche Bank said: 'In Germany, 25 percent before taxes yields 16 percent after taxes. This is the absolute minimum today, the best banks far exceed this,' cited after 'Ackermann verteidigt Stellenabbau bei der Deutschen Bank', *Wirtschafts-Woche*, 26 February 2005. http://www.wiwo.de/unternehmer-maerkte/ackermann-vertei-digt-stellenabbau-bei-der-deutschen-bank-91671/.

[24] Again calculated according to the rule of thumb. More precisely, the rate of return is only 23.75%. As equity increases to 6.25 at a probability of 99% and is zero at a probability of 1%, the expected equity at the end of the period is $(99\% \times 6.25) + (1\% \times 0) = 6.1875$, implying a rate of return of 23.75% on an initial equity of 5, as $6.1876/5 = 1.2375$.

The special feature of this business model is that the high rate of return on equity is generated by the mere risk, i.e. not from the bank's assets yielding a genuine risk premium. According to the assumptions, the expected average rate of return of the risky strategy is not higher, at 5 per cent, than that of the safe strategy. Responsible for this result is the limitation of liability, which implies that in case of failure the losses are passed on to others.

These others are the creditors of the bank. The creditors were promised a nominal rate of return of 5 per cent, but they only receive this return if everything goes well, i.e. at a probability of 99 per cent. At a probability of 1 per cent, they will not get their money back because the bank is bankrupt. Their expected average rate of return is therefore only 4 per cent.[25]

The above example clarifies why the Bloos Rule or limited liability represents the core of the business model with which the American investment banks achieved their high profits. It is of much greater relevance, however, as most banks work according to a similar pattern, in America as well as in Europe and elsewhere. Thus, American mortgage banks, which foisted mortgages on homeowners for risky projects (Chapter 5), as well as European banks, which acquired securities from these banks that were based on such mortgages (Chapter 6), acted on a similar principle. The only difference from the investment banks is that the investment banks had to consider fewer regulatory barriers in their business and therefore incurred even more risks, resulting in higher profits than can be achieved by regular banks. Whereas regular banks in continental Europe were satisfied with a still considerable return on equity of 15 per cent, American investment banks had a minimum target of 25 per cent.

All banks make profits by taking on risks. They not only achieve normal risk premiums like those determined by the market for risky investments compared to less risky ones, but generate their returns also from the chance of passing the risk of losses onto other shoulders in view of the minute equity asset ratios with which they work. The losses to be borne by the banks' creditors in case of failure appear in the normal course of business as special profits that can be proudly reported on the balance sheet, to the delight of the shareholder.

---

[25] As the borrowed funds rise from 95 to 99.75 at a probability of 99% and decline to zero at a probability of 1%, the expected value of the creditors' claims is 98.75 at the end of the period, yielding a rate of return of 3.95% on the initial lending volume of 95.

While the artificial incentive for risk-taking shown in the example results from limited liability as such, an even stronger incentive would prevail if the bank can reckon on the government helping out if something goes wrong. If the bank anticipates that the government will consider it too big to fail and therefore bail it out in the case of equity losses, the bank's expected rate of return with the risky business model will even be higher. Suppose the 5 units of equity assumed in the example are the minimum that the supervision agency requires and that the government will cover any loss beyond that to protect the equity base of the bank. The worst that can happen to the bank now is that it is unable to earn a return on its equity, ending the period with the same 5 units with which it started. In this case, the 1 per cent chance gives a rate of return of 0 per cent instead of −100 per cent, and the expected (average) rate of return is nearly 25 per cent.[26] The bail-out guarantee increases the artificial incentives for risk-taking even further.

It increases these incentives only a bit, however, as the protected equity is close to zero anyway, if compared with the bank's business volume. In the above example, the bail-out guarantee makes the rate of return to equity just one percentage point higher, 25 per cent instead of 24 per cent, which is not a big difference. The only important difference could lie in the behaviour of the banks' creditors. As the bail-out guarantee reduces their interest in distinguishing between risky and safe banks, they would not be available as potential guards helping to ensure more prudent bank behaviour. However, for reasons that will be explained below (in the section on *Lemon trade*), it is unlikely that they can perform such a control function satisfactorily anyway, due to lack of information.

Why sustainability was lost sight of

The extent to which banks consciously choose to gamble is difficult to determine. For regular banks, ignoring catastrophic risks is not even a conscious decision of the executives. Rather, this lax approach is 'business as usual' that has emerged from market conditions. Bank executives plan for

[26] With a probability of 99% the equity is 6.25 at the end of the period, and with a probability of 1% it is 5. Thus the expected end-of-period equity is 6.2375 which is 24.75% higher than the initial equity of 5.

the normal case and in their minds push aside the catastrophic case that only occurs with a small probability anyway. That is also why it remains unclear whether practising bankers have ever been aware of the calculations based on the Bloos Rule, presented in Figure 4.1. When asked before the crisis about the chance of a systemic catastrophe wiping out market partners, bank managers responded by the shrugging acknowledgement that these would be strokes of fate that could not be averted anyway. The fact that in that case the creditors or the state would have to pay the bill was implicitly accepted. In any case, they were not willing to reduce their aspirations for their normal business only to reduce the excess of losses over equity in the improbable case of catastrophe. Whether losses would be incurred that would be bigger than equity by a factor of twenty or only by a factor of ten, as in the example considered above, was completely irrelevant, in the same way as it is irrelevant whether following an earthquake the ruins of one's home burn down or not. In the course of normal business the topic was simply irrelevant and not subject to serious consideration by the bank's supervisors. The bankers may not have acted deliberately, but their actions were certainly based on ignorance and the imitation of others' temporarily successful behaviour, as is common in business life and in life in general.[27]

The formal models of risk theory used by the banks' investment managers did not consider the case of a systemic catastrophe, not even as a distant possibility. The investment managers derived their data on profit fluctuations only from normal situations of recent years, taking account only of short-term frequencies resulting in changes of direction from one day to the next. Even the risk of business cycles with typically one upswing and one downswing per decade was not adequately taken into account. As a rule, in calibrating the models the managers were content with statistical data covering only five years, if only because the supervisory authorities did not ask for more. For the periods during which investment bankers earn their money, business cycles already

---

[27] Economists in general leave it open why they assume that people behave rationally, whether it is because of cognitive decisions or only because there are cultural rules of behaviour that people imitate because they seem to work. Milton Friedman once called this the 'as if' approach, see M. Friedman, 'The Methodology of Positive Economics', in M. Friedman, *Essays in Positive Economics* (University of Chicago Press, Chicago, 1953), 3–43. See also G. Kirchgässner, *Homo Oeconomicus* (Mohr Siebeck, Tübingen, 2000).

represent a small eternity. That is why risks of a century, like those that led to a collapse of the banking system in 1929 and 2008, were not covered. Only the daily ups and downs of stock prices and the normal loan loss ratios of customers were transformed into a probability distribution of total profits. That was the basis of their risk estimates. Other risks, especially those that theoretically result in a collapse of the system once in 100 years, played no part in the datasets and were ignored. The fact that such deficient models were able to prevail is the result of a competitive selection process taking place in fair weather periods only. All of the data generated by these models on the so-called value at risk, the loss limit that would be exceeded at a probability of 1 per cent, underestimated the truth by a multiple factor.

The actors in these processes, the bank executives and their staff, were part of the 'business as usual' and were unable to defy the customary practices of the banking business. Even if they had wanted to, they had no possible means of counteracting and choosing a conservative investment strategy with a lower return on equity, because the financial markets would have immediately punished their behaviour by a markdown of the stock price. The analysts would have denounced the management and demanded its immediate replacement. In addition, a conservatively managed bank would have become at once the target of a hostile takeover by other banks, which knew that they could achieve the usual, higher returns with a change of the business model. Managers of big banks live in constant fear of their company being taken over by competitors. The concentration process is also advancing at great speed in the banking sector, and sometimes one bank swallows another one to prevent being swallowed by an even bigger fish.[28]

There are many good reasons for takeovers, and most of them are based on the possibility of increasing profits by implementing better business models and exploiting economies of scale. One of the reasons, however, is certainly also the attempt to pocket the profits from the described gamble. Banks that rely on conservative business models with high safety and low

---

[28] The fear of takeovers and mergers was especially great in Germany in recent years, as the abolition of capital gains taxation on the sale of corporate equity cross-holdings by the Schröder government in 2002 set in motion great changes in the company structure. Although this was successful, it did intensify the chase for short-term profits and changed the attitude towards banking business in Germany substantially.

profits are the natural victims of hostile takeovers. For reasons presented above, such business models do not maximize the value of the company and shareholder value but aim at stability and a long life of the company. If a clever management takes over a hitherto conservatively managed bank and then applies the described gambling strategy, the bank can achieve higher earnings and a higher company value because the stockholders are given additional dividends at the expense of the creditors and at the expense of the state. The stockholders of the acquiring bank can share the increase in the company value that is generated by the change in strategy.[29] In view of the permanent danger of being swallowed by someone else, the management of a bank has no choice but to take on risk and to implement the gambling strategy.

Sometimes it is argued that the behaviour of bankers violated the economic rationality assumption and that irrational behaviour or animal spirits are necessary to explain what happened.[30] Such factors may also have contributed to certain aspects of the crisis. However, the excessive risk-taking that results from gambling with limited liability does not necessitate such explanations. The strategy described is highly profitable precisely when banks act rationally, be it conscious rationality or unconscious rationality, as a result of simply imitating successful behaviour. As is often the case in economic decision-making, individual rationality breeds collective irrationality if externalities are involved. In the case at hand, it is the negative externality that bankers impose on their creditors and possibly the taxpayers that induces excessive risk-taking, producing private profits and social losses.

Puppets on a string

It cannot be stressed enough that the explanation of the banks' gambling is not primarily the false incentives of the bank executives but the false incentives of the shareholders. After all, it is the shareholders who benefit from limited liability. They demand from their banks risky and profitable

[29] Empirically, the stockholders of the acquired bank profit more, however, than the stockholders of the acquiring bank, as a so-called control premium must be paid. See, for example, B. G. Baradwaj, D. R. Fraser, and E. P. H. Furtado, 'Hostile Bank Takeover Offers: Analysis and Implications', *Journal of Banking and Finance*, 14 (1990), 1229–42.

[30] G. A. Akerlof and R. Shiller, *Animal Spirits: How Human Psychology Drives the Economy, and Why it Matters for Global Capitalism* (Princeton University Press, Princeton, 2009).

business models that only function because they entail the advantage of socializing the risk of losses that exceed equity. The problem was not that bank managers did not act in the interest of shareholders, but that shareholders gambled with the money of creditors and taxpayers.

It was the shareholders who forced executive boards to meet high profit targets and banks' supervisors to design the remuneration systems for the managers to induce them to implement the appropriate business models. If the chairman of a bank announces a profit target of 25 per cent, then he does so because the analysts and institutional investors are on his back. Often, the relevant shareholders of the banks are not individuals who do not know the rules of the game but professionals, representatives of the big pension funds and investment companies, who are after the fast high profits. And even if there are no big shareholders, there are the analysts chasing the bank managers. The board chairmen of the big banks spend a substantial part of their time travelling through the world and presenting their strategies to the analysts of the various countries at so-called road shows, trying to convince them of the performance of their companies and to induce them to give 'buy' recommendations to investors for the stocks of their banks.

The much criticized short-termism of the remuneration systems stems from the interest of the shareholders in achieving high profits for the normal case, neglecting the long-term systemic risk for which one is not liable anyway. The remuneration systems of managers are usually constructed in such a way that there is a basic salary enlarged by bonuses in the case of high profits and stock price increases but no 'malus' when losses are made. For example, Anshu Jain, the investment banker resident in London, who used to achieve fairy-tale profits for Deutsche Bank, is said to have frequently earned a multiple of the income earned by the chairman of the management board, Josef Ackermann. Whereas Ackermann earned an income of markedly more than 10 million euros in good years, an investment banker is thought to have earned triple this amount or more, of course without having to fear a loss of wealth in case of failed speculation.[31] The asymmetry of the shareholders' sharing in profits and losses of a company that exists due to

[31] Cf. *Frankfurter Allgemeine Zeitung*, 3 April 2004, p. 21: 'He is said to have earned more than 100 million euros last year', and *Süddeutsche Zeitung*, 25 March 2006, p. 4: 'It is conjectured that he gets perhaps three times as much as the 11.9 million euros that Ackermann took home last year.' (Author's translations.)

limited liability is matched and even exceeded by the asymmetry of the remuneration systems of the bank managers. Under these circumstances it is no wonder then that investment bankers try to gamble in the interest of their shareholders.

Proposals by politicians to create new remuneration systems for managers to induce them to pursue a sustainable business policy, such as those made by some European governments at the G-20 summit on banking regulation in Pittsburgh in September 2009,[32] are not wrong but ineffective because the core of the problem is not the false incentive systems for managers but for shareholders. It is the shareholders who benefit from the Bloos strategy explained above, and it is they who design the incentive schemes for their managers in such a way that they act as soldiers of fortune. In economic terms, they are the principals and the managers are the agents. Or even more bluntly: the shareholders pull the strings in the puppet theatre, and the managers, whom the public blames for the evils they have witnessed in this crisis, are only the puppets. To be sure, sometimes the managers are more than puppets in reality, neglecting the preferences of shareholders. The strings occasionally seem flexible, like rubber bands, and the puppeteers have difficulties controlling the behaviour of the puppets. However, to explain the excessive risk-taking that caused the crisis, it is not necessary to dwell on the subtleties of economic principal–agent models. It is the shareholder value concept itself that points to the heart of the problem. Maximizing shareholder value is not the same as maximizing a bank's contribution to social welfare because of the massive externalities involved in the bank's risk decisions.

The heart of the problem lies in the shareholders' ability to get rid of the liability risk by minimizing their equity capital. A reform of banking supervision must therefore start with the equity rules, as will be described later on in this book, especially since policy-makers have no meaningful way to prescribe remuneration rules to shareholders and their representatives among the banks' supervisors. If shareholders had to be liable with more equity than today, they would prefer less risky business models, as they

---

[32] See Federal Government of Germany, *EU to Speak with One Voice in Pittsburgh,* Information from the government, 17 September 2009, online at www.bundesregierung.de, accessed on 20 October 2009.

would have to bear a higher fraction of the losses, and consequently they would also remunerate their investment bankers and bank executives in a way that would bolster their interest in a sustainable business policy.

These considerations show that an anonymous systemic fault exists, similar to the systemic faults that result in overfishing the world's oceans, the increase of the greenhouse effect, or the overcrowding of roads. In all these cases the search for the guilty parties who could be taken to court or made morally responsible makes no sense, because their misconduct has become the normal case and shows up in thousands of decision-makers, and no single individual can or should be held responsible. Only a change of the institutional framework of doing business, as specified in laws and rules, can solve the problem. This does not mean that those who have violated the laws should not be held responsible. If bankruptcy approaches, tricks are applied and criminal offences pile up. Individual offences must be prosecuted and punished wherever they occur. But the deficiencies of the banking system will not be corrected on these minor battlefields.

Lemon trade

Some may think that the views expressed in this chapter are too pessimistic. After all, there are still creditors of banks who execute a certain control function that eliminates the risk preference of banks or at least limits it in their own interest. What if the creditors do not want to play the game? What if they do not accept an average rate of return of only 4 per cent instead of the rate of return of 5 per cent promised in the example above? What if they lend their money only to those banks that select safe investment strategies or demand higher interest rates to compensate them for the risk? Would not the shareholders have to bow to this counterpressure?

With similar reasoning, the argument that banks try to minimize their equity in order to shift potential losses to their creditors could be countered: after all, the creditors could change the bank if they consider their transactions too risky. This is indeed the content of the so-called Modigliani–Miller Theorem,[33] to which financial theory accords much importance. According

---

[33] F. Modigliani and M. H. Miller, 'The Cost of Capital, Corporation Finance, and the Theory of Investment', *American Economic Review*, 48 (1958), 261–97.

to this theorem, banks are indifferent to financing their business by equity or by debt because a reduction of the equity asset ratio induces the creditors to demand higher interest rates to compensate for the additional risk they have to bear. Thus, the expected return on equity cannot rise when leveraged banks take more risks, as the increase in interest rates they have to offer their creditors would offset any advantage. In the above example, the creditors would demand a nominal rate of interest of 6 per cent rather than 5 per cent if the bank chooses the risky investment option (abstracting from risk aversion which would imply an even higher demanded rate of interest). This would keep their average rate of return at 5 per cent and limit the bank's average rate of return on equity also at 5 per cent.

The hope for such counteraction is doomed to failure, however. One reason is the implicit government bail-out warranty that creditors expect. If the creditors of the bank can reasonably hope that they will get their money back because the government will not allow a systemically relevant bank to go bankrupt, they do not have to care what the bank really does with their money. For the bank this means that the expected rate of return on equity is lower, the higher the bank's equity stock is, because additional equity reduces the support coming from the state in the case of catastrophe.

Another is the creditors' lack of information. The banking business is much too complicated for outsiders to be able to assess the bankruptcy risk of individual banks. Although creditors are aware of the possibility that banks may go bankrupt and will therefore react to changes in the expected bail-out guarantee (as the Lehman Brothers case has shown), they are not able to differentiate among banks regarding the size of their idiosyncratic bank-ruptcy risk resulting from the respective business model. As each bank will claim that the money will be safe with it, the creditor cannot rely on the banks' statements. A look at equity asset ratios and the volume of assets also says little about the risk if one does not know how the bank does its investments, how it protects itself against losses by means of credit insurance or derivatives, and how such ratios are to be interpreted.

One could argue that the buyers of financial products are able to rely on experience and reputation and only buy the financial products of those banks with which they or other customers had been satisfied in the past. But this argument fails the test for the sole reason that bankruptcy is an extremely rare event and that one cannot, therefore, gather the necessary experience.

In the example mentioned, the investment strategy of the banks may be successful for ninety-nine years until bankruptcy occurs in the hundredth year. That is far too much time to be able to learn from experience, especially since numerous changes in the management and in the shareholder structure quickly devalue such long-term experiences.

That is why practitioners can only smile at the Modigliani–Miller Theorem. For them it goes without saying that highly leveraged banks achieve a higher return on equity than banks that operate with large equity asset ratios, even though they may not be aware that this is so, because leveraging means increasing the burden on taxpayers and creditors to the benefit of the bank's owners.

In order for creditors to be able to react to the risk of leveraging they would need profound knowledge of a bank's internal structure and the subtleties of accounting rules, knowledge that only a few specialists possess. Private rating agencies, which evaluate the creditworthiness of banks and investment strategies, employed such specialists and they should have been able to shed light on the investment risks. For reasons to be discussed later in Chapter 6 below, they failed miserably, however.

The bank creditors could have benefited from interpreting the risk coefficients the bank is obliged to publish according to the so-called Basel rules. These are an internationally agreed system of risk weighting of investments, controlled by state supervisory authorities. Very risky investments receive a weight of one, practically safe investments like government bonds receive a weight of zero, and the remaining investments are placed in between according to their riskiness. Dividing equity by the sum of such risk-weighted investments or 'risk positions' yields the so-called Tier 1 ratio that gives the bank's creditors some idea of their risks. However, the USA has not yet implemented the Basel agreement in their domestic banks. Customers of US banks were not even informed about Tier 1 ratios. And in Europe, too, few buyers of bank securities know what a Tier 1 ratio really means, because the complicated structure of the risk weights is difficult to understand.

Financial products issued by investment banks are, therefore, obviously a prime example of lemon goods, a term coined by Nobel laureate George Akerlof.[34] A bad used car is called a lemon. The fact that used cars for sale

---

[34] See G. A. Akerlof, 'The Markets for Lemons: Quality, Uncertainty and the Market Mechanism', *Quarterly Journal of Economics*, 84 (1970), 488–500, and H.-W. Sinn, *The New Systems*

are of poorer quality on average than all cars of the same age was explained by Akerlof with the better information of the sellers of used cars. Someone who knows that his car has a hidden defect, like high oil consumption or spark plugs easily clogged by carbon particulates, is more likely to sell it than someone whose car is in good order. Because the buyer cannot easily find the defect when he makes his decision, used cars in good working order do not achieve a higher price than used cars with hidden defects. This is the reason why more than a fair share of used cars with hidden defects wind up on the used-car market, while the good ones continue to be driven by their owners.

The case of bank securities is similar to that of used cars: conservatively managed investment banks selling safe financial products are pushed out of the market, and only a market for lemon products remains. As the conservative banks cannot explain the safety advantage over their competitors to their customers, they will lose their customers when they try to endow their products with a lower rate of interest, as would be appropriate given the higher safety. Or they will lose their shareholders when competition forces them to offer their customers the same rate of interest as the competitors do, because the rate of return on equity that the shareholders could earn is too low. Thus, they will ultimately disappear from the market, being crowded out or taken over by banks that choose more risky business models. This is the key economic problem of the lemon trade. Investment banks and other banks that aimed at high rates of return have been seduced into gambling by the combined effects of limited liability and information deficits and have thereby caused the world financial crisis.

Competition, 136–9 and 150–77. See also H.-W. Sinn, 'Limited Liability, Risk Taking and the Competition of Bank Regulators', and H.-W. Sinn, 'Lemon Banking', *Project Syndicate*, April 2008, published in 27 national newspapers in the respective languages, see www.cesifo.de, Ifo Viewpoint No. 94, 2008.

CHAPTER 5

Main Street also Gambled

Non-recourse loans

Not only Wall Street succumbed to gambling; Main Street did too. Mr Jones and his home also benefited from limited liability, which induced him to gamble.

If, in Europe, someone takes out a mortgage to buy a home they know that they must repay it, if necessary until their death. If they become insolvent, the bank auctions off their home to recover the loan. If the proceeds of the sale do not cover the loan, the bank has recourse to other assets and to the future labour income of the homeowner.[1] That is why Europeans are cautious when buying a home and can only sleep peacefully again when the mortgage is repaid. Not so in America. There, only a fool does not incur debt.

In the USA, the liability of the homeowner is limited because, as a rule, home mortgages are given as so-called non-recourse loans. If something goes wrong, the bank can repossess the house but cannot get hold of other property, let alone the labour income of the debtor. There are special anti-deficiency laws in eight states that enforce these rules. And in states where there are no anti-deficiency laws, non-recourse loans are nonetheless the

---

[1] In Europe, mortgage contracts are commonly collateralized by land charges. The land charge, according to which payment of a given amount of money including interest out of a piece of real estate may be demanded, only serves as collateral for the contractual debt. In all cases of collateralization, the contract consists of a loan agreement that then presupposes a personal debtor with unlimited liability.

common form, maybe because banks are compelled by competition or because in the USA the declaration of private insolvency, which precludes recourse to other assets, is easy anyway. A non-recourse loan means that when the homeowner stops paying mortgage interest, the bank may only claim the home and nothing else. States like California and Arizona, where recourse to other assets of the mortgage holder is legally restricted, report an exorbitantly large number of foreclosures, as many homeowners simply stop payment in the event that the home is over-mortgaged.[2]

In Europe, non-recourse loans to private persons are extremely uncommon. They may be found sometimes in the case of commercial lessors, when these establish a separate limited liability firm for each of their buildings and then take out mortgages on behalf of each of these firms.[3] This legal trick resembles non-recourse loans, as it also ensures that in case of conflict the bank only has the right to the mortgaged unit. Moreover, in the UK, much property lending to companies is non-recourse. However, everywhere in Europe, even in the UK and Ireland, essentially all mortgage loans to private households are personal. Only in America are homeowners protected from banks as if their home was a limited liability firm owned by the family.

Traditionally, in the USA non-recourse mortgages were given on a down payment of 20 per cent. Hence, the buyer only had to finance one-fifth of the purchase price with his own equity; the lending ceiling for the mortgage thus amounted to 80 per cent. In recent years, however, banks did not demand any down payments, permitting full credit financing of the homes.

One hundred per cent mortgage financing is no problem for the bank as long as house prices are rising. That was the case for a long time, as shown in Chapter 2 (Figure 2.8), but the trend changed in the winter of 2006/7. Home prices slumped, and millions of homeowners became overly indebted as the value of their homes fell below the value of their mortgages. Estimates put the figure of American homes that had fallen 'under water' at 12 million by the end of September 2008.[4] The banks, whose mortgages were no longer covered, had to write down the value of their credit claims correspondingly

---

[2] See T. J. Zywicki and J. Adamson, 'The Law & Economics of Subprime Lending', *University of Colorado Law Review*, 80 (2009), 1–86.

[3] I am grateful to Oswald Braun for this information.

[4] See M. M. Zandi, *Homeownership Vesting Plan*, December 2008, Moody's Economy.com, online at www.economy.com, accessed on 3 March 2009.

and in this way lost immense amounts of equity. This made the banking crisis and its many contagion effects inevitable.[5]

How Mr Jones became a gambler...

Protection against recourse to other assets is not only a problem because of the loss of equity, but primarily because it induced Mr Jones to incur risk and overreach himself when buying a home. He did not even shrink from the most expensive properties that far exceeded his means. And he did not act overly negligently, but, on the contrary, tried to make a profit in a rational way. Nobody should be blamed for accepting an offer that he cannot refuse.

Imagine that Mr Jones has no money but would like to buy a home. He is offered a property that he thinks is too expensive. He knows that if he accepts, he will need a 100 per cent mortgage, but he could make his fortune. Everything would depend on the evolution of house prices.

Should house prices rise, Mr Jones would be in good shape. He could resell the house after a few years, repay his mortgage, and make a profit equal to the capital gain. Or he could go to the bank, refer to the increased value of his home, and correspondingly raise the size of his mortgage. From the new loan he could buy another car or finance a vacation.

Should prices fall, however, Mr Jones would be out of luck but would face no insurmountable problem. As the mortgage would exceed the value of the home, putting the house 'under water', as one says, he could simply leave the key to his house with the bank and write a letter declaring the surrender of his property and the non-servicing of his mortgage. Banks used to call these letters *jingle mail*, because the key jingled in the envelope like a little bell. Beyond that, Mr Jones would not have anything to do with the affair. He would move to another home that was for rent in the neighbourhood and live again as before.

All of this was on Mr Jones's mind when he decided on the purchase of the house and he knew that he could do no wrong in buying a house on credit.

---

[5] That falling home prices would lead to immense problems was first projected by N. Roubini. Cf. N. Roubini, 'Trends and Forecasts for the U.S. and Global Economy in 2006', *Nouriel Roubini's Global EconoMonitor*, 28 January 2006, online at www.rgemonitor.com, accessed on 9 February 2009.

Even the most ramshackle property could still turn a profit as long as house prices continued to rise with a certain probability. With this probability he could gain, whereas the probability of loss did not even enter his mind, as there was no recourse liability. Obviously, in the worst case, he would move out and give up his old living quarters, but it would be cheaper to rent a home in the neighbourhood than continue the high debt service.

These truly bizarre incentive structures led to unrestrained purchase decisions of American private households. They may be considered the microeconomic core of the American housing bubble. American private households became real estate speculators, and—in spite of all the energy problems—vast satellite towns developed in which the American dream of one's own home became reality for millions of people. People ran in droves to real estate agents, and the construction industry was hard pressed to meet the rising demand, especially since land for building in preferred locations was scarce. As a consequence, house prices continued to rise. Every year in which house prices climbed fed the subjective expectations of home buyers that prices would continue to rise in the future and further fuelled the speculation.

Especially clever were John and Lauren Visconsi of Portland, Maine, he a lawyer, she the owner of a small textile store.[6] In March 2006, the couple bought their first home. Although they only earned average incomes, they purchased another home just two years later in order to rent it out. Although they could not raise the initially demanded down payment of 20 per cent on the mortgage, in an environment of rising house prices, a bank offered to reduce the down payment by half by combining two mortgages. The expected rent served as collateral for the payment of the correspondingly high mortgage rates. Things worked out so well that the Visconsis repeated the procedure two more times within one year. And they were lucky. Home prices continued to rise, and within a few years the couple was able to amass housing assets of $1.4 million. In the meantime they are likely to have lost the houses again, but they surely had a good time living the good life. In any case, they did nothing wrong.

---

[6] See C. Hawn, *The Low-Down-Payment Empire*, CNN Money.com, 1 September 2005, online at www.money.cnn.com, accessed on 22 January 2009.

The economic reason for the excessive risk preference of homeowners like the Visconsis is, similar to what it was for gambling banks, the limitation of liability that shields against losses. The lower end of the probability distribution of profits was cut off by the lack of direct liability beyond the mortgaged asset. And since only the upper end was still relevant, involvement became all the more attractive the bigger the uncertainty about the future value of the properties. It was uncertainty *per se* that created the private profits, not a natural risk premium such as that usually offered by business for courageous economic decisions. Even if, on average, a falling house price was expected, limited liability created profits for the homeowner, because profits were privatized and losses were socialized, in this case initially at the expense of the banks.

... and lived beyond his means

The question arises as to whether the statement that banks were willing to finance the homes at 100 per cent was not a bit exaggerated. But it was indeed common practice. Figure 5.1 presents the website of a bank with offers that were still common practice in July 2007. Obviously, the bank was willing to provide mortgages of up to 125 per cent of the value of the house, and it also was generous regarding the creditworthiness of the customers.

Fig. 5.1 How loans were chasing borrowers

Source: LoanWeb advertisement shown on many US loan or credit-card related websites during 2007, and as a pop-up on the company's own website. The website has been deactivated in the meantime.

'Borrow up to 125 per cent of your home's value' and 'No initial credit check' are statements found on the website. The offers could be used for purchases or for adding on to the loans if house prices rose.

If banks were more conservative and did not permit loans of over 100 per cent of the home price, the buyers sometimes used tricks by entering into so-called cash-back contracts with the sellers. In the written part of the contract they would show an overblown purchase price in order to make the bank grant the corresponding mortgage, then agreed in a second contract that at the time of the sale, part of the purchase price transferred to the sellers was to be refunded in cash to the buyers who could now use it for consumption. This was a common cheat, not only tolerated by real estate brokers but even actively promoted by them in order to be able to earn higher brokerage fees. That the subsequent securitization of these loans meant that the buyers of American financial products were cheated is yet another story (see Chapter 6).

Banks also tried, however, to induce people to take out loans at official terms by inventing all kinds of bizarre financial instruments. Common were, for example, the so-called *teaser-rate mortgages* that started with low fixed interest rates that were later raised to market level. And then there were the *interest-only loans* on which borrowers did not have to make capital repayments for several years. Borrowers were even allowed to add on to their loans over time instead of repaying them. For that purpose the banks offered *payment-option loans*, for which borrowers could decide themselves whether to pay interest or make repayments or to add on to the loan, or *piggybacks* that explicitly included the option of add-on debt for consumption purposes if home prices kept rising.[7]

All of these business practices helped Americans live the high life during the time of the housing bubble. The possibility of adding to the mortgage debt on their homes, whose value kept on rising, was actually used by many people to enjoy a standard of consumption that was not commensurate with their income.

Figure 5.2 shows that in the years before the crisis the volume of US mortgage loans far exceeded residential construction, at times by over 60 per cent.

---

[7] According to B. Rudolph, presentation at the Protestant Congregation of Gauting, Germany, on 24 January 2009.

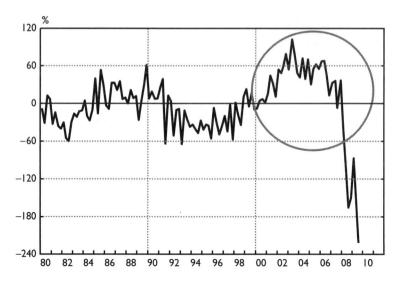

Fig. 5.2 Excess of mortgage loans over residential construction in the USA (1st quarter 1980–3rd quarter 2009)

Note: Shown is the percentage difference between mortgage loans granted and private residential construction. Positive values show excess borrowing for consumption purposes, negative values show mortgage loans below residential construction and hence restrained consumption. The area in the circle underneath the curve measures the entire additional consumption enjoyed by homeowners out of mortgage loans during the years 2000–7, about $7.4 trillion in total.

Source: Federal Reserve Board, *Flow of Funds Account*, D.2 Borrowing by Sector, F.100 Households and Non-profit Organizations, Ifo Institute calculations.

Before then, this surplus had never been so large and sometimes even negative, as should be expected, because in other countries part of the funds needed for new homes is usually financed by equity instead of debt. What happened in America in the period from roughly 2001 to 2007 is beyond any notion of healthy business.

The situation pictured in Figure 5.2 fits in with Figures 2.1 and 2.2 of Chapter 2, which depicted the macroeconomic side of the events, with the US savings rate tending toward zero and gigantic capital imports ballooning to 5 per cent of GDP, breaking all historical records. Homeowners who took out more loans than needed to finance their homes had a negative savings rate; they consumed more than their disposable income. Of course, there were also thrifty households that saved part of their disposable income. But they only just about balanced the spendthrift households, as average savings, as macroeconomic statistics indicate, did approach zero.

It is a fact that American households in their entirety no longer saved and that they had to look to foreigners to get the loans for their investments in real estate and equipment as well as for financing the government budget deficit. This is what caused the huge capital imports that were absorbing more than half of total world capital exports. America's gigantic current account deficit, in other words, the surplus of imports of goods and services over exports, was the necessary counterpart to this development, as you need capital from abroad if you want to live beyond your means.

In the meantime, this development has come to a halt. As shown in Figure 5.2, the surplus of mortgages over residential construction has disappeared and turned into a deficit. The flow of loans to homeowners has run dry, as the financial crisis forced the banks to scale down their operations. Americans have had to tighten their belts, and their savings rate has risen sharply. While from a long-term perspective this was a sorely needed correction, it also brought about a slump in current consumer demand, triggering a crisis in the real economy. To counteract the crisis, the government began putting together gigantic recovery packages and borrowing the money that ordinary citizens were no longer able to borrow (see Chapter 10).

Now that the government is the borrower and not its citizens, US capital imports have shrunk substantially. While capital imports hit a record of more than \$800 billion in 2008, the shrinkage of the US trade deficit, shown in Figure 1.8, and other preliminary information suggest that they may have been cut by one-third in the meantime.

Apart from the flow of funds drying up, the depreciation of the dollar against the euro and other currencies, which was a consequence of an oversupply of American securities on world financial markets over a long period of time, has also contributed to a reduction of capital imports. This depreciation has made American exports cheaper abroad and imports more expensive at home. Both price changes have, after an initial opposite effect,[8] contributed to reducing the surplus of imports of goods and services over exports that Americans must finance with foreign loans; this will continue to be so in the coming years.

---

[8] Depreciation initially, at still unchanged quantities, leads to higher prices of imports in terms of domestic currency and thereby increases the current account deficit (J-curve effect). A normal reaction of the current account, where an increase in the volume of exports and a decline in the volume of imports prevails over the mere change in value of imports, takes about two years.

The adjustment process of the US economy will be cumbersome and time consuming, as it involves building up a new export industry and replacing imports with domestic products, if possible. By the time America and the entire world economy has found a new equilibrium, more than one term of a US President will have passed. Americans must say goodbye to the *American dream*, the dream of a high standard of living for the masses, announced by President Franklin D. Roosevelt in the 1930s. New economic structures must emerge that are compatible with a more balanced current account and a higher savings rate. A full adjustment cannot be accomplished within one cyclical recovery, which will probably occur in the meantime. But with things as they are, the process seems irreversible, because the world is no longer willing to play the American game.

The banks as gambling partners

Let us get back to microeconomic events. The riddle is why the banks participated in this game at all, a game that went so sour for them. Two reasons come to mind: gambling and legal coercion. Let us look at each in turn. Gambling was already described in the previous chapter. It is based on the artificial risk preference of banks that has its cause in the banks over-extending the privilege of limited liability by minimizing their equity. If you can cut off the negative parts of the probability distribution of profits and pass them on to others, you seek widely dispersed distributions and become a gambler. You behave like a gambler in a casino, but you are at the same time much better off because, in contrast to the casino gambler (and lottery player), you are participating in a game with positive outcomes on average.

For gambling you need partners. Banks can gamble with one another by placing mutual bets. That is what they actually did in great style under the *credit default swaps* (CDS) banner, as will be explained in Chapter 8. Better partners, however, were the homeowners, in whose gamble revolving around rising house prices the banks participated by means of mortgage loans. Banks promoted the risky actions of homeowners, because they knew that they could turn a tidy profit from a continuation of the housing boom and could not lose more than the little equity they had if the trend turned around.

Their calculation was simple: in the case of further increases in house prices they would profit because their loans would remain covered and the homeowners would service their debt. They may have been aware of the fact that the debt service would be partly financed by new loans, but they did not find this problematic as they assumed that the new loans would also be serviced. By contrast, in the case of falling home prices the banks would of course have a problem, because their customers could return their homes without repaying their loans. But they knew that if this did occur, the problem would equally affect the whole banking industry. In addition, even this unfavourable development would have only limited effects on the wealth of their own shareholders thanks to the limited liability of the corporations and their minute stocks of equity. In case of doubt they would ask the government for help or close down the bank and leave part of the losses to their own creditors. Before that happened, however, they would make big profits and distribute them to their stockholders. Each year in which business was good was a year won for their own bank and their own shareholders, and even if some day the fiasco of falling home prices was to occur, the shareholders would still have made their profits. Strategies which promise gigantic profits at a 99 per cent probability also pay off if one's equity is lost at a 1 per cent probability, because the bank's equity is not identical to the bank owners' wealth.

Who knows whether the banks planned for the case of falling house prices or only closed their eyes to it in the course of doing business as usual? If you have limited liability and work almost without any equity that could be lost, you do not go wrong by restricting yourself to fair-weather strategies. It does not pay to plan for the catastrophe and make provisions because you would have to forgo profits during good times without being able to exert a significant influence over the effects of the potential catastrophe on your own wallet.

The right to play the lottery: Clinton's law

Limited liability combined with minimal stocks of equity and the resulting gambling fever explains why banks allowed homeowners to fully finance their homes, although homeowners, too, benefited from contractual limited liability. The explanation is incomplete, however, as the banks amazingly also gave mortgages to homeowners from financially weak social strata, who could not be expected to repay their loans with any realistic probability even if the economic development of the housing market had not been disrupted. The tinkling of the jingle letters could already be heard when the loan contract was signed. The explanation becomes more complete if the second reason for the generous mortgage lending is considered.

This second reason was simply that the banks *had* to grant mortgage loans. There was a special federal law that forced them, the Community Reinvestment Act (CRA). The programme was introduced in 1977 under President Jimmy Carter in order to counteract the dilapidation of entire neighbourhoods and the creation of slums. It was intended to help disadvantaged strata of the population to invest in homes in order to revitalize the neighbourhoods. This followed the old idea, already promulgated by the New Deal of President Franklin D. Roosevelt, that every American should own his home.

Due to an amendment passed in 1995, three years after President Clinton's election, the law became substantially more effective and pressured banks to give mortgages also to customers with little creditworthiness. The bus driver, the hairdresser, the assembly-line worker, and really everyone should be able to buy a home, which was a laudable goal in itself. The Community Reinvestment Act thus became de facto a basic right to participate in the lottery described in the preceding section, where nothing could go wrong due to non-recourse loans.

The amendment, initiated by Clinton against the recommendations of economists,[9] had been preceded by the politically articulated concern about the decay of American cities. This was said to be due to *red lining*, the practice of American banks in granting mortgage loans. Internally, banks used to mark entire blocks on city maps red and exclude them from mortgage lending, because of their bad experience with collateralizing the loans due to the debasement of the properties. That was, understandably, anathema to the policy-makers, and the Clinton administration wanted to end this practice by forcing banks by law to grant housing loans evenly to all social and ethnic groups also in economically underdeveloped areas.

The banking supervisor was asked to ensure adherence to the measures by means of a special reporting system and an especially created

---

[9] See e.g. W. A. Niskanen, *Repeal the Community Reinvestment Act*, Testimony of William A. Niskanen, Chairman, Cato Institute, before the Subcommittee on Financial Institutions and Consumer Credit, Committee on Banking and Financial Services, United States Senate, 8 March 1995.

rating system.[10] The rating received by the banks was taken into account in permitting mergers and acquisitions and the granting of deposit insurance by the supervisory authorities. It forced the banks to actually implement the easing of mortgage lending to disadvantaged groups that was expected of them.[11] Additional pressure to adhere to the legal provisions of the Community Reinvestment Act was exerted by the publication of the results of the rating process by the Federal Financial Institutions Examination Council.

One of the consequences of these legal measures was the partial abandonment of credit checks that banks normally resort to prior to granting a mortgage in order to protect against losses. The increase of the loan percentage and the introduction of the interest-free loans described above were, at least in part, the consequence of the new political requirements. The banks did everything necessary to improve their statistics regarding the social strata shunned in the past. Mortgage brokers, who received premiums from the banks for each loan contract completed, actively chased down households that did not yet own a home. The mortgage standards were softened until neither records of income nor of net worth were necessary to receive a mortgage loan. In the end even low-wage and unemployed people, who had neither assets nor income to service the debt, were able to buy homes. The mortgages so acquired were called NINJA loans. No Income, no jobs or assets—no problem.[12]

[10] The Federal Financial Institutions Examination Council (FFIEC) publishes the results of the rating processes of the four supervisory bodies, the Office of the Comptroller of the Currency (OCC), the Board of Governors of the Federal Reserve System (FRB), the Office of Thrift Supervision (OTS), and the Federal Deposit Insurance Corporation (FDIC). On the basis of a number of criteria, the banks are rated regarding their meeting the goals of the Community Reinvestment Act. See www.ffiec.gov for a survey of the rating process.

[11] See e.g. Federal Deposit Insurance Corporation, *FDIC Law, Regulations, Related Acts*, Part 345—Community Reinvestment, Effect of CRA performance on applications, online at www.fdic.gov, accessed on 10 February 2009.

[12] See A. Dodd and P. Mills, 'Outbreak: U.S. Subprime Contagion', *Finance and Development* (June 2008), 14–18. At the height of lending it was evidently no longer necessary to be still alive. Thus in the state of Ohio 23 mortgages were awarded to people already deceased. See A. Blumberg, A. Davidson, and I. Glass, 'A Giant Pool of Money', *Chicago Public Radio*, broadcast on 9 May 2008, transcript available online at www.nzzfolio.ch, accessed on 18 February 2009.

If banks refused without good reasons to grant NINJA loans, they could be taken to court and accused of discrimination. Even Barack Obama used to participate in such trials as a lawyer. For example, in 1995, in *Buycks-Roberson* v *Citibank*, he successfully represented the prosecution, accusing Citibank of having systematically rejected credit applications of ethnic minorities.[13] He also worked for the Association of Community Organizations for Reform Now (ACORN), which actively promoted the application of the Community Reinvestment Act and helped poor people to receive mortgage loans.

The Clinton amendment even allowed class action suits, in which a group of residents from disadvantaged communities or organizations like ACORN or NCRC (National Community Reinvestment Coalition) could take the banks to court if they could prove that the banks granted fewer loans in that particular neighbourhood than elsewhere. This option led to a large volume of lawsuits in ensuing years that forced the banks to change their lending practices. The organizations even succeeded in being granted co-determination rights in awarding the mortgage loans.

President Clinton's amendment to the Community Reinvestment Act was a complete success. As shown in Figure 5.3, the share of households owning their homes surged during the ensuing ten years from 64 per cent to 69 per cent. The goal of helping the disadvantaged ethnic groups was achieved. Whereas the total number of homeowners rose by 6 per cent during this period, homeownership by Afro-Americans increased by 13 per cent and that by Hispanics by 18 per cent.[14]

Obviously, this negligence in lending practices could not end well. As the prices of the homes together with the volumes of mortgages rose faster than household incomes, it became more and more difficult, especially for poorer people, to service their mortgage debt. Frequently the borrowers were not even able to make the first payment. The new market segment of the

---

[13] See Washington University, St Louis, School of Law, *The Civil Rights Litigation Clearinghouse, Settlement Agreement, Buycks-Roberson vs. Citibank Fed. Sav. Bank,* 94C-4094 (n.d. Ill. 16 January 1998), online at www.clearinghouse.wustl.edu, accessed on 2 February 2009.

[14] See US Census Bureau, *Housing Vacancies and Homeownership (CPS/HVS), Annual Statistics 2007*, table 20, online at www.census.gov, accessed on 17 February 2009.

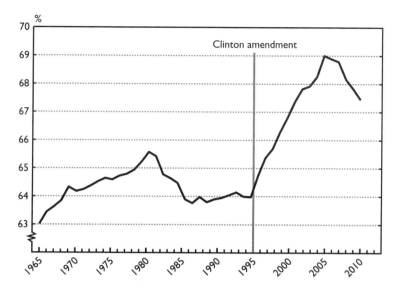

Fig. 5.3 Share of US households owning their homes (1965–2009)

Source: US Census Bureau, *Housing Vacancies and Homeownership* (CPS/HVS), Historical Tables, table 14, online at www.census.gov, accessed on 2 February 2010.

problem loans was called the *subprime market* in order to distinguish it from the prime market where loans with good credit risks were awarded. Subprime loans were mortgages with a financing ratio of more than 90 per cent or those that were awarded to persons whose debt service exceeded 45 per cent of their before-tax income and/or who did not have a clean credit record.[15] Figure 5.4 shows how dramatically the number of subprime mortgages surged in the late phase of the housing bubble. Whereas in 1998 there were hardly any subprime loans, their number had exploded to more than six million by 2006.

The value of subprime loans relative to that of total mortgages also rose substantially, as shown in Figure 5.5. Adding the so-called Alt-A loans (alternative A mortgages), which are close to subprime loans because their borrowers do not meet all credit criteria either, yields an increase from 10 per cent in 2001 to 34 per cent in 2006. Then the growth screeched to a halt, because the banks pulled the emergency brake and stopped awarding new loans to problematic customers. Home prices also stopped rising from then on (see Figure 2.8).

[15] This delineation of prime and subprime loans is based on the definition of conforming loans, accepted by Fannie Mae and Freddie Mac. There is no uniform definition of subprime loans.

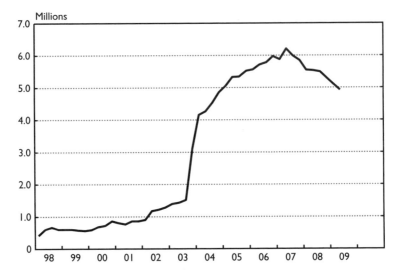

Fig. 5.4 Number of mortgage loans in the subprime market (1st quarter 1998–2nd quarter 2009)

Source: Mortgage Bankers Association of America, *National Delinquency Survey*.

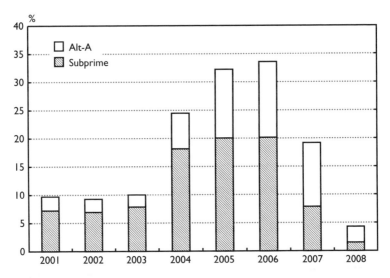

Fig. 5.5 The value share of subprime loans in the total value of mortgages (2001–2008)

Source: Inside Mortgage Finance Publications, *The 2009 Mortgage Market Statistical Annual* (Bethesda, MD, 2009).

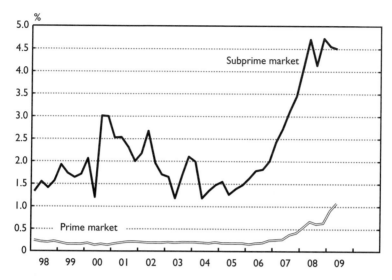

Fig. 5.6 Foreclosures of homes in the USA (1st quarter 1998–2nd quarter 2009)

Note: Share of homes being foreclosed in total stock of mortgages.

Source: Mortgage Bankers Association of America, *National Delinquency Survey*.

As banks were no longer willing to extend or renew maturing loans, many homes were foreclosed. Figure 5.6 shows that foreclosures in the subprime segment of the mortgage market have surged since the end of 2006, while there were still relatively few foreclosures in the prime market. As these foreclosures were the most tangible trigger of the worldwide financial crisis, the financial crisis was initially also called the subprime crisis.

The immediate cause of, albeit not the true reason for, the difficulties of the subprime market may be traced to rising American interest rates, as already described in Chapter 2. The American central bank had initially kept its short-term interest rates extremely low until early 2003 in order to counter the economic downturn after the attack on the World Trade Center in 2001. When the success of this policy materialized and the economy started to recover in the winter of 2003/4, the Fed raised interest rates again to forestall any risk of inflation. Although it did not raise interest rates to the level of the past boom, the increase caused difficulties for many of the poorer households that Clinton's policy had turned into homeowners, at least those for whom the initial grace period had already expired and who now had to pay variable interest rates. They were fully hit by the rapid increase of the variable interest rates shown in Figure 2.12. Many of them used the high monthly burden, which they could no longer shoulder, as an opportunity to leave their house keys with the banks, which forced the banks into foreclosuring.

From the subprime market the crisis spread to the entire housing market, because speculative bubbles are unstable. As long as the market agents believe that prices will continue to rise, the latter actually do so because buyers and sellers behave accordingly. But when doubts have arisen, the turnaround can set in fast. That is what happened when the American housing bubble burst. The bad news was an incentive for many people to sell their homes at still good prices. This first led to a slowdown of the price increase and then to the turnaround. Prices began to tumble, and home-owners with average solvency were driven into excess indebtedness. Banks refused a prolongation or increase of mortgages and foreclosures were now forced on those homeowners, too. This increased the downward pressure on prices and further depressed expectations, driving more and more borrowers into giving up. At the same time the pessimism spread to the stock market. Stock prices fell, giving rise to a feeling of panic as described in Chapters 1 and 2. The consequences were a general reluctance to consume and an economic recession.

In 1980, in a paper that became famous, Janos Kornai, the Hungarian economist, traced the weakness of the Communist system to the soft budget constraints.[16] One of the secrets of the market economy's success consists of having the monetary system break down actual resource constraints of an economy to the level of the individual: in the form of the time available for working and property rights in real capital, land, and natural resources. Thus, every individual learns by way of prices about the actual scarcity in the form of a budget constraint and is induced to use his or her scarce monetary resources with caution. Under Communism, the budget con-straints were eased time and again, whenever the politicians considered it opportune. Upon the command of the leadership, projects were undertaken without making sure that free production capacity was available or noting what had to be sacrificed elsewhere in the economy. That was one of the reasons for the inefficiency of this economic system, a form of inefficiency

---

[16] See J. Kornai, *Economics of Shortage* (North-Holland, Amsterdam, 1980).

that, as we know now, is not limited to the Communist system. It is an irony of history that the soft budget constraints, which destroyed Communism, were re-established by the Community Reinvestment Act in the heart of the epitome of capitalism, the United States of America, triggering the crisis of the American financial system that has grown into a crisis of the world economy in the meantime.

CHAPTER 6

Hot Potatoes

The securitization trick

The mortgage banks, forced to grant subprime loans because of the Community Reinvestment Act tightened under President Clinton, knew of course how risky the repayment claims were that they acquired, and sought remedies. They also became increasingly anxious about regular loans they had granted to wealthier households as warnings became louder that the housing bubble might burst. The solution they found consisted of securitizing their mortgage loans. Instead of keeping them against the homeowners and nervously waiting for uncertain repayments, the banks (including the brokers and other originators) divided their debtors into different categories of creditworthiness and sold the loans in the financial markets to other banks or financial investors. For this purpose they created securities based on claims to the homeowner's payment of principal and interest. The claims were only serviced to the extent to which the homeowners were able to meet their obligations.

In the USA the securitization of loans of all kinds was a popular method to free the balance sheets of banks from the credit risk. Altogether, 28 per cent of outstanding loans in the US were securitized by early 2009, while in Europe the corresponding figure was 6 per cent. Most of the securitizations concerned mortgage loans, and most of the mortgage loans were securitized. By 2009 about 60 per cent of the outstanding stock of residential mortgage credit, a value of $7.2 trillion, had been securitized,[1] and the share of new mortgage credit securitized was above 80 per cent, occasionally even above 90 per cent, in the years before the crisis (2000 to 2007).[2] From 2002 to the onset of the crisis in 2007, private mortgage securitization trebled in the USA, before collapsing during the crisis.[3]

Securitization covered credit claims of various degrees of creditworthiness, but was especially attractive to the seller in cases of low creditworthiness that were to be removed from the books. Therefore, nearly all subprime risks were securitized and sold. Figure 6.1 shows the dramatic surge in the share of subprime loans and the related Alt-A loans (alternative A mortgages) in the total value of securitized mortgages from 2001 to 2008. Whereas both categories accounted for about 7 per cent of all mortgage securitizations in 2001, their share had risen to 42 per cent by 2006. After a significant reduction in 2007, the market for securitized subprime and Alt-A mortgages collapsed in 2008 to only 0.35 per cent of all securitized mortgages. For all practical purposes, it has ceased to exist.

The securities created from claims against homeowners were called *mortgage-backed securities* (MBS). For European investors, the term 'mortgage-backed security' evokes positive associations with the German *Pfandbrief*, a covered bond backed by real estate. This may be one of the reasons why in Germany so many investors were keen to put their money into such securities or their derivatives in recent years. The initial impression is wrong, however. Whereas Pfandbriefs represent legal claims against the issuing bank, which are additionally collateralized by real estate, buyers of an MBS in the end only acquire a claim against the real estate. In fact, the owner of a Pfandbrief holds a threefold claim. First he holds a claim against the bank. Second, if the bank goes bankrupt, he holds a claim against the bank's mortgage debtor. Third, if the debtor files for personal bankruptcy, the owner of the Pfandbrief has a claim against the real estate, which he can satisfy by selling it to the highest bidder. The claims held by the buyer of an MBS hold little similarity with this. The buyer holds no claim against the bank and not even against the

---

[1] International Monetary Fund, *Global Financial Stability Report* (October 2009), 30.

[2] J. Krainer, 'Recent Developments in Mortgage Finance', *FRBSF Economic Letter* 2009-33, 26 October 2009, figure 3, www.frbsf.org, accessed November 2009.

[3] See International Monetary Fund, ibid.

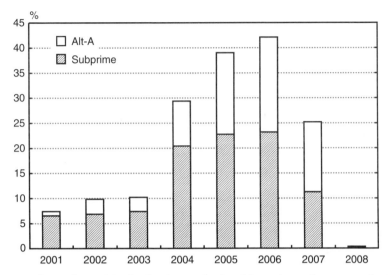

Fig. 6.1 Share of securitized subprime and related loans in total mortgage-backed securities (2001–2008, flows)

Source: Inside Mortgage Finance, *The 2008 Mortgage Market Statistical Annual*, vol. ii.

debtor, as the debtor is protected by the non-recourse nature of the mortgage debt and can choose to not redeem his debt if his home has fallen 'under water'. The buyer indeed only holds a claim against the real estate property itself and bears the risk of declining house prices.

The Pfandbrief was introduced in 1769 in Prussia, and since then not a single Pfandbrief has failed. Small wonder that this financial instrument spread quickly across Europe in various forms of covered bonds. While the Pfandbrief has a trustee security status, an MBS is just a risky asset. Its possession only implies a claim to cash flows that depend on the extent to which the securitized loan is serviced by the primary debtor with interest payments and principal repayments. The gain or loss to the buyer depends exclusively on the development of house prices and the payment behaviour of the homeowner. The bank itself is not liable for a homeowner's eventual default or the losses from a possible foreclosure.

MBSs further expanded the limited liability that financial institutions already enjoyed. In most cases the issuing institution itself did not even hold any of the risky securities, but got rid of the risk completely. Therefore, it did not have to be concerned about borrowers who appeared to be unreliable customers. The bank had little incentive to select reliable customers *ex ante* and to secure the repayment flow through legal actions *ex post*. The whole securitization business took place in a haze of carelessness and irresponsibility.

MBSs are similar to so-called *asset-backed securities* (ABS). Sometimes they are even considered as a sub-category of such securities. Asset-backed securities also present a claim of the issuer against a borrower, without the issuer himself having any legal obligation to service the paper. In a strict sense, however, in ABSs the legal claim is not necessarily tied to real estate. For example, ABSs are created from car leasing contracts, credit-card transactions, or any similar mass credit business.

Securitization in itself is not a bad thing for capital markets, but a potentially useful instrument that permits the distribution of financing risks onto many shoulders and thus their consolidation, as one says in insurance economics. This reduces the risk premium that the lender must charge its customers as part of the interest rate and allows the customers to assume productive entrepreneurial risks that they would not have dared to touch otherwise. The willingness to bear and manage risk can be seen as one of an economy's most important factors of production.[4]

Risk consolidation, however, is always accompanied by a watering down of responsibility, making moral hazard effects more likely. That is why it is never a good idea to assume all the risks of a decision-maker, regardless of the economic decision. Real estate financing is certainly no exception. In the present case, excessive securitization of credit risks by mortgage lenders fuelled a substantial dose of carelessness on their own part and on the part of their credit customers in dealing with risk. The customers bought overpriced homes, and the banks did not care. The banks were after new business and offered mortgages to the most dubious customers, since they knew that they could subsequently sell the claims and could remove such potentially toxic assets from their balance sheets.

---

[4] See H.-W. Sinn, 'Risiko als Produktionsfaktor' (inaugural lecture LMU Munich), *Jahrbücher für Nationalökonomie und Statistik*, 201 (1986), 557–71, and H.-W. Sinn, 'Gedanken zur volkswirtschaftlichen Bedeutung des Versicherungswesens', *Zeitschrift für die gesamte Versicherungswissenschaft*, 77 (1988), 1–27.

Fannie and Freddie

Securitization of mortgage loans on a grand scale was initially done by Fannie Mae and Freddie Mac. Both institutions covered about half of the US mortgage securitization market. Although these institutions were privately organized, they were non-profit organizations with the status of *Government-sponsored Enterprises* (GSE). Their objective was to acquire credit claims from mortgage institutions if the risks attached to these claims did not exceed a certain threshold. In order to consolidate the existing risks, they securitized and sold part of these claims as mortgage-backed securities on the market. This permitted the customers of mortgage lenders to borrow at better terms and contributed for a long time to the strong growth of the American housing market.[5]

The non-profit banks still kept many credit claims on their books and bore the attached risks, which turned them, as described in Chapter 3, into the first victims of the financial crisis. Fannie and Freddie were nationalized in early September 2008, before the collapse of Lehman Brothers. By August 2008 they had already made write-downs and valuation adjustments amounting to $20 billion, and this was only just the tip of the iceberg. According to estimates by the International Monetary Fund (IMF), the value of the uncollectable claims of the American non-profit financial institutions may amount to about $250 billion.[6] Since the nationalization, the total liabilities of the American taxpayers have risen to about $5,000 billion, equal to the total mortgage loans of the two institutions.

That these two GSEs had to be nationalized is remarkable in that they had not bought the typical subprime loans, as these had not met their conditions. They had not even touched the Alt-A loans, mentioned in the

---

[5] Government-sponsored Enterprises also include the monoline banks that are active in community financing and whose core business is the insurance of mortgage risks. For regular mortgage banks this insurance not only meant protection against a debtor's payment default, but above all a better rating, which allowed them to refinance on the capital market at more favourable terms. Especially institutional investors, like the big American pension funds, were always keen on finding safe investments and were therefore willing to put money into such insured mortgage banks.

[6] See International Monetary Fund, *Global Financial Stability Report: Responding to the Financial Crisis and Measuring Systemic Risks* (April 2009), 28, table 1.3, footnote 2.

previous chapter. These inferior credit claims were directly securitized and sold by the mortgage institutions or big investment banks.[7] The fact that nationalization had been necessary, although the riskiest bits of the American housing market had not been unloaded there, shows only the dimensions of the crisis.

The securitization cascade

Although Fannie and Freddie were heavily affected, the financial crisis centred on the private banking system. That is where the subprime and Alt-A risks wound up and where substantial parts of the risks securitized by Fannie and Freddie were also placed.

The private banks, which purchased MBSs from the mortgage institutions, were lured by hefty price reductions and the high effective rates of return that would be achieved in the most favourable case. But, of course, these banks also had no illusions about the creditworthiness of the securities. That is why they quickly tried to pass them on. The claims against the homeowners had the character of hot potatoes that nobody wanted to hold in their hands.

The buyers of MBSs, typically internationally active business and investment banks, applied a trick similar to that used by the mortgage lenders, namely to securitize once again the already securitized claims.[8] For this

---

[7] 95% of all securitizations were done by the 25 biggest issuers. These included Countrywide Financial, Washington Mutual, and Lehman Brothers, which went bankrupt or were taken over in 2008. (Cf. Inside Mortgage Finance, *The 2007 Mortgage Market Statistical Annual*, online at www.imfpubs.com, cited after A. Ashcraft and T. Schuermann, 'Understanding the Securitization of Subprime Mortgage Credit', Federal Reserve Bank of New York, *Staff Report* no. 318, March 2008, online at www.newyorkfed.org, accessed on 3 February 2009.)

[8] Detailed descriptions of securitization strategies may be found in B. Rudolph, 'Die Finanzkrise aus mikroökonomischer Perspektive', unpublished manuscript, University of Munich, Department of Business Economics, February 2009; M. Hellwig, *Systemic Risk in the Financial Sector: An Analysis of the Subprime-Mortgage Financial Crisis* (Jelle Zijlstra Lecture, Netherlands Institute for Advanced Study in the Humanities and Social Sciences (NIAS) and Free University of Amsterdam, November 2008); W. Münchau, *Kernschmelze im Finanzsystem* (Hanser, Munich, 2008); and F. Kübler, 'Die Krise der amerikanischen Hypothekenverbriefungen: Ursachen und Herausforderungen', in S. Grundmann et al. (eds.), *Unternehmensrecht zu Beginn des 21. Jahrhunderts*, Festschrift für E. Schwark zum 70. Geburtstag (Beck, Munich, 2009), 499–510.

purpose they added a name, combined good and bad MBSs in one pool, and issued securitized claims against the contents of the pool that they in turn sold on to other banks. These pools resided in so-called *special purpose vehicles*, separate entities mostly organized as non-profit foundations with little equity that were equipped by the parent company with a guarantee against losses. The MBSs themselves had been put together in a similar fashion, by pooling good and bad claims, and been created largely by such special purpose vehicles. These entities resided in foreign low-tax jurisdictions or even in tax havens. The Bahamas and Ireland ranked among the preferred locations on account of their low or non-existent corporate tax rates.

The special purpose vehicles did not design the claims against the pool in such a way that acquiring them would mean receiving a completely mixed portfolio against all ABSs in the pool. Rather, they created a hierarchy of tranches, a process called *structuring*. Already the ABSs were structured so as to define different risk categories of securities. However, the full complexity of the structuring process was only applied to the so-called *collateralized debt obligations* (CDOs).

Whereas the underlying securitized claims backing up the original MBSs consisted only of mortgage loans, the CDOs contained all sorts of financial products. A CDO could, for example, consist of other securities, such as ABS, corporate bonds, or even CDO tranches themselves. The CDOs often also involved *credit default swaps* (CDS). Credit default swaps are credit guarantees that insure against the default of financial claims. Credit default swaps were included in CDOs mainly in a way that made the investor an insurer, effectively selling protection to others and receiving premiums in exchange (CDS contracts in so-called synthetic CDOs). Sometimes, some of the assets underlying a CDO or even the CDOs themselves were insured by other CDS contracts to improve their rating and hedge against default risk. (A detailed discussion of these securities may be found in the last section of Chapter 8.)

As already explained in Chapter 2, the cash flow from servicing the debts making up such a composite pool of claims, whether MBS or CDOs, which constituted the current income of the special purpose vehicle, was first applied to servicing the best tranche, the so-called AAA or *senior tranche*, at the agreed terms. Any funds left over were to service the second best tranche, the *mezzanine-A tranche*, and when all obligations had been met there, it was the turn of the *mezzanine-B tranche*. At the very end, it would be the turn of the worst of all tranches. This was called the *equity tranche*, because, like the equity of a business, it was to be serviced after the borrowed funds. The scaling described has often been compared to a waterfall that flows from basin to basin, fills the basins one after the other, and only flows to the next basin when the preceding one has been completely filled.

The claims were structured according to the waterfall principle because many institutional investors, especially the pension funds, which manage the money of American employees, were obliged to invest the largest part of their capital in securities of the very best category. Structuring allowed turning rather dubious MBSs at least in part into AAA papers by granting them the right to be serviced with first priority out of the loan repayments. Even if the loans themselves constituted uncertain claims against homeowners, the assumption was that not all of them would default at the same time, so that a subset of CDO buyers could be granted nearly risk-free claims, of course at the expense of a deterioration of the claims of the other buyers. AAA-rated MBSs and CDOs were sold primarily to such investors as the American pension funds. But banks all over the world also acquired them in the course of their so-called proprietary trading (see Chapters 3 and 8).

The CDOs were equipped with different rates of return according to their risk class, in order to make them attractive enough to the investors. The equity tranche, which was expected to be the first tranche hit by any loss, was given by far the highest rate of return, while the senior tranche, which was the safest category, was endowed with a correspondingly low rate of return. But even the senior tranche rate of return was still markedly higher than the bond rate. For example, buyers of AAA-rated CDOs were promised in 2004 an average annual yield about one percentage point higher than that of government bonds of a comparable maturity.[9] No wonder that so many investors believed they were getting a very good deal. They had hopes and expectations that possible losses would only hit the worst tranche and overlooked the true risks that could arise from a collapse of the entire housing market. Their trust was nourished by the fact that house prices had

[9] See F. Packer and P. Wooldridge, 'Overview: Low Yields in Robust Economies', *BIS Quarterly Review*, March 2005, online at www.bis.org, accessed on 20 February 2009.

continuously risen for years and that banks used generally accepted econometric models to calculate the probabilities of default.

American banking market insiders were more sceptical, however. They were aware of the shortcomings of such econometric models, for instance the fact that the tranches had been calculated on the assumption of stochastically independent risks. With independent risks, the probability distribution for repayments of a sufficiently large number of bundled loan claims is a Gaussian normal distribution, and for that distribution one could calculate that the securities of the senior tranche would be serviced with an extremely high probability. The only problem was that the actual risks were far from being stochastically independent. The major risk did not stem from individual homeowners becoming insolvent due to personal circumstances, but from the collapse of the entire housing market. This risk could not be eliminated by bundling many small risks. It was intentionally ignored in calculating the tranches, just as it was left out by risk-theoretical models used by the banks' investment departments for their own purposes, as criticized in Chapter 4.

It is symptomatic that Warren Buffet, the famed investor and speculator and one of the richest men alive, already in 2003 had said that he considered derivatives, including securities created from mortgage loans by way of structuring, to be 'weapons of mass destruction'.[10]

Because they distrusted the calculations, insiders pushed the securitization process forward rather than keeping the CDOs on their books. They pocketed the honorariums and management fees and passed on the hot potatoes to the next bank. Buyers of the various tranches of CDOs, in particular of the mezzanine tranche, defined new pools, in which they mixed the CDOs of different issuers with original subprime MBSs as well as ABSs, and again defined a hierarchy of claims of different degrees of creditworthiness, structured according to the waterfall principle, and sold them on. They again calculated the risks on the erroneous assumption of stochastic independence and negligible systemic risks. The products thus generated were called CDOs of the second generation, or also CDO^2 securities. And so the game continued.

---

[10] 'In our view, however, derivatives are financial weapons of mass destruction, carrying dangers that, while now latent, are potentially lethal.' W. Buffet, *Letter to Berkshire Hathaway Shareholders 2003*, online at www.berkshirehathaway.com, accessed on 18 February 2009.

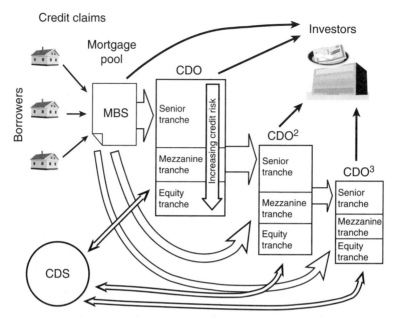

Fig. 6.2 The securitization cascade

The senior tranches of CDO² securities were sold to final customers and the mezzanine tranches of various issuers were again combined by other banks with MBSs and ABSs in order to create new CDOs with a hierarchical structure: CDOs of the third generation, CDO³. Up to six securitization stages were not uncommon in order to squeeze out some more AAA papers for the customers from the ever more insubstantial mush of claims. A member of a leading international auditing firm told me that he had seen CDOs that had gone through twenty-four stages of securitization, and a leading banker revealed that he had seen securities with forty stages. Figure 6.2 shows, by way of example, a simplified version of the process of securitization.

The securitization cascade could turn an initial portfolio of mortgage loans of medium quality into a portfolio with a relatively big share of assets with an AAA rating and a smaller share of assets with a high probability of default. This was no open fraud, as the mathematical calculations it was based on were comprehensible and logical in themselves. Unfortunately the basic assumption of stochastically independent risks was not fulfilled. Those readers interested in the mathematical details of structuring and the importance of the assumption of independent risks are directed to the footnote.[11]

The final products emerging from this process could no longer be understood by anybody. The cascade of interlinked claims created was opaque even to the cleverest investment banker. Looking back to the starting point of the cascade, one could see far away the blurred picture of Mr Jones and all the other private borrowers with their homes. But it was nearly impossible to assess the probability of repayment with any degree of accuracy. Presumably, the final buyers of the CDOs would never have touched these securities if they had been able to inspect these home loans more closely in the first place.

The most prominent victims in continental Europe were arguably the banks of the German federal states (*Landesbanken*). They invested more than 100 billion euros in the purchase of such securities. According to an older estimate of the rating agency Standard & Poor's of September 2007, the banks had put the majority of the securitized instruments, amounting to about 97 billion euros, into special purpose vehicles, reporting only a small

---

[11] An example may clarify the problem of the calculation. Assume there are initially two portfolios with two mortgages each, each with a nominal value of one and, independently of each other, having a 10% probability of default. In the first securitization stage, each portfolio is divided into a senior tranche and an equity tranche. The senior tranche is defined such that it incurs a loss only if both underlying mortgages default. According to the multiplication rule for probabilities, the probability of joint default of both mortgages is 10% times 10%, i.e. to 1%. In contrast, the equity tranche, for which cuts are implemented first, already suffers a loss if at least one of the mortgages defaults. According to the addition rule for probabilities, the probability of a loss is: $10\% + 10\% - (10\% \times 10\%) = 19\%$. In the second securitization stage the equity tranches of the two structured portfolios are combined into a new portfolio. Hence, this portfolio is now based on four mortgages. Another tranche is formed out of the two equity tranches that only suffers a loss if both default together. This creates a second generation senior tranche that has only a very low probability of default, although two equity tranches with high probabilities of default were combined. According to the multiplication rule, the probability of default of the new senior tranche is now $19\% \times 19\% = 3.61\%$. In contrast, the probability of default of the newly formed second generation equity tranche is $19\% + 19\% - (19\% \times 19\%) = 34\%$. In total, out of four underlying mortgages with a 10% probability of default each, three AAA securities were created with a probability of default of less than 5% and one extremely bad security with a probability of default of 34.39%. The error in this calculation lies in the assumption of independent risks, as the probabilities of default of the senior tranches would become much higher under the assumption of correlated risks. In the extreme case of perfectly correlated risks, the probability of default of the very first securitization stage would already amount to 10% instead of 1%, because the joint default of both mortgages is as probable as the default of a single mortgage.

portion of them on their balance sheets, and this figure is likely to have risen further in the meantime.[12] But even German private banks were busy buyers. Up to 2008, German banks had probably invested a total of up to 300 billion euros in such securities, as much as their total stock of equity, which was 305 billion euros in 2007.[13] As even AAA-rated CDOs lost two-thirds of their value during the crisis (see Figure 2.7), this corresponds to a loss of about 240 billion euros, equivalent to about $350 billion. Fortunately for the German banks, these are not net losses, as the banks had bought large-scale CDS insurance against the default risk. So a substantial fraction of the losses is lying elsewhere in the worldwide financial system. The example shows, however, the dimensions that the CDO problem had assumed. More details about the international distribution of losses will be provided in Chapter 8. One can only wonder what was going through the head of banks' management board members when they decided to order the acquisition. The banks' executives had believed they would be able to make a fortune, but obviously had no idea of what they were doing. Their acquisition of CDOs was a prime example of lemon banking discussed in Chapter 4.

Figure 6.3 shows the enormous growth of the stock of outstanding CDOs in just one decade, the period from 1996 to 2006. Until 1996, this kind of security was practically non-existent, but then CDOs ballooned and reached a volume of about $2.4 trillion in 2008, before the market collapsed. More on this later.

The trick with honorariums and cash-back credits

An important motive for the cascade of securitizations were the honorariums earned by the banks that granted the initial mortgage loans and then did the structuring. No institution wanted to keep the hot potatoes in its own books, but instead passed them on quickly. They had a sneaking suspicion

---

[12] Cf. S. Best, M. Brennan, and H. Semder, 'German Banks' Subprime Mortgage and Structured Vehicle Exposure Concerns Are Overstated', *Standard & Poor's Ratings Direct*, September 2007, online at www.standardandpoors.com, accessed on 10 February 2009.

[13] According to a secret survey of the Bundesbank which an insider revealed to the press. See 'Bankenkrise: Weitere Verluste', *Der Spiegel* (19 January 2009), 16; 'Jetzt geht die Krise richtig los', *Die Zeit* (22 January 2009), 20.

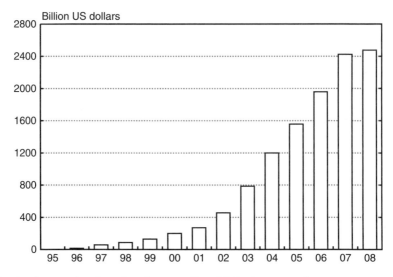

Fig. 6.3 International stocks of outstanding CDOs (1995–2008)

Note: Including the nominal value of their derivatives.

Sources: A. Pierron, *Collateralized Debt Obligations Market, Technical Report*, Celent, October 2005, online at www.celent.net, accessed on 26 February 2009, and Securities Industry and Financial Markets Association, *SIFMA Global CDO Issuance Data*, online at www.sifma.org, accessed on 3 February 2009.

that something was foul. Every time the hot potatoes changed hands, processing fees were generated that had to be paid out of the earnings.

For the first securitization in the USA, substantial honorariums and fees for credit checks, credit brokerage, consultation, and much more became due that, measured by European standards, are extortionate. These honorariums, as mentioned in the preceding section, were included in the mortgage used to start the securitization cascade. Thus, in the case of 100 per cent financing, the buyer of a CDO did not have a claim to the nominal value printed on the security, but only a claim against the value of a home that fell short of that nominal value by the amount of the fees. This distortion was unknown even to most bankers and greatly contributed to the later bewilderment of the CDO buyers. The bankers knew that undercollateralization was formally excluded in the creation of MBSs, which meant that the value of the MBSs issued could not exceed the underlying value of mortgage loans. However, many overlooked the fact that the mortgage claims themselves might have exceeded the underlying home values because of the honorariums that were also financed with such mortgages.

The problem was exacerbated by the practice of cash-back credits, also already mentioned in the previous chapter. Here the buyer and seller of a house inserted a higher price in the signed contract under the provision that the seller refunded some of the price in cash without a receipt upon signing the formal contract. This was plain fraud, as it artificially inflated the reported house value and induced banks to provide and securitize higher mortgage loans.

The deal was highly advantageous to home-buyers. First, they actually received an uncollateralized consumer loan at an interest rate that was much lower than the rate on normal consumer loans. Second, they were able to deduct the interest on the outstanding debt from their taxable income, quite in contrast to regular consumption loans. Third, the home-buyers were able to lower their capital-gains tax liability. In the USA, realized capital gains on homes are subject to income taxes, unless they are used to buy another home. This tax liability may be lowered if the price of the new home can be exaggerated above what it actually is, provided the seller has not yet exhausted his own tax exemptions.

According to insiders, these tricks implied that in many cases the mortgage loans on the books were up to 50 per cent or even 60 per cent above the amounts that were actually used for home financing. This means that the value of the houses that served as collateral fell short of the mortgage loans by up to one-third, without considering the decline in house prices by a further one-third during the crisis (see Figure 2.8). This turned the MBSs and CDOs into empty shells even in the early stages of securitization. Buyers of these securities were cheated as they paid good money for claims that were not covered by real assets and which borrowers could get rid of at any time thanks to the instrument of non-recourse mortgage loans.

The deception of customers and the public spread all the way to the official statistics. The official US home price indices were calculated on the basis of data that the mortgage banks reported to the statistical offices, which included fees and hidden cash-backs. As these ploys expanded and the distance between mortgages and the actual scarcity price of homes increased, the statistics reported price increases that themselves no longer had any real basis and led home-buyers to believe in capital gains that did not exist.

Further distortions were introduced by the honorariums and processing fees that fell due at every step in the securitization process.

These honorariums were paid out of interest differentials made possible by the alleged consolidation of risk of bad securities as a result of bundling them into a CDO. Risky securities of low creditworthiness burdened by high interest rates were made to seem safer through the bundling process and could, thanks to their better rating, be placed at lower interest. And of course all those clever managers were keen on seeing their honorariums serviced preferentially from the repayment flow, even before the senior tranches of the securities sold around the world at an AAA rating. In the end, what the buyer of such a repeatedly securitized CDO actually acquired was a large chunk of banking services instead of a repayment claim against a homeowner.

The failure of the rating agencies

The only people who could have shed light on the economic interlinkages and assessments were those who worked at the nationally recognized rating agencies like Moody's, Standard & Poor's, or Fitch Ratings.[14] It was, after all, the rating agencies that evaluated the issuers of CDOs using a sophisticated rating system, in order to provide their customers with information on the creditworthiness of their business partners. They also rated the ABSs and CDOs themselves. At the end, they did start downgrading in August 2007, as was mentioned earlier, but by then house prices had already fallen. That was after and not before the debacle. If the rating agencies had functioned as expected, they would have recognized the systemic risks contained in these securities and reported them to their customers. But in fact they failed miserably.

American rating agencies are entirely privately held. They assess real-economy companies, banks, countries, and financial products. At Standard and Poor's, for example, assessments range from the best quality AAA or 'triple A', through A + for good quality, BBB + for medium quality, BB +

---

[14] The 'nationally recognized statistical rating organizations' (NRSRO) are: Moody's Investor Services, Inc. ('Moody's'), Standard & Poor's Rating Services ('S&P'), Fitch, Inc. ('Fitch'), A. M. Best Company, Inc. ('A. M. Best'), Dominion Bond Rating Service Ltd. ('DBRS'), Japan Credit Rating Agency, Ltd. ('JCR'), Rating and Investment Information, Inc. ('R&I'), Egan-Jones Rating Company ('EJR'), LACE Financial Corp. ('LACE'), and Realpoint LLC ('Realpoint').

for speculative bonds, all the way to CCC for junk and D for default. Although the rating agencies call their ratings mere 'opinions', these opinions have legal power insofar as pension funds, boards of trustees of charities, and other institutions are required by law to hold only 'investment grade securities'. Moreover, all companies active in financial markets are obliged, according to a rule of the American securities regulation agency SEC, passed in 1975, to be rated by at least two of the nationally approved agencies.

A look at the example of Canada can give a clear impression of the power of the rating agencies. The new Liberal government in 1994 had inherited a very bad and fast deteriorating fiscal situation whose seriousness it did not understand. Its budget was timid and badly received, and the currency came under pressure. The press called the Canadian dollar the 'Hudson Bay Peso'. Then, in 1994, the government tried to counteract the depreciation of its currency by cutting expenditures and raising taxes. Moody's declared these measures insufficient and announced that it would analyse the country with respect to a possible downgrading. The consequence was a massive sell-out of Canadian government bonds and an even greater depreciation of the currency.

Germany, too, bowed to the power of the rating agencies. When the German parliament changed the country's constitution on 29 May 2009 in order to limit the federal government budget deficit to a maximum of 0.35 per cent from 2016 on, and to ban borrowing by lower-tier government levels completely from 2020 onwards, the fear of being downgraded by the rating agencies was an argument used explicitly by its finance minister.[15]

Remarkably, the rating agencies helped their customers, for a fee, with their so-called indicative rating to structure the securities they owned, that is, to assign them to different CDO tranches, so as to be able to sell them in the market. While the rating agencies claim that this did not constitute a consulting service, they cannot deny that they did evaluate hypothetical CDO constructs for a fee and gave the banks the possibility, when a given instrument did not make the grade, of reconstructing it and putting it to the test time and again until the coveted AAA rating could be applied to as many CDO securities as possible. It is akin to admitting a student to an oral

---

[15] See Bundesministerium der Finanzen, *Rede des Bundesministers der Finanzen Peer Steinbrück anlässlich der zweiten/dritten Lesung des Gesetzes zur Änderung des Grundgesetzes und des Begleitgesetzes zur zweiten Föderalismusreform am 29. Mai 2009 im Deutschen Bundestag*, online at www.bundesfinanzministerium.de.

examination again and again until he passes the test. Whether this is to be formally described as consulting is more a matter of semantics and judicial nit-picking than a question of economic substance. In any event the rating agencies helped the banks design the tranches in such a way as to maximize the volume of AAA tranches and the revenue from selling the CDOs. For this they used the mathematical models criticized above that assumed stochastic independence of the risks, in order to just remain below the prescribed maximum probabilities of default for the tranches. For consulting and auditing, the rating agencies employed armies of analysts and other staff, who were sent to the banks for weeks to get the required information. In 2007, Moody's, Standard & Poor's, and Fitch employed about 14,000 people between them, covering 95 per cent of the rating market.[16]

The problem was, however, that the calculations and the ratings thus generated were wrong. While mathematically consistent, they were flawed by assuming stochastic independence, neglecting the systemic risk of collapse of the entire market. In mysterious ways the structuring had primarily created AAA tranches, although most of the original mortgage loans to the homeowners were of much lower quality. The IMF estimates that no less than 80 per cent of the volume of all CDOs issued belonged to the senior tranche, the AAA category, and only 2 per cent to the bad equity tranche.[17] In the same way in which a bad teacher cheats employers and universities if he gives all his students top grades, the rating agencies cheated the banks' customers by awarding much too good ratings to the CDOs. Financial investors and savers from all over the world would certainly not have contributed to financing the US current account deficit to such an extent if they had known what kind of junk they were being offered.

The size of the ploy was revealed by an investigation by Harvard economists Efraim Benmelech and Jennifer Dlugosz.[18] The two authors analysed 4,000 CDOs that contained claims to loan portfolios, that is ABS instruments. They found that 70 per cent of the CDOs had a triple-A rating,

---

[16] B. Balzli, M. Schiessl, and T. Schulz, 'Trio Infernale', *Der Spiegel*, 47 (16 November 2009), 72–8.

[17] See International Monetary Fund, *Global Financial Stability Report: Containing Systemic Risks and Restoring Financial Soundness*, April 2008, online at www.imf.org, accessed on 3 February 2009.

[18] E. Benmelech and J. Dlugosz, 'The Alchemy of CDO Credit Ratings', *Journal of Monetary Economics, Carnegie-Rochester Conference*, 56 (2009), 617–34.

Table 6.1 Ratings of US investment banks by Standard & Poor's and Moody's in 2007

	Standard and Poor's long	Moody's long
Bear Stearns †	A	A2
Goldman Sachs	AA −	Aa3
Lehman Brothers †	A +	A1
Merrill Lynch †	AA +	A1

Source: Annual reports of investment banks 2007.

although the average rating of the ABSs that had been used to form the CDO pools was only a B +, which would have made the CDOs unmarketable if the rating had been also applied to them. The authors called this 'alchemy' in the title of their paper, as one must indeed believe in alchemy if by simply mixing securities and defining tranches on the basis of rather poor initial data such a tremendous improvement in risk could be achieved. Evidently, the American financial system and its rating agencies had found the formula for turning lead into synthetic gold.

A look at Table 6.1 also confirms the catastrophic picture presented by the American rating agencies. It shows the ratings given by the agencies to the big American investment banks as late as 2007. Even those banks that went under in 2008 and are marked by daggers in the table still got good ratings by Standard & Poor's and Moody's. Lehman Brothers, for example, received an A + and an A1, while not the best, still extremely good ratings. Lehman Brothers still held an A + rating until the last week before its collapse.

One may well ask how such false ratings could have come about. Part of the reason may be the fact that the rating agencies are themselves big private firms, listed corporations, that want to pursue their business and are paid by the companies they are rating. As they receive high honorariums for the employees they send to the companies to rate and give advice, while they themselves pay only modest salaries, they achieve substantial profits. Of course, they largely try to do their work conscientiously, if only not to lose their good reputation. They probably thought twice, however, before upsetting a good customer like Lehman Brothers or Merrill Lynch by giving poor ratings and risking losing them. It was much easier to rate some small banks in Europe correctly instead, and so burnish their objectivity credentials.

People's Republic of America

'You can fool all the people some of the time, and some of the people all the time, but you cannot fool all the people all the time.' This proverb attributed to Abraham Lincoln applies well to the US system of mortgage finance, for its deficiencies were ultimately detected, and then it collapsed. By 2008 the market for new CDO issues had disappeared, and so had the market for the underlying MBSs, which had a much bigger volume. This is shown in Figure 6.4, which gives the annual new issues of all types of securitized products in the USA: CDO, MBS, ABS, and ABCP. As mentioned earlier, ABSs are asset-backed securities, which, narrowly defined, may be collateralized with anything but real estate, such as company loans, leasing contracts, or credit-card debt. ABCPs are *asset-backed commercial papers*, typically short-term securities that banks and special purpose vehicles issue to finance their investments. They are collateralized with assets that the issuer possesses, possibly even those that he buys with the revenue from

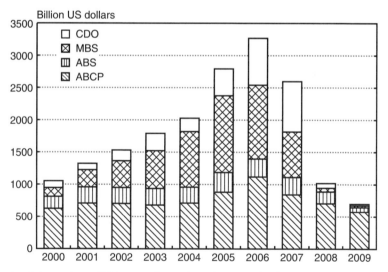

Fig. 6.4 New private US issues of securitized papers (without GSE)

Note: The graph shows the privately issued securities and therefore does not include the issues of Fannie Mae and Freddie Mac, the two US Government-sponsored Enterprises that serve as the backbone of the US real-estate market. Their CDO and ABS issues amounted to about $2 trillion in 2003 and $750 billion in 2009. See International Monetary Fund, *Global Financial Stability Report* (October 2009), figure 2.7.

Source: International Monetary Fund, *Global Financial Stability Report*, October 2009.

selling the ABCPs. Obviously, only the markets for ABCPs and ABSs survived the crisis, albeit at a reduced scale. The CDO market vanished completely, and the MBS market shrank to a tiny residual.

The precise point of collapse was in the summer of 2007, between the second and third quarters of that year.[19] The reason was that rating agencies, after long hesitation, one year after house prices had begun to collapse, reacted to the emerging real-estate crisis by downgrading the CDOs and MBSs radically, sometimes by even three grades, as described in Chapter 3. This resulted in a loss of demand and a price decline for these securities and a temporary interruption of interbank trade in August 2007. While interbank trade was soon re-established thanks to the joint efforts of central banks, the securitization process quickly dried up.

Only in Europe is it possible today to find a few CDO issues and sizeable ABS issues. However, the European CDO issues do not count in this regard, as they are not traded. The European banks securitize their credit claims against companies to be able to give the so-constructed CDOs to the European Central Bank as collateral for short-term funds they borrow.

Overall, the new issues of privately issued securities of US origin declined from $3.269 trillion in 2006 to an estimated $697 billion in 2009, that is, by nearly four-fifths of its previous volume. The joint market volume of (mostly mortgage-based) CDOs and MBSs even declined from $1,874 billion in new issues in 2006 to an estimated $53 billion in 2009, a decline of 97 per cent. There is hardly anything that describes the crash of the American system of mortgage finance more clearly than these figures.

Their enormity is enhanced by the fact that the market for non-securitized mortgage lending, which was never very significant, also largely disappeared. In the years before the crisis, this market covered about 15 per cent of overall mortgage lending, and by mid-2009 it accounted for just 2 per cent.[20]

In Chapter 2 it was shown that in the years before the crisis Americans bought an immense amount of foreign goods and services on credit. Now it

---

[19] See Securities Industry and Financial Markets Association, *SIFMA Global CDO Issuance Data*, online at www.sifma.org.

[20] Krainer, 'Recent Developments in Mortgage Finance' (see n. 2 above).

becomes clear why they had been able to do so with such lack of restraint. They issued securitized claims to non-recourse loans that resembled lottery tickets more than fixed interest claims. As it became impossible to sell these lottery tickets any further, the model of finance on which the American dream was based collapsed.

The closure of the main private channels of mortgage finance has forced the government to help out. Fannie Mae and Freddie Mac, now 79.9 per cent state owned, have stepped in to secure mortgage finance for ordinary home-owners by issuing and guaranteeing an even larger fraction of MBSs, almost 60 per cent, by mid-2009. In addition, the Government National Mortgage Association (GNMA), also known as Ginnie Mae, a government-owned insurance institution that until then had played a minor function in the market, is now backing about a third of newly issued MBSs, primarily of the subprime variety, with a sharply rising trend. Together, these three government-owned institutions in October 2009 secured almost 95 per cent of mortgage lending in the USA.[21] Once economies with such a percentage of government finance used to be called socialist. People's Republic of America.

[21] J. Krainer, 'Recent Developments in Mortgage Finance' (see n. 2 above).

CHAPTER 7

Policy Failure

Henry Paulson and the SEC

If rating agencies were unable or unwilling to warn about CDOs, why did the supervisory authorities of the countries also fail to point out the danger? In the USA, after all, the FDIC and the Federal Reserve oversee commercial banks and the Securities and Exchange Commission (SEC) banks' activity on the stock exchange; in Europe responsibilities lie with the central banks or special supervisory authorities established for this purpose. None of these institutions sounded the alarm in the years before the crash or took appropriate action to curtail the high-risk activities of the banks.

Beyond that, in the USA a dubious SEC decision on capital requirements of 28 April 2004 even increased the dangers. Since 1975 regulation had been in place that induced the broker-dealer units of investment banks to keep at least one-fifteenth of their debt in the form of *net capital* or, alternatively, 2 per cent of their deposits.[1] Net capital is a construct that basically captures liquid securities and cash, and is only loosely related to equity.[2] While the

---

[1] See SEC Rules 15c3-1 and 15c3-3. In addition, there are early waning limits that require net capital to exceed one-twelfth of debt or 5% of deposits, respectively. See E. R. Sirri, Director, Division of Trading and Markets US Securities and Exchange Commission, *Remarks at the National Economists Club: Securities Markets and Regulatory Reform*, April 2009, Washington DC, online at http://www.sec.gov/news/speech/2009/spch040909ers.htm, accessed on 25 November 2009.

[2] The construct derives from equity by adding qualifying subordinated loans and deducting illiquid assets such as fixed assets, goodwill, real estate, and unsecured receivables.

SEC maintained the net capital rules as such, it decided in 2004 to no longer define the net capital itself, but to give the investment banks the freedom to use their own net capital definitions.[3] As a consequence, the investment banks calculated themselves liquid and sharply leveraged their operations. By 2006 they had expanded them to a multiple of 22 (Merrill Lynch) and even 31 (Morgan Stanley) of their equity capital, which corresponded, as was shown in Table 4.1, to equity asset ratios of 3.2 per cent to 4.6 per cent.

This had been preceded by intensive lobbying by the five leading US investment banks. The investment banks had argued that after the introduction of the Basel II system their European competitors would be able to do business with much lower equity and therefore achieve higher rates of return. In addition, they maintained that American banks needed no regulation, as all of their customers were professional investors who were able to assess any potential risks. In order to continue to be able to offer these customers high rates of return, lower equity asset ratios were indispensable, they maintained. It was in the interest of each bank itself to see that it had a sufficient stock of equity capital to ensure the necessary security. Furthermore, they argued, sophisticated computer models were available to calculate the probabilities of default so that any risk of bankruptcy could be effectively prevented.[4] Instead of relying on government regulation, it was better to trust the self-regulating powers of the market.

The successful lobbyists, whose arguments led to a weakening of capital regulation, also included Henry Paulson. From 1999 to 2006, Paulson had been CEO of Goldman Sachs, the largest US investment bank, with assets of $707 billion.[5] This is the same Paulson who became Treasury Secretary under President George W. Bush and who made the decision, in September 2008, not to save his former competitor Lehman Brothers, thus triggering the banking crisis that almost led to the collapse of the world's financial system. His former bank, Goldman Sachs, is one of two big investment banks that survived the crisis, and this bank will presumably emerge victorious after the

---

[3] See Sirri, *Remarks at the National Economists Club*.

[4] See S. Labaton, 'How SEC Opened Path for Storm in 55 Minutes', *International Herald Tribune* (5 October 2008), 15.

[5] See S. Labaton, 'Agency's '04 Rule let Banks Pile Up New Debt', *New York Times*, 2 October 2008, online at www.nytimes.com, accessed on 1 April 2009.

destructive fall-out from the present crisis settles. Already in the second quarter of 2009, the bank reported profits of $3.44 billion.[6]

Madoff, Spitzeder, Ponzi, et al.

The SEC's inability to carry out its regulatory responsibility is also demonstrated by the Madoff scandal. Bernard Madoff, now a convicted ex-New York banker, ran a Ponzi scheme dating back to 1990 with his financial company, Bernard Madoff Investment Securities LCC. He asked his customers for capital that he supposedly would invest well and repay later with a high rate of interest. Whereas in the 1990s corporate bonds, rated AAA by Moody's, yielded 7.7 per cent interest on average,[7] Madoff offered his customers rates of 10 per cent to 15 per cent.[8] As news of the high rates of interest spread, Madoff gained more and more customers. Old customers were so enchanted by his performance that they reinvested their earnings and did not ask for cash. The fraud consisted in Madoff not actually achieving any returns, but simply crediting his permanent customers' accounts and repaying those who wanted out with the funds received from new customers. Madoff had not bought any securities and hence had not earned any additional interest income for thirteen years.[9] The fraud became evident when during the financial crisis many customers suddenly wanted their money back, while at the same time fewer new customers invested their money with him and Madoff became insolvent.

Behind this scandal lies a failure of the SEC that had early on received a number of warnings, as was admitted by Christopher Cox, former SEC chairman.[10] On the basis of these warnings, the SEC had investigated

---

[6] Goldman Sachs, *Goldman Sachs Reports 2009 Second Quarter Earnings Per Common Share of $4.93*, quarterly earnings releases, 14 July 2009, online at http://www2.goldmansachs.com/, accessed on 5 October 2009.

[7] Federal Reserve, H15, *Selected Interest Rates, Corporate Bonds, Moody's Seasoned,* Aaa http://www.federalreserve.gov/releases/h15/data/Annual/H15_AAA_NA.txt.

[8] B. Iginla, 'Ponzi Squared', *The Economist*, 15 December 2008, online at www.economist.com, accessed on 27 February 2009.

[9] 'Madoff kaufte seit Jahren keine Papiere', *Süddeutsche Zeitung* (23 February 2009), 20.

[10] See 'Sins of the Commission', *The Economist*, 19 December 2008, online at www.economist.com, accessed on 27 February 2009.

Madoff as early as 2003 and had found some irregularities.[11] Nonetheless the issue was not pursued further, and Madoff was allowed to continue his fraudulent activities until 2008. Whether the negligence resulted from the fact that the SEC was simply underequipped to supervise all US stock exchange activity with a staff of only 3,500, or the fact that Madoff was formerly chairman of NASDAQ (National Association of Securities Dealers, a self-regulatory organization) or that Shana Madoff, one of Madoff's nieces, who worked as a compliance officer in Madoff's company, was engaged to Eric Swanson, an SEC lawyer, remains an unanswered question.[12]

When Madoff's firm declared bankruptcy, he owed his investors $50 billion, offset by assets of only $200 million to $300 million. The conned creditors of his investment firm are distributed all over the globe. They also included a number of Jewish foundations and non-profit organizations like the Elie-Wiesel Foundation. Banks and investment companies in Geneva alone lost $4.22 billion.[13]

Although the Madoff case is the biggest snowball scheme in history, it is not the only one. Indications are that the Texan banker Robert Allen Stanford piled up suspected losses of about $8 billion with a similar method.[14] And Madoff had historical predecessors. They include Adele Spitzeder, an actress and speculator, who used a snowball or chain-letter scheme in Munich in the nineteenth century. The Spitzeder Private Bank paid its customers, most of whom were farmers from the Munich hinterland, fantastic rates of interest that stemmed from the deposits of new customers. Farmers sold their farms to invest the revenues at the bank, and Adele Spitzeder became a famous personality who, similarly to Madoff, was renowned for her generous charitable contributions. The fraud blew up when several creditors collaborated and demanded their money simultaneously. In the end, 31,000 citizens were defrauded of a total of 8 million guilders, and Adele Spitzeder was sentenced to a three-year prison term.[15]

---

[11] http://www.cnbc.com/id/28242487, accessed on 22 March 2009.

[12] See S. Labaton, 'Unlikely Player Pulled into Madoff Swirl', *New York Times*, 18 December 2008, online at www.nytimes.com, accessed on 1 April 2009.

[13] 'Geneva Banks Lost More than 4 Billion to Madoff', *Reuters*, 13 December 2008.

[14] A. Mühlauer and H. Wilhelm, 'Das Universum des Sir Allen Stanford', *Süddeutsche Zeitung* (26 February 2009), 26.

[15] See A. Spitzeder, *Geschichte meines Lebens: Der große Münchner Bankenskandal 1872* (Buchendorfer Verlag, Munich, 1998).

The notorious case in America is that of the fraudster Charles Ponzi, who pulled his tricks in Boston in the early 1920s. Ponzi was an Italian immigrant who, having worked in the financial business in Montreal, set up an investment business in Boston in 1920. He too promised extraordinarily high rates of interest, with which he attracted more and more depositors, paying his old customers out of the deposits of new ones. This scheme worked for some time, but in the end Ponzi left behind losses amounting to $4.3 million.[16] In the world of finance, the terms 'Ponzi scheme', 'snowball system', or 'chain letter system' are now used synonymously.[17]

In terms of volume, Bernard Madoff topped them all. His scheme had little to do with the financial crisis, other than that the crisis and the liquidity needs of his investors emanating from it caused it to blow up. It is relevant to the extent to which it revealed the unbelievable deficiencies of the US financial supervisory system.

Basel also failed

The true reason for the obvious deficiencies in financial oversight is the belief in the self-regulation of markets. This belief is responsible for the government's understaffing of the supervisory authorities and its failure to allocate the tasks in order to achieve effective control.

Although the belief in the self-regulation of markets was particularly strong in the USA, it was also widespread in Europe. For example, this belief underlay discussions in 1996 on the introduction of model-based risk assessments as part of the European regulatory system Basel I. Basel I is an accord established in 1988 under the auspices of the Bank for International Settlements (BIS) in Switzerland, which has meanwhile been signed by more than 100 countries. Motivated among other things by the collapse of the German Herstatt Bank in 1974, the idea was to ensure, by prescribing a minimum equity share, that banks would have a sufficiently large buffer in times of crisis to prevent bankruptcy. Toward that end, Basel I did not set a

---

[16] See G. Braunberger, 'Internationale Antwortscheine als heißes Spekulationsobjekt', *FAZ.Net*, http://www.faz.net, read on 25 February 2009.

[17] In economic terms, the pay-as-you-go statutory pension insurance could also be seen as a Ponzi scheme, since here the funds contributed by new 'customers' are not invested but used to meet the claims of the old ones. It is not, however, since it is run by the government.

minimum ratio for required equity capital that was simply related to total assets, but developed a weighting scheme to take account of the degree of risk of the various assets in the balance sheet, that is, loans granted and financial investments. For example, loans to firms were given a risk weight of 1.0, loans to normal banks a weight of 0.2, and seemingly fail-safe sovereign loans a weight of zero. To calculate the equity share, the bank's required equity capital was divided by the sum of risk-weighted assets, the quotient being called the 'capital ratio'. Later, this sum was supplemented by various market risk positions valued in monetary units, such as currency risks, interest change risks, and stock price risks. The total sum is called the 'risk position'.

Two capital ratios were distinguished, and this distinction still applies today: the *Tier 1 ratio*, which must equal at least 4 per cent, and the *Tier 2 ratio*, which must amount to at least 8 per cent. The Tier 1 ratio is derived by dividing core capital by the sum of all risk positions. Tier 1 capital essentially consists of the paid-in capital stock, the accumulated retained earnings of the past (reserves), and preferred stock, that is, equity without voting rights. The Tier 2 ratio differs from the Tier 1 ratio only by a broader definition of capital, including a number of items such as undisclosed reserves or subordinated debt.[18]

At the time, banks disliked the obligation to stick to the fixed, simple valuation systems of the supervisory authority. They proposed instead to calculate the market price risks using their own computer models, in order also to take account of the potential risk consolidation due to combining verifiably independent risks within different risk categories, and to reduce their equity capital base, presumably without incurring more risk. This request was met in the EU by an amendment to Basel I in 1995 and 1996 (Capital Adequacy Directive of the EU). Accordingly, in Europe, banking supervision only had to audit the internal risk models of the banks themselves rather than the assignment of assets to individual risk classes. In 1996 the main argument in favour of deregulation was again that the bankers had the know-how and the experience to implement such self-regulation. Bank representatives asserted that the supervisory authorities need not worry.

---

[18] Subordinated debt is debt that, according to the contract, will only have to be serviced by the bank after all other liabilities to customers and credit institutions have been met. Concerning the risk it bears, it stands between the bank's equity capital and its normal debt capital.

By replacing the previously rigid rules by their internal risk models, the banks could now preclude bankruptcies with even greater certainty, they argued. The banks utilized their new flexibility to an extent, however, which the legislature had certainly not foreseen. According to a report of the Scientific Advisory Council to the German Economics Ministry, the use of internal risk models resulted in a dramatic mushrooming of banks' activities relative to their equity capital, which increased the banks' risks rather than reducing them.[19]

In this way, the Basel I system was given more flexibility and was perhaps also designed more accurately for the actual risks. The accuracy was not great enough for the banks, however, as the risk classes were rather broad, lumping together different risks that should have had different equity capital backing. Consequently, within the risk classes the banks preferred to deal with customers of low creditworthiness, as these customers were also willing to pay higher interest rates in view of their higher risks.

To eliminate the defects, banks and supervisory authorities aimed for a change in Basel I, which was to address the different risk classes in a much more detailed way. After years of negotiations between representatives of banks and governments, which again took place on the BIS premises, the so-called Basel II accord was agreed, a document of 333 pages that meticulously defines the risk classes and weighting schemes with which the risk-weighted assets (or risk positions) were to be calculated. For example, loans to other banks received a weight of 0.2 if these banks resided in countries with high creditworthiness (AAA rating), and up to 1.5 if the country rating was very poor. All banks from EU countries received a weight of 0.2. A similar procedure was applied to loans to non-financial companies. Companies rated good to very good received risk weights from 0.5 to 0.2. Risk weights of more than one were only given to loans to companies that were rated lower than BB−. Furthermore, the internal risk models were expanded from market risks to credit risks. In addition to the 'credit risk standard approach' (CSA) available for the latter, the possibility was created to calculate the credit risks according to an 'internal ratings-based approach' (IRB), that is, an approach

---

[19] Scientific Advisory Council to the German Ministry of Economics, *Zur Bankenregulierung in der Finanzkrise*, letter to Minister Glos of 23 January 2009, online at www.bmwi.de/ BMWi.

based on internal risk assessments of the banks' customers. The basic concept of the accord, including the 8 per cent rule for the Tier 2 capital ratio and the 4 per cent rule for the Tier 1 ratio, remained intact. A novelty, however, was that the so-called operational risk in the form of possible losses from business mistakes and fraud was to be backed by required equity capital.

The Basel II accord was adopted by Switzerland and the EU and made obligatory in corresponding directives for all EU countries as of 1 January 2008.[20] Meanwhile Australia, Canada, Hong Kong, Japan, Korea, Singapore, and South Africa also implemented the Basel II accord in national law. Only the United States hesitated. Although the USA had pushed for the acceptance of Basel II, it then surprised the world by deciding only to make internationally active banks subject to the Basel II system. In the current financial crisis, it is still unclear whether the system will ever be implemented by the USA.

However, the USA has a very similar supervisory system for its commercial banks. Whereas investment banks were only loosely regulated, commercial banks are required to have a *Tier 1 risk-based capital ratio* greater than 4 per cent and a *total risk-based capital ratio* greater than 8 per cent. The Tier 1 based capital ratio is basically the same as the Tier 1 ratio in the Basel system, that is, the ratio of core capital to the sum of risk-weighted assets.[21] The total risk-based capital ratio is similar to the Basel Tier 2 ratio, dividing a more broadly defined equity stock by the sum of risk-weighted assets. While there are many details in the definition of capital and risk-weighted assets that limit the comparability, it seems that an additional element has made the US regulatory system for commercial banks even stricter than the Basel system: the provision that the so-called *Tier 1 leverage ratio* exceed 4 per cent in the normal case (or 3 per cent in the case of banks, satisfying additional safety criteria).

---

[20] EU Directives 2006/48/EG and 2006/49/EG.

[21] Cf. United States Securities and Exchange Commission, Office of the Chief Accountant, Division of Corporate Finance, *Report and Recommendations Pursuant to Section 133 of the Emergency Economic Stabilization Act 2008: Study on Mark-to-Market Accounting*, especially 99–100, http://www.sec.gov/news/studies/2008/marktomarket123008.pdf. Cf. also P. van Doorn, *Regulatory Capital Categories for Banks and S&Ls*, online at http://www.thestreet.com/story/10462318/regulatory-capital-categories-for-banks-and-sls.html, accessed on 25 November 2009.

The Tier 1 leverage ratio is what in this book is called the *equity asset ratio*. The equity asset ratio is the inverse of the *leverage ratio*, that is, the ratio of total assets to equity capital. Although the equity asset ratio is only a very rough indicator of the security that a bank can offer its customers, it has the advantage of being a simple measure that everyone understands. It also seems to be more effective than the Tier 1 ratio in curbing the creative abilities of risk managers and investment bankers. That is why it has increasingly been favoured in policy debates since the outbreak of the banking crisis.

Unfortunately, neither the American regulatory system nor the Basel system was able to prevent the storm of the financial crisis from cutting big swaths in the American and European banking landscape and driving many banks into ruin or into the arms of the state, as described in Chapter 3. Apart from the weakening of the net capital rule for investment banks mentioned above, there are several reasons for this political failure.

The trick in calculating the capital ratio

The first reason for the failure of the supervisory systems was simply that the designated capital ratios were much too small and not at all sufficient to cover the risks. Equity asset ratios amounting to 3 to 4 per cent, required in the USA as a minimum, do not provide an appropriate buffer if something goes wrong with the bank's assets. And a Tier 1 ratio of 4 per cent, as demanded by the Basel system, is even less impressive. As shown in Table 7.1, a Tier 1 ratio can easily be four times as large as the equity asset ratio. For example, in 2007 the United Bank of Switzerland (UBS) and Deutsche Bank both had Tier 1 ratios of more than 8 per cent, while their equity asset ratios were only 1.9 per cent.

Before Basel I, that is up to 1988, different national rules applied in Europe, which tended to be more restrictive and required higher equity asset ratios. In Germany, for example, at least 4 per cent of loans had to be backed by equity capital, similar to the USA today. This explains why the country's largest bank, Deutsche Bank, had an average equity asset ratio of 5.5 per cent between 1985 and 1987.[22] In 2007, before the crisis,

---

[22] Deutsche Bank, *Geschäftsberichte 1985–1987*, online at www.bankgeschichte.de, accessed on 5 March 2009.

Table 7.1 Equity asset ratios* and Tier 1 ratios** in 2007

	Equity asset ratio (%)	Tier 1 ratio (%)
US banks		
Citigroup	5.2	7.1
Wachovia	9.8	7.4
Freddie Mac	3.4	–
Fannie Mae	5.0	–
Merrill Lynch	3.1	–
Washington Mutual	7.5	6.8
Bank of America	8.6	6.9
Wells Fargo	8.3	7.6
US banking system***	8.7	
Swiss banks		
UBS	1.9	8.8
Credit Suisse	3.2	11.1
Swiss banking system	4.0	
British banks		
Barclays Bank	2.1	7.5
HBOS	3.3	7.4
HSBC	5.4	9.3
Lloyds TSB	3.4	9.5
Royal Bank of Scotland	4.8	7.3
British banking system	5.3	
German banks		
Deutsche Bank	1.9	8.6
Commerzbank	2.6	7.0
HypoVereinsbank (UniCredit)	5.7	17.9
Hypo Real Estate	1.5	7.0
LB Baden-Württemberg	2.3	8.3
German banking system	4.0	
Further euro banks		
Santander	5.7	7.7
Unicredit Group	5.6	6.6
BNP Paribas	3.2	7.3
Credit Agricole	3.3	8.1
KBC	5.2	9.0
Dexia	2.7	9.1

Table 7.1 (Continued)

	Equity asset ratio (%)	Tier 1 ratio (%)
ING Group	3.0	7.4
Fortis	8.0	30.7
Euro banking system	6.7	

*Equity capital divided by total assets (inverse of the so-called leverage ratio).

**Tier 1 capital divided by the sum of risk positions.

***Commercial banking, savings institutions, security brokers and dealers, Government-sponsored Enterprises.

Notes: The capital assumed for calculating the Tier 1 ratio differs from the equity capital shown in the balance sheet, since according to the Basel II rules, immaterial assets (e.g. the difference between purchase price and the book value of the equity capital of an acquired firm) as well as own stocks must be deducted from equity capital.

Sources: Annual Reports of the banks, Board of Governors of the Federal Reserve System, Schweizerische Nationalbank, Bank of England, Deutsche Bundesbank, European Central Bank.

the same bank had an equity asset ratio of only 1.9 per cent, as Table 7.1 shows.

It is puzzling that today the 4 per cent rule still applies in the Basel system and that nevertheless the equity asset ratio can be below 2 per cent. The reason is of course that the Tier 1 ratio is not the same as the equity asset ratio. While there are minor differences in the numerators of these ratios, the main differences lie in the denominators. To calculate the Tier 1 ratio, equity capital is not divided by the simple sum of all assets but by the sum of risk positions, that is, essentially by the sum of risk-weighted assets. The term 'risk weighting' does not sound bad, as one automatically thinks of a weighting scheme for which the average weight remains unchanged and a differentiation is made only for the weights according to the risk classes. The term is misleading, however, as the average weight of the assets fell dramatically along with the differentiation of weights because in practice there are hardly any weights above one but many very low weights. If in the standard approach the credit claims against other banks have a weight of 0.2 and claims against states (sovereign claims) a weight of zero, because they are considered intrinsically safe, it is no wonder that the sum of risk-weighted assets represents only a fraction of the actual assets and the Tier 1 ratio is thus inflated.

This effect was exacerbated by the already mentioned circumstance that the banks have been permitted, since 1996, to apply their own models for calculating their investment risks. The creative scope they gained often induced them to use model varieties that mathematically yielded a rather high Tier 1 ratio given the business volume, and hence allowed a larger business volume with any given amount of equity capital.[23]

Another reason for downgrading the risk weights is credit insurance, more precisely the credit default swaps (CDS) that banks can acquire to hedge against the default of debtors. If the bank insures its credit claims, it may replace the risk weight of the debtor with that of the insurer, which has the advantage that less equity is needed to support the business. If the insurer, typically another bank, has an AAA rating, the risk weight is reduced to 20 per cent. The potential downside is that the insurer must include the guarantee according to the creditworthiness of the debtor in its own risk positions, but this only matters if the insurer itself is subject to a corresponding regulation.

The world's largest credit insurer for such deals was the American International Group (AIG). AIG was not controlled by anyone when selling CDS insurance. Rather, AIG took advantage of a gap in the American regulatory system that allowed it to transact its insurance business without any equity capital regulation. In spite of this, the company received an AAA rating by the rating agencies. Because of this good rating and the lack of any supervision, European customers of AIG, which were subject to the Basel system and applied the standard risk approach, were able to reduce the risk weights of even the most dubious loans to 20 per cent and thus increase their business volume relative to their equity capital by a factor of five for debtors who otherwise would have been allocated risk weights of one without AIG having to scale down any of its other business activities in exchange.

As reported in Chapter 3, a sizeable fraction of the losses due to non-paying debtors, which was incurred in the course of the crisis, showed up at AIG. The company's record loss amounting to $99.29 billion in 2008 has its causes here.[24] However, as AIG has now been nationalized, the American

---

[23] See J. Baetgen, T. Brembt, and P. Brüggemann, 'Die Mark-to-Mode-Bewertung des IAS 39 in der Subprime-Krise', *Die Wirtschaftsprüfung*, 21 (2008), 1001–10; M. Hellwig, 'Systemic Risk in the Financial Sector: An Analysis of the Subprime-Mortgage Financial Crisis', Jelle Zijlstra Lecture, *Preprints of the Max Planck Institute for Research on Collective Goods*, no. 2008/43, November 2008.

[24] See American International Group, *Annual Report 2008*, 36, online at http://www.aig.com, accessed on 5 October 2009.

taxpayer is footing the bill. European banks like Deutsche Bank are among the beneficiaries. For the accounting year 2008 alone, Deutsche Bank received almost $12 billion from AIG.[25]

Deutsche Bank is an extreme example of the extent to which risk weighting according to the Basel system can lead to an optical improvement of the balance sheet. In 2008, total assets of 2.2 trillion euros shrank to only 308 billion euros of risk positions, that is, to only about 14 per cent.[26]

Because of its confusing complexity of risk weights and the lack of a constraining leverage ratio, the Basel system unfortunately has had the effect that many European banks seem to be capitalized even less than their US counterparts. As total assets of all banks in the euro area were 22.3 trillion euros in 2007 and total equity was 1.49 trillion euros, the average equity asset ratio of the euro banking system was 6.7 per cent.[27] In the USA, on the other hand, aggregated assets were $19.9 trillion, and the aggregate equity capital was $1.73 trillion, yielding an equity asset ratio of 8.7 per cent, 2.0 percentage points higher than the European one.[28]

While these aggregate figures should be roughly comparable, certain reservations are in order when individual banks are compared, as the US accounting rules (US GAAP) generate shorter balance sheets than European ones. For example, mutual credit claims between two banks may be offset, leaving only net claims on the balance sheet. This may explain part of the differences in the company-specific capital ratios between Europe and the USA. In some cases, this effect may be enormous. Deutsche Bank, for example, demonstrated that its balance sheet as of 30 June 2009 would shrink from 1.7 trillion euros to 928 billion euros if it switched from the European to the American accounting system.[29] However, its equity asset ratio would not really be comfortable in this case, increasing from the official

---

[25] 'Deutsche Bank erhält 12 Milliarden Dollar', *FAZ.Net*, http://www.faz.net, read on 16 March 2009.

[26] See Deutsche Bank, *Annual Review 2008*, 247.

[27] See Europäische Zentralbank, *Monatsbericht Januar 2009*, Statistik des Euro-Währungsgebiets, 11.

[28] See Board of Governors of the Federal Reserve System, online at http://www.federalreserve.gov/releases/z1/Current/z1.pdf, accessed on 2 February 2010.

[29] J. Ackermann, *Die Finanzkrise und die Deutsche Bank: Eine vorläufige Bilanz*, 14. Handelsblatt Jahrestagung, Frankfurt, 9 September 2009, online at http://www.deutsche-bank.de/presse/de/downloads/JA_Handelsblatt_deutsch_final.pdf, accessed on 5 October 2009.

2.0 per cent to 3.8 per cent, a number which according to Table 7.1 would still be much lower than that for US banks and a bit lower than the 4 per cent that US supervisory rules for commercial banks require. European banking supervisors ought to give heed to this issue. While it is true that the banking crisis arose in the USA because of the collapse of the US housing market and weak banking regulation, the USA would probably have suffered even more under the crisis had it adopted the European Basel system. This system is much too lax to serve as a model, and Europe can be grateful that its banks were only indirectly affected.

Overall, European capital ratios do not diverge too much from the 5 per cent used in the example in Chapter 4, which showed how to generate high rates of return out of the privilege of limited liability and the chance to offload catastrophic burdens onto creditors and taxpayers. Even if all banks were to report this ratio, it would be much too small to ensure the stability of the banking system.

The pro-cyclical effects of the mark-to-market method

The second common reason for the failure of European and American regulatory systems lies in the pro-cyclical effect of the mark-to-market or fair-value valuation method, that is, the fact that this method amplifies the ups and downs of the business cycle. The method follows, as already explained in Chapter 4, the International Financial Reporting Standard (IFRS), the new accounting system patterned after the USA, which all big (listed) European corporations had to adopt in recent years. As, according to this method, the assets of the bank are valued at current values, whereas the loans raised by them are normally booked at nominal values, the size of profits and the accounting equity is subject to large fluctuations.[30] In an economic upswing, when all asset prices are rising, high profits are shown, even if no money is coming in, and in downturn phases accounting losses may be reported, although banks actually have a good performance. As a consequence, a bank that in good times adjusts its equity to the minimum capital

---

[30] This statement needs to be qualified insofar as there are circumstances under which the IFRS allows a company to even depreciate its reported debt if the market value of debt has declined. However, this possibility is more a curiosity than a common rule.

ratio by distributing dividends or repurchasing its own stocks will be con-
fronted with deficient equity in a downswing and be forced to limit its
lending, in so doing hurting real investment and intensifying the downswing.

There are attempts to block these effects by so-called prudential filters,
that is, precautionary measures in assessing balance sheets. Furthermore,
German banks can still resort to the old German commercial law with its
lowest value principle for the purpose of supervisory accounting, even if they
use IFRS for the purpose of corporate accounting. All of this, however, has
hardly been able to constrain the pro-cyclical nature of the mark-to-market
method which, after all, is the most widely used accounting rule today, even
for supervisory accounting.

The particular problem of the pro-cyclical effect of the mark-to-market
method is its enormous multiplier effect emanating from small capital ratios.
To illustrate, let us look at the example of a bank with a Tier 1 ratio of 8 per
cent and an equity asset ratio of 2 per cent. If in bad times the bank loses 1
per cent of its total assets due to general stock price declines, something that
can easily happen, equity shrinks by half. If the bank wants to get back to a
capital ratio of 2 per cent (or, assuming a constant asset structure, to a core
capital ratio of 8 per cent), it must reduce its assets by half, that is, by 50 per
cent. Since a 1 per cent depreciation loss becomes a 50 per cent reduction of
assets, the multiplier is 50 (=1 : 2 per cent). In other words, if the bank loses a
billion euros in assets and loans, it must, unless it can raise additional capital,
reduce the volume of its assets and loans (including this one billion) by 50
billion euros. Correspondingly, to use another example, a multiplier of 20
(=1 : 5 per cent) results if a balance sheet capital ratio of 5 per cent is to be
held. A loss of assets and loans by one billion euros forces the bank in this
case to reduce its assets and loans by 20 billion euros.

The balance sheet multiplier, whether it is 50, 20, or anything in between,
results in dramatic consequences for private business that must rely on
bank loans for financing investment. If book profits occur and are not
distributed, the banks can increase their loans to companies according to
the multiplier. They are generous in their lending, and the companies invest
as much as possible, boosting economic activity and driving up asset
demand. The increased asset demand raises asset values in the balance sheets
of banks and creates another increase in lending, causing an upward spiral.
If, by contrast, book losses from lending occur, economic activity drops,

leading to even bigger losses of banks, forcing them to reduce their lending and so on. The mechanics of accounting rules according to the mark-to-market method thus lead to an unhealthy overheating of the economy or, in the worst case, to a vicious downward cycle.

This defect was pointed out early on by Charles Goodhart and others.[31] Martin Hellwig calls this a regulatory paradox, because the state wants to make the financial system more crisis-proof by means of minimum capital ratios, but in connection with the mark-to-market method actually designs it in a way that the crisis is exacerbated, a problem that will be discussed in more detail in Chapter 11.[32] The International Monetary Fund has also distinctly criticized this aspect of the regulatory systems.[33]

In order to diminish the pro-cyclical effects of the mark-to-market valuation within the Basel II system in the current recession, the International Accounting Standard Board (IASB), and with it the EU, decided in October 2008 to permit different valuations for some bank assets and to defer the valuation adjustments that would be necessary according to a tight market valuation. Technically this was done by permitting the banks to rebook their problematic assets by 1 November 2008 from the trading book to the banking book and to do so retroactively to 1 July 2008.[34] In this way the balance sheet valuations of the concerned assets were frozen at the level of July 2008, that is, the time *before* the Lehman Brothers collapse. With this ruling the IASB wanted to counteract the pro-cyclical effect of mark-to-market accounting. This is similar to the use of the lowest value principle. The only difference is that the lowest value principle creates hidden reserves, whereas the new IASB rule implies hidden losses due to the waiver of write-downs. It is hard to imagine that the IASB has thereby contributed to the stabilization of the banking system.

No matter how these problems are overcome, one thing is clear: if the banks of the world had to do their accounting according to the rules of the

---

[31] See C. Goodhart, 'Are Central Banks Necessary?', in F. Caprie and G. E. Wood (eds.), *Unregulated Banking: Chaos or Order?* (Macmillan, London, 1991), 1–21; Scientific Advisory Council to the German Ministry of Economics, *Zur Bankenregulierung in der Finanzkrise*; M. Hellwig, 'Systemic Risk in the Financial Sector: An Analysis of the Subprime Mortgage Financial Crisis', *De Economist*, 157(2) (2009), 129–207.

[32] M. Hellwig, foreword to H.-W. Sinn, *Risk Taking, Limited Liability and the Banking Crisis* (Selected Reprints, Ifo Institute, Munich, 2009).

[33] International Monetary Fund, *Global Financial Stability Report 2008*, 109–34.

[34] European Commission, Amendment to IAS 39 and IFRS 7, *Reclassification of Financial Assets*, www.ec.europa.eu/internal_market/accounting.

lowest-value principle, the multiplier process and its related vicious circle in the interaction of the banking system and the real economy could not have arisen. A substantial part of the losses could have been offset, without being reflected in the balance sheets, by realizing hidden reserves by way of selling some undervalued assets, and all the uproar could have been avoided.

A look at the European roots of the lowest-value principle and, in particular, Germany's experiences, is revealing in this regard. The principle dates back to Louis XIV and his finance minister Colbert.[35] Germany adopted this principle in the nineteenth century after a cumbersome trial-and-error period. Initially Prussia had introduced the mark-to-market principle in 1861. This was not long-lived, however, as the Great Panic of 1873 had made the perils of using near-market valuations evident. Such valuations had allowed excessive distributions of dividends during the economic boom that preceded the crisis and led to an undercapitalization of firms, resulting in many bankruptcies with huge losses of creditors' assets. The blame was placed on the company executives, who had exaggerated the value of their assets by near-market valuations of unsold assets and later were no longer able to repay their loans. In the German-speaking countries the term 'founders' fraud' is used to characterize their behaviour, as most of the companies affected had only recently been founded. As a consequence, in order to better protect the creditors, the market valuation was abolished in 1884 and replaced by the lowest value principle.[36] The lowest value principle created much stability for Germany until it was replaced by the IFRS system in 2002 in compliance with

---

[35] The lowest value principle was first encoded in the 'Ordonnance de Commerce'. According to this commercial code, French merchants were obliged to keep a journal and to conduct an inventory every two years of all mobile and immobile assets, all claims and debts. The Ordonnance was itself based on Jacques Savary (1622–90) who determined the lowest value principle as the valuation rule in a work of reference in 1675. See K. Blaufus, *Fair Value Accounting: Zweckmäßigkeitsanalyse und konzeptioneller Rahmen* (Deutscher Universitäts-Verlag, Wiesbaden, 2005), 39 f.

[36] The 1861 edition of the Prussian Commercial Code (Art. 31, section 1) says: 'In recording the inventory and the balance sheet, all assets and claims are to be assigned the value they had at the time of recording.' The 1884 edition of the Commercial Code of the German Reich says instead: 'For setting up the balance sheet the general rules of Article 31 are to be applied: Securities and goods having a market price may at most be valued at the stock exchange or market price at the time the balance sheet is set up, but if this exceeds the purchase or production price it must be valued at most at the latter.'

an EU directive.[37] It is an irony of history that the world first had to relive the same bitter experience of late nineteenth-century Germany and Austria before it was possible to challenge the mark-to-market method.

Dynamic company valuation is also pro-cyclical

Additional pro-cyclical effects are created by the dynamic valuation method of borrowers within the Basel II system. Whereas Basel I schematically regulated the backing of company loans by equity capital, Basel II makes the required capital ratios dependent on the creditworthiness of the customers. The bank, which determines its risk weights according to internal risk models (IRB method), must regularly evaluate its debtors according to prescribed procedures and assign them to risk categories that must be multiplied by given weights and combined into the sum of risk positions. That is not implausible in principle, but this dynamic valuation creates in turn a strong pro-cyclicality in the banking business. As the profits of the banks' customers rise in an upswing, so does their creditworthiness. The bank must then back each loan with less equity and is therefore able to lend more, accelerating the boom. The reverse happens in the downswing, and that, unfortunately, is what has just happened. In the course of a crisis, more and more borrowers slip into the loss zone, their creditworthiness shrinks, and the banks must back existing loans by more equity capital. This reinforces the contractionary effect on the volume of loans that is due to the banks' own capital losses. Loans coming due are prolonged only hesitantly and new loans are scarcely granted. Therefore, real investment declines, producers of capital goods experience a fall in orders; workers are laid off, they consume less, and the downswing accelerates.

This problem resembles that which was noted in the preceding section regarding the mark-to-market principle. The practical difference is only that, in contrast to the mark-to-market method, dynamic company valuation

---

[37] The directive applies to companies that are subject to EU law and also use the issue of tradable securities for their financing. For all practical purposes this means all bigger banks and insurance companies. See *Official Journal of the European Community*, Regulation (EC) No 1606/2002 of the European Parliament and of the Council of 19 July 2002 on the Application of International Accounting Standards, online at www.eur-lex.europa.eu, accessed on 3 February 2010.

does not unfold its contractionary effect at once but only after a lag. Thus, because of the crisis, company balance sheets deteriorated substantially in 2009. From the second half of 2010, contractionary effects of credit constraints can therefore be expected that may be traced to the 2009 recession in the real economy. That will hit business hard at a time when it wants to move beyond the crisis.

The effect is substantial. For example, Deutsche Bank estimates that its own risk positions will rise by 40 per cent due to this effect. Other banks report lower estimates ranging from 20 per cent to 30 per cent. A 20 per cent higher valuation of the stock of risk positions means that the bank must reduce this stock by 17 per cent if it wants to keep its risk positions unchanged, and a 30 per cent higher valuation requires a quantitative reduction of 23 per cent. It is essential that this problem be taken into consideration in a reform of banking regulation.

Special purpose vehicles and hedge funds

Other deficiencies of the Basel II regulatory system consist in the exceptions allowed by the system. The major exceptions concern special purpose vehicles and hedge funds. It is surprising that precisely these highly risky instruments were excluded from the regulation.

As already described in Chapter 3, in Europe special purpose vehicles are often Irish subsidiaries of established banks that make their money with big portfolio deals. Ireland was in many cases the preferred location because of its low taxes, but there are other tax havens, too. The special purpose vehicles were primarily financed by short-term secured bonds, so-called asset-backed commercial papers (ABCP) that were sold in the money market. If necessary, they also received loans from their headquarters or 'sponsors', but for less than one year so that the loans did not have to be carried in the balance sheets. The special purpose vehicles typically invested the funds received in long-term derivatives of American mortgage loans, essentially in the CDO and ABS securities described in Chapter 6. The maturity transformation they performed allowed them to realize substantial profit margins. Because their business volume was not carried on the books of the parent company and hence did not have to be backed by equity capital, they could engage in big deals and achieve giant profits for their parent company, as long as things went well.

Excluding special purpose vehicles from Basel II was an obvious regulatory error, as the parent company was obliged, as a rule, to assume all the risks (for conduits) or part of the risks (for the so-called structured investment vehicles, SIV), in order to give the special purpose vehicles the creditworthiness needed for their operations.[38] For example, in its Annual Report for 2006, Deutsche Industriebank (IKB) reported credit lines to special purpose vehicles of about 12 billion euros, the majority of which were meant for the American special purpose company Rhineland Funding Capital Corporation. This corresponded to almost one-quarter of the total assets of IKB.[39] As we know today, the maturity transformation of the special purpose vehicles described above doomed IKB, Hypo Real Estate, and Sachsen LB, to name only a few, because in the wake of the collapse of interbank transactions it had become impossible to sell new short-term ABCP securities to service the expiring securities with the sales revenue.[40]

Interestingly, in Europe only the supervisory authorities of Spain and Italy had seen the risk and insisted that the transactions of special purpose vehicles also had to be backed by equity capital. Not surprisingly, the Spanish bank Santander and the Italian UniCredit Group are among the banks with the highest balance sheet capital ratios in all of Europe, as shown in Table 7.1.

Hedge funds are peculiar financial institutions that conduct their capital market business in unstandardized ways and are usually short-lived. They were exempted from the capital regulation upon the request of Great Britain, probably also because the country feared to lose even more domestic funds to the Cayman Islands or other offshore financial centres.

'To hedge' means to cover risks. For this purpose hedge funds offered banks and other financial institutions insurance against well-defined business

---

[38] SIVs limited the majority of their investment to listed securities with high ratings that were considered very liquid. That is why it was considered sufficient for the parent company to assume a liability of only 20% of the value of the assets.

[39] See IKB, *Annual Report 2006/2007*, online at www.ikb.de, accessed on 2 March 2009.

[40] See especially B. Rudolph, 'Die Finanzkrise aus mikroökonomischer Perspektive' (Institut für Kapitalmarktforschung und Finanzierung, University of Munich, unpublished manuscript, January 2009).

risks, which was a very useful function. The funds were sometimes even in the reinsurance business and as such were subject to insurance supervision.

Over time they made more and more risky transactions and no longer limited themselves to insuring against risk but instead became increasingly involved in problematic speculative business. Particular specialties of hedge funds are the so-called short sales that promise profits from falling stock prices, although these usually create losses. The fund borrows securities of a special kind and promises to return them including a borrowing fee at a later time. Then it sells the borrowed securities in the market, hoping to repurchase them at a lower price to return them at the predetermined date. This is frequently successful because the fund not only throws its own securities on the market but the borrowed ones as well. In this way it can exert quasi-monopolistic power and develop a strong leverage effect that causes the price of the securities to fall. The falling price generates herd behaviour by raising further devaluation expectations and causing other buyers to also leave the market, again depressing the price. If the hedge fund is clever, a panic breaks out, at whose height it can repurchase the securities at a very low price and subsequently return them to their owner. If the repurchase price is below the selling price by more than the fee, the fund makes a profit.

The hedge funds moved centre stage when a fund belonging to the multi-billionaire Georges Soros in 1992 speculated with short sales against the British pound, forced the Bank of England to depreciate the currency, and made huge profits. Soros had borrowed pounds sterling and sold them against dollars in the currency market in order to put the pound under pressure. The Bank of England tried to stem the tide by buying pounds for dollars from its reserves. Soros knew, however, that the national bank's stocks of dollars were limited and threw more and more borrowed pounds onto the market until the Bank of England was out of dollars and could no longer prevent the devaluation. Soros then repurchased the devalued stock of pounds at a fraction of the dollar revenue he had collected by selling the pounds in order to return them to his creditors. This deal enriched Soros by around £1.1 billion sterling and the Bank of England was wiser for the experience.[41] The pound was forced to leave the European currency band

---

[41] See H. G. Mankiw and P. Taylor, *Economics* (Thomson Learning Services, London, 2006), 757.

('the snake in the tunnel'), which was one of the reasons the UK did not join the euro system. The impact that a single speculator had on the course of history was astonishing.

In the collapse of Lehman Brothers, which nearly touched off a breakdown of the world financial system, short sales also played a role. Thus, Richard Fuld, the former CEO of Lehman Brothers, at a hearing before the House of Representatives, mentioned that naked short selling, that is, noncovered short sales, were one of the reasons for the crash of Lehman Brothers stocks and the downfall of Bear Stearns.[42] In contrast to normal short selling, in the case of naked short selling the seller has neither acquired ownership of the sold stock nor a claim to a transfer of ownership at the time of the sale. One sells what one does not own, thereby driving down the stock price, and subsequently buys back in the market the devalued stocks in the very last second, before the already sold stocks have to be supplied in order to fulfil one's supply obligation. Obviously these are highly speculative and risky transactions that are baffling for the layman. Gambling pure and simple.

The price of Lehman shares had temporarily stabilized during the period of the first prohibition of naked short sales by the supervisory authority that was effective between 21 July and 12 August. After the end of the prohibition, the price continued to fall and thus generated the loss of confidence that led to the downfall of Lehman Brothers. The markets viewed the plunge of stock prices as the unmistakable sign of the imminent end of the bank, and therefore hardly anybody was willing to lend the bank any additional funds. This made insolvency inevitable.

Among the few that still gave loans was the German Credit Bank for Reconstruction (KfW), a public bank dating back to the post-war period whose function is to extend subsidized funds and low-interest loans. On the day after the insolvency was announced, on Monday, 15 September 2008, it transferred more than 300 million euros to Lehman Brothers, part of an earlier agreed hedging transaction. Although the responsible staff had already learnt at the end of the preceding week that Lehman's bankruptcy was inevitable, they had overlooked that the payment was already in the pipeline.

---

[42] See United States House of Representatives, *Statement of Richard S. Fuld, Jr. before the United States House of Representatives Committee on Oversight and Government Reform*, 6 October 2008, online at www.house.gov, accessed on 12 March 2009.

In the course of Monday attempts were made to rescind the payment, but it was too late. The money was gone.

The American banking supervisor reacted to the collapse of Lehman Brothers by again prohibiting short sales of important securities on 17 September. BaFin, the German banking supervisory authority, issued a similar prohibition the same day.

An accurate description of other hedge fund transactions is difficult as they are so manifold and erratic. The investment bankers they employ, the 'masters of the universe', are constantly looking for uncommon business models and unique profit opportunities. That is another reason why hedge funds are so opaque. In addition, there are no published statistics, annual reports, or balance sheets that provide insights into their business practices. What is known is that these funds are organized as limited liability companies and evidently work with extremely little equity capital. The trick described in Chapter 4, of leveraging one's own equity to shift losses, in case of bankruptcy, onto other shoulders, has been perfected by hedge fund owners. They usually divide their involvement into several individual hedge funds, in order to avoid the mutual spillover of losses. For this reason, the speculator Soros also does not operate one hedge fund but many. If hedge funds were economically useful vehicles that made risks controllable by mixing and consolidating them, similar to the way insurance companies do, they would tend to merge into big agglomerates, but this is not the case. They are prime examples of the gambling described in Chapter 4 that is generated by the limitation of liability.

With their business model, the funds generated huge profits in the past, but are now, in the current crisis, going broke on a large scale or are being closed down. About 1,500 of the around 10,200 funds that existed in 2007 disappeared from the market by the end of 2008.[43] And that surely is not all. Insiders expect the majority of hedge funds to disappear during this crisis, something that would entail only a minimal loss for the owners because of the minimal equity used by these firms.

---

[43] See Hedge Fund Research, *Hedge Fund Liquidations Accelerate in the Third Quarter*, online at www.hedgefundresearch.com, accessed on 2 March 2009.

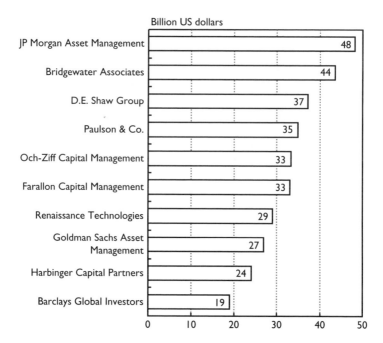

Fig. 7.1 The ten biggest hedge funds—managed assets (June 2008)

Note: The figure contains independent unregulated hedge funds and hedge funds that are subdivisions of regulated firms.

Source: European Economic and Social Committee (EESC), *Data Collection Study on the Impact of Private Equity, Hedge and Sovereign Funds on Industrial Change in Europe*, 2009, 22, www.eesc.europa.eu/sections/ccmi/externalstudies/documents/Final_Report_Data_Collection.doc.

In 2007 hedge funds managed about $1.9 trillion of assets. One year later the funds managed had fallen by $500 billion to only $1.4 trillion.[44] Figure 7.1 shows the allocation of the assets ($329 billion) of the ten biggest hedge funds, most of which are located in the USA, at the end of June 2008, shortly before the collapse of Lehman Brothers and the interbank market. These are independent hedge funds that are entirely unregulated, as well as hedge funds that are subdivisions of regulated firms (like Goldman Sachs Asset Management).

The business of hedge funds is in some respects not too dissimilar to that of banks. Therefore one could very well have subjected this kind of financial institution to capital regulation according to the Basel system. The fact that

---

[44] See Hedge Fund Research, *Record Number of Hedge Funds Liquidate in 2008*, press release of 18 March 2009, online at www.hedgefundresearch.com, accessed on 5 October 2009.

this was not done is one of the reasons why the financial system has become so unstable and why hedge funds were hit especially hard by the crisis.

The competition in laxity

The core question is: why did the regulators fail? Some answers offered deal with the subtleties of the political process and the lack of democratic controls of the regulatory agencies. The key for understanding the problem, however, lies in a statement of a high-level representative of the Banque de France at a conference in Paris in October 2008 regarding the decisions of his house with respect to the approval of financial products:[45] 'We had resolved to approve a financial product only if at least one of us understood how it worked. We were unable to adhere to this principle, however, as we always had to fear that it would then be approved by the English or German authorities. So we closed our eyes and gave the approval.' This confession dramatically expresses the tragedy of banking supervision. Regulators did not want to apply stricter regulations than other countries as they feared that the banking business would move there.

The French central banker was certainly not alone in his observation, which addresses a fundamental problem when state supervisory authorities fear losing out in the competition for financial centres. There is always an incentive for the supervisory authority to regulate domestic banks more generously than is done in neighbouring countries, in order to strengthen the domestic financial centre and to ensure in this way income and employment in the banking sector. As such an incentive exists for the supervisory authorities of all countries, however, the authorities mutually underbid one another, and there is a race to the bottom in regulatory standards. In this race, every supervisory office does the right thing from a national point of view, given the conduct of other authorities. But in the end, the regulation that results is too generous in the overall view of all authorities. An authority would gladly be stricter than it is if it knew that the other authorities would be just as strict, but the assurance that this is indeed the case could only be given in an international agreement and not when regulatory systems compete.

[45] Cited almost verbatim from memory.

The competition of governments or regulatory authorities degenerates to a competition in laxity.

I examined the theory of this phenomenon in my Yrjö Jahnsson Lectures.[46] The topic was the competition of national governments regarding tax rates, business infrastructure, social legislation, environmental regulation, product standards, national competition laws, and finally also bank regulation. In all of these cases it could be shown that competition among countries has become a competition in laxity that in the final analysis no longer meets the requirement of efficient regulation and constitutes a substantial policy failure.

The cause of the policy failure may be found in the disadvantages that decisions of individual countries entail for other countries. These disadvantages lead to a distortion of incentive structures, as they are not considered in the plans of individual countries' regulatory authorities. Only if they are given attention and weight, as one ought to expect from a collective decision of a supranational authority, can competition in laxity be avoided.

In the case of banking regulation, the disadvantage of regulatory competition is shown in particular in permitting the banks to conduct their business with little equity backing, which reduces liability and saddles taxpayers and creditors with high risks. The smaller the capital ratio, the smaller is that part of the losses that is covered by equity in case of bankruptcy and the bigger is the other part that must be offset by creditors and the state. In addition, bankruptcy is more likely when there is little equity capital, as the buffer against losses is smaller and the banks, as was shown in Chapter 4, are induced to gamble.

---

[46] H.-W. Sinn, *The New Systems Competition*, Yrjö-Jahnsson Lectures, Helsinki, 1999 (Blackwell, Oxford, 2003). The chapter on banking regulation was also published as H.-W. Sinn, 'Risk Taking, Limited Liability and the Competition of Bank Regulators', *FinanzArchiv*, 59 (2003), 305–29, triggering a critical discussion with more liberal economists who, in contrast to me, were of the opinion that reliance on competition among national banking regulation systems was warranted. See E. Baltensperger, 'Competition of Bank Regulators: A More Optimistic View. A Comment on the Paper by Hans-Werner Sinn', *FinanzArchiv*, 59 (2003), 330–5; P. Spencer, 'Can National Banking Systems Compete? A Comment on the Paper by Hans-Werner Sinn', *FinanzArchiv*, 59 (2003), 336–9; H.-W. Sinn, 'Asymmetric Information, Bank Failures, and the Rationale for Harmonizing Banking Regulation: A Rejoinder to Comments of Ernst Baltensperger and Peter Spencer', *FinanzArchiv*, 59 (2003), 340–6. A summary of my contributions plus an introductory statement by Martin Hellwig may be found in H.-W. Sinn, *Risk Taking, Limited Liability, and the Banking Crisis* (Selected Reprints, Ifo Institute, Munich, 2009).

Such disadvantages would be no problem for the incentives of the national regulatory authority if taxpayers and creditors consisted only of citizens of the home country. After all, the decision-makers, from the manager of the regulation authority to the members of parliament, who enact the regulations, must be answerable to these citizens. But this condition is not met in the financial sector in particular, as asset owners try to diversify their capital across borders in order to minimize country risks. Securities issued by a bank, by means of which it has financed itself, are traded on international financial markets and distributed all over the world. If banks collapse, burdens are distributed in the form of non-serviced credit claims and in the form of ensuing damages all over the globe. Therefore, a national regulatory authority does not benefit much from being strict. Stricter rules would only result in the loss of domestic jobs, profits, and tax revenues, while advantages of diminishing external burdens are being enjoyed somewhere far away by the citizens of other countries.

Figure 7.2 shows the percentage share of national debts of the banking systems that each country has abroad. The data shown are gross figures, as they are important with respect to the question of disincentives. It is evident that the smaller countries and Great Britain, which has specialized in financial business, owe a substantial share of their debt to foreigners. In the case of Great Britain, the share amounts to 54 per cent, in the case of Switzerland, Ireland, and Luxembourg to 62 per cent, 64 per cent, and 70 per cent, respectively. In Germany the share is 30 per cent, in Italy only 19 per cent.

From a theoretical point of view one may argue that a threatening loss of international reputation will prevent the national regulatory authorities from being less strict than in the case just presented in which all creditors live in the home country. Thus, there is not really a problem, and systems competition will work. This argument resembles the one that was discussed in Chapter 4 in the context of lemon competition among banks, and it does not hold for the same reasons as discussed there. First of all, details of national regulatory authorities are much too complex to be understood by buyers of bank bonds, especially CDO certificates and related products. As the complexity of financial products and regulatory systems exceed by a multiple the complexity of other products people buy, Akerlof's 'theory of lemons', discussed in Chapter 4, applies especially well to banking. Secondly, in view of the rarity of systemic catastrophes, there is no chance to achieve the necessary

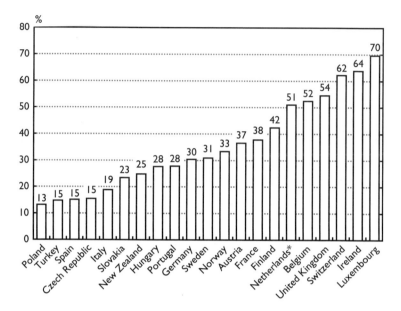

Fig. 7.2 The share of foreign liability in total liabilities of national bank balance sheets (2007)

*2003.

Note: Amounts of foreign liabilities of banks in percentage of their total liabilities. Unfortunately the OECD statistics do not contain any data for the USA.

Source: OECD, *Banking Statistics*, table C, database, accessed on 5 October 2009.

experience by observation. If the quality of regulation is reflected in whether a systemic catastrophe, which occurs once in 100 years, can be prevented, observation and experience do not help. One would have to observe events over centuries: this is not possible, however, as there will always be systemic breaks and evolutionary changes in regulatory systems that exacerbate or even prevent drawing analogous conclusions from the past to the present.

In order to overcome deficiencies in competition among countries, transnational agreements are necessary. In this context, Basel I and Basel II were important steps in the attempt to weaken incentive effects of international externalities by setting minimum capital ratios. Experience also shows, however, that past efforts in this regard do not suffice by any means. The result of the negotiations on the Basel accord was no more than the smallest common denominator of the countries involved. As the business areas of the national banks differ quite a bit, each country saw to it in the negotiations that regulations that affected areas in which the country was strong did not become too strict. As a result, only a rather lax overall regulation came about. Incidentally, the USA and large parts of the rest of the world participated little or not at all in the agreements, which for the signatory states created the incentive not to be too strict with themselves. The forces of laxity competition were also effective in the negotiations on the Basel accords and the 2004 decision of the SEC and prevented an optimal outcome. This should not discourage policy-makers from trying again. The crisis may indeed help them to reach sufficiently strict international agreements that would help reduce the risk of a repetition of the crisis; but more on this in the last chapter.

The selection principle and neoliberalism

For some it was surprising that competition among regulatory authorities failed in the final analysis. After all, it is the competition principle to which the market economy owes its success. The astronomical increase in the standard of living of the broad masses since the nineteenth century and the victory over Communism clearly demonstrate the advantages of the competition principle.

But there is more to competition than just laissez-faire. To make it work, a functioning framework for competition is required, that is, a system of rules of the game to which the players in the competition are subject. This, in turn, requires a strong state that defines the rules of the game and oversees their adherence. After all, the market economy is not a state of anarchy, where everyone can do what they want. A football match would be frustrating if there were no fixed rules enforced by a competent referee.

To be sure, a market economy is also not a central planning system that prescribes all the moves of the players in detail, which still today is implicitly called for by some leftist politicians. Setting up the rules of the game is not the same as detailed control of the game. It is, therefore, not a contradiction to argue against the *self-regulation* of the market economy but argue in favour of *self-organization* within a regulatory framework.

The rules of the market economy include the price system, property rights, the monetary system as well as, in particular, the civil code that determines which forms of contract are permitted and which are not. Such a system is supplemented by numerous special laws that limit the free decisions of individuals. These do not include, however, any laws that limit the free determination of prices and wages; such laws would lead to market imbalances in the sense of excess supply or excess demand that entail serious inefficiencies.

Within a well-designed framework of rules, the market, more specifically the free forces of prices and wages, can correctly signal scarcities and coordinate the actions of millions of people seeking their individual advantage within an orderly whole, as if steered by an invisible hand. This view of Adam Smith[47] is well known and was subsequently proved by Kenneth Arrow and Gérard Debreu using a formal mathematical model, for which they were awarded the Nobel Prize in Economics.[48]

We still have no superior authority, however, to define an appropriate framework of rules for the interaction of states, let alone an enforcement mechanism for the compliance with such rules. It is even unclear theoretically whether such rules can ever be designed. To the contrary, there is reason to fear that competition among states cannot function in principle because the states administer the exceptions to the rules of competition. Since states become active where the private market fails, we must fear that the reintroduction of the market through the back door of systems competition would again lead to the old market errors that originally called for the state's intervention. This phenomenon I once termed the 'Selection Principle'.[49]

In the systems competition of banking regulators the Selection Principle proves true to the fullest extent. If state regulation was originally called for to make competition among banks function despite the information deficit of

[47] A. Smith, *An Inquiry into the Nature and Causes of Wealth of Nations* (W. Strahan and T. Cadell, London, 1776).

[48] Kenneth Arrow (together with John Hicks) received the Nobel Prize in 1972 'for their seminal work on the general theory of the economic equilibrium and on welfare theory'; Gérard Debreu received it in 1983 'for the introduction of new analytical methodologies in economic theory and for a rigorous new formulation of the theory of the general equilibrium of markets'.

[49] H.-W. Sinn, 'The Selection Principle and Market Failure in Systems Competition', *Journal of Public Economics*, 66 (1997), 247–74; H.-W. Sinn, 'Der neue Systemwettbewerb', *Perspektiven der Wirtschaftspolitik*, 3 (2002), 391–407; H.-W. Sinn, *The New Systems Competition*, chapter 1.

the banks' customers, then one must be concerned that the same information deficit will again arise on the level of systems competition and will direct this competition into the wrong channels. The place of the bank that takes advantage of the information deficit of its customers, in order to pass on lemon bonds to them, is taken by the national regulatory authority that does the same with foreign bank customers by pursuing a hands-off approach to the national banks.

Although the Selection Principle leads to a sceptical assessment of systems competition, it is fully compatible with a neoliberal world view. 'Neoliberalism', as defined at a colloquium in Paris in 1938, grew out of the experiences of the Great Depression and emphasized time and again that competitive processes can only function within a strong, state-controlled framework of rules.[50] The emphasis on the framework of rules and a strong state defining the public order is what differentiates neoliberalism from the so-called 'paleoliberalism' or Manchester liberalism. Because of the importance accorded to order, neoliberalism in Germany is often also called 'ordoliberalism'. Paleoliberalism relied on the self-regulation of an economy, without assigning to the state a bigger role than employing night watchmen to protect the property. Neoliberalism relies on the self-ordering forces of the market within a framework of rules, but does not believe that this framework of rules can be created by the market itself. According to the neoliberal

---

[50] Le Colloque Walter Lippmann, 26 to 30 August 1938, which the philosopher Louis Rougier convened, marks the birth of neoliberalism. The concept itself was defined at this conference by the German economist Alexander Rüstow. Rüstow had formulated his ideas even earlier, at the 1932 meeting of the German Economic Association: 'The new liberalism, which is defensible today and which I represent together with my friends, demands a strong state, a state superior to business, superior to special interests, there where it should be. And with this commitment to a strong state in the interest of liberal economic policies and to liberal economic policies in the interest of a strong state—for this is mutually determined— with this commitment let me end.' (Author's translation.) See F. Boese (ed.), *Deutschland und die Weltkrise: Verhandlungen des Vereins für Sozialpolitik in Dresden, 28. und 29. September 1932*, Auftrag des Vereinsvorstandes, Schriften des Vereins für Sozialpolitik 187 (Duncker & Humblot, Munich, 1932), 62–9, here 69. The Verein für Socialpolitik (temporarily also Verein für Sozialpolitik) was founded in 1873, dissolved in 1936 after the Nazis seized power, and re-founded in 1948. It laid the foundations of the social reforms of Otto von Bismarck in the 1880s in Germany that served as the pattern for similar reforms in Europe and many countries of the Western world (public pension insurance, health insurance, and workplace injury insurance).

view, the responsibilities of the state therefore include the regulation of markets, the limitation of economic power, and the provision of justice and security by means of social policies.[51] From a neoliberal viewpoint it is not surprising that competition among states does not function unless there is a framework of rules for the states.

[51] See W. Eucken, *Grundsätze der Wirtschaftspolitik*, 1st edn. (Francke und Mohr, Bern, 1952), 7th edn. cited here (Mohr Siebeck, Tübingen, 2004), chapter 17, pp. 291 ff. and chapter 18, pp. 312 ff.

CHAPTER 8

The Extent of the Damage

Bank losses to date: US banks at the centre

The financial crisis has forced huge depreciation losses onto the banking system, calling into question its very existence. In 2008 and 2009 an avalanche of losses rolled over the banking world that, as described in Chapter 3, overwhelmed hundreds of banks worldwide, driving them into the arms of competitors, the state, or into receivership. This chapter will attempt to assess the quantitative importance of these events and to evaluate the risk situation of the banking system as a whole on the basis of Bloomberg and IMF data.

The term *depreciation loss* covers what, according to accounting rules, is called *depreciation and market value losses*. For accountants, depreciation means write-offs arising from expected defaults of debtors or actual default of payment, whereas market losses result from the devaluation of traded contractual claims and assets for which a price is known. For economists the terms depreciation, write-off, or write-down are defined more broadly, also covering market value losses.[1]

---

[1] From an economic view, there is no basic difference between depreciation and market value losses. In fact, true economic depreciation is defined as a loss in market value. See the seminal work on the economic theory of depreciation by P. Samuelson, 'Tax Deductibility of Economic Depreciation to Insure Invariant Valuations', *Journal of Political Economy*, 72 (1964), 604–6, and also H.-W. Sinn, *Capital Income Taxation and Resource Allocation* (North-Holland, Amsterdam, 1987), 119–23. The different use of the terms in economics and accounting frequently results in confusion. This is why it is explained here at the very beginning.

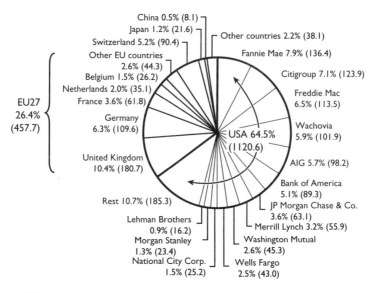

Fig. 8.1 Worldwide distribution of depreciation losses of financial institutions during the financial crisis ($1.737 trillion or 1.244 trillion euros as of 1 February 2010)

Notes: The list contains the total worldwide depreciation (market value and write-offs) of financial institutions since 2007 on CDO, ABS, MBS, and similar financial instruments as well as the defaults of commercial loans, bonds and debentures, loans to banks, bank bonds, and bank debentures incurred from 2007 to 1 February 2010, as officially reported by the institutions. The depreciations began with sizeable amounts in the third quarter of 2007. Only about $5 billion stem from the first half of 2007.

In parentheses: billions of dollars.

Source: Bloomberg list, read on 1 February 2010.

Figure 8.1 provides an overview of the depreciation in financial assets broadly defined that has been incurred by banks and insurance companies worldwide in the course of the financial crisis. Covered are all write-offs during the period from July 2007 to January 2010. The data were extracted from the Bloomberg database on 1 February 2010.[2] Bloomberg evaluates the quarterly reports of the major financial institutions of all countries, looking for any depreciation on direct and indirect, that is, securitized, credit claims. These include monetary claims held by public and private financial institutions like banks, real-estate brokerages, and insurance companies against households, firms, including other financial institutions, and the state. Covered are CDO, ABS, MBS, and similar securitized credit claims as well as commercial bonds, government bonds, bank bonds, company loans, and loans to banks

---

[2] The data are not available in printed form and cannot be printed from the screen.

and consumers. Assets that do not involve fixed monetary claims, such as equity stakes, are not taken into account. The data refer to gross equity losses due to depreciation on financial claims without netting these losses out with government rescue measures, retained earnings, revenue from new share issues, and other ways to compensate for the equity losses. Chapter 9 will deal with the rescue measures in detail. Even though the Bloomberg list is not entirely free of inconsistencies, it provides the most comprehensive and, in fact, only overview of the actual depreciation losses of the world financial system broken down into countries and institutions. All data stem from officially reported statistics published by the institutions themselves. They are not simply estimates or forecasts.

According to the Bloomberg list, on 1 February 2010 depreciation totalled $1.74 trillion for all financial institutions (1.24 trillion euros, valued at the exchange rate of that day). This figure is only a snapshot of a growing stock of depreciation, as many distressed loans do not become visible until the debtor fails to meet his obligations, and banks hesitate to write them down prematurely, before the accounting rules require them to do so.

The International Monetary Fund does similar calculations of actual write-offs on an aggregate level, but in addition it makes forecasts of such write-offs, as will be reported below. The most up-to-date statistics on actual depreciation on loans and securities held by banks (including brokers and non-US state banks, excluding insurers and US GSEs) inside or outside the USA was published by the IMF in October 2009 and concerns a subgroup of buyer countries, that is, the USA, the euro area, the UK, other Western European countries (Denmark, Iceland, Norway, Sweden, and Switzerland), and Asia (including Australia, Hong Kong, Japan, New Zealand, and Singapore).[3] According to the IMF statistics, by the end of the second quarter of 2009 the depreciation on these assets had amounted to $1.3 trillion. This number is smaller than the $1.74 trillion depreciation according to Bloomberg, as it refers to a subset of financial institutions and to a slightly shorter period. The Bloomberg figure closest to the IMF data is the write-down on financial products by banks including brokers but without US Government-sponsored Enterprises that amounted to $1.25 trillion by 1 February 2010.

[3] International Monetary Fund, *Global Financial Stability Report: Navigating the Financial Challenges Ahead* (October 2009), 9.

As expected, the Bloomberg statistics report the lion's share of the financial institutions' losses, at 64.5 per cent, in the USA, where the crisis began. In second and third place follow Great Britain, at 10.4 per cent, and Germany, at 6.3 per cent, of worldwide losses. Losses of US financial institutions add up to $1.12 trillion or 802 billion euros, losses of British financial institutions to $181 billion or 129 billion euros, and losses of German institutions to $110 billion or 79 billion euros. Great Britain occupies the second place on the list because London is the European financial centre, and Germany follows at only a short distance, perhaps because it was the biggest capital exporter worldwide after China (see Figure 2.3 in Chapter 2).

China hardly plays a role in the Bloomberg list, with depreciation amounting only to 0.5 per cent of total worldwide losses or $8.1 billion in absolute terms. This may be surprising in view of China's huge capital exports, but it is corroborated by the statement made in Chapter 2 that the Chinese invested primarily in US government bonds that are not affected by price declines. A similar remark applies to Japan, which accounts for only 1.2 per cent of worldwide losses, or $21.6 billion, even though it recently was the world's third largest capital exporter (see Figure 2.3). The experience with the Asian crisis seems to have created more prudence in that part of the world.

The US losses are not only large because the USA is a big country; the losses are also substantial relative to the size of the country. As becomes evident in Figure 8.2, the US financial institutions have thus far accumulated a loss of 8.0 per cent of the US gross domestic product. In an international comparison this percentage is only exceeded by very small countries.

The $1.12 trillion losses made by American financial institutions can be attributed to a few well-known names and a great many smaller institutions. As is shown in Figure 8.1, over half of the losses (51.2 per cent) were incurred by Fannie Mae ($136.4 billion), Citigroup (123.9), Freddie Mac (113.5), Wachovia (101.9), and AIG (98.2).

None of these institutions has survived without making substantial changes in its legal status and without accepting the government as a co-owner. As will be explained in more detail in the next chapter, the overall equity contribution of the US government to its public and private banking

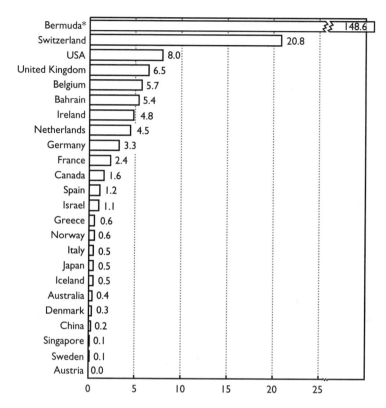

Fig. 8.2 Depreciation losses of the financial systems relative to their 2007 gross domestic products (by 1 February 2010, %)

*Bermuda estimate as of 27 February 2009, as the data are no longer reported by Bloomberg.

Sources: Bloomberg list, read on 1 February 2010; IMF, *World Economic Outlook Database*, October 2009; World Bank, *World Development Indicators online*; Ifo calculations.

systems, including AIG, up to the end of 2009 was $445.1 billion, or 19 per cent of the aggregate equity stock.

UK, Germany, and France

British financial institutions have also had to realize substantial write-off losses relative to the country's output. Among the bigger countries, the UK with a loss of 6.5 per cent of GDP was far ahead of Germany, which lost 3.3 per cent (see Figure 8.2). As shown by Figure 8.3, the British losses consisted primarily of depreciation losses incurred by the Royal Bank of Scotland

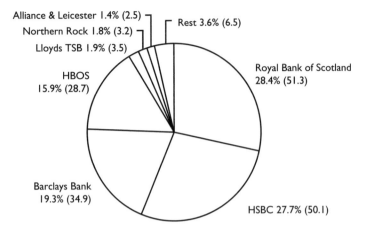

Fig. 8.3 Crisis-caused depreciation of British banks and insurance companies ($181 billion or 129 billion euros as of 1 February 2010)

Note: In parentheses: billions of dollars.

Source: Bloomberg list, accessed on 1 February 2010.

($51.3 billion, 28.4 per cent), the HSBC ($50.1 billion, 27.7 per cent),[4] Barclays ($34.9 billion, 19.3 per cent), and HBOS ($28.7 billion, 15.9 per cent),[5] which together accounted for 91.3 per cent of total British write-off losses.

Given that Great Britain was a net importer of capital (see Figure 2.3), this may seem surprising at first glance. However, the city of London is a financial intermediator with financial transactions moving in all directions. So there is no contradiction between being a net capital importer and having invested substantial funds in structured US financial products that were the source of the losses.

French losses, amounting only to 2.4 per cent of GDP or $61.8 billion, were recorded primarily by BNP Paribas ($19.5 billion, 14.0 billion euros, 31.6 per cent), Société Générale ($19.4 billion, 13.9 billion euros, 31.4 per cent), and Crédit Agricole ($9.1 billion, 6.5 billion euros, 14.7 per cent). As the figures indicate, France's losses were comparatively minor.

By comparison, Germany was more severely hit. As shown in Figure 8.4, the largest part of the losses of German financial institutions, amounting to $109.6 billion (79 billion euros), was accounted for by Deutsche Bank ($21.3 billion, 15.3 billion euros, 19.4 per cent), BayernLB

---

[4] Hong Kong Shanghai Banking Corporation.
[5] Halifax Bank of Scotland.

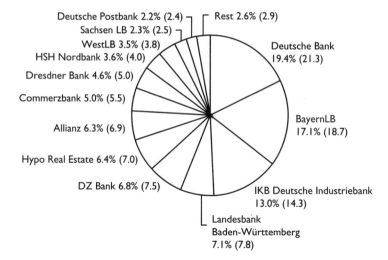

Fig. 8.4 Crisis-induced depreciation of German banks and insurance companies ($110 billion, 79 billion euros as of 1 February 2010)

Note: In parentheses: billions of dollars.

Source: Bloomberg list, accessed on 1 February 2010.

($18.7 billion, 13.4 billion euros, 17.1 per cent), and IKB ($14.3 billion, 10.2 billion euros, 13.0 per cent). These were followed by Landesbank Baden-Württemberg (LBBW), Allianz, DZ Bank, Hypo Real Estate, Commerzbank, Dresdner Bank, HSH Nordbank, WestLB, and Sachsen LB. The banks of Germany's federal states (including IKB) together accounted for write-down losses of 37.9 billion euros or 48.3 per cent of total losses of German banks and insurance companies although, in 2007, they owned just about one-fifth of the equity of the entire banking system. They lost 58 per cent of their capital as reported in the 2007 aggregate balance sheet.[6]

Switzerland, the Netherlands, Belgium, and Austria

It is amazing how hard hit small countries like the Netherlands, Belgium, and Switzerland were by losses of their financial institutions. Measured by an absolute loss of $35.1 billion (see Figure 8.1), the

---

[6] The total equity stock of all banks of the federal states, including Deutsche Industriebank (IKB), a largely government-owned bank, amounted to 65 billion euros in 2007. (To be precise, this figure refers to IKB, LBBW, BayernLB, Helaba, Nord/LB, Landesbank Berlin, Bremer Landesbank, HSH Nordbank, WestLB, Landesbank Saar, Landesbank Rheinland-Pfalz, Sachsen LB, and Deka Bank.) See Deutsche Bundesbank, *Bankenstatistik* (January 2009), 13, and IKB, *9-Monatsbericht 2007/2008, 1. April–31. Dezember 2007*, 2.

Netherlands ranks sixth worldwide after the USA, the UK, Germany, Switzerland, and France. The losses were primarily caused by the ING Group (52.4 per cent of the Dutch total) and AEGON (30.2 per cent), a large life insurance and pension group. By 1 February 2010, the country had, as is shown in Figure 8.2, already lost 4.5 per cent of a year's GDP.

Belgium, too, ranks relatively high in the loss statistics with a depreciation loss in the order of $26.2 billion, only a little less than the Netherlands. Expressing this loss relative to GDP shows that Belgium was one of the most severely hit economies in the world, ahead of Bahrain, Ireland, and the Netherlands (see Figure 8.2). The losses stem from the KBC Group (40.1 per cent of the Belgian total), Fortis Bank (34.7 per cent),[7] and Dexia (25.2 per cent). The KBC Group is an integrated bank-insurance group, and Dexia a bank specializing in public finance. Fortis, a normal, widely diversified bank, was one of the first victims of the crisis (cf. Chapter 3). It was sold at the last minute to the governments of the Netherlands, Belgium, and Luxembourg as well as to BNP-Paribas to prevent bankruptcy.

Among the small countries, however, Switzerland is the most remarkable case. At $90.4 billion or 5.2 per cent of worldwide losses, the country ranks fourth in the international loss statistics shortly after Germany and far ahead of France. Switzerland's financial institutions have, as shown in Figure 8.2, already lost 20.8 per cent of one year's GDP as a result of the financial crisis. That is a singular international position only topped by a tax haven like Bermuda.

Hidden behind the immense losses in Switzerland is, as shown in Figure 8.5, the huge loss, at 63.5 per cent of the total, of the United Bank of Switzerland (UBS) and at 22.8 per cent the loss of the Credit Suisse Group. UBS, which in 2007 had a balance sheet of 2.27 trillion Swiss francs, was endowed with an equity capital of only 43.8 billion Swiss francs and incurred a write-off loss of 60.3 billion Swiss francs or $57.4 billion. UBS would have gone bankrupt had it not been saved with a broad-based rescue operation injecting into the bank 34.6 billion francs ($36.3 billion), six

---

[7] Fortis was a Dutch-Belgian company with headquarters in Utrecht and Brussels. Bloomberg considers the company Belgian.

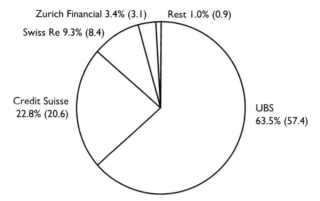

Fig. 8.5 Allocation of the losses of Swiss banks and insurance companies (as of 1 February 2010)

Note: In parentheses: billions of dollars.

Source: Bloomberg list, read on 1 February 2010.

billion of which came from the Swiss government budget, 13 billion from sovereign wealth funds,[8] and 15.6 billion from a private capital increase.[9]

With its openness to foreign financial capital, Austria could be expected to emulate Switzerland in many respects. But fortunately it managed to avoid the Swiss mistakes. The losses of the Austrian financial institutions amount to just $0.1 billion, which is close to nothing, even for a small country like Austria. It is too early, however, to be sounding the all clear for Austria, as it may still be affected by the repercussions of the real economy crisis on the Eastern European countries, where Austrian banks are heavily involved. This topic will be discussed in detail in Chapter 10 (see Figure 10.5).

How stable are the banks?

Since the banks of the Western world have already lost considerable substance in the crisis, the question arises as to their ability to survive. How much of their equity has already been exhausted, and does the rest suffice for a normal, healthy banking system?

[8] The money that flowed in 2008 from Sovereign Wealth Funds originated with the Government of Singapore Investment Corporation Pte Ltd. (11 billion Swiss francs) and an unidentified Near East investor (2 billion francs), see UBS, *Annual Report 2008*, 349.

[9] The capital increase was subscribed by the stockholders.

An important piece of information required to assess these questions is presented in Table 8.1. The table compares the depreciation losses of a selected group of banks, based on the Bloomberg list of capital asset ratios as shown in Table 7.1. Column A repeats the equity asset ratio for 2007, the year before the peak of the crisis. The capital asset ratio is the ratio of the equity capital shown in the balance sheet to total assets; it is the inverse of the so-called leverage ratio. Column B represents the depreciation losses as a percentage of the equity capital, and Column C represents them as a percentage of total assets. Column D shows the calculated equity asset ratio after deducting the depreciation, which indicates how strong the effect was on the individual banks.

As an orientation aid, all figures below an equity asset ratio of 4 per cent are shown in bold characters. The 4 per cent threshold is set arbitrarily and has no supervisory significance. It is of certain relevance, however, as before the introduction of Basel I in 1988 some countries required a minimum of 4 per cent equity relative to the credit volume (e.g. Germany). In the Basel system, criticized in the previous chapter, the 4 per cent threshold for the equity asset ratio lost its significance. It was replaced by a 4 per cent rule for the Tier 1 ratio that is based on entirely different measurement concepts. Nevertheless, the number provides a useful orientation.

Please note that these figures are based on a purely fictive calculation that does not take into account the profits or losses in 2008 and 2009, special aspects of accounting rules, new share issues, or state rescue programmes. The purpose here is not to present a forecast of capital ratios but rather an unadulterated picture of the original state of risk, without analysing the effectiveness of private or public rescue operations to date.

According to the information shown in Table 8.1, the losses reported by Bloomberg took on large dimensions when set in relation to equity, and must have been causing severe problems for many banks. The table shows that the US banks in particular had huge equity losses due to the write-offs caused during the crisis. Of the large banks, Freddie Mac was hit most severely with a loss of 424.7 per cent of its 2007 stock of equity capital ($113.5 billion). The world's largest bank, Citigroup, lost 109.1 per cent of its equity capital, ending up with a calculated equity asset ratio of − 0.5 per cent before being rescued by the US government. Wachovia, the fourth biggest

Table 8.1 The relative importance of crisis-caused depreciation by 1 October 2009 for selected banks (excluding increases in equity and state support) (%)

	A Equity asset ratio 2007	B Write-off losses rela- tive to equity 2007	C Write-off losses rela- tive to total assets 2007	D Calculated equity asset ratio after losses[*]
US banks				
Citigroup	5.2	109.1	5.7	−0.5
Wachovia	9.8	132.6	13.0	−3.7
Freddie Mac	3.4	424.7	14.3	−12.7
Fannie Mae	5.0	309.9	15.5	−12.4
Merrill Lynch	3.1	175.1	5.5	−2.5
Washington Mutual	7.5	184.3	13.8	−7.3
Bank of America	8.6	60.8	5.2	3.5
Wells Fargo	8.3	90.3	7.5	0.9
US banking system[**]	8.7	53.6	4.7	4.2
Swiss banks				
UBS	1.9	141.7	2.7	−0.8
Credit Suisse	3.2	50.1	1.6	1.6
Swiss banking system	4.0	58.6	2.4	1.7
British banks				
Barclays Bank	2.1	94.5	2.0	0.1
HBOS	3.3	80.1	2.7	0.7
HSBC	5.4	39.1	2.1	3.4
Lloyds TSB	3.4	17.9	0.6	2.8
Royal Bank of Scotland	4.8	34.8	1.7	3.2
British banking system	5.3	29.7	1.6	3.8
German banks				
Deutsche Bank	1.9	39.6	0.8	1.2
Commerzbank	2.6	24.4	0.6	2.0
HypoVereinsbank (UniCredit)	5.7	1.8	0.1	5.6
Hypo Real Estate	1.5	82.5	1.3	0.3
LB Baden-Württemberg	2.3	53.6	1.3	1.1
German banking system	4.0	23.9	1.0	3.1
Further euro banks				
Santander	5.7	18.1	1.0	4.7
Unicredit Group	5.6	7.7	0.4	5.2
BNP Paribas	3.2	26.0	0.8	2.4

(cont.)

Table 8.1 (Continued)

	A Equity asset ratio 2007	B Write-off losses rela- tive to equity 2007	C Write-off losses rela- tive to total assets 2007	D Calculated equity asset ratio after losses[*]
Credit Agricole	3.3	14.0	0.5	**2.8**
KBC	5.2	40.7	2.1	**3.2**
Dexia	2.7	28.8	0.8	**1.9**
ING Group	3.0	33.3	1.0	**2.0**
Fortis	8.0	29.9	2.4	5.7
Euro banking system	6.7	12.2	0.8	5.9

[*] Column A minus column C relative to total assets reduced by losses. Bold = equity asset ratio of less than 4%.

[**] Commercial banking, savings institutions, security brokers and dealers, and government-sponsored banks.

Note: Note that column D is not to be understood as a forecast of actual equity ratios, as new share issues, public support, retained earnings, and many other balance sheet details are not considered. The data refer only to banks rather than financial institutions. Thus, e.g., AIG which acted as both a bank and insurance company is not included.

Sources: Bloomberg list, accessed on 1 February 2010; Annual Reports of the banks, Board of Governors of the Federal Reserve System, Schweizerische Nationalbank, Bank of England, Deutsche Bundesbank, European Central Bank; Ifo calculations.

US bank, lost 132.6 per cent of its equity, ending up with a calculated equity asset ratio of −3.7 per cent. Similarly, Fannie Mae, Merrill Lynch, and Washington Mutual all had write-offs far exceeding their equity capital resulting in negative equity asset ratios. This demonstrates very clearly the point made in Chapter 4 that banks do incur risks that in the worst case scenario far exceed their liable equity stock and result from the sort of gambling predicted by the Bloos Rule.

The overall losses of the US banking system were not as dramatic as those of the large banks mentioned. Nevertheless, the US banking system, including the government-sponsored banks, lost one-half of its stock of equity capital (53.6 per cent) as is reported in Column B, which is $929.2 billion of $1.73 trillion available in 2007. This information is also repeated in Figure 8.6, which however provides a more extensive international comparison of banks' relative equity losses than does Table 8.1. As shown by Columns A and D in Table 8.1, the USA experienced a shrinkage of its

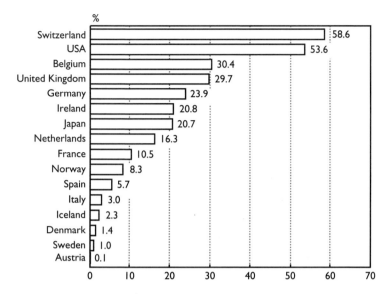

Fig. 8.6 Percentage equity capital losses of the banking system

Notes: Banks' losses according to Bloomberg during the crisis, as shown in Figure 8.1, divided by the banks' equity capital according to their aggregate annual balance sheets in 2007.

Whereas Figure 8.1 refers to the depreciation of the entire financial sector including insurance companies, in this figure the numbers refer only to the depreciation (write-off losses and market value losses of financial claims) of the banks divided by the total equity capital of the respective national banking systems. The data include government-sponsored banks and exclude AIG.

Source: Bloomberg list, accessed on 1 February 2010; banking statistics of the respective central banks.

calculated equity asset ratio from a seemingly comfortable 8.7 per cent in 2007 to 4.2 per cent, again without taking into account the effects of rescue packages, new share issues, and retained earnings.[10]

Huge losses also had to be borne by German and British banks that lost 23.9 per cent or 29.7 per cent of the 2007 equity stocks, respectively. These losses pushed the calculated equity asset ratios of these countries below the

[10] There is some ambiguity in the IMF data insofar as the Global Stability report changed its database, switching from the federal statistics *Assets and Liabilities of Commercial Banks in the United States*, which provided a total stock of equity for 2007 of $1.15 trillion, to the statistics *Flow of Funds Data for Commercial Banks, Savings Institutions, and Broker-Dealers*, which reported a sum of $1.640 trillion. If the equity of GSE is added (esp. Freddie Mac and Fannie Mae), a total of $1.733 trillion results. The depreciation, $929.2 billion (banks + GSE) according to Bloomberg, therefore amounts to 53.6% of the aggregate equity stock according to this new database.

critical 4 per cent limit, the British one from 5.3 per cent to 3.8 per cent and the German one from 4 per cent to a meagre 3.1 per cent.

In Germany, Hypo Real Estate lost 82.5 per cent of its equity capital during the crisis. Landesbank Baden-Württemberg lost 53.6 per cent and Germany's biggest bank, Deutsche Bank, lost 39.6 per cent. Except for HypoVereinsbank (UniCredit), all German banks mentioned in the table were pushed below the 4 per cent threshold and must be rated as under-capitalized. This is a particular problem insofar as, unlike British banks, German banks have thus far hesitated to accept the equity capital provided by the government rescue plan (see Chapter 9).

Nevertheless, British banks were severely hit. Barclays lost 94.5 per cent of its equity, HBOS 80.1 per cent, and HSBC 39.1 per cent. The British banks listed in Table 8.1 are all undercapitalized.

Switzerland had an aggregate equity loss of 58.6 per cent primarily because of UBS. As was mentioned above, the bank would have gone bankrupt had it not been rescued with Swiss and foreign state money. UBS lost 141.7 per cent of its equity capital and ended up with a calculated equity asset ratio of −0.8 per cent. Without massive government help it would have gone bankrupt, like so many of the large US banking corporations.

A surprising role is played by Belgium. The country not only ranks high in terms of its loss relative to GDP (Figure 8.2) but also with regard to its loss relative to the pre-crisis equity stock of its banking system. As is revealed by Figure 8.6, its banking system lost 30.4 per cent of its aggregate equity stock and would have been in deep trouble without government help. As was mentioned above these losses stem primarily from KBC, followed by Fortis and Dexia. KBC incurred write-off losses of 7.5 billion euros ($10.5 billion) that diminished its pre-crisis equity stock of 18.5 billion euros by 40.7 per cent. All three banks had to be supported with massive government equity help.

Figure 8.6 confirms that Swiss and US banks in particular overextended themselves. They all lost more than half of their equity capital during the crisis. Granted, these are gross losses that do not take into account that additional capital, which ensures the functioning of the Swiss and US banks, and which has been raised in the meantime. Yet the hypothesis of the self-regulating banking system, which was disseminated especially by economists from these countries, is by no means confirmed by the data in the figure.[11]

At 53.6 per cent, the relative capital losses of the US banking system are only marginally lower than the Swiss values. Since the banking system of the USA represents the heart of the entire financial system of the Western world, this is an ominous fact portending great danger.

Hidden write-offs

In view of the size of the depreciation, the question arises whether the financial system of the Western world can survive the crisis in its old form. The losses reported in Table 8.1 and Figure 8.6 are not forecasts, but the depreciation figures on loans and securities already published by the banks, including valuation adjustments and losses in market value resulting from the accounting rules of the respective countries. The losses have forecasting character only insofar as they include depreciation on market value that depends on the expectations about the future of market partners or depreciation due to credit defaults that are considered highly probable.

Various people and institutions, especially the International Monetary Fund (IMF), have attempted to forecast the overall write-offs that banks will have to recognize during this crisis on the basis of balance sheet analyses and macroeconomic considerations. As the crisis has resulted in a rapid increase in bankruptcies, company loan defaults will also rise sharply in wholesale banking, similar to the period after 2001. In addition, rising unemployment will drive many employees into insolvency resulting in their inability to repay their consumer loans. The relevant forecasts or projections made at different points in time are assembled in Figure 8.7. The IMF forecasts refer both to claims against worldwide debtors and to US debtors alone, as is indicated by the asterisks. The other forecast statements are less specific. The details are explained in the footnote.

For the sake of comparison, the graph also shows the Bloomberg data on actual write-offs on claims that worldwide financial institutions hold against worldwide debtors. These data are represented by the three vertical lines,

---

[11] Compare the economic controversy, already cited in the previous chapter, between Ernst Baltensperger, Peter Spencer, and the author in the journal *FinanzArchiv* from 2003.

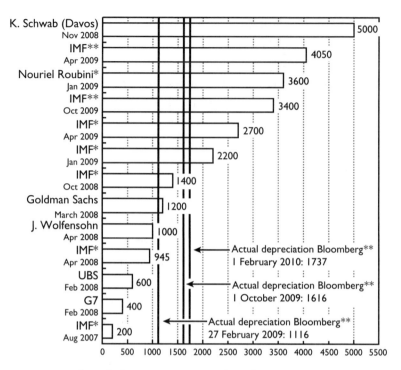

Fig. 8.7 Projected total depreciation required at financial institutions in billion US dollars

* Write-offs on worldwide financial claims against US debtors.

** Write-offs on worldwide financial claims against worldwide debtors.

Notes: All projections are for depreciation in the balance sheets of financial institutions. Nevertheless they are not identical nor clearly defined. The IMF projected both the total of the worldwide write-offs on claims against US debtors and on write-offs on claims against worldwide debtors. Schwab, UBS, and Wolfensohn referred generally to write-offs in financial markets, Goldman Sachs to global losses, Roubini to write-offs at US institutions, the G-7 to subprime losses.

Sources: International Monetary Fund, *Global Financial Stability Report*, October 2007, April 2008, October 2008, January 2009 (Update), April 2009, and October 2009; International Monetary Fund, *World Economic Outlook Update*, January 2009; D. Pilling and J. Soble, 'Subprime Losses Could Rise to $400 bn', *Financial Times*, 10 February 2008; A. Moses and Y. Onaran, 'Financial Firms Face $600 Billion of Losses, UBS Says', *Bloomberg*, 29 February 2008; B. Swint, 'Wolfensohn "Pessimistic" as Financial Losses Rise', *Bloomberg*, 28 April 2008; H. Meyer and A. Daya, 'Roubini Predicts U.S. Losses May Reach $3.6 Trillion', *Bloomberg*, 20 January 2009; 'Goldman Sees Credit Losses Totalling $1.2 Trillion', Reuters, 26 March 2009; 'Kosten der Finanzkrise—5.000.000.000.000 Dollar', *Süddeutsche Zeitung*, 28 November 2008.

referring to 27 February 2009, to 1 October 2009, and to 1 February 2010, the dates when their dynamically changing database was read.

What is surprising is the enormous dispersion of the projected write-offs, ranging from $200 billion to $5 trillion. It may be explained primarily by the time at which these projections were made. For example, the IMF suspected in August 2007, at the first signs of the banking crisis, that the worldwide financial system, including the American financial institutions, would have to shoulder a depreciation of claims against American debtors amounting to $200 billion. In April 2008 this forecast rose to $945 billion, in October 2008 to $1.4 trillion, and in January 2009 to $2.2 trillion. According to the IMF estimate of April 2009, the forecast for write-offs on US securities held by financial institutions worldwide climbed to $2.7 trillion.

In addition to financial products originating in the USA, from April 2009 the IMF extended its projection of depreciation figures also to financial products originating in Europe and Japan. In its Financial Stability Report of April 2009 it estimated that a total of $4.054 trillion of depreciation was to be expected for the world's financial system, but in its October 2009 report it revised this estimate downward to $3.4 trillion to be written off by the end of 2010, due to a perceived cyclical recovery in the world economy. Apart from the fact that some countries and institutions have been omitted, this figure may be interpreted as a forecast analogous to the actual figures of Bloomberg, according to which by 1 February 2010 a worldwide depreciation total of $1.737 trillion had accumulated in the balance sheets of banks (including brokers) and insurance companies. The alarming implication is that by this date not more than 51.1 per cent of the expected total depreciation of financial institutions worldwide had been realized. Looked at in this way, it means that in winter 2009/2010 the world was not at the end but right in the middle of its financial crisis.

This of course is a shocking piece of news for the American banking system. As that system had already lost 53.6 per cent of its 2007 stock of equity capital (Figure 8.6), total losses of 105 per cent of that stock could be expected (53.6 per cent/51.1 per cent). However, such an estimate would be misleading as the USA and, in particular, US banks seem to have recognized a larger fraction of their total write-offs than the world financial system as whole. In its October 2009 Global Financial Stability Report the IMF also published regional forecasts for private bank write-offs. According to this forecast, the private US banking system will have to reckon with overall write-offs by 2010 on the order of $1.03 trillion, while the Bloomberg data indicate that US private banks had actually recognized write-offs of $679.3 billion by 1 February 2010, that is, 66.3 per cent of the $1.03 trillion expected.[12] Assuming the same percentage of recognized write-offs for the Government-sponsored Enterprises, the entire US banking system can be expected to lose 81 per cent of its 2007 equity capital during the crisis (53.6 per cent/66.3 per cent).[13] This is a somewhat better figure than would result by making the forecast with the IMF world-wide data, but nevertheless alarming. Whatever the truth turns out to be: a lot of public money has already flowed, and much more will have to flow to rescue the American financial system (see Chapter 9).

Similar calculations can be made for Europe. While the IMF did not break down its forecasts by country, tentative calculations on the basis of its forecast for Western Europe are also revealing. 'Western Europe' in the IMF statistics includes the euro area, UK, Switzerland, Sweden, Denmark, Norway, and Iceland. The IMF forecast that the banking systems of these countries (including government-sponsored banks like Germany's state banks) will have to write off $1.62 trillion by the end of 2010—50.2 per cent of their joint 2007 balance sheet equity capital, which was $3.23 trillion. The IMF also calculated that by mid-year 2009 the actual write-offs of the banks of these European countries amounted to $685 billion. This was 21 per cent of the 2007 stock of equity capital or 42 per cent of the anticipated write-offs (the above-mentioned $1.62 trillion), indicating that $934 billion in write-offs still have to be recognized.

The Bloomberg figures about actual write-offs of the same set of European countries are a bit smaller than the IMF figures ($511.9 billion by 1 February 2010), as Bloomberg seems to leave out some of the smaller financial institutions. Nevertheless they are useful because they are the only ones that break down the write-off figures by country. Scaling-up Bloomberg's national write-off percentages given in Figure 8.6 with the ratio of the European IMF forecast figure and the European Bloomberg figure on actual write-offs (1,619/511.9) would imply, for example, that the total write-off of

---

[12] This is only a bit more than the IMF's own calculations of actual write-offs by mid-year 2009, which amounted to $608 billion.

[13] The equity capital of the US banking system in 2007 was $1.733 trillion including the Government-sponsored Enterprises, and $1.640 trillion without them. Given the IMF forecast of overall write-offs in the order of $1.03 trillion, the private US banking system can be expected to lose 63% of its 2007 equity stock.

Belgian banks will be 96 per cent of their 2007 equity stock, of British banks 94 per cent, of German banks 76 per cent, of Irish banks 66 per cent, and of Dutch banks 51 per cent. French banks, on the other hand, would have to write off only 33 per cent, Italian banks 9 per cent, Danish 4 per cent, and Swedish 4 per cent.[14] Caution is called for, however, insofar as these estimates neglect potential differences among the European countries with regard to the extent to which they have already recognized the necessary write-offs as well as to the deviations between the Bloomberg and IMF data on actual European write-offs. Nevertheless, the figures are unbiased forecasts that would be true if these differences and deviations were the same in relative terms for all countries. Given that a breakdown of the IMF figures by single European countries is not available, better forecasts cannot be made at this stage. Policy-makers and supervisory authorities need to be aware of major problems that still might show up in their national balance sheets.

This could be particularly true for Germany. Before the acute stage of the crisis (June 2008), German banks held the biggest foreign loan portfolio of all countries, at $4.6 trillion, followed by the French banks, at $4.2 trillion, and the British banks at $4.1 trillion.[15] $790 billion of the German loan portfolio were accounted for by claims against the USA. According to an internal survey by the Bundesbank and the German supervisory agency (BaFin) at the turn of the year 2008/9, which was divulged to *Der Spiegel* and *Die Zeit*, the twenty biggest banks were said to have 305 billion euros of extremely toxic CDOs on their books.[16] Assuming a repayment value of one-third of these assets (see Figure 2.7), the overall write-off loss of the German banking system would be 203 billion euros. Perhaps even more alarming was a secret list of problematic assets presumably produced by

[14] These forecasts are calculated by dividing the percentages given in Figures 8.6 by 31.6%, the ratio of overall Bloomberg write-offs and the overall IMF forecast. This is a best-guess forecast, assuming in the absence of better information, that the degree of recognizing the country-specific ultimate write-offs by 1 February 2010 is the same in all countries and that the percentage of write-offs not captured by the Bloomberg figures relative to the IMF figures is also the same in all countries.

[15] See Bank for International Settlements, *BIS Quarterly Review* (December 2008), Statistical Annex, table 9B.

[16] 'Bankenkrise—weitere Verluste', *Der Spiegel* (19 January 2009), 16; 'Jetzt geht die Krise richtig los', *Die Zeit* (22 January 2009), 20.

the German supervisory agency BaFin, which the newspapers *Frankfurter Allgemeine* and *Süddeutsche Zeitung* reported in spring 2009. According to that list, the seventeen biggest German banks had a combined volume of dubious credit claims worth at least 816 billion euros on their books.[17] A somewhat smaller, though still disturbing, figure of 650 billion euros in dubious credit claims in the balance sheets of big German banks was reported in a secret study by Merril Lynch, as reported by *Der Spiegel* in October 2009.[18] It is unclear how large the write-off losses would be that these press reports imply, if true, but they are frightening nevertheless. Unfortunately, they are consistent with the information given in the previous paragraph, according to which the German banking system's overall write-off on financial claims during the crisis will turn out to be 232 billion euros, equivalent to 76 per cent of its 2007 stock of banking equity (306 billion euros).

The credit-card problem

Another reason why the banking crisis has not yet been overcome and why the IMF presents such horrendous projections is the credit-card problem. Parallel to the growth of mortgage loans, Americans have availed themselves of more and more credits via credit cards in recent decades. There are, on average, no fewer than twelve credit cards per household, including those issued by supermarkets and department stores.[19] In the USA, credit cards offer substantial credit availability, because credit-card companies do not require that incoming bills be paid immediately. An American has a credit limit of $18,000 available on average, which used to be good business for credit-card companies due to the high interest rates charged.[20] Things are

---

[17] H. Steltzner, 'Banken ohne Zukunft', *Frankfurter Allgemeine Zeitung* (22 April 2009), 1. The *Süddeutsche Zeitung* also reported this: 'Die erste Bilanz des Banken-Desasters', *Süddeutsche Zeitung* (25/6 April 2009), 1.

[18] W. Reuter and C. Schwennicke, 'Bad Bank Germany', *Der Spiegel* (19 October 2009), 74.

[19] 'Kreditkarten bringen die Banken in Bedrängnis', *Die Welt*, 26 November 2008, online at www.welt.de, accessed on 11 March 2009.

[20] B. Bucks, A. Kennickell, T. Mach, and K. Moore, 'Changes in U.S. Family Finances from 2004 to 2007: Evidence from the Survey of Consumer Finances', *Federal Reserve*

very different in Europe, because there the full amount of credit is deducted from the charge account at the end of the month, and the overall credit card debt is negligible.

The volume of consumer loans based on credit cards in the books of commercial banks nearly doubled in the USA from mid-2000 to early 2009, from $200 billion to $392 billion.[21] Credit-card borrowing has contributed to the fall of American households' savings rate to almost zero in recent years (see Figure 2.1 in Chapter 2).

Demand for credit cards has risen rapidly especially since the collapse of the American mortgage market, as in many American households the flow of housing loans has ended quite abruptly. The constraints on mortgages meant difficulties for those who had become accustomed to financing their consumption from housing loans (see Figure 5.2 in Chapter 5) and for those who were simply looking for follow-up financing for housing loans coming due. Similar difficulties arose for people whom the banks denied follow-up financing for car leasing contracts. They all plundered their credit cards. The credit-card companies then attempted to erect barriers by tightening their credit standards, at least this is what two-thirds of the credit-card banks said in a survey in the month of September 2008 after the demise of Lehman Brothers.[22]

The tightening of the standards could not, however, alter the fact that because of the financial crisis and rising unemployment more and more credit-card debtors defaulted. From the second quarter of 2007 to the third quarter of 2009 the default or charge-off rate for US credit cards rose from 3.85 per cent to 10.10 per cent, increasing by 162 per cent.[23] While, as is shown in Figure 8.8, the charge-off rates for all kinds of loans have been rising during the crisis up to the time of writing, the charge-off rate for the credit cards exceeds them all by far. This reiterates the point made

Bulletin, 95 (February 2009), online at www.federalreserve.gov, accessed on 12 March 2009; see further http://www.creditcards.com/credit-card-news/credit-card-industry-facts-personal-debt-statistics-1276.php.

[21] Federal Reserve, *Assets and Liabilities of Commercial Banks in the United States H.8*, online at www.federalreserve.gov, accessed on 11 March 2009.

[22] Federal Reserve, *Senior Loan Officer Opinion Survey on Bank Lending Practices*, online at www.federalreserve.gov, accessed on 11 March 2009.

[23] Federal Reserve, *Charge-off and Delinquency Rates on Loans and Leases at Commercial Banks*, online at www.federalreserve.gov, accessed on 3 February 2010.

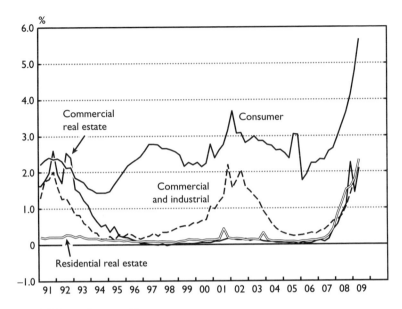

Fig. 8.8 US loan charge-off rates

Source: International Monetary Fund, *Global Financial Stability Report* (October 2009), 6.

frequently in this book that, while the worst of the real crisis will hopefully be over at the time of publication, the banking crisis is likely to continue for quite some time.

The increasing number of credit-card defaults has hit the credit-card companies hard. The stock price of American Express dropped, and the difficulties of Citigroup described above have to do with uncollectable credit-card claims. Egg Banking plc, the world's largest internet bank and a subsidiary of Citigroup, was even forced in early February 2008 to cancel the credit cards of 160,000 customers, which was a unique event.[24] American Express became a commercial bank in order to access the direct credits that, in contrast to earlier practice, the Federal Reserve has been granting to commercial banks since 2008.

Credit-card companies and banks that had supplied credit cards and car loans securitized most of their credit claims and sold them as asset-backed securities, similar to housing loans that were securitized as mortgage-backed

---

[24] 'Web-Bank zieht Kreditkarten ein: UBS drohen Ermittlungen', *Spiegel online*, 3 February 2009.

securities (MBS). Like MBSs, the securitized credit-card claims were subsequently included in the construction of synthetic securities of the CDO type that were sold all over the world. As these credits have now increasingly become non-performing, many countries will have to suffer losses for a long time.

There is one argument, according to which the credit-card problem is not of the same calibre as the housing loans: as the credit-card debtors are not relieved from personal liability by the legal concept of non-recourse loans, securities based on credit cards might be safer than those based on mortgage contracts. Credit-card debt is not limited to the value of a collateralized object, but must be serviced out of a person's entire wealth and labour income. However, the counterargument is that the credit cards are not collateralized at all and are used as a source of credit primarily by the poorer segment of the population, where the banks have little recourse in the case of payment default because there is nothing to take. Personal bankruptcy because of poverty is fairly easy in America, and it limits liability in a similar way to the legal concept of non-recourse loans. Time will tell how the credit-card risk will appear in future annual accounts.

Graveyard insurance

Additional, incalculable risks still exist for the so-called credit default swaps (CDS). Originally these were guarantees that one bank granted another bank as insurance against losses. If a bank had a risky credit claim against a debtor, it could protect itself against payment default by buying insurance from another bank. It paid the insuring bank an annual fee in the amount of a given percentage of the credit volume, usually of 0.5 per cent to 1 per cent. And if the debtor defaulted, the insuring bank serviced the debt in his stead.

In Europe, too, bank guarantees are common whenever the loan cannot or will not be secured by real property. Typically, the debtor buys the guarantee to provide security for the creditor. The special aspect of CDS insurance is that the creditor himself may insure against the default of a credit. It is customary for the creditor to buy a CDS from another bank to provide insurance for his claim, and the latter bank in turn insures itself against a possible default by buying a CDS from a third bank.

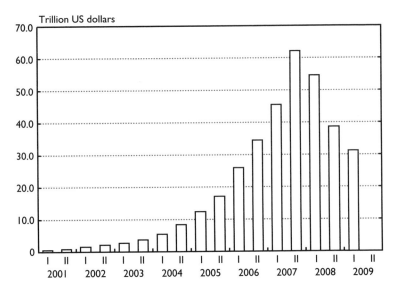

Fig. 8.9 Outstanding CDS contracts

Note: Shown is the volume of outstanding credit default swap contracts, which corresponds to the nominal value of the sum of insured credit volumes.

Source: ISDA, International Swaps and Derivative Association, online at www.isda.org, accessed on 8 October 2009.

These insurance contracts create a long chain of mutual obligations that are difficult to unravel, like the cascade of CDOs.

The volume of such hedging contracts based on credit default swaps was and is huge. As shown in Figure 8.9, the volume rose to over $60 trillion by the second half of 2007. This was more than the gross national product of the world (about $55 trillion) in 2007.[25] Since 2008, the volume of CDS contracts has been falling, however, as indicated by the last column in Figure 8.9. In the first half of 2009 the aggregate volume dropped to $31.2 trillion. One of the reasons for this is that in response to the crisis the banks made every effort to undo the mutual hedges (compression). Another reason is a partial collapse of the market due to the fear that the insurance contracts would not be serviced.

Credit default swaps have an important economic function as they distribute the risk of a real investment, which the debtor finances with his loan, onto several shoulders, thereby making it controllable. Courage and

---

[25] International Monetary Fund, *World Economic Outlook Database*, October 2009, online at www.imf.org, accessed on 3 February 2010.

risk-taking are known to pay off, but in view of bearing the possible losses by oneself, courage is quickly reduced to faintheartedness. That is why insurance and other vehicles like CDS hedges are most useful to economic growth. By sharing gains and losses in a fair way, they enlarge the total risk that investors may incur, thereby generating economic and business returns that otherwise would not have been possible.[26]

Unfortunately, however, over time credit hedges in the form of credit default swaps lost all connections to their original function of insuring the creditor. Today it is possible to negotiate CDS contracts to insure economic events that have no effect on the policyholder, and those transactions are apparently done frequently. While no statistics exist to clarify the issue, experts estimate that 90 per cent of the CDS market volume involves contracts of this type. Insurance has mutated to mere gambling and is nothing but useless speculation.

This development may again be traced to limited liability in connection with minimal equity asset ratios. Similar to what was shown in Chapter 4, limited liability generates excessive risk-taking on the part of the guaranteeing banks if the market partners have insufficient information, because profits in the form of insurance premiums are privatized and insured losses are either not fully borne or left to the taxpayer. Under the Bloos Rule, the banks involved in CDS transactions have developed into speculators who try to outwit one another, mostly without any economic utility whatsoever. Gambling has become their normal business model.

Truly perverse is the opportunity to insure, by means of a CDS, against the bankruptcy of another firm, even though this bankruptcy does not inflict any damage on the insurance purchaser. You pay a current premium to the 'insurer', and he pays you the insurance or guarantee amount if the other firm goes bankrupt. It is easy to see the consequences if the 'insured party' has the financial means to influence the probability of bankruptcy by his own actions. For example, one can 'insure' against the bankruptcy of a competitor and then try to bring about this bankruptcy by predatory pricing, short selling the competitor's stock, slander, or other infamous tricks, which are not uncommon market strategies nowadays.

---

[26] See H.-W. Sinn, *Risiko als Produktionsfaktor*, Inaugural lecture, University of Munich, published in: *Jahrbücher für Nationalökonomie and Statistik*, 201 (1986), 557–71.

An event that I learnt of may shed light on this issue. A colleague, a renowned economist, made a laudatory comment in a British newspaper about a certain firm, characterizing it as stable. After the newspaper appeared, he received a call from a lawyer who told him to be more cautious. Did he really know what he had said? The firm in question was not at all stable but was facing bankruptcy, the lawyer argued. If he, as an expert, praised this firm in public, he might face costly consequences. The lawyer was speaking for a hedge fund that had bought 'insurance' against the bankruptcy of the firm concerned, or better, underwritten a bet on it, and now expected the indemnification payment that would become due in case of bankruptcy.

All of this is reminiscent of the so-called graveyard insurance described in 1906 by Irving Fisher in his book on the life insurance market, *The Nature of Capital and Income*.[27] Normally a life insurance policy is taken out on one's own life to the benefit of individuals who are close or who are owed money. In America of the nineteenth century it was possible, however, to take out life insurance on a neighbour's life, with the policyholder choosing himself as the beneficiary. The policyholder paid the premium and, when the neighbour died, he received the insurance sum from the insurance company. It does not take much to imagine the implications of these insurance policies in the Wild West, where the Colt sat loosely in its holster.

In medieval Italy there were also similar insurances. But they were limited to the life of the king, as it was assumed he was protected well enough to preclude danger to life and limb.

Graveyard insurance was an episode in American history. After everyone had realized the incentives it created, it was prohibited. All the worse to think that graveyard insurance is experiencing a renaissance in the market of CDS hedges, with the main participants being banks and other firms. In any case, in view of such possibilities and in view of the huge sums involved, the CDS problem holds an unbelievable risk potential for business and society that must be urgently restricted by regulating the CDS market and guiding it into proper channels.

[27] I. Fisher, *The Nature of Capital and Income* (Macmillan, New York, 1906), 294 f.

CHAPTER 9

Rescue Attempts

Bank rescue

How many independent private banks would have survived the crisis without the government rescue measures and whether the market economy itself would have survived is anybody's guess. Undoubtedly, however, right after the new Black Friday, on 10 October 2008, when one of the worst stock market weeks of all time ended, the countries of this world put together comprehensive rescue packages for their banking systems that exceeded even the wildest expectations. The G-7 summit in Washington, DC, on 11 October and the EU conference in Paris on the following day set the course for a bail-out mission in favour of the banks that, while it rescued the world's economies, also burdened future generations with gigantic new public debt.

In the meantime, some of the amounts committed then have even been increased. The USA, for example, had passed rescue packages amounting to $1.3 trillion financed by government agencies by September 2009, of which $700 billion stemmed from TARP (*Troubled Assets Relief Program*) and $600 billion from a loan guarantee programme of the Federal Deposit Insurance Corporation (FDIC).[1] Not included are various market

---

[1] In total, the US Department of the Treasury provides up to $100 billion equity for the Public Private Investment Program (PPIP) by means of TARP resources. Half of this sum is expected to be devoted to the Legacy Loan Programme, which will be leveraged by a factor 12 with private debt (i.e. $600 billion) guaranteed by the Federal Deposit Insurance Corporation (FDIC). See US Department of the Treasury, *Treasury Department Releases Details on Public*

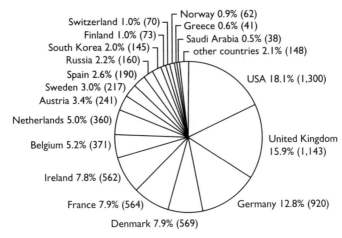

Switzerland 1.0% (70) — ┌ Norway 0.9% (62)
Finland 1.0% (73) ┐ ┌ Greece 0.6% (41)
South Korea 2.0% (145) ┐ ├ Saudi Arabia 0.5% (38)
Russia 2.2% (160) ┐ │ ┌ other countries 2.1% (148)
Spain 2.6% (190)
Sweden 3.0% (217)
Austria 3.4% (241)
USA 18.1% (1,300)
Netherlands 5.0% (360)
Belgium 5.2% (371)
United Kingdom
15.9% (1,143)
Ireland 7.8% (562)
France 7.9% (564)
Germany 12.8% (920)
Denmark 7.9% (569)

Fig. 9.1 Government-financed bank rescue packages (totalling $7,174 billion)

Notes: Excluding central bank rescue packages.

In parentheses: absolute amounts in billions of dollars, converted at the exchange rates of December 2009.

Sources: For EU countries (approved public interventions in the banking sector): European Commission, *Economic Crisis in Europe: Causes, Consequences and Responses*, European Economy 7/2009. The European Commission figure for Denmark was corrected and downsized according to information received from Peter Birch Sørensen, Danish Council of Economic Advisors. For the USA: Congressional Budget Office, *The Troubled Asset Relief Program: Report on Transactions through December 31* (2008), 1; US Department of the Treasury, *Public-Private Investment Program*, 4; US Department of the Treasury, *Treasury Department Releases Details on Public-Private Investment Program: Fact Sheet*, 23 March 2009, online at www.treasury.gov, accessed on 27 October 2009; for the remaining countries: *Der Spiegel* (10 November 2008), 61; Ifo calculations.

liquidization programmes of the central banks, of which the US TALF programme alone has a volume of $1 trillion (see below, section *Monetary policy*), as well as Keynesian-type economic recovery programmes that aim at stabilizing income levels.

Figure 9.1 gives an overview of the guarantees and supports to banks to which the countries have committed themselves. They add up to $7.1 trillion (5 trillion euros) and include guarantees, loans, subsidies, and capital assistance. About nine-tenths of the European bank rescue programmes that are contained in it are likely to consist of guarantees and loans. The remaining one-tenth is additions to capital.[2] In the American bail-out programme, too, government guarantees and loans account for the lion's share.

Private Investment Program: Fact Sheet, 23 March 2009, online at www.treasury.gov, accessed on 27 October 2009.

  [2] European Commission, *Economic Crisis in Europe: Causes, Consequences and Responses* (European Economy 7/2009), 63.

It must be emphasized that the amounts mentioned are not to be equated to actual government expenditures. The guarantees frequently serve only to make it possible for the banks to continue their maturity transformation function, providing security to the creditors who extend short-term loans to the banks for relending. Under the most favourable circumstances of a quick stabilization, the government may even turn a profit, as it can collect guarantee fees. However, realistically, a substantial fraction of the guarantees will have to be honoured. In the Savings & Loan Crisis of 1991, the overall rescue package of $519 billion in the end involved a true cost for the taxpayer of only $124 billion, about 24 per cent of the total, while the thrift industry itself bore another $29 billion.[3] If this percentage is taken as a yardstick, the crisis could cost the governments of the world $1,720 billion in terms of bank rescue packages alone.

The true nature of the guarantees becomes especially clear if Ireland is taken as an example. At $562 billion (386 billion euros) the country put together one of the largest rescue packages in the world. However, in 2009, Irish GDP was only $229 billion (164 billion euros), less than half (41 per cent) the size of the guarantees it pledged to provide. Given the large number of banks and special purpose entities resident in Ireland, the size of the Irish rescue package is understandable, but it is entirely implausible, promising much more than the country could ever pay. Obviously, Ireland assumes that only a tiny fraction of the guarantees will ever become due. And indeed, by 1 February 2010 the Irish write-offs had only reached 5 per cent of GDP.

The same, though to a lesser extent, is true for Denmark. The country put together a rescue package of $569 billion (390 billion euros), but its GDP was only about $314 billion (225 billion euros) in 2009, just 55 per cent of the guaranteed sum. The size of the package is surprising, given that Danish write-downs on securities and loans have been minute, as was shown in the previous chapter, at just 0.3 per cent of GDP by 1 February 2010, whereas the ratio of Belgium, for example, stood at 5.7 per cent. If Denmark is lucky it will get off lightly in terms of its true depreciation. If it is unlucky, it will have to take responsibility for the entire amount mentioned, which, however, is out of the question.

---

[3] T. Curry and L. Shibut, 'The Cost of the Savings and Loan Crisis: Truth and Consequences', *FDIC Banking Review*, 13/2 (2000), 26–35.

The three countries most heavily involved in absolute terms, the USA, Germany, and Great Britain, had put together combined rescue packages worth $3,364 billion by 2009. It is remarkable that Germany and Great Britain, at a combined total of $2,064 billion, top the total of the substantially larger USA, at $1,300 billion (890 billion euros). Nevertheless, the US package is, of course, by far the biggest for any one country.

The US package

To help its financial sector recover, the American government rolled out its main programme, TARP, on 14 October 2008. The programme's original volume of $250 billion was later extended to $700 billion, and is to be spent through twelve separate sub-programmes. TARP funds allow the government to buy mortgage-backed securities and residential loan claims, insure troubled assets, subsidize homeowners, support the automotive industry, and provide equity capital to banks.

By December 2009, about $205 billion had been injected as equity capital into the US banking system (including the quasi-bank AIG) via the *Capital Purchase Program* (CPP) alone. The largest amounts were invested into Citigroup, Bank of America, JPMorgan Chase & Co., and Wells Fargo, at $25 billion each. The two investment banks Morgan Stanley and Goldman Sachs, which had adopted the status of commercial banks after the collapse of Lehman Brothers, received $10 billion each. All in all, more than 600 banks received equity via the CPP. Another $40 billion was injected into Citigroup and Bank of America via the *Targeted Investment Program* (TIP), in equal parts. Citigroup received an additional $5 billion through the *Asset Guarantee Program* (AGP), increasing its total public funding to $52 billion. Being classified as a system-relevant institution, AIG received $69.8 billion of equity capital via the so-called *SSFI program* (Systemically Significant Failing Institution program).[4]

Summing up all programmes, up to December 2009 the US government contributed a gross amount of $262.7 billion of equity capital to its private

---

[4] US Department of the Treasury, *Troubled Assets Relief Program: Transaction Report*, online at www.financialstability.gov, and Office of the Special Inspector General for the Troubled Asset Relief Program, *Quarterly Report to Congress: July 21 2009*, online at www.sigtarp.gov, accessed on 12 October 2009.

banks excluding the Government-sponsored Enterprises and excluding AIG,[5] which amounted to 12 per cent of the aggregate equity stock (third quarter 2009) of \$2.19 trillion.[6] If AIG, which acted like a bank although it was an insurance company, is included, another \$69.8 billion of state equity is added,[7] bringing the government's equity contribution to its private banking system to a total of \$332.5 billion or 15 per cent of the equity capital. The nationalization of Fannie Mae and Freddie Mac, which administer about half of US mortgage portfolios, brought the US government's potential liabilities to something in the order of \$5 trillion and implied a further equity contribution of the government in the order of \$112.6 billion.[8] Thus during the crisis, the overall equity contribution of the US government to its public and private banking systems, including AIG, by the end of 2009 was \$445.1 billion, or 19 per cent of the aggregate equity stock of the public and private banking systems available at the time (third quarter 2009), namely \$2,331 billion.[9]

In spring 2009 stress tests were performed on the US banks to find out whether their equity capital would be sufficient if a further deterioration of the economic situation and further write-offs on toxic assets occurred (the so-called Supervisory Capital Assessment Program, CAP). The result, published on 7 May of that year, was that despite the government equity injections a further \$74.6 billion of equity capital would be required.[10] Ten of the nineteen banks tested needed additional capital. Topping the

---

[5] Capital Purchase Program and Targeted Investment Program.

[6] See Board of Governors of the Federal Reserve System, *Flow of Funds Accounts of the United States*, Flows and Outstandings Third Quarter 2009, tables L.109, L.114, L.124, and L.129.

[7] See American International Group, Inc., *Financial Supplement* Third Quarter 2009, 9. After the equity injection AIG's equity was \$76.5 billion in September 2009.

[8] See Freddie Mac, *Third Quarter 2009 Financial Results Supplement*, 4, and Fannie Mae, 2009 *Third Quarter Results*, 9.

[9] The aggregate stock of equity of the banking system including AIG and Government-sponsored Enterprises was \$2,331 billion by the end of the third quarter of 2009 (the most recent data point available at this writing). See Board of Governors of the Federal Reserve System, *Flow of Funds Accounts of the United States*, Flows and Outstandings Third Quarter 2009, tables L.109, L.114, L.124, and L.129, and American International Group, Inc., *Financial Supplement* Third Quarter 2009, 9.

[10] US Department of the Treasury, *The Supervisory Capital Assessment Program: Overview of Results*, 7 May 2009, online at www.financialstability.gov, accessed on 30 September 2009.

list was the Bank of America, with $33.9 billion, followed by Wells Fargo and GMAC (General Motors Acceptance Corporation), with $13.7 and $11.5 billion respectively. These banks entered into a commitment to issue a CAP convertible preferred security to the US Department of the Treasury in an amount sufficient to meet the capital requirement determined by the stress test. Each institution was permitted up to six months to raise private capital in public markets to meet this requirement, and would be able to cancel the capital commitment without penalty. The ten banks were required to submit a capital plan to the supervisors by 8 June 2009, to be completed by 9 November 2009. Nine of them succeeded. Only the General Motors bank GMAC did not. It received $3.8 billion equity from the Treasury, a sum which is included in the above figures.

As the crisis subsided in early summer 2009 and several banks were once again profitable, some banks bought back a portion of the government-owned shares. Bail-out fund repayments totalled $161.9 billion by the end of 2009, implying a net government equity contribution of $283.2 billion or 12 per cent of the aggregate stock of equity of the US banking system.[11] The world's centre of capitalism and entrepreneurship had effectively national-ized substantial parts of its banking system.

The Geithner Plan

The biggest US support package is to be provided by the *Public-Private Investment Program* (PPIP) of Treasury Secretary Timothy Geithner, an-nounced in March 2009. It partly draws on TARP, partly on the TALF programme run by the Federal Reserve (see below), and partly on a guaran-tee programme of the Federal Deposit Insurance Corporation (FDIC), protecting up to $600 billion of private loans. PPIP aims at inducing private investors to purchase troubled assets from the banks with public support.

---

[11] The figure is calculated as follows: $204.9 billion (Capital Purchase Program) + $40 billion (Target Investment Program for Citigroup and BofA) + $69.8 billion (SSFI Program AIG) + $60.9 billion (Fannie Mae) + $51.7 billion (Freddie Mac) + $17.8 billion (Automotive Industry Financing Program for GMAC and Chrysler FinCo) = $445.1 billion (gross). $445.1 billion – payback (–$121.9 billion (CPP) – $40 billion (TIP)) = $283.2 billion (net). See US Department of the Treasury, *TARP Transaction Reports*, online at www.financialstability.gov, accessed on 25 January 2010.

For this plan, a total of up to $1 trillion is to be spent by the government and the Federal Reserve on equity capital, loans, and credit guarantees.[12]

The Geithner Plan offers a 50 per cent government equity share to private investors who purchase toxic claims that are still on the banks' books, and grants them at least twice this share as a non-recourse loan. The idea is to employ the private know-how of financial investors in order to remove the toxic assets from the banks' books at prices that are as correct as possible. In this way, the market is to be stimulated, and the bank balance sheets are to be relieved of their liabilities inherited from the housing crisis. This is a bit reminiscent of the medical strategy of strengthening the body's own defences by enabling the antibodies to target the germ causing the illness, in principle not a bad approach.

The Geithner Plan distinguishes between two types of liabilities inherited from the housing crisis that are still lying dormant on bank balance sheets: direct loan claims (legacy loans) against homeowners, and indirect claims in the form of ABSs, CDOs, and similarly constructed securities (legacy securities). Whereas public equity shares amount to 50 per cent in both cases, the additional credit is in the first case twelve times and in the second case double the government equity. In the case of legacy loans the credit comes from the private sector and is guaranteed by the FDIC. In the case of legacy securities, it comes directly from the government. It is this kind of government credit or guarantee that makes up the true public aid, as it is the government that bears the loss if something goes wrong.

The plan is best understood if one imagines that the government partners with private investors to establish a multitude of limited liability firms, supported by additional public loans, in order to buy toxic claims from the banks. Such firms are not actually established, but partnership contracts are signed that have characteristics similar to those of limited liability firms. The private investor and the government inject equal shares of equity, and the government then extends or guarantees additional loans to the partnership. The partnership acquires the toxic assets from a bank and its business consists of receiving the interest and collecting the claims upon maturity. It can also resell the claims to others. The partnership uses its capital and the funds made available by the state to buy the assets, paying interest on the state funds. Profits are distributed

[12] US Department of the Treasury, *Public-Private Investment Program*, online at www.financialstability.gov, accessed on 12 October 2009.

equally to both owners. Losses first eat up the capital. If they exceed the capital, the state as creditor or insurer must either waive repayment of the loans it provided or pay out the guaranteed sum. The private investor has no liability extending to any other assets beyond his equity share.

The Geithner Plan evidently copies the basic construction of a corporation that, thanks to a combination of limited liability and high leverage, can derive private profit from mere risk, similar to what was described in Chapter 4. And again, the potential private profits are the mirror image of potential losses for the government. An example of the functioning of the plan, constructed on the basis of official data, may illustrate this.[13] A bank holds toxic claims whose expected value is $84, as the market assumes that the nominal value of the claims, $168, may be collected at a probability of 50 per cent, while at the same probability the claims would default with no repayments at all. The bank now sells these claims at market value to the public–private partnership. The private investor and the state contribute $6 each as equity capital, and FDIC, in addition, guarantees twelve times its equity share, that is, $72. In the best case, the capital of the two partners grows from $12 to $96 ($168 minus the $72 of the loan), which means that each partner's capital increases from $6 to $48. In the worst case, the capital will be used up completely, and the loan is repaid by FDIC. The private investor can expect total average earnings of $24 on his investment of $6 ($= 0.5 \times 48 + 0.5 \times 0 = 0.5 \times 48 = 24$), which corresponds to a rate of return of 300 per cent. For the government, the tally does not look quite so good. The best case, if it also earns $48 on its investment of $6, is outweighed by the risk of it losing its equity investment and having to service the guarantee. In the latter case, the earnings on the investment of $6 is −$72: its equity is gone, and it has to repay the loan. On average, the state must assume that its capital of $6 will yield a final return of −$12 ($= 0.5 \times 48 - 0.5 \times 72$), corresponding to a return on capital of −300 per cent. The private investor may thus expect a huge profit and the government a huge loss.

---

[13] See US Department of the Treasury, *Treasury Department Releases Details on Public-Private Partnership Investment Program*, press release of 23 March 2009, online at http://financialstability.gov; for the example see also at the same address the White Paper titled 'Public-Private Investment Program: $500 Billion to $1 Trillion Plan to Purchase Legacy Assets'.

Small wonder then that Wall Street celebrated and share prices surged when the plan was announced (see Chapter 2).

The Geithner Plan can only combat the insolvency problem if the government loses money from its participation and if this money actually benefits the banks. That it will lose money is likely, for the reasons discussed above. It is not obvious, however, how much of it will go to the banks and how much of it will instead wind up with the buyers, who are likely to consist primarily of pension funds and hedge funds.

In the example, in which the claim is sold at $84 and this amount has a fifty-fifty chance of doubling or disappearing into thin air, the entire advantage of the government intervention accrues to the buyers, who may expect a fantastic rate of return. Not a cent would go to the banks and the plan would not contribute to solving the liquidity crisis of the banking system. To be realistic, one must assume, however, that the private investors' demand induced by the high rate of return will drive up the toxic assets' price above the $84. This will lower the buyers' rate of return, and the bank will also profit from the public money. But this effect will not result in the entire funds invested by the government winding up with the banks. Rather, in the normal case, one may expect the market to find an equilibrium in which both market partners will share the public subsidies.[14]

This does not bode well for the Geithner Plan. If the prime purpose was to prevent an insolvency crisis, direct government money given to the banks would make more sense, as it would ensure that the public funds did not partly flow to the hedge funds, but ended up entirely with the banks, replenishing their capital.

---

[14] The economic model of market equilibrium between demand and supply shows in general (except for pathological cases) that a subsidy, no matter to which market partner it is granted, always leads to a change in contract conditions so that the market partners end up sharing the subsidy. The rule is that the partner whose desired exchange quantity reacts relatively less to price changes gets a higher portion of the subsidy. Only in the extreme case, in which one side of the market acts thoroughly insensitively to price, does the entire subsidy wind up with that side of the market. In the present example this means that the public funds only benefit the banks in their full amount if the quantity of assets they want to sell, instead of keeping them on their books, does not react to a change in market price. If they are willing, however, to sell just about everything when the price rises just a little, the public funds will wind up entirely with the buyers. The real world is somewhere in between.

But why should the government give away money in the first place? It would only be fair if it received stocks in exchange for the funds it makes available, effectively turning the taxpayer into a stockholder. In that case, there would at least be expectations of dividends or later proceeds from selling the stocks. Looked at it this way, the Geithner Plan is in fact only a third-best political option to deal with the solvency crisis of the American banking system. First-best is providing equity capital against shares. Second-best is providing equity as a gift to the banks. Third-best is providing equity as a gift that is split between the banks and the hedge funds. It is understandable, therefore, why the critics of the plan accuse the government of having only looked for a hidden way to give taxpayer money to influential special interest groups.[15]

The plan started to be implemented in September 2009. By the end of 2009 it was not clear to what extent investors would make use of it. In principle, there should be an overwhelming interest because of the extremely favourable terms granted by the government. However, the problem is that the purchases will reveal the true market value of the assets and may therefore force banks to recognize hidden losses in their balance sheets, which they cannot afford because the reported equity would then fall short of the required regulatory minimum and trigger insolvency. Even though US banks seem to have revealed the truth faster than their European counterparts, the previous chapter showed that just 66 per cent of the necessary write-offs had been recognized in the USA by 1 February 2010, implying a stock of hidden write-off losses for all banks excluding the Government-sponsored Enterprises and AIG in the order of $346 billion.

Germany

As shown in Figure 9.1, at a total of $899 billion (630 billion euros), Germany passed the third-biggest bank rescue package after the USA and UK. The country enacted its programme (*Finanzmarktstabilisierungsgesetz*) on 17 October 2008, creating a special agency, the SoFFin (*Sonderfonds*

---

[15] See J. Stiglitz, 'Obama's Ersatz Capitalism', *New York Times* (1 April 2009), A31, New York edition, and P. Krugman, 'Financial Policy Despair', *New York Times* (23 March 2009), A21, New York edition.

Finanzmarktstabilisierung) for its implementation. Before this, it had already provided substantial support to various banks of the federal states (*Landesbanken*), the semi-public IKB (Deutsche Industriebank), and HRE (Hypo Real Estate).

The German programme is essentially a guarantee programme. At the time of writing, guarantees amounting to a total volume of 400 billion euros had been made available. Of the 218 billion euros applied for, 176 billion euros had been approved.

The German federal programme also includes equity capital for needy banks in the order of 100 billion euros. At the time of writing, 28 billion euros had been extended, not counting the contributions that the Länder made to their *Landesbanken,* which had grown to 15 billion euros by the end of 2009 and the 1.25 billion euro equity capital that the state-owned KfW provided to IKB, one of the first victims of the crisis.[16] The lion's share of this, at 18.2 billion euros, went to Commerzbank, 3 billion euros to WestLB, the Landesbank of North-Rhine Westphalia, and 525 million to Aareal Bank, a small bank active in real-estate financing. Furthermore, the government nationalized Hypo Real Estate, injecting 6.3 billion euros of equity capital (in addition to providing guarantees in the order of 95 billion euros). Unfortunately, apart from these four banks, which probably would have gone bankrupt without the government money, German banks did not find the equity offers attractive. This is astounding as, according to the information given in Chapter 8, by 1 February 2010 those German banks observed by Bloomberg already had acknowledged write-off losses in the order of 79 billion euros; all German banks may in the end have to acknowledge an aggregate loss of about 230 billion euros, two-thirds of their 2007 equity stock. The 28 billion euros that helped the four banks above simply represents the wrong order of magnitude.

The reason for the refusal of public capital may be found in the penalties attached to its acceptance. One condition for receiving public capital is that representatives of government bodies would sit on supervisory boards, have a voice there, and participate in internal bank discussions. Another condition is that management salaries would be limited to 500,000 euros ($750,000)

---

[16] For example, Bayern LB received 10 billion euros from the Free State of Bavaria, and HSH Nordbank received 3 billion from the states of Hamburg and Schleswig-Holstein. For IKB see www.ikb.de/content/de/ir/news/ad-hoc-mitteilungen/alle/08_02_16_Ad-hoc-Mitteilung.pdf.

per annum. For executives of big German banks, whose yearly salaries most recently averaged 2.2 million euros, this means a substantial reduction.[17]

The supervisory boards show no interest in public equity either, as the shareholders whose interests they represent do not benefit from the government as co-owner meddling in the banks' policy just to stabilize the size of the balance sheet. If the government demands a fair rate of return on its investment, then the rate of return on the private capital invested will not rise.

The banks, therefore, prefer to react to their equity losses by scaling down their business.[18] For example, Deutsche Bank reduced its balance sheet by 371 billion euros, or 18 per cent, from the first to the second quarter of 2009—more than three times the volume of German annual net investment.[19] Deutsche Bank has repeatedly rejected any public capital with which it could avoid scaling down its business volume. Thus, Josef Ackermann, its chief executive, is known to have said that he would be ashamed if his bank had to rely on public support.[20] Others share his opinion but are not courageous enough to make it public.

German politicians will have to come up with new ideas to remove this design flaw from the rescue package. Regardless of how intensively the wish for 'fair' manager salaries is voiced in public, nobody will be willing to pay the price for it in terms of an extreme slump of the real sector. The logical solution to the problem is either to abandon the cap on manager salaries or rescind the voluntary nature of capital increases. The last chapter will present an argument in favour of the second alternative.

On 22 July 2009 Germany, in addition, also implemented a plan for a so-called bad bank whose purpose was to remove the toxic assets from the private banks' balance sheets. Each private bank was given the option of creating a special purpose entity that would assume the role of the bad bank,

---

[17] The annual reports of Deutsche Bank, Commerzbank, Dresdner Bank, HypoVereinsbank, and Deutsche Postbank for 2007 show average yearly salaries of 2.23 million euros.

[18] The chairman of the board of Deutsche Bank, J. Ackermann, declared: 'We...are firmly determined to shorten our balance sheet and thereby improve the leverage ratio.' See Deutsche Bank, press release of 30 October 2008.

[19] See Deutsche Bank, press release of 28 July 2009.

[20] 'I would be ashamed if we had to accept public funds in the crisis,' said Ackermann according to *Der Spiegel*; see 'Deutsche Bank rückt von Renditeziel ab', *Der Spiegel*, 18 October 2008, online at http://www.spiegel.de/wirtschaft/0,1518,584925,00.html

and to sell the toxic assets to this entity in exchange for interest-bearing securities, in order to avoid the otherwise necessary write-offs on bank balance sheets.[21] As the securities are insured by SoFFin for a fee, they are AAA rated, require only small risk weights, and, therefore, only little equity needs to be held against them.

The exchange is to take place at 10 per cent below the book value of the toxic assets, which normally is still above their potential, but unknown, market value. An expert committee will calculate the so-called *fundamental value* in order to arrive at an estimate of the market value. The difference between the reduced book value and the fundamental value as well as any further losses that might result from an overly favourable assessment of the fundamental value must be repaid with interest to the special purpose entity over time out of the original bank's dividend flow.

The construction so described does not entail a recognizable asset gain for the bank, especially as all losses of the bad bank are carried forward at the market rate of interest. The construction does, however, offer an apparent balance sheet gain for the bank in its relationship with the supervisory authorities, as the bank will be able to include the securities received on its balance sheet as reserves against potential losses, without also having to include its debts to the bad bank.

At the time of writing, the German bad bank model had not met with much interest among private banks. Only some public banks were willing to set up bad banks. WestLB, one of the German public banks hardest hit by the crisis, created a bad bank on 14 December 2009, outsourcing a sizeable 85 billion euros in non-strategic assets. HRE, Germany's big nationalized mortgage bank, applied for a bad bank with a volume of 210 billion euros on 21 January 2010. And the Bavarian Landesbank expressed interest in setting up a bad bank as well. Rumour has it that private banks have so little interest in bad banks because even the initial 10 per cent write-off is more than they can afford, given the regulatory minimum equity constraints and given the amounts already written off by the banks. In addition, there is no

---

[21] Law on the Further Development of Financial Market Stabilization, draft bill of the Federal Government of May 2009. This is elucidated in: Deutsche Bundesbank, 'Zum "Bad Bank"-Modell der Bundesregierung', *Monthly Report* (May 2009), 56–9. Unfortunately this text remains unclear regarding important details of the draft contract.

real advantage for the firms in present value terms, as all losses of the bad bank will in any case have to be covered, including the interest.[22]

The true monetary advantage that remains for the bank is that it must only offset the losses of its bad bank if it pays out dividends and that it has the right to issue preferred stock against the claims of the bad bank. This advantage permits the bank to procure equity capital even in difficult times, but it raises the bankruptcy probability of the bad bank, which would have to be footed by SoFFin.

How big this advantage is for the original bank is debatable. Basically, the German bad bank is a bookkeeping trick that hides the true problems of the banks and pretends there is more capital than in fact exists. Reducing the regulatory minimum equity ratios would have been an equivalent, but more honest policy measure in economic terms. The bad bank policy upholds the functioning of the original banks, but instead of really strengthening them, it plants the seed of the next banking crisis.

The British way

In view of the rescue package acceptance problems in Germany it is useful to learn how Britain tried to rescue its banks. The UK, one of the first European countries to be hit by the crisis, has undertaken measures that one would never have believed possible in such a liberally inclined country. While Germany, with its bad banks, in fact chose a temporary reduction of equity requirements, the British went the opposite way. In the midst of the crisis they convinced eight of the biggest banks to participate in a rescue plan that contemplated an increase in the Tier 1 ratio from the Basel II minimum of 4 per cent to 9 per cent.[23]

---

[22] Initially, the bad bank plan had foreseen that losses above the difference between the reduced book value and the fundamental value would be carried forward interest-free such that SoFFin, the government rescue fund, would have had to bear the losses. This provision was heavily criticized in the first (German) edition of this book and was abolished in the final version of the bad bank law.

[23] See 'Führung der Royal Bank of Scotland muss gehen', *Frankfurter Allgemeine Zeitung* (14 October 2008), 17; 'Brown nimmt die Banken an die Leine', *Handelsblatt* (14 October 2008), 3.

At first glance, such an increase in the equity requirements appears a counter-productive measure in the midst of the crisis, because it aggravates the liquidity shortage and would thus promote a credit crunch. At a second glance, however, things look a bit different. First, arrangements were made so that banks could not simply meet the new requirements by reducing their loans to home-buyers and firms. Secondly, the government helped the banks in fulfilling the minimum capital ratio. The banks had the right to first try to raise the required equity capital in the market, and would have to accept the co-ownership of the government only in case they did not succeed, as the case turned out to be.

The government did indeed eventually become a partner in most major UK banks, except for HSBC and Barclays, which ranked first and third by the size of their 2007 balance sheets. It acquired a share of more than 70 per cent of the stock of the Royal Bank of Scotland, once the biggest European banks, and a share of 65 per cent in Lloyds TSB, which had acquired HBOS (Halifax Bank of Scotland), and in the meantime carries on business under the name of Lloyds Banking Group. In October 2008 a total of £50 billion, equivalent to about $83 billion (58 billion euros), were made available out of the public budget.[24] Before that, the British government had already taken over 100 per cent of Northern Rock, affected in the autumn of 2007 by the first bank run of the crisis (see Chapter 3). The total expenditure of the British government for the acquisition of bank equity had amounted to £94 billion or $136 billion (106 billion euros) by March 2009, which was 25 per cent of the stock of equity reported in the aggregate 2007 balance sheet of the British banking system.[25] These measures have stabilized the big banks in a sustainable way. At present, they have substantially more Tier 1 capital than the 4 per cent that is required for an orderly banking business, according to Basel II.

In addition, the British government also offered its more robust commercial banks an insurance solution with the so-called *Asset Protection Scheme* (APS).[26]

---

[24] See Council of Economic Experts, *Die Finanzkrise meistern: Wachstumskräfte stärken* (Annual Report 2008/9), 154. Conversion into euros at the exchange rate of August 2009.

[25] See 'Global Downturn: In Graphics', *BBC News*, online at www.bbc.co.uk, accessed on 13 April 2009. See Deutsche Bundesbank, *Exchange Rate Statistics* (March 2009), 9.

[26] See GHM Treasury, *Statement on the Government's Asset Protection Scheme*, 19 January 2009, online at www.hm-treasury.gov.uk, accessed on 17 April 2009.

The objective of APS was to insure the losses of loans, ABS, and CDOs as well as the related derivative business so as to reduce the Basel II risk weights and hence the need to hold equity against the assets. To participate, the banks must be solvent, well capitalized, and sufficiently big to be considered system-relevant (total assets of more than £25 billion). Those which did not qualify had to participate at once in the government's equity programme. The toxic claims were evaluated and insured by the government for a fee, and the banks had to accept a deductible bracket. This implies that they take responsibility for losses up to a given amount, with the government chipping in thereafter. Of the losses that exceed the deductible, the banks will have to bear at least 10 per cent as co-insurance.[27] These limitations on the degree of government insurance were set so as to induce the banks to continue making efforts to get back their money from the debtors, instead of leaving it to the government to collect the debts. At the time of writing, the UK government had insured about £585 billion ($968 billion, 678 billion euros) of structured instruments on the balance sheets of the Royal Bank of Scotland and the Lloyds Group via the APS Programme.[28]

Monetary policy

The central banks have also made enormous efforts to keep the banking sector afloat and enable it to service the real sector with cheap credit. In 2008 the US Federal Reserve System increased the monetary base by 97 per cent, essentially doubling it, while the European Central Bank (ECB) increased its money supply by no less than 37 per cent and the Bank of England by 31 per cent.[29]

---

[27] The Royal Bank of Scotland, which had invested £325 billion in ABS securities, succeeded in negotiating a reduction in the co-insurance ratio to 6%. Cf. A. Seager, 'How Many Bucks can you Pass?', *The Guardian*, 7 March 2009, online at www. guardian.co.uk, accessed on 17 April 2009.

[28] *The Economist*, Recovery ward, 24 September 2009, online at www.economist.com, accessed on 13 October 2009.

[29] See Federal Reserve Bank of St Louis, *Monetary Trends* (March 2009), 16, European Central Bank, *Monthly Report* (January 2009), S 9, and Bank of England, *Narrow Money and Reserve Balances*, online at www.bankofengland.co.uk, accessed on 19 October 2009. The monetary base consists of currency in circulation as well as reserve deposits and deposit facilities of private banks with the central bank. Money supply M1, in contrast, is composed of currency in circulation and demand deposits of private non-banks with commercial banks.

In addition, central bank interest rates were drastically reduced. In the USA they reached zero by December 2008, in the UK 0.5 per cent by March 2009, and in the eurozone 1.0 per cent by May 2009 (see Figure 2.11), the lowest level since the introduction of the euro.

In the course of the crisis, the Fed as well as the ECB had increasingly become intermediaries for interbank transactions. As discussed in Chapter 3, banks lost trust and stopped lending to each other after the collapse of Lehman Brothers. The central banks reacted by borrowing from banks and lending to other banks, thereby securing the transactions (see Figure 3.3).

The Bank of England, as the British central bank is officially called, had initially been reluctant to stop the bank run on Northern Rock (see Chapter 3), but it learned its lesson after the event and injected extra reserves into the banking system. For the first time in its history it issued *Bank of England bills*. Bank of England bills are marketable securities with a maturity of usually only one week, issued to provide lending banks with a safe investment option. It also introduced so-called *Operational Standing Facilities*, special credit lines for banks that wanted to borrow. Most importantly, in April 2008, it introduced the *Special Liquidity Scheme* to allow banks and building societies to exchange, for up to three years, currently illiquid assets rated 'high quality' for treasury bills. Use of the scheme has been considerable, totalling treasury bills in the amount of £185 billion ($306 billion, 214 billion euros). As financing conditions remained difficult for banks and building societies, the Bank of England introduced a permanent *Discount Window Facility* to provide liquidity insurance to the banking system, as part of a series of changes to its procedures for operating in sterling money markets.[30]

The Federal Reserve, in turn, implemented a number of programmes designed to support the liquidity of financial institutions and improve conditions in financial markets. These new programmes have led to a significant lengthening of the Federal Reserve's balance sheet. First, the Fed provided short-term liquidity to banks and other depository institutions and financial institutions under the *Term Auction Facility* (TAF), the *Term Securities Lending Facility* (TSLF), and the *Primary Dealer Credit Facility* (DCF). Second, the Federal Reserve also approved bilateral currency swap agreements with

---

[30] See Bank of England, *Annual Report 2009* (May 2009), 17.

fourteen foreign central banks. These swap arrangements assist these central banks in their provision of dollar liquidity to banks in their jurisdictions to prevent an appreciation of the dollar. Third, the Fed provided liquidity directly to borrowers and investors in key credit markets, buying up ABSs and MBSs. For this it maintained a gigantic and spiralling set of programmes, bearing such names as the *Commercial Paper Funding Facility* (CPFF), the *Asset-Backed Commercial Paper Money Market Mutual Fund Liquidity Facility* (ABCP MMMF), the *Money Market Investor Funding Facility* (MMIFF), and the *Term Asset-Backed Securities Loan Facility* (TALF); this last facility alone has a volume of up to $1 trillion. In addition to the purchases of debt issued by government-sponsored banks ($200 billion) and of mortgage-backed securities ($1.25 trillion), these operations included $300 billion worth of purchases of longer-term treasury securities.[31] The purpose of all these measures was to fight a potential credit crunch and ensure that private firms and the government were able to get the money they needed for their respective investment and expenditure programmes.

In addition to reducing its main refinancing rate, the ECB pursued a policy that it called *enhanced credit support*.[32] The enhanced credit support facility consisted of five pillars: first, the provision of unlimited liquidity to banks at the main refinancing rate (fixed rate full allotment). Second, a dramatic expansion of the list of assets that banks could present as collateral when borrowing from the ECB. Third, a lengthening of the maturity of the funds lent by the ECB to one year. Fourth, the provision of dollar loans following the corresponding Fed policy aiming at a stabalization of the dollar. Fifth, direct purchases in the order of 60 billion euros of covered bonds including AAA-rated mortgage bonds (*Pfandbriefe*), but also more dubious products that received at least a BBB–/Baa3 rating by one of the major rating agencies (Fitch, Moody's, S&P, or DBRS).[33]

---

[31] See Federal Reserve, *Credit and Liquidity Programs and the Balance Sheet*, online at www.federalreserve.gov, accessed on 19 October 2009.

[32] See J.-C. Trichet, *The ECB's Enhanced Credit Support*, lecture at Munich Economic Seminar of CESifo and Süddeutsche Zeitung, 13 July 2009, published as *CESifo Working Paper* No. 2833, October 2009, online at http://www.cesifo-group.de/wp.

[33] See European Central Bank, *Purchase Programme for Covered Bonds*, press release of 4 June 2009, online at www.ecb.int

A common objective of the strategies of these three central banks was to do more than just cut their respective key interest rates, because they knew that the scope of such a measure is limited by the simple fact that nominal interest rates cannot become negative, as people would hoard cash instead of lending it out. A situation where the rates are close to zero is called a *liquidity trap*, as all the extra liquidity that the central bank might pump into the economy will end up being hoarded rather than spent on the purchase of real consumer or investment goods. During the crisis, the UK, the USA and the eurozone definitely found themselves in such a liquidity trap, with central bank interest rates being either zero or close to zero.

The credit crunch

The additional measures initiated by the central banks definitely have helped mitigate the crisis and keep the credit flow up to some extent. However, there are two major reasons why their effects were limited and ultimately unable to prevent a credit crunch.

First, the huge equity losses discussed in Chapter 8 forced the banks to scale down their operations. The provision of liquidity by the central banks did, of course, help the banks keep lending to the real sector. However, this measure could not prevent the current solvency crisis that is characterized by a lack of capital on bank balance sheets. When equity capital is lacking, banks simply cannot channel the cheap liquidity offered to them by the central bank to the real sector, because this would expand their balance sheets and hence violate the regulatory minimum equity requirements enforced by the supervisory agencies (see Chapter 7).

Second, and most importantly for the USA, central banks possess no tools with which to overcome the loss of trust in the securitization business. As shown in Chapters 4, 5, and 6, the combination of non-recourse mortgage loans, undercollateralized securities, wrong mathematical models for structuring CDOs, and incompetent rating agencies has destroyed the supply chain of funds that for many years had flowed from worldwide savers to US home-owners. The gigantic flow of private mortgage securitizations on which about half of the US system of housing finance was built has practically ground to a halt, and homeowners have been unable to extend or refinance their mortgage loans. As already mentioned, the flow of new issues of privately securitized mortgages (MBSs and CDOs) declined by 97 per cent in the period from 2006 to 2009, from $1.9 trillion to just $50 billion (Figure 6.4). Likewise, the market for subprime loans (Figure 6.1) disappeared completely, and millions of American households could not renew their existing loans, let alone receive new loans to purchase new houses. More and more existing houses were sold, prices plummeted, and sales of new houses fell to an all-time low (see Figures 2.9 and 5.2). Central banks are powerless when it comes to revitalizing the securitization process. To regain the lost confidence, better laws and regulations must be instituted that ensure more liability and prudence on the part of the banking system creating the securities. Perhaps a Europeanization of the American mortgage market with a change to covered mortgage bonds would be a possibility (see Chapter 11).

A credit crunch causes distress not only to homeowners and the construction industry but also to other firms in the real sector that need bank loans to finance their investment. The leverage effect of a low equity asset ratio that is responsible for today's high rates of return has large repercussions on the real sector. Firms that want to purchase new equipment to modernize or expand their production capacity rely on the banks passing the savings of the private households on to them. If the flow of loans comes to a halt, massive problems result. There is both a lack of productive capacity for future growth and a decline in the demand for capital goods. Producers of machinery, software, shipbuilding, and other branches of the capital goods industry all the way to the construction industry are affected.

In other countries the situation is less severe than in the USA, but there are also signs of credit constraints, predominantly because of the equity losses of banks and the resulting negative multiplier process via the bank balance sheets as described in Chapter 7. For example, when banks try to preserve an equity loan ratio of 4 per cent, each dollar of equity loss implies $25 of lending cuts.

Apart from the obvious collapse of the US mortgage market, there are other indicators of the extent of the credit crunch currently weighing down the Western economies. One is the so-called *financing gap* calculated by the IMF. The financing gap is the excess of ex-ante financing needs of the sovereign and private non-financial sector over the projected credit capacity of the financial sector. The IMF forecasts that in 2009 and 2010 the gap will be 15 per cent of nominal GDP in the UK, 3 per cent

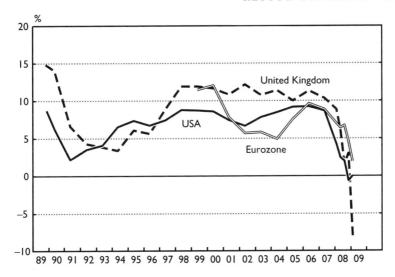

Fig. 9.2 Private-sector credit growth (4th quarter 1989–1st quarter 2009)

Note: Private sector borrowing as a percentage of debt outstanding, quarter-on-quarter annualized, seasonally adjusted; from 1990 to 2007 quarterly data were converted to annual averages.

Sources: International Monetary Fund, *Global Financial Stability Report* (October 2009), 25, data available online at http://www.imf.org/external/pubs/ft/gfsr/2009/02/index.htm; Ifo calculations.

in the eurozone, and 2.4 per cent in the USA.[34] The figure is surprisingly low for the USA. One reason could be that the equity injections pushed through by the US government, as described above, have worked and re-established the lending capacity of US banks. Another reason is probably that the rapid decline of residential construction during the housing crisis has reduced the demand for funds in line with the decline of lending capacity. This would be compatible with a latent credit constraint that will bite as soon as the economy begins to recover and investors demand more credit.

Whatever the truth may be, it is worth noting that US credit growth appeared to have stopped entirely during 2009. This is shown in Figure 9.2, which presents the ratio of private sector net borrowing as a percentage of the outstanding stock of debt. Whereas British credit growth is clearly the outlier with strongly negative numbers in 2009, even US and eurozone credit growth has sharply declined during the crisis.

---

[34] International Monetary Fund, *Global Financial Stability Report*, October 2009, p. 34.

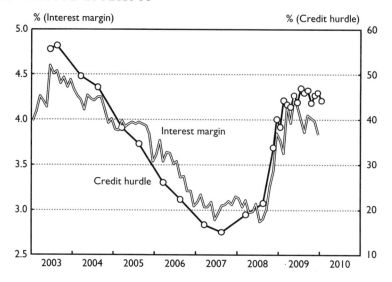

Fig. 9.3 Credit hurdle and overdraft interest margin (Germany, June 2003–January 2010)

Note: The credit hurdle is the share of firms in the Ifo Business Survey (manufacturing industry) that describe the banks' lending attitudes as 'restrictive'. The Ifo survey on lending has been conducted half-yearly since 2003 and monthly since November 2008. Normally 4,000 firms respond to the credit hurdle survey, choosing among 'restrictive', 'normal', and 'generous' as possible answers. The interest margin shown in this diagram is the difference between the banks' overdraft rate and the main refinancing rate of the ECB.

Sources: Ifo Institute; Deutsche Bundesbank, MFI Interest Rate Statistics, *Interest Rates and Volumes of German Banks (MFI's)*, New business, loans to non-financial corporations, accessed on 5 February 2010; Eurostat, Database, Economy and Finance, *Interest Rates, Central Bank Interest Rates*, accessed on 5 February 2010.

Further light is shed on the credit crunch by Figure 9.3, which depicts results of the Ifo Business Survey of German manufacturing firms. Every month the Ifo Institute asks about 7,000 firms whether they find the credit policy of their banks restrictive, normal, or favourable.[35] The solid curve shows the percentage of answers that indicate that the policy was restrictive, called the *credit hurdle*. It can be seen that the credit hurdle rose sharply during the crisis, much more than it came down during the last boom. As can be seen

---

[35] The survey was initiated by Frank Westermann, who had written his habilitation (postdoctoral) thesis on the implications of the Japanese credit crunch that broke out in the wake of the banking crisis of the 1990s: F. Westermann, *From Credit Boom to Credit Crunch: Facts and Explanation of the Japanese Boom-Bust Cycle* (Ludwig-Maximilians University of Munich, Economics Department, 2004). Cf. also A. Tornell and F. Westermann, *Boom-Bust Cycles and Financial Liberalization* (MIT Press, Cambridge, Mass., 2005), and R. Ranciere, A. Tornell, and F. Westermann, 'Systemic Crises and Growth', *Quarterly Journal of Economics*, 123 (2008), 359–406.

on the right-hand scale, about 45 per cent of firms indicated that the banks' lending behaviour is restrictive in the most recent survey at the time of writing. The percentage of big German corporations (not shown in the chart) indicating that banks were restrictive increased to 54 per cent in September 2009, an all-time high, and has since stayed above 50 per cent.

For comparison, on the left-hand scale we can see the German banks' interest margin for overdraft loans, defined as the difference between the overdraft rate and the main refinancing rate of the ECB. Obviously, the interest margin follows a similar path as the credit hurdle. Regardless of whether or not this is called a credit crunch, there is little doubt that the credit conditions of the real sector have worsened sharply during the crisis.

Interestingly enough, the German government and the Bundesbank keep denying the existence of a credit crunch in Germany.[36] They do this despite the information given above, despite the fact that credit growth in Germany has come to a standstill,[37] and despite the fact that in March 2009 the government found it necessary to introduce a programme to provide state loans and guarantees to German business worth 115 billion euros, in order to mitigate just this credit crunch whose very existence it is denying.[38]

Gaining weight

The rising interest margin is not only a phenomenon in Germany but in the entire Western world. This is illustrated in Figure 9.4, which presents banks' interest margins in the USA and in the eurozone. Here, the interest margin is defined as the difference between the interest rate at which banks lend short-term funds to private business (rather than the overdraft rate) and the short-term interest rate at which they can themselves borrow from their respective central banks. The graph covers the period up to the third quarter of 2009.

---

[36] See Deutsche Bundesbank, *Monthly Report* (September 2009), 17 f.

[37] See Deutsche Bundesbank, *Monthly Report* (October 2009), Statistical Annex, 24.

[38] The programme includes 15 billion euros exclusively allotted as credits to small and medium-sized businesses, 25 billion euros as credits to larger companies, and credit guarantees to domestic companies amounting to 75 billion euros. See German Ministry of Economics (BMWi), *Der Wirtschaftsfonds Deutschland*, online at www.bmwi.de, accessed on 15 October 2009.

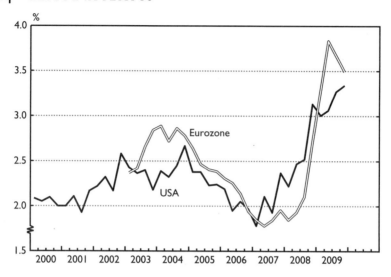

Fig. 9.4 Interest margins in the USA and in the eurozone

Notes: USA: Difference between commercial and industrial loan rates, all loans (average loan size: US $687,000, average maturity weighted by loan size: 500 days) and federal funds rate of the Federal Reserve System.

Eurozone: Difference between company loan rates (volume up to 1 million euros, fixed interest 1–5 years) and ECB main refinancing bid rate.

Source: Federal Reserve, Survey of Terms of Business Lending, *Commercial and Industrial Loan Rates Spreads over Intended Federal Funds Rate, by Loan Size*, online at www.federalreserve.gov, accessed on 5 February 2010, and Deutsche Bundesbank, *Time series database*, accessed on 5 February 2010. http://www.bundesbank.de/statistik/statistik_zeitreihen, Ifo calculations.

Obviously, interest margins rose sharply during the crisis and recently were significantly above 3 per cent, much higher than during the economic slump from 2001 to 2004, during which many companies had also complained about a credit crunch.

The huge interest margins which banks are enjoying during the crisis are a clear indication of a credit crunch, as they result in all likelihood from the reduction of credit supply due to the banks' equity losses and the balance sheet multiplier. As in all markets, the reduction of supply increases the market price, and in the present case this means an increase in the rate of interest at which banks are willing to lend out their funds to private business. As this happens while the central banks are expanding the money supply, the margin increases sharply. Normally, monetary easing increases the quantity of loans that banks offer in the market and hence reduces the lending interest rates. However, the destruction of bank equity makes such a reaction impossible, given the regulatory systems, leading to an adverse movement of the banks' lending and borrowing rates, thus increasing the margins. The equity losses effectively operate like a cartelization of commercial banks which would also result in a curtailing of supply and an increase in the difference between price and marginal cost in order to maximize profits.

This quasi-cartelization effect, resulting from the equity losses and the support provided by the central banks' interest rate cuts, implies a strong increase in the rates of return on equity that banks can earn during the crisis, given the losses written off on their toxic assets. This allows banks to gradually put on weight and to grow out of the mess the crisis has meant for them. Small wonder then that the big investment and commercial banks on both sides of the Atlantic have been reporting a surge of operating profits in the second and third quarters of 2009. Bygones are bygones. From now on, the best that can happen to the banking system is to just wait and see how the huge margins gradually fill up their stocks of equity.

The policies of the central banks to mitigate the solvency crisis of the banking system, by lowering their key interest rates and so helping the banks increase their interest margins, is a cumbersome and time-consuming method of recapitalizing the banks. It will take years before the banks will have grown out of their undercapitalization and will have put on enough fat to return to normal lending behaviour.

This method of recapitalizing the banks is also costly, as it implies that the interest income earned by the central banks and transferred to the government budget is lower than it could be at the same level of credit. Basically, it means that the taxpayers gradually recapitalize the banks over time without receiving bank shares in exchange. While there is nothing wrong with a policy of keeping interest rates low in a recession like this one, it is necessary to combine it with a strategy of recapitalizing banks with direct equity injections. The last chapter of this book will analyse such a strategy in detail.

The Keynesian recovery packages

In view of the limited power of monetary policy, Keynesian deficit policies to directly stimulate aggregate demand have also been used to combat the crisis. Basically, these are debt-financed recovery programmes, ranging from tax cuts to infrastructure projects. All of these programmes aim to support aggregate demand in order to stabilize the flow of company orders and employment. The measures were recommended by John Maynard Keynes in the 1930s to help overcome the Great Depression, following the recommendations of a number of academic predecessors.[39] They have since become a fixed component of economic theory and are the major policy tool to overcome the current crisis in all countries affected.

Economics knows a multitude of deficiencies or diseases of the economy, just as medicine knows a multitude of diseases of humans. And just like medicine, economics has different therapies for different illnesses, including among others the Keynesian therapy. While there is no real disagreement among economists over the usefulness of the Keynesian therapy under appropriate circumstances, there is disagreement over when it should be applied. Economic recovery programmes are like biting a nitroglycerine capsule to prevent a stroke. They can help to boost performance in the short term and to overcome a crisis, but in the long term they are rather damaging, as they result in higher public debt and distort economic incentives. One certainly does not need a Keynesian therapy if one already has high blood pressure. Keynesian recipes are also equally unable to help against chronic unemployment and a myriad of other economic diseases. However, they are appropriate to fight a crisis featuring deficient demand and an excessive preference for money hoarding, such as the current one.

In contrast to monetary policy, which works via interest rates and liquidity provision, the key idea of Keynesian policies is to offset recession-caused demand gaps using credit-financed government demand and income support measures. As private liquidity preference is nearly unlimited, aggregate demand cannot be stimulated by providing ever more liquidity, but only by absorbing the

---

[39] See J. M. Keynes, *The General Theory of Employment, Interest and Money* (Macmillan/ Cambridge University Press, Cambridge, 1936). Keynes had a number of important predecessors from whom he had adopted the theory of the multiplier as well as the basic policy recommendations. For an overview of the history of economic thought see: D. Laidler, *Fabricating the Keynesian Revolution* (Cambridge University Press, Cambridge, 1999). For important developments of Keynesian theory, reconciling this theory with neoclassical theory, see R. Barro and H. Grossman, 'A General Disequilibrium Model of Income and Employment', *American Economic Review*, 61 (1971), 82; E. Malinvaud, *The Theory of Unemployment Reconsidered* (Blackwell, Oxford, 1977); O. Blanchard, 'Is There a Core of Usable Macroeconomics?', *American Economic Review*, 87 (1997), 244; and G. A. Calvo, 'Staggered Prices in a Utility-Maximizing Framework', *Journal of Monetary Economics*, 12 (1983), 383.

existing liquidity by way of borrowing and spending the funds on real goods and services. The government can borrow to purchase goods in the private sector, to cut taxes, or to make such transfer payments to the citizens as pensions, student aid, or welfare. The important element is that it chooses debt financing, for if it were to finance its expenditures by tax increases, consumption cutbacks would reduce the expansionary effect or even eliminate it entirely.[40]

The surest policy is a debt-financed direct increase of purchases from the private sector, for example for infrastructure projects. In this case the private suppliers to the government will experience a direct increase in demand. This increase in demand will cause more economic activity in the construction sector, leading to more income and employment there that is likely to generate second-round or multiplier effects on private consumption. Tax cuts and increases in transfer payments are somewhat less effective in comparison, as they only cause second-round effects. However, tax cuts and increases in transfer payments have the advantage of spreading the demand widely, leaving the spending decisions to the private households and avoiding local overheating. They are like a warm blanket, while infrastructure projects are more like a hot-water bottle placed on the belly.

It is, however, debatable whether there will be any notable second-round effects. If the people fear that they will have to service the additional public debt in the future, they may save for this purpose from the start and consume correspondingly less. Only if they fail to see the connection, or if the government announces credibly that it will offset the additional public debt at a later date by cutting its own consumption, may second-round effects be expected.

In contrast to the labour unions' claim, frequently heard in Europe, the Keynesian medicine does not include wage increases. Wage increases are not an effective means to increase demand for the reason that they depress the returns to many investment projects below the profitability threshold and

---

[40] Because of the so-called Haavelmo Effect, demand could even be boosted if purchases in the business sector were financed via tax increases. This is so because government purchases are direct demand and they raise disposable income in the industries in which the government buys in the same measure as the disposable income of the taxpayers declines. Although there is no multiplier effect via a revival of consumption, the primary effect of the higher government purchases in the business sector remains. See T. Haavelmo, 'Multiplier Effects of a Balanced Budget', *Econometrica*, 13 (1945), 311–18.

thereby reduce the demand for capital goods. This has immediate unfavour-able consequences for the intake of orders in the capital goods industries, including the construction sector, and also has a negative effect on the demand for consumer goods as jobs are destroyed and with them the sources of wage income. Keynes himself never recommended wage increases to stimulate economic activity and probably would consider them a parody of his theory.

Figure 9.5 provides an overview of the magnitudes of the Keynesian recovery programmes introduced in various parts of the world since the outbreak of the crisis in 2008.

According to the IMF, the economic recovery programmes of the G-20 countries totalled $1,443 billion in the years 2009 and 2010 together, corre-sponding to about 2.6 per cent of the world's 2007 gross domestic product ($55 trillion).[41] In 2009, measures amounting to 1.5 per cent of the world's gross domestic product have been put into effect.

The most important programme, according to IMF calculations, is the American recovery programme, at $525 billion, $276 billion of which (193 billion euros) were to be spent in 2009.[42] At 2 per cent of US gross domestic product ($13,808 billion in 2007), the programme is one of the biggest in the world. The four largest EU countries combined only arrive at 1.1 per cent of their gross domestic product ($10,836 billion in 2007), with a programme volume of 83 billion euros ($118 billion) in 2009.[43]

At first glance, these figures might suggest that Europe is not fighting the crisis as energetically as the USA and is restricting itself to the role of free rider on the American recovery policy. This impression is wrong, however, as the

[41] The G-20 comprises: Argentina, Australia, Brazil, The People's Republic of China, Germany, France, Great Britain, India, Indonesia, Italy, Japan, Canada, Mexico, Russia, Saudi-Arabia, South Africa, South Korea, the United States, Turkey, and the European Union. Individual (or summary) data for the European Union are not contained in the IMF compilation.

[42] According to American data, the volume of the recovery programme in the period 2009 to 2019 amounts to $787 billion; for 2009 a total of $185 billion was noted. See Congressional Budget Office, *Estimated Macroeconomic Impacts of the American Recovery and Reinvestment Act of 2009*, online at www.cbo.gov, accessed on 16 March 2009.

[43] According to plans of the EU Commission, the amount is to consist of additional budget funds of the member states amounting to 170 billion euros and EU funds amounting to 30 billion euros. See Commission of the European Communities, *Communication from the*

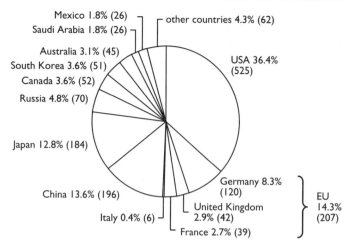

Fig. 9.5 Keynesian recovery programmes of the G-20 countries 2009–2010 ($1,443 billion)

Note: In parentheses: absolute amounts in billions of dollars.

Sources: International Monetary Fund, *Group of Twenty: Global Economic Prospects and Effectiveness of Policy Response*, online at www.imf.org, accessed on 19 October 2009; Ifo Institute.

social policies of the European countries with their unemployment compensation schemes and their diverse social protection systems generate an additional budget deficit and hence a substantial automatic expansionary force for the world economy. According to estimates of the EU Commission, this effect amounted to more than 1.5 per cent of gross domestic product in 2009,[44] implying a total expansionary effect of about 2.5 per cent in that year. Nonetheless, the size of the American programme is impressive for a country that is usually more sceptical about government intervention.

One should not harbour any illusions about the nature of the American programme, however. As explained in Chapters 2 and 5, America has lived beyond its means for years. American households got deeper and deeper into debt via housing loans and enjoyed a standard of consumption that they could not have afforded on their own. That brought about a temporary economic boom that has now collapsed. Figuratively speaking, America

Commission to the European Council: A European Economic Recovery Plan, 6. In addition to the countries listed here, Spain in particular is contemplating an extensive package that, according to EU data, amounted to about 12 billion euros in 2009. See European Commission, *Interim Forecast* (January 2009), 25.

[44] European Commission, *Interim Forecast*, 14.

smoked opium and now is suffering from withdrawal symptoms. To solve the problem, the American government is now providing a new supply of opium by indebting itself on behalf of its uncreditworthy citizens. That makes sense because you cannot subject an addict to a cold-turkey withdrawal. But ultimately there is no way around a withdrawal therapy. Opium cannot be supplied forever if the patient is to recuperate.

Why governments should not bail out GM and Opel

Some want governments to do even more, by saving individual firms that have run into trouble. With the same justification that is used for saving the banks, they should also save General Motors and other big companies, so the thinking goes.

Unfortunately, this wish cannot be endorsed by economists. A bank rescue cannot be avoided. Not a single big bank can be left to perish without sending a shock wave through the world financial system. The Lehman Brothers bankruptcy in the autumn of 2008 is the cautionary example. In 2007 Lehman had total assets worth $691 billion (468 billion euros) and thus was only a little bigger than, for example, Germany's Hypo Real Estate (HRE), which had assets of $589 billion (400 billion euros).[45] Had HRE not been nationalized, the European mortgage bond market would have broken down, with catastrophic implications for the European housing market and construction industry. In addition, hopes for confidence in the ability of banks to survive and in the recovery of interbank transactions would have been buried, with dire consequences for the standard of living of millions of Europeans. No other industry except perhaps agriculture and food processing comes near the importance of the banking sector. The monetary system is of crucial significance for the settlement of economic transactions and thus for the economy's entire exchange system, including the labour market.

By contrast, rescue actions targeted at individual firms in the real sector no longer conform to the Keynesian policy recipe and are to be strictly rejected from an economic point of view. The government cannot and should not manage businesses. If a government rescues individual firms

---

[45] Calculated at the exchange rate on the day of the balance sheet.

like General Motors or its German subsidiary Opel, it distorts the market and reduces the overall welfare of its citizens. The best sermons about the company's productivity and efficiency, that it does not deserve to perish and so forth, do not help. If GM really had been an efficient company it would have profited enough from the economic recovery programmes to survive. However, it filed for bankruptcy protection under chapter 11 on 1 June 2009 and offered Opel for sale. There is nothing in this process that would have called for further government action. If GM and Opel had been building economically sound cars, they would have found investors to take over the companies without any government help. In fact, however, the US government has invested a total of $50.7 billion in GM via the Automotive Industry Financing Program (AIFP) and now owns a 60.8 per cent stake in the new company.[46] The German government, in turn, supported Opel by offering a credit of 1.5 billion euros ($2.1 billion; Opel took 1.1 billion euros) and contemplated offering a further 3 billion euros if Spain, the UK, and Poland participated in support of the Opel subsidiaries located there. In the meantime, GM withdrew its offer to sell Opel, hoping that it would be able to use the government subsidies itself.

The bankruptcy, which GM filed under chapter 11 of the US Bankruptcy Code, effectively converted the debt of GM into equity and allowed the debtors to take over the company as so-called debtors in possession. The debtors in possession often successfully revitalize companies, because they can procure financing and loans at favourable terms by giving new lenders first priority on business earnings. United Airlines and Delta Airlines were also rescued in recent years by making use of chapter 11. German insolvency law, too, would have provided good opportunities for a new start for Opel, as it basically provides the same sort of flexibility. The insolvency laws of most countries are not designed for the destruction of firms, but—on the contrary—to enable them to make a fresh start that offers the workforce the best chance of retaining their jobs.

---

[46] See General Motors, *The New General Motors Company Launches Today*, press release of 10 July 2009.

Of course, continued operations of a firm are not always possible. In that case, plant and equipment are sold separately and assigned to new uses. This is good, as the firm's property, capital, and labour are scarce factors of production that ought to be put to the best possible uses. Only the best technological processes, for which the sales proceeds exceed the costs to the firm, are realized in a market economy. Everything else remains in the archives of the engineers as blueprints or goes to museums as prototypes. A lot of what has been tried for several years and made temporary sense will subsequently be excluded again from the production process. It is this very selection function that explains the superiority of the market economy over alternative economic systems. It explains why the market economy has been able to beat Communism with respect to growth in standard of living.

This does not mean that the market can solve all problems. The state is needed for curtailing such external effects as environmental pollution, for public infrastructure projects, for setting the rules of the market game, and for many other tasks. But these are not the tasks that GM, Opel, and so many other needy firms demand. These firms produce normal marketable goods and therefore do not need the help of the state.

In order to properly evaluate the rescue policy, one must realize that the resources GM and Opel receive from the state must be withdrawn from other uses. After all, the state cannot rely on a *deus ex machina* to finance its recovery programme. Whatever funds the government makes available after weighing all the pros and cons: the money that (temporarily) saves jobs at GM or Opel is lost to other branches of industry and leads to job losses there.

The 4.5 billion euros contemplated as aid for Opel correspond to an average of 180,000 euros for each of its 25,000 employees, to 142 per cent of the capital invested per person in the German manufacturing industry, or to the price of an apartment of at least 100 square metres in the towns where Opel cars are produced.[47] This same sum is likely to have saved many more jobs in other parts of the economy.

---

[47] In September 2009 the average price of a 100-square-metre apartment in Rüsselsheim (the biggest Opel location) was about 171,000 euros, in Bochum (the second biggest location) it was about 147,000 euros, in Kaiserslautern 118,000 euros, and in Eisenach 88,000 euros. www/immowelt.de, 20 October 2009.

The decision regarding the financial scope of the recovery programme is up to the government, but the government does not have the capacity to take the decisions on how to allocate the funds in detail. Neither can politics usefully process the quantity of information that is necessary for appropriate structural decisions, nor have politicians the necessary incentives to decide efficiently. It is not those who produce the best goods who are rescued in a state-run economy but those who scream the loudest, are the biggest, and the best organized politically. Among automotive suppliers, about as many jobs have been lost in the past year or so as were to be saved at Opel. But such firms were too small and too unknown to attract the attention of the media and politicians. They had to close down, although their jobs might have been saved with less money than the Opel jobs.

All of this concerns the basic question of whether the state ought to slow down the structural change in the economy. There is nothing static in business. Firms and branches of industry must reinvent themselves again and again and prevail in competition. Firms come and go, and even entire industries shrink while new ones come into being. Structural change is the secret of progress, and—of course—it does not take place during booms, but during recessions. Ailing structures, which may just about survive in good times, break down in a crisis. Weaker firms disappear and make room for new ones that establish themselves in the next recovery phase. If there had been no structural change in Europe or the USA, the vast majority of the population would still be employed in agriculture, as in the middle of the nineteenth century, rather than the 6.2 per cent in the European Union and 1.4 per cent in the USA in 2007, and all of us would be as poor as church mice. Structural change is accompanied by great pain for those affected, but in the European welfare states nobody falls through the cracks. One of the strengths of the social market economy is the very fact that those who are affected by structural change can rely on the protection provided by public unemployment insurance and are not left unsupported if unemployment should last longer. The existence of the welfare state is one reason why politics ought to stay out of the entrepreneurial decisions at GM, Opel, and similar companies.

Scrapping the scrap premium

The same is true of the scrap premiums that a number of governments, including those of the USA, Austria, France, Italy, Portugal, Romania, Spain, and Cyprus, passed during the crisis, following the German example. While the USA reserved $3.5 billion for its *Cash for Clunkers* programme, Germany spent as much as $7.1 billion (5 billion euros). Those who scrapped an old-enough car and replaced it with a new one with hopefully lower energy consumption received a cash premium from the government. In the USA, for example, the premium amounted to between $3,500 and $4,500, in France $1,430 (1,000 euros), and in Germany $3,570 (2,500 euros). Politicians from all these countries celebrated the scrap premiums as a great success.

And a great success it was for the producers of small cars.[48] According to the German Federal Automotive Office, new Fiat Panda registrations rose by 202 per cent in February 2009 year on year and those for Toyota's Aygo by 196 per cent. The highest growth rate, at 359 per cent, was recorded by the VW Polo or Fox, which leads in terms of the absolute number of new registrations. The Ford Fiesta, at an increase of 295 per cent, and the Skoda Fabia, at 169 per cent, also benefited.

Even if the programme seemed to work, it could hardly be called a success. For one, specific support measures always look like more than they are because people tend to cut their expenditures on other things. The money now spent at the car dealership will no longer be there for a new washing machine or refrigerator. Even though econometric analyses are still lacking, one can assume that the net effect on aggregate demand will only be a fraction of the sum spent on the new cars. So, in effect, the automobile industry is propped up at the expense of the rest of the economy. No wonder that the refrigerator producers are demanding a scrap premium for refrigerators.[49]

Furthermore, from an economic perspective it is perverse to subsidize the destruction of economic goods. Casino capitalism is being combated by throw-away capitalism. What a weird economic logic! The scrap premium

[48] See Kraftfahrt-Bundesamt, *Monatliche Neuzulassungen*, Neuzulassungen von Personenkraftwagen im Februar 2009 nach Segmenten und Modellreihen, online at www.kba.de
[49] See 'Abwrackprämie für Kühlschränke', *Süddeutsche Zeitung* (7 March 2009), 23.

mocks the human endeavour for affluence and the ecological goal of sustainable economic activity. It makes the taxpayer poorer and damages the environment.

Keynes, with his British humour, tried to explain his theory to his readers by way of an example. Assume that the state puts banknotes in bottles, buries them in a mine, fills up the mine with garbage and then lets private businesses dig the bottles up. This would get the economy going again, unemployment would fall and real income would rise, he quipped. How amused he would have been if he had known that so many governments would actually take his plan seriously. Giving people up to $4,500 for destroying a still-serviceable old car so that they can buy a new one is, as far as the economic core of the action is concerned, just like burying the Keynesian bottles and digging them up again.[50]

Nine- or ten-year-old cars are far from being clunkers. An accident-free BMW or Lexus can stay on the road for twenty years, and a VW Rabbit can easily run for fifteen years. The engines of premium cars run for 300,000 kilometres and more. With a yearly average of 20,000 kilometres, a nine-year-old car clocks in at only 180,000 kilometres. Furthermore, since the 1980s the steel used for the chassis has been galvanized, so that rust is no longer a problem. Some car-makers even give a thirty-year guarantee against corrosion. Scrapping nine-year-old cars, therefore, makes no economic sense whatsoever.

Western countries used to sell their used cars on a large scale to countries in Africa, Eastern Europe, and Central Asia, which teem with second-hand Western vehicles. In 2008, Germany alone exported 423,000 used cars, earning 5.6 billion euros.[51] In 2009, the German government paid 5 billion euros for rerouting some of these exports to the scrap heap.

Some people believe scrapping old cars is good for the environment. For example, a leading German newspaper (*Süddeutsche Zeitung*) cited on its title page experts who asserted that the scrap premium serves environmental protection because it promotes the replacement of old gas guzzlers by modern, fuel-efficient cars. This, the article maintained, would even be

---

[50] J. M. Keynes, *The General Theory of Employment, Interest and Money* (Macmillan, London, 1936), chapter 10, The Marginal Propensity to Consume and the Multiplier, part VI, here cited after the 2006 reprint, p. 116.

[51] See Federal Statistical Office, *Außenhandel* (GENESIS-Online, Wiesbaden, 2009).

the case if we take into account that the production of a new VW Rabbit costs 25,000 kWh of energy and a premium car 50,000 kWh.[52]

Let's look at this more closely. A new gasoline-powered VW Rabbit (Golf IV) with a 1.4-litre engine consumes 6.4 litres of gasoline every 100 km (a mileage of 37.8 miles per gallon). Assuming it travels 12,000 kilometres annually, it will burn 768 litres per year and emit 1,790 kg of CO_2 through the exhaust pipe.[53] Given that, as the newspaper says, 25,000 kWh of energy are consumed to produce the car, then with a plausible split of this energy between electricity and fuel (50 per cent from the typical German electricity generation mix at 40 per cent efficiency, and 50 per cent from fuels produced at a 5 per cent efficiency loss) the likely CO_2 emissions for producing this car are 10,790 kg, which translates into 1,199 kg per year if the new car also runs for nine years. Thus, the production-related emissions add 67 per cent to the CO_2 that the new engine emits on the road.[54] If we replace an old car with a new Rabbit, the environment will benefit only if the old car's fuel burn was more than 67 per cent higher than that of the new Rabbit.[55] This could be the case if the new Rabbit replaces a gas-guzzling big car. However, if the new car replaces one with a similar-sized engine, this saving cannot be attained, because a fuel-burn improvement of this magnitude has simply not been achieved yet. Ten years ago, the 1.4-litre Rabbit, the most popular model, consumed the same 6.4 litres of gasoline every 100 km as a brand-new Rabbit

[52] 'Grüne Schrottpresse', *Süddeutsche Zeitung* (16 January 2009), 1.

[53] These annual CO_2 emissions are derived from burning 768 litres of gasoline multiplied by 2.33 kg of CO_2 per litre of gasoline (2.33 kg of CO_2 are emitted by burning one litre of gasoline).

[54] The CO_2 emission for the production of a Rabbit (Golf VI) is calculated as follows: given a factor of 0.6 kg CO_2/kWh energy, which represents the average efficiency and the fuel mix for energy generation, the 12,500-kWh electricity input yields 7,500 kg of CO_2 emissions; analogously, given an average factor of 0.2632 kg/CO_2/kWh fuel from the 12,500-kWh fuel input yields 3,290 kg of CO_2. Added together, the production of one car thus generates 10,790 kg of CO_2.

[55] Under environmental considerations it would make sense to drive all cars very much longer, as the longer the replacement cycles are, the lower the CO_2 emissions generated by the production of the replacement vehicles will be. Allocating this emission to the individual years of service life of the new car is the key to finding the optimal time of replacement. This is the point in time when the production-caused emission per year of the new car plus its emissions on the road equals the direct annual emissions of the old car on the road (excluding the emissions generated during its production).

with the same engine size does now. The efficiency gains of the new engine are used to propel a heavier car instead of bringing down fuel burn. For this reason, replacing an old Rabbit with a new one entails an increase of around two-thirds in annual CO_2 emissions, despite the new Rabbit's more efficient engine.

We can consider any number of other factors in these calculations and the result will still be the same. Even with 20,000 kilometres travelled annually and a fifteen-year service life for the new car, the critical percentage for the higher gasoline consumption of the old car vis-à-vis the new Rabbit is still 24 per cent. For vehicles of the same engine size this percentage will just not be reached. The calculation is even clearer for large, luxury cars. Here replacing an old car with a new one makes even less sense, because the energy consumed producing the luxury car relative to the fuel savings on the road is even higher than for small vehicles. Whichever way you look at it: in all plausible scenarios CO_2 emissions rise if an old car is scrapped and replaced with a similar-sized new one. If we are serious about protecting the environment and rescuing our economy, we should scrap the scrappage schemes instead of our old cars.

CHAPTER 10

Will the West Retain its Stability?

The new top debtors

The gigantic bank rescue and economic recovery packages described in the previous chapter have been nearly exclusively financed by debt thus far. In addition, the built-in flexibility of the public tax and expenditure systems has led to growing public deficits in the recession as more unemployment benefits were paid out and taxes fell together with taxable incomes. Now that the crisis of the private economy has been overcome, a crisis of the public sector is looming. Handling the growing public debt will be the major challenge countries will have to meet.

Figure 10.1 shows the indebtedness of OECD and EU countries. The left part of the diagram shows that Japan is alone at the top of the list with an estimated debt-to-GDP ratio of 189 per cent in 2009. It is followed at some distance by Iceland (118 per cent), Italy (115 per cent), Greece (113 per cent), and Belgium (97 per cent). Austria, France, Germany, Portugal, and the UK are among the countries that somewhat exceed the 60-per-cent Maastricht limit.

The debt-to-GDP ratios rapidly increased during the crisis for almost all countries, as real output of most countries shrank and, as the right-hand part of Figure 10.1 shows, substantial budget deficits resulted. According to the figure, thirty-two of the thirty-six countries listed are expected to exceed the 3 per cent ceiling in 2010, among them twenty-six EU countries. This ceiling is the maximum allowed for the euro countries by the 1996 Stability and Growth Pact and is one of the admission criteria for joining the euro,

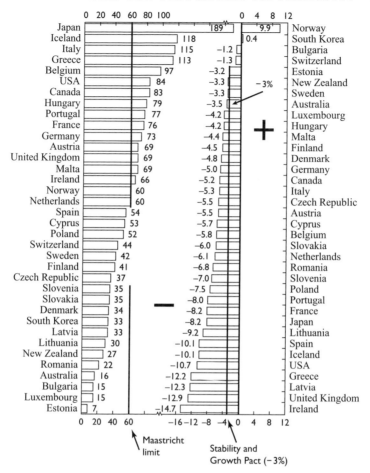

Fig. 10.1 Public debt 2009 and expected public deficits 2010 relative to GDP for the OECD and EU countries (%)

Sources: EU countries: European Commission, *Economic Forecast* (Autumn 2009), Statistical Annex, table 37 and table 42, other countries: *OECD Economic Outlook Volume 2009/2*, 86 (November 2009), appendix, table 27 and table 32.

according to the Maastricht Treaty. The EU is obliged to formally open deficit procedures against euro area countries that continue to breach the 3 per cent rule when economic growth recovers. Although it is unlikely that the sinners will mutually punish one another, the large number of countries in breach of the pact shows how unusual and worrisome the situation is.

Extreme situations are being faced by Ireland, the UK, and Latvia, where deficits of 14.7 per cent, 12.9 per cent, and 12.3 per cent, respectively, are expected. Among these countries only Latvia can afford the deficit, as total debt is still far below the 60 per cent ceiling, whereas the debt-to-GDP ratio of Ireland and the UK surpassed this ceiling by the end of 2009. The British have always been against accession to the euro area, as they hoped that the pound would be the stronger currency in the long run. These hopes have been buried for the time being: from August 2007 to December 2009 the exchange rate of the pound plunged from 1.48 euros to 1.11 euros, that is, by 25 per cent. And in view of the EU Commission forecast, in 2010 the UK would not even be allowed to join the euro area because it would violate both ceilings.

Especially worrisome is the situation in the USA. A few years ago, the USA boasted a debt ratio of around 50 per cent. Because of the financial and economic crisis, this ratio has now spiralled to a level of nearly 84 per cent, which is high in an international comparison. In coming years the ratio will continue to rise sharply, as the extensive rescue operations of the US government will make for huge budget deficits. The OECD expects a US budget deficit for 2010 of 10.7 per cent of GDP, more than three times the percentage allowed for the European countries by the Stability and Growth Pact. With a growth rate of 2 per cent or so in 2010, this means that the American debt-to-GDP ratio will reach a level of more than 92 per cent by the end of 2010. In all likelihood, therefore, the US debt-to-GDP ratio will surpass the 100 per cent level in 2011 or early 2012.[1]

These frightening figures for the once so proud leading world power explicitly confirm once again the assessment of Chapters 2 and 5 that the USA is living beyond its means. First, its citizens went into debt way above their heads with mortgage loans, then they were refused new loans, and now the government is piling on debt in their stead, hopefully not to the point at which it, too, becomes overly indebted. Although American debt policy is not 'the road to hell', as Mirek Topolanek, the former EU Council President

---

[1] See OECD, *Economic Outlook Volume 2009/2*, 86 (November 2009), Annex, table 32. US internal statistics sometimes point out lower debt-to-GDP numbers for the USA, because government debt is netted out with government claims against the private sector. However, the OECD statistics uniformly apply to gross rather than net debt figures for all countries, given that there is a continuum of ways to net out liabilities with assets and that government assets are often endowed with artificially low interest rates and limited repayment probabilities, which makes them incomparable to assets that have to be serviced at the market rate of interest. Moreover, the 60% rule of the Maastricht Treaty refers to gross rather than net government debt. Focusing on net debt would make the US debt figures non-comparable with European figures.

and Czech Prime Minister, said in a speech to the EU parliament, it is dangerous all the same.[2]

Europe at risk

One must worry about some countries not only because of their public debt level as such but in particular because they might face acute insolvency problems as a result of the crisis. That this is a serious risk is confirmed by the fact that the G-20 countries decided at their London Summit in April 2009 to raise the equity capital of the International Monetary Fund (IMF) by $250 billion and its credit lines by $500 billion.[3] The funds are to serve, among other things, troubled countries with assistance loans.

As already stated in Chapter 3, *Iceland* was virtually insolvent in the autumn of 2008, when it was unable to pay off a 750-million-euro bond of the troubled and already nationalized Glitnir Bank. It could only be saved from national bankruptcy by loans from the International Monetary Fund. In 2009 its GDP shrank by 8.5 per cent, and its current account deficit declined to more than 5 per cent relative to GDP.[4]

Ireland was also hard hit. As in the United States, the housing bubble burst there, too, and as was shown in Chapter 2, its house prices had still not stopped declining at the time of this writing in January 2010 (see Figure 2.10). In addition, the country is closely intertwined with the United States and was severely affected by the crisis. Ireland depends in large measure on foreign capital that it was able to attract by an extraordinarily loose regulation of its financial sector. The Hypo Real Estate Bank and Sachsen LB, Germany's first victims in the crisis (see Chapter 3), had also expanded in Ireland with special purpose entities. Irish banks were very active players in the trade with securitized mortgages. The total of outstanding loans, derivatives,

---

[2] See *The Washington Post*, 'E.U. President Blasts U.S. Spending', 25 March 2009, online at www.washingtonpost.com, accessed on 28 October 2009, and *The Guardian*, 'Obama's Rescue Plan is "Road to Hell", Claims EU President', 25 March 2009, online at www.guardian.co.uk, accessed on 28 October 2009.

[3] *Declaration on Delivering Resources through the International Financial Institutions: London, 2 April 2009*, online at www.g20.org, accessed on 13 April 2009.

[4] See International Monetary Fund, *World Economic Outlook Database*, October 2009, accessed on 23 October 2009.

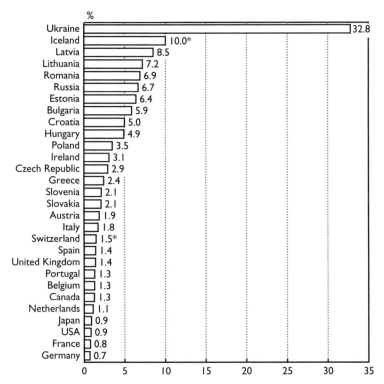

Fig. 10.2 Premiums for ten-year government bonds for insurance against country risks (credit default swaps) as a percentage of the credit volume at the peak of the crisis (February 2009)

Note: *Five-year duration.

Source: Bloomberg.

and mortgages of Irish banks, at a volume of $840 billion (656 billion euros) in January 2009, was four times the country's GDP (164 billion euros in 2009).[5] As mentioned in Chapter 9, the country's bank rescue package alone, at 385 billion euros, is more than twice the size of its GDP and therefore completely non-credible. As a consequence, credit default swaps for ten-year Irish bonds rose above 3 per cent during the crisis. If an investor wanted to insure Irish government bonds worth one million euros against default, he would have to pay a premium of 31,000 euros per annum. Figure 10.2 shows the insurance premiums as a percentage of the insured loans for some problem

---

[5] See Central Bank of Ireland, *Monthly Statistics, January 2009*, online at www.centralbank.ie, accessed on 15 March 2009.

countries compared to others that are considered quite stable. In 2009, Ireland's GDP shrank by about 7.5 per cent.[6]

The crisis posed a particularly severe threat to the stability of Eastern Europe, with possible repercussions for those western countries exposed to financial claims against that part of the world.

Hungary faced substantial payment difficulties that could only be overcome with loans from the European Central Bank, the IMF, the World Bank, and the EU, totalling 30 billion euros. Responsible for the progressive drying up of the market for Hungarian government bonds were the high deficits in the current account and government budget, which amounted respectively to 6.8 per cent and 5.0 per cent of GDP in 2007.[7] From February 2008 to February 2009 the Hungarian forint lost about 12 per cent of its value against the euro and 19 per cent against the Swiss franc. It is true of course that depreciation may be useful for a country in economic difficulties, as it makes the country more competitive: as exports become cheaper abroad and imports more expensive at home, the demand for the products of domestic firms rises, boosting the economy. However, the devaluing country will have a problem if it has incurred debt in foreign currency. This was the case for Hungary, where no less than 31 per cent of all loans and almost 60 per cent of all household loans were denominated in Swiss francs.[8] Devaluation then made these debts rise in forint terms, rendering debt service in many cases unbearable, and burdening the balance sheets of many Hungarian firms. This contributed substantially to the fact that in 2008 more than 11,300 firms were pushed into insolvency, 16 per cent more than in the preceding year.[9] In 2009, Hungary's GDP shrank by an estimated 6.5 per cent.[10]

Hungary's problems are reminiscent of the Asian crisis in the second half of the 1990s. At the time, the banks of many Asian countries, especially of Thailand, Indonesia, South Korea, Malaysia, the Philippines, and Singapore,

---

[6] See International Monetary Fund, *World Economic Outlook Database*.

[7] See Eurostat, Statistics Database, *Economy and Finance*, online at http://epp.eurostat.ec. europa.eu, accessed on 16 November 2009.

[8] 'Der Schweiz droht der Bankrott', Interview with C. Habicht, *Tagesanzeiger*, 17 February 2009, www.tagesanzeiger.ch, accessed on 8 March 2009.

[9] Creditreform, *Insolvenzen in Europa 2008/09*, February 2009, online at www. creditreform.de, accessed on 13 March 2009.

[10] See European Commission, *Economic Forecast* (Autumn 2009), Statistical Annex, table 1.

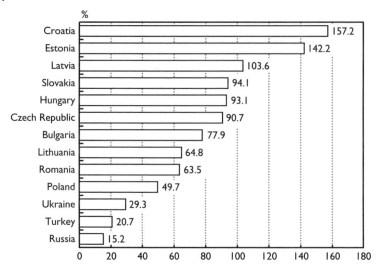

Fig. 10.3 Foreign bank debt of Eastern European countries as percentage of GDP (2007)

Source: A. Maechler and L. Ong, 'Foreign Banks in the CESE Countries: In for a Penny, in for a Pound?', *IMF Working Papers*, 54 (2009).

had taken out dollar loans abroad at favourable interest rates in order to relend them at home in domestic currency at high interest rates. When the dollar, after years of weakness, appreciated from 1995 on, the value of foreign debts recorded in the balance sheets rose. This pushed a great many Asian banks into insolvency. The consequence was a severe economic recession in 1998 that was only gradually overcome. South Korea, Indonesia, and Thailand received assistance totalling $39 billion, made available by the International Monetary Fund.[11]

Other Eastern European EU countries have also been suffering from similar problems, as most of them are highly indebted abroad, as shown in Figure 10.3. Since a part of these debts is denominated in foreign currencies, the same negative mechanisms kick in as in Asia then and in Hungary today.

For example, due to markedly lower interest rates, in *Poland* about 80 per cent of mortgage loans were also denominated in Swiss francs.[12] Because the zloty fell by 23 per cent against the euro from February 2008 to February

[11] See International Monetary Fund, *Recovery from the Asian Crisis and the Role of the IMF*, June 2000, online at www.imf.org, accessed on 22 March 2009.

[12] See B. Holland, L. Cochrane, and B. Penz, 'Panic Strikes East Europe's Borrowers as Banks Cut Franc Loans', October 2008, online at www.bloomberg.com, accessed on 13 March 2009.

2009, after relentless short sales by hedge funds had put it under pressure, droves of Polish homeowners also became excessively indebted. This was aggravated by the ebbing of remittances from the two million Poles who used to work abroad and returned home in large numbers during the crisis. About half of these worked in Great Britain, where the crisis was raging with special force. In 2007, the remittances were $4.4 billion or 1.0 per cent of Polish GDP, not a negligible amount.[13] However, Poland seems to be recovering quickly. With an estimated GDP growth of 1.2 per cent in 2009 it survived the crisis surprisingly well.[14]

The *Czech Republic* showed light and shadow during the crisis. Although the Czech koruna fell by 11 per cent against the euro from February 2008 to February 2009 and the country's foreign debt amounted to 90 per cent of GDP, the country did not suffer from a crisis like Hungary, because it had only taken out an insignificant amount of foreign-currency-denominated loans (4 per cent).[15] The reason may have been that the Czech Republic, in contrast to other Eastern European countries, protected its banking system against acquisition by foreigners following the collapse of Communism. The Czech labour market also was stable. The German old-car scrappage scheme in 2009 even allowed Skoda production to run at full steam, benefiting the extensive supplier industry located in the country. Nevertheless, however, Czech GDP probably declined by 4.8 per cent in 2009.[16]

Slovakia and *Slovenia* were also financially stable. They were protected against currency turbulences because they, in contrast to Poland, the Czech Republic, and Hungary, belong to the euro area. Consequently, at 2.1 per cent, the insurance premiums for their ten-year government bonds were the lowest, in February 2009, of all Eastern European countries. However, being closely linked to the shrinking German industry, Slovenian GDP shrank by an estimated 7.4 per cent in 2009, while Slovakian GDP shrank by 5.8 per cent.[17]

Croatia found itself in an extremely precarious situation, with a foreign debt of nearly 160 per cent of GDP, as shown in Figure 10.3. However,

---

[13] See World Bank, *World Development Indicators Online*, accessed on 26 October 2009.

[14] See European Commission, *Economic Forecast* (Autumn 2009), Statistical Annex, table 1.

[15] See 'Abwärtstrend in Russland gestoppt?', 3 March 2009, online at at.e-fundresearch. com/article.php?aID=12045, accessed on 28 October 2009.

[16] See European Commission, *Economic Forecast* (Autumn 2009), Statistical Annex, table 1.

[17] See ibid.

fortunately, the domestic currency remained stable during the crisis. From February 2008 to February 2009 the kuna lost only 2 per cent against the euro. Besides Turkey and Macedonia, Croatia is one of three countries officially accepted as candidates for EU membership. After Croatia and Slovenia agreed to a procedure for resolving their border dispute, the country entered the final stage of accession negotiations in 2009.[18] Croatia's GDP in 2009 shrank by an estimated 5.2 per cent.[19]

Romania, whose currency depreciated against the euro by 15 per cent from February 2008 to February 2009, was caught up in the turbulence. With a population of 21.5 million, the country is the second biggest of the Eastern European EU countries after Poland. In Romania, too, high foreign debt contributed to the problems. Its current account deficit, which measures net borrowing abroad, amounted to a huge 13.4 per cent of GDP in 2007.[20] Because of growing private indebtedness, the rating agencies Standard & Poor's and Fitch lowered the country's rating to 'non-investment' as early as October 2008. Hence, investors were being warned not to get involved there. Consequently, the insurance premiums for ten-year government bonds had risen to 6.9 per cent by February 2009, one of the highest levels overall. On 10 March, Romania asked for an assistance loan by the European Union and the International Monetary Fund.[21] On 25 March a consortium consisting of the International Monetary Fund, the European Union, the World Bank, and the European Bank for Reconstruction and Development agreed to grant immediate aid amounting to a total of 20 billion euros.[22] The Romanian economy probably shrank by 8.0 per cent in 2009.[23]

---

[18] See 'As the EU Grows: Who's Next? Croatia Could Wrap up Entry Talks with the EU Next Year', *European Commission, External Relations and Foreign Affairs*, 14 October 2009, online at http://ec.europa.eu, accessed on 22 October 2009.

[19] See International Monetary Fund, *World Economic Outlook* (October 2009).

[20] See Eurostat, Statistics Database, *Economy and Finance*.

[21] See R. Marinas and I. Wissenbach, 'Rumänien bittet EU und IWF um Finanzhilfe', *Reuters*, 10 March 2009, online at www.reuters.de, accessed on 13 March 2009.

[22] See International Monetary Fund, 'IMF Announces Staff-Level Agreement with Romania on €12.95 Billion Loan as Part of Coordinated Financial Support', 25 March 2009, online at www.imf.org, accessed on 26 March 2009.

[23] See European Commission, *Economic Forecast* (Autumn 2009), Statistical Annex, table 1.

Bulgaria, too, was hard hit by the financial crisis, but it was still classified as just investment-grade by the rating agencies. While the current account deficit, at a truly gigantic 25.2 per cent of GDP in 2007, was the highest of all EU countries, the Bulgarian government was able to report a tiny budget surplus.[24] The Bulgarian economy in 2009 also shrank, by about 5.9 per cent.[25]

The Baltic countries were affected early by the financial crisis due to their extensive linkages with foreign countries. At 22.3 per cent of GDP, the current account deficit of *Latvia* even exceeded that of *Lithuania* and *Estonia,* which reported deficits of 14.5 per cent and 17.8 per cent respectively.[26] As Figure 10.3 shows, Estonia had an extremely large foreign debt, at 142.2 per cent of GDP. In Latvia the recession, which started relatively early, gave rise to serious social and political tensions. On 13 January 2009 more than 10,000 people protested against the government in Riga, the Latvian capital, and on 20 February the government stepped down. Between 2000 and 2007 Latvian economic growth averaged 9 per cent per annum, more than that of any other EU country. In 2005 and 2006 house prices surged by 60 per cent each year,[27] and by the end of 2007 foreign debt had risen to 103.6 per cent of GDP, the second highest figure in the EU, after Estonia. Correspondingly dramatic was Latvia's collapse in the crisis. As early as 8 November 2008, the Latvian government had assumed a controlling interest in the Parex Bank, the country's second largest, at a symbolic price of three euros. A consortium consisting of the European Union, the International Monetary Fund, and a number of individual countries aided Latvia with a rescue package amounting to 7.5 billion euros. Paul Krugman has already called Latvia the 'new Argentina'.[28]

Because of their high foreign-currency debts, Lithuania and Estonia are exposed to similar payment difficulties. In Lithuania 84 per cent of all loans were denominated in euros. Thus the central banks of the countries intervened

---

[24] Eurostat, Statistics Database, *Economy and Finance*.

[25] See European Commission, *Economic Forecast* (Autumn 2009), Statistical Annex, table 1.

[26] Eurostat, Statistics Database, *Economy and Finance*.

[27] See International Monetary Fund, 'Republic of Latvia: Request for Stand-By Arrangement—Staff Report', *IMF Country Report*, January 2009, online at www.imf.org, accessed on 13 March 2009.

[28] See P. Krugman, 'European Crass Warfare', *New York Times*, 15 December 2008, online at www.nytimes.com, accessed on 13 March 2009.

to preserve the exchange rate, spending between 3.2 per cent (Lithuania) and 5 per cent (Estonia) of their foreign currency reserves by February 2009.[29] A depreciation of the national currencies would have pushed many firms into bankruptcy and mortgage debtors into insolvency.

In 2008 the three Baltic states had to cope with an insolvency wave twice as large as in the other Eastern European countries,[30] and all three economies are forecast by the European Commission to have shrunk at unprecedented rates in 2009: Estonia by 13.7 per cent, Latvia by 18 per cent, and Lithuania by even a bit more than 18 per cent.[31]

The problems of the non-EU countries of Eastern Europe that were once part of the Soviet Union were even more serious. *Ukraine*, for example, suffered most from the increased prices of gas from Russia and the collapse of demand for steel. The Ukrainian currency, the hryvnia, depreciated by 38 per cent against the euro between August 2008 and December 2009. In order to provide support, the International Monetary Fund extended a credit totalling $16.4 billion.[32] Still, the country was threatened by insolvency like no other. Risk premiums for ten-year government bonds, at 32.8 per cent, were by far the highest of all countries (see Figure 10.3). Country default insurance would thus cost one-third of the nominal value of a bond per year, which is astronomical. Accordingly, the rating agency Standard & Poor's assigned the country a CCC+ rating, the worst of all European countries, putting it on the same level as Pakistan. GDP shrank by an estimated 14 per cent in 2009.[33]

The economy of *Russia* was also impacted by the financial crisis. The Russian central bank used up a substantial part of its foreign currency reserves between October 2008 and March 2009 to prop up the rouble. As a consequence, its foreign currency reserves shrank from $600 billion to $384 billion. But the central bank still failed to prevent a depreciation of the rouble by 23 per cent during the same period. Although Russia's foreign

[29] See 'Währungen: Baltische Staaten beharren auf Eurobindung', *Die Presse*, 23 February 2009, online at www.diepresse.com, accessed on 13 March 2009.

[30] Lithuania had 115, Estonia 108, and Latvia 99 insolvencies per 10,000 firms in 2008. Creditreform, *Insolvenzen in Europa 2008/09*, February 2009, online at www.creditreform.de, accessed on 22 October 2009.

[31] See European Commission, *Economic Forecast* (Autumn 2009), Statistical Annex, table 1.

[32] See International Monetary Fund, 'IMF Approves US $16.4 Billion Stand-By Arrangement for Ukraine', 5 November 2008, online at www.imf.org, accessed on 26 March 2009.

[33] See International Monetary Fund, *World Economic Outlook*, October 2009.

debt was relatively modest by international comparison, at 6.7 per cent, the risk premium for its government bonds was relatively high, even higher than that of Estonia. Russia's GDP shrank by about 7.5 per cent in 2009, while its inflation rate was about 12 per cent.[34]

Just as serious are the problems of the Central Asian countries that formerly belonged to the Soviet Union. Destabilization and political unrest cannot be precluded, an analysis of which is beyond the scope of this book. The problems indeed transcend borders.

The payment problems of the Eastern European countries could affect *Austria*. Austrian banks extended a large volume of loans to Eastern Europe and they own many banks there. At about 230 billion euros, Eastern European countries accounted for almost half of the foreign investments of the Austrian banking sector in 2008.[35] This corresponds to a good 80 per cent of the country's GDP. If taxpayers had to underwrite the full amount of the loans, this would correspond to about 27,500 euros for each of the 8.35 million Austrians.

Figure 10.4 shows the unusually exposed position of Austria. No other country has so many credit claims against emerging countries relative to its GDP. The reason is historical. Austria has exploited its old connections in the areas of the former Austro-Hungarian Empire and has established a Western-type banking system there. Its banks, led by the Raiffeisen Central Bank Austria, Erste Bank, and Bank Austria, part of the UniCredit Group, acquired ownership of many East European banks and established an extensive network of branches.[36] The credit claims of these branches account for the lion's share of the amounts shown in Figure 10.4.

High credit claims reflect Austria's strength as a direct investor in Eastern Europe. But in times of crisis strength can turn into weakness. This happens when Eastern Europe encounters payment difficulties. At least this is how markets see it. As already shown in Figure 10.2, Austria had to pay a guarantee premium of 1.9 per cent in February 2009. This was more than Italy.

---

[34] International Monetary Fund, *World Economic Outlook*, October 2009.

[35] See Bundeskanzleramt, *Informationen aus Österreich, Bankenpaket: Finanzminister Pröll auf Osteuropa-Visite*, online at www.austria.gv.at, accessed on 10 March 2009.

[36] The three banks mentioned account for almost 90% of the total assets of the Austrian bank subsidiaries in Central and Eastern Europe. See Österreichische Nationalbank, *Die Bedeutung Zentral- und Osteuropas für Österreichs Banken*, online at www.oenb.at, accessed on 20 March 2009.

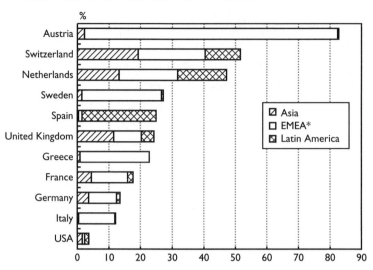

Fig. 10.4 Bank claims (September 2008) against emerging countries in percentage of GDP in 2007

Note: *EMEA: Europe, Middle East, and Africa.

Source: BIS Consolidated Banking Statistics and calculations of the Ifo Institute.

Nevertheless, the rating agencies have not touched Austria's excellent AAA rating, and rightly so. As shown in Chapter 8, Austria certainly has no prominent position on the Bloomberg list of crisis-caused write-offs. Above all, account must be taken of the fact that credit claims of subsidiaries of Austrian banks against East Europeans are offset by the deposit business with East Europeans, which has been highly profitable and will again be so after the crisis is over. In addition, all Austrian parent banks are protected against an avalanche of losses by liability limits, as their Eastern European subsidiaries are independent institutions for whose debt they will not be liable in case of bankruptcy. The Austrian banks may be politically liable, but they are not legally liable, and that can make a difference if push should come to shove. In 2009, Austria's GDP declined by 3.7 per cent, which was less than the average shrinkage rate of the euro countries (4.0 per cent).[37]

The situation in *Switzerland*, listed in second place in Figure 10.4, is still unclear. As mentioned, taking out loans denominated in Swiss francs used to be very attractive for the citizens of Eastern Europe because of their low interest rates. An analysis by the Swiss National Bank shows that at the end

[37] See European Commission, *Economic Forecast* (Autumn 2009), Statistical Annex, table 1.

of 2007 Swiss franc loans amounting to 75 billion francs circulated in Central and Eastern Europe, corresponding to nearly 15 per cent of Swiss GDP.[38] If the loans cannot be repaid, debtors and creditors alike will have problems. But these figures do not necessarily imply that the loans had actually been issued from Switzerland. In many cases the lenders were located in quite different countries and only denominated their credit contracts in Swiss francs. In these cases, insolvency of the debtors would lead to losses there and not in Switzerland. The issue should not be taken lightly, however, since Switzerland, as shown in Figure 8.2, has by far the highest write-offs of credit claims relative to its size, with the exception of the pure tax shelter, Bermuda. In Switzerland the American subprime crisis and the crisis of Eastern Europe came together, with the risk of becoming a tidal wave. While Swiss GDP shrank only slightly in 2009, at 2 per cent,[39] in February 2009 the country ranked worse than Spain or Portugal in terms of high premiums to hedge against country default (see Figure 10.2).[40] Who would have thought this of a country that for such a long time was the epitome of solidity and security in the world? Tempora mutantur—the times are changing.

Will Greece and Italy have to be bailed out?

Although the world economy emerged from recession in early summer 2009, investors became increasingly nervous about the creditworthiness of some western countries. In winter 2009/10, the fears focused on *Greece,* a remarkable development considering that Greece is one of the euro countries. The Greek current account deficit in 2008 was 13.8 per cent,[41] by far the highest of all euro countries, and, as shown in Figure 10.1, the country's debt-to-GDP ratio had reached 113 per cent by the end of 2009, from 99 per cent a year earlier, which made it the second highest of all euro countries except for Cyprus. For 2010 the budget deficit is forecast to be 12.2 per cent, way above the 3 per cent that the Stability and Growth Pact allows. Given that Greek

[38] 'Der Schweiz droht der Bankrott', *Berner Zeitung,* 17 March 2009, online at www.bernerzeitung.ch, accessed on 26 March 2009.

[39] See International Monetary Fund, *World Economic Outlook* (October 2009).

[40] See International Monetary Fund, *World Economic Outlook.*

[41] European Commission, *European Economic Forecasts* (Autumn 2009, Annex, table 49).

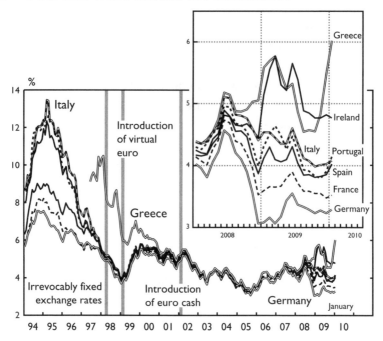

Fig. 10.5 Ten-year government bond rates (January 1994–January 2010)
Source: National central banks.

GDP is likely to shrink in 2010, this will increase the debt-to-GDP ratio to more than 125 per cent by the end of 2010 and earn Greece a dubious trophy in the eurozone.

In the light of these prospects, the euro came under pressure, and investors demanded high interest rates for Greek government bonds as compensation for the perceived investment risk. In January 2010 Greece had to pay an interest rate of 6.02 per cent on ten-year government bonds, while Germany's rate was only 3.29 per cent. The 2.73 percentage-point difference was reminiscent of pre-euro times. This is shown in Figure 10.5.

In pre-euro times, different interest rates primarily reflected uncertainty over exchange rates rather than specific doubts regarding countries' credit-worthiness. The bonds were issued in national currencies, and international investors sought protection against the risk of currency depreciation.[42]

---

[42] R. Koll and H.-W. Sinn, 'The Euro, Interest Rates and European Economic Growth', *CESifo Forum*, 1/1 (2000), 30–1.

This interpretation is suggested by the fact that interest rates started to converge in 1995, after it had been determined which countries would join the euro, and converged up to within a few tenths of a percentage point after the exchange rates were irrevocably fixed at the beginning of 1998. Obviously, the bond rates of the euro latecomer Greece adjusted to the same euro-area level after the conversion rate of the Greek drachma into euros had been fixed in 1999 and the entry of Greece into the euro area was decided on in 2000. It stayed there until the crisis emerged.

In the very early stages of the crisis, until autumn 2008, many observers had argued that Greece would be safe, given that the Greek banks were exposed in Turkey rather than in the USA and did not have many toxic assets of American origin in their accounts. However, as the figure shows, the interest spread began to rise sharply after the crisis broke out in September 2008, reaching a temporary peak in February and March 2009. In January 2009, Standard & Poor's had lowered its rating of Greek government bonds from A to A−, and Moody's changed the rating outlook at the end of February 2009 from 'positive' to 'stable', which sounds better than it was meant to be.[43] The interest surcharge for ten-year government bonds over Germany's in March 2009 was 2.70 percentage points, and as Figure 10.2 shows, the insurance against the default of ten-year government bonds in February 2009 was 2.4 per cent. After March 2009 the situation eased again substantially, and until August the Greek interest surcharge over Germany fell to 1.21 percentage points. However, this was only a temporary relief, as information kept piling up that the Greek fiscal situation was much worse than anticipated. This prompted the Fitch rating agency on 7 December 2009 to downgrade the country's creditworthiness from A− to BBB+, just on the verge of a concrete insolvency.[44] On 16 December 2009, Standard & Poor's followed suit and gave the country the same rating.[45] This caused the interest surcharge over German government bonds to reach the 2.73 points measured in January 2010 mentioned above.

---

[43] See Moody's, 'Rating Action Report: Moody's Changes the Outlook for Greece's A1 Rating to Stable', online at www.moodys.com, accessed on 10 March 2009.

[44] Spiegel Online, *Griechenland büßt an Kreditwürdigkeit ein*, 8 December 2009, www.spiegel.de, accessed on 19 January 2009.

[45] See Handelsblatt Online, *Auch S&P stuft Griechenland herunter*, 17 December 2009, www.handelsblatt.com, accessed on 19 January 2009.

Apart from the large public debt figures for Greece, the reason for the obvious mistrust in the creditworthiness of Greece was a misleading, if not fraudulent, information policy of the Greek government. Greece's conduct was hair-raising, but successful. As is well known, Greece gained access to the eurozone in 2001 thanks to doctored government financial data.[46] In order to qualify for the euro, the Greek government had asserted that its budget deficit stood at 1.8 per cent of GDP in 1999. That was enough to meet the 3 per cent Maastricht criterion, but it had no base in reality. After the euro banknotes with Greek motifs had already been printed and distributed, Eurostat, Europe's statistics agency, reported that Greece's real deficit had actually been 3.3 per cent in that year, and even that information seems to have been too optimistic, as Eurostat later also withdrew this revised number from its statistics. Today, no official figure on the budget deficit in 1999, the year on which the EU based its decision about Greece's entry, is available.

The reports issued by Greece in the crisis year of 2009 were similarly misleading. Greece had claimed in its stability programme published towards the beginning of 2009 that its deficit would be around 5.1 per cent for 2009. However, in its autumn forecast the European Commission said the deficit would be 12.7 per cent for that year. The data conveyed by the statistical office of Greece were so unreliable that Eurostat felt forced to express 'reservation on the data reported by Greece due to significant uncertainties over the figures notified by the Greek statistical authorities' and the European Commission even states 'a case of deliberate misreporting of figures'.[47] The direct consequence of all this was that what Greece had intended to avoid with its dodgy data, namely the rise in spreads for Greek state bonds, was exactly what took place.

If no support comes from abroad, Greece will soon become insolvent. Technically speaking, Greece would have to announce a formal debt moratorium. With a debt moratorium, a sovereign state declares that it

---

[46] Frankfurter Allgemeine Zeitung, *Griechenland erschwindelte Euro-Beitritt*, 16 November 2004, No. 268, 11, and EU, *Preparation of Eurogroup and Council of Economics and Finance Ministers, Brussels, 15–16 November 2004*, Memo/04/258, 15 November 2004.

[47] Eurostat, *Euro Area and EU27 Government Deficit at 2.0% and 2.3% of GDP respectively*, press release on 22 October 2009. European Commission, *European Commission Report on Greek Government Deficit and Debt Statistics*, Brussels, 8 January 2010, p.22 and p.26.

will only service a part of its debt, as was done by Mexico and Brazil in 1982 or Germany in 1923 and 1948.[48]

However, the EU will not let Greece go under, because it fears a domino effect similar to the one triggered by the insolvency of Lehman Brothers among the banks that had stopped trusting one another. If Greece went bust, investors from all over the world could lose their trust in the stability of the weaker EU countries. In an extreme case, this could mean that they would immediately stop lending. A milder variant of the possible scenarios involves sharply increased interest surcharges on government bonds, which would increase the governments' budget deficits and make the public debt grow even faster, fuelling a corresponding risk of later insolvency.

The endangered countries could include Ireland, Portugal, Spain, Belgium, or Italy, because they also have high debt-to-GDP ratios and/or high deficit ratios (see Figure 10.1). The end of the euro could be among the consequences of such a development.

Let us look at the Italian case to see what could happen in what would hopefully only be a worst-case scenario. Although Italy is not caught in an acute crisis, comparable to Iceland, Greece, Ireland, or some Eastern European countries, the country gives rise to concerns because of its extremely high public debt. By the end of 2009, its debt-to-GDP ratio, as shown in Figure 10.1, was 115 per cent. In absolute terms, the Italian public debt amounted to 1.76 trillion euros and was thus as high as the German national debt (also 1.76 trillion euros), although Italy is a smaller country, with a lower national income per capita and only 64 per cent of Germany's GDP in 2009.[49]

In February 2009, the guarantees for ten-year Italian government bonds already cost 1.8 per cent of the insured amount, and the government had to pay an interest rate 1.38 percentage points higher than Germany's, which would have been 24 billion euros per year on the debt mentioned had all debt been revolved at that point in time. In the meantime, the interest surcharge for Italy fell a bit until November 2009. However, in January

[48] See D. Bayaz, *Staatspleiten in Europa?*, February 2009, online at www.tagesschau.de, accessed on 18 March 2009.

[49] See European Commission, *Economic Forecast* (Autumn 2009), Statistical Annex, table 1, table 14, and table 42; Eurostat, *Annual National Accounts*, database, accessed on 11 February 2010.

2010 it was still 0.79 percentage points. This was equivalent to an extra interest burden for Italy in the order of 14 billion euros relative to a situation where it would only have had to pay the German rates on its debt.

In the mid-1990s, Italy had to pay bond rates that were up to six percentage points higher than those for Germany. As Figure 10.5 shows, in 1995 Italy had to pay the highest bond rates of all euro countries and therefore benefited most from the interest rate convergence that resulted from eliminating the exchange risk under the euro.

It is often argued that Italy brought about this benefit through its own thriftiness. After all, it seemed that Italy had tried hard to meet the entry criteria for the euro, reducing its budget deficit by 4.7 percentage points, from 7.4 per cent of GDP in 1995 to only 2.7 per cent in 1997, the reference year for euro qualification, and thus below the 3 per cent threshold for accession to the euro area.[50] However, this is a misconception, as the announcement of the euro itself reduced the budget deficit, without any effort being exerted on the Italian side, by bringing down the interest burden in the Italian public budget. A back-of-the-envelope calculation shows why this was so. Since the Italian public debt amounted to 125 per cent of GDP at the beginning of 1995, the reduction of the interest margin by 5.2 percentage points that took place from 1995 to 1997 in and of itself relieved the government budget deficit by 6.5 per cent of GDP, other things being equal. This was even more than the actual reduction of the deficit by 4.7 percentage points, indicating that the country had, in fact, relaxed its fiscal discipline in the years during which it had to qualify for the euro. Not the politicians but the euro itself saw to it that Italy met the euro entry conditions.

And politicians have done little, if anything, in the meantime to promote the country's financial recovery. On the contrary, even in 2006, a boom year, the Italian deficit ratio, at 3.4 per cent, exceeded the critical 3 per cent ceiling. Italy's debt-to-GDP ratio in 2010 will still be 117 per cent, according to EU estimates,[51] despite the fact that the Maastricht Treaty has imposed a 60 per cent constraint for the government debt not only for euro qualification but also for a continued membership in the euro club. It is no wonder that investors demand high interest rates from the Italian government before deciding to purchase its bonds.

---

[50] See Eurostat, Statistics Database, *Economy and Finance*, accessed on 11 February 2010.

[51] See European Commission, *Economic Forecast* (Autumn 2009), Statistical Annex, table 42.

During the crisis, it was no longer the fear of exchange rate fluctuations that forced Italy to offer an interest rate mark-up, but the fear of a country default that had been nourished by the lack of effort on the part of the Italian government to actively fight for a sounder financial situation. Buyers of Italian government bonds were afraid that Italy might soon be unable to revolve its debt and therefore demanded high interest mark-ups. After all, Italy had to renew loans for about 344 billion euros in 2009 alone.[52]

At the time of writing, the Italian situation is again under control because the recession has ended and the world economy is recovering. However, the potential domino effect resulting from a collapse of Greece is a new danger on the horizon. The EU will, in all likelihood, stabilize Greece if only to prevent Portugal, Ireland, Spain, and Italy from becoming one of the next victims. While a formal bail-out of Greece may not be likely because the Maastricht Treaty explicitly excludes any mutual bail-out obligations of euro countries,[53] indirect bailing out strategies might be invented. One such strategy is the so-called 'eurobond'.

Eurobonds

Eurobonds are bonds to be issued on its own account by the European Investment Bank in Luxembourg in order to be able to extend credit to individual euro countries. These bonds do not yet exist, but they could be created by the EU to help the weak euro countries borrow at lower interest rates. The idea was originally proposed by Giulio Tremonti, the Italian finance minister and, small wonder, it was also endorsed by the Greek finance minister George Papaconstantinou.[54] The creditworthiness of eurobonds

[52] See Dipartimento del Tesoro, *Next 12 Months Redemptions 31.01.2009*, online at www. dt.mef.gov.it, accessed on 22 March 2009.

[53] Official Journal of the European Union, *Consolidated Version of the Treaty on the Functioning of the European Union*, Article 123.

[54] 'Now my feeling—I am speaking of a political issue not an economic issue—is . . . now we need a union bond,' said Tremonti according to *Business Week* at the World Economic Forum in Davos, see www.businessweek.com/globalbiz/content/feb2009/gb2009022_614778. htm. ' "It is not something Greece has proposed, but it is an interesting proposal," the Nikkei's Sunday edition quoted Greece's finance minister, George Papaconstantinou, as saying in an interview in Davos, referring to the idea of a euro zone common bond', see www.reuters.com/ article/idUSTOE60U00U20100131.

corresponds to that of the average for the EU, as all EU states jointly provide a guarantee. Thus, the European Investment Bank will probably have to offer international investors a sort of average of the current interest rates of the EU countries. While the eurobonds would obviously enable the weak European countries to borrow at lower interest rates, they would at the same time hurt the stronger countries, as these would face an increase in the interest rates on their own debt. In addition, the stronger countries would face a disadvantage insofar as they would have to stand in if the weaker countries failed to redeem their debt, as the buyers of the eurobonds would be protected by the EU. The implicit international redistribution resulting from the eurobonds could be substantial.

Another look at the interest rate curves in Figure 10.5 illustrates the importance of interest pooling. On the right-hand side of the graph not only the Greek and Italian bond rates but the bond rates of a large number of euro countries are diverging upward from the German level, which is the lowest of all. At times, during the crisis it appeared that Europe was standing at the beginning of a development in the course of which the old pre-euro times would re-emerge. In the autumn of 2009 the situation had apparently eased again somewhat. However, in the following winter some of the rates began to diverge substantially once again.

Greece and Italy were not the only problem, however. Ireland's interest surcharge remained high, and the surcharges of Portugal and Spain began to increase substantially, indicating the increasing doubt that markets placed on their financial stability. Even Austria, France, and Finland had to encounter persistent interest surcharges over Germany's rates.

It is understandable that the Italian proposal to introduce eurobonds finds more and more supporters under these circumstances. The chairman of the Socialist Parties in the European Parliament, which account for 25 per cent of the votes, emphatically endorsed the introduction of eurobonds, arguing the EU should not 'abandon the country to the mercy of world markets'.[55]

Eurobonds effectively imply a socialization of the credit risk of the problematic countries and will surely become expensive for Europe's more

---

[55] 'Urgent Call for Eurobonds to Support Greece in Economic Crisis', *Newsroom News*, 28 January 2010, online at www.groupesocialiste.eu/gpes/public/detail.htm?id=133640&section=NER&category=NEWS&startpos=0&topicid=-1&request_locale=EN

financially solid countries. Suppose the bond rate divergence of January 2009 shown in Figure 10.5 had continued to prevail without the eurobonds. Assume further that the interest rate on eurobonds will settle on a level given by the GDP-weighted average of national interest rates. In that case, Italy would enjoy an interest rate relief of 0.71 points which, given a public debt level of 1.76 trillion euros in 2009, would imply an annual cost advantage of 12.5 billion euros. Similarly, Greece would have a relief of 1.76 percentage points or 4.8 billion euros per year, Ireland one of 1.32 percentage points or 7.5 billion euros, Spain one of 0.30 percentage points or 1.7 billion euros, and Portugal one of 0.48 percentage points or 600 million euros. Other European countries would have to pay for that. Germany, for example, would experience an interest increase of 0.74 percentage points, amounting to an annual loss of 13 billion euros, given its 2009 debt, and France a rate increase of 0.23 percentage points, amounting to a loss of about 3.4 billion euros per year.

An alternative calculation based on the same logic and the same 2009 debt level, but with the interest data for January 2010, a year later, implies that per year Italy would gain 6.2 billion euros, Greece also 6.2 billion euros, Ireland 6.0 billion euros, Spain 1.7 billion euros, and Portugal 500 million euros, while Germany would lose 7.7 billion euros and France 3.1 billion euros.

Some of the proponents of eurobonds argue that the interest rates of the eurobonds would not converge at the average of national bond rates but at the lowest of them, so that there would only be advantages for some countries and no disadvantages for anyone. They say further that national government bonds and eurobonds could exist side by side. Then it would become evident that the bonds directly issued by countries that currently have below-average interest rates would have to grant the same interest rates to investors as the eurobonds, which would prove that eurobonds do not bear an interest-rate disadvantage for anyone.

This argument is not convincing, however. If the more stable countries agree to a Community bond, thereby providing a guarantee for the weaker countries, they reduce their own creditworthiness and must therefore pay higher interest rates also on the national bonds they issue, presumably at rates similar to those being offered on eurobonds. As it is unknown what they otherwise would have had to have paid, it will be impossible to ever find out about the true redistribution effect of the eurobonds. This is exactly the appeal that such a solution may have for some politicians.

The introduction of eurobonds would open the floodgates and jeopardize stability in Europe. If the costs of not exercising self-discipline can be farmed out to other countries, all discipline will vanish. Then Greece and Italy can continue their unsound budget policies with impunity and the contagion of national bankruptcy will spread all over Europe.

To date, European countries are protected against the assumption of foreign debts by Article 103 of the Treaty of Rome that established the European Community, which in the course of the agreement on Monetary Union, together with the Maastricht Treaty, was included in the Treaty on European Union in 1992. The article determines explicitly that the countries of the EU are not mutually responsible for the debts they have incurred.[56] Political pressure could become very strong, however, to change the situation.

European politicians will probably argue that the risk of insolvency would push the countries of the eurozone into the arms of the International Monetary Fund and would thus make them dependent on countries that do not belong to the euro area. This should not be permitted, and therefore eurobonds would have to be issued for a limited time and limited purposes. It would not be a permanent solution. Later on, other politicians would then argue that there was no other possibility but to issue eurobonds permanently. If they were not wanted, they should have been rejected from the outset. Once made permanent, it would be too late. This is a familiar procedure. Such are the laws of politics.

Eurobonds would mean a fundamental change in the way the EU is organized, granting the EU's decision-making bodies the implicit right to redistribute income and wealth from the richer to the poorer countries. It would require a reformulation of the Maastricht Treaty, which in turn requires the unanimous agreement of all countries. Thus a more plausible scenario involves bilateral support for Greece from the stronger EU countries, accompanied by EU measures to limit Greek budget sovereignty and enforce the necessary thrift. The austerity rules that the IMF advocates when it provides support to endangered countries could be a guideline for EU policy in this regard.

---

[56] See European Commission, *Consolidated Version of the Treaty Establishing the European Community*, online at www.eur-lex.europa.eu, accessed on 10 March 2009.

Americans may travel to Italy, Europeans to Japan

Never before have so many billions of dollars and euros been forked out by so many governments and central banks as today. In the years 2009 and 2010, the United States will pump $525 billion into its economy, Europe $207 billion, and China $196 billion (this amounts to 359, 142, and 134 billion euros, respectively). The Federal Reserve increased the stock of central bank money by 97 per cent in 2008, the European Central Bank (ECB) by 37 per cent. The discount rate in the USA is near zero, and the main refinancing rate in the euro area is at an all-time low of 1.0 per cent (see Figure 2.11). The Fed grants commercial banks direct access to its loans, while the ECB no longer rations the money supply, but makes as much liquidity available as the banks demand. Since October 2008, the rescue packages for banks have reached a worldwide volume of more than $7 trillion—a breathtaking level.

Many people now fear that, because of the additional debts and the enormous injection of money, inflation is imminent. In Germany, which suffered from hyperinflation in 1923, there is widespread fear that people could again lose all their savings and would have to start over from scratch. Other countries share these concerns, albeit to a lesser extent.

But are these fears well founded? Obviously, the risk of inflation requires that the central bank *wants* inflation and *is able to* make it happen. It is not self-evident that these conditions are satisfied.

It is true that finance ministers of indebted nations would like to have inflation and to pull the Italian card to erode the real value of public debt. Before the euro was introduced, Italy had regularly succeeded in escaping its growing public debt by inflating the economy through loose monetary policy and devaluing the lira in order to preserve international competitiveness. But it is doubtful whether the finance ministers will be able to convince the central bank presidents. Perhaps the American finance minister will be able to get the chairman of the Fed on his side because the latter has a flexible set of goals and is not fully independent. However, the European Central Bank will never be able to aim at inflation because the pursuance of price stability is the only goal it has been given by the Maastricht Treaty. Before the ECB Governing Council could adopt an inflationary policy, all twenty-seven EU countries would have to agree to a change of its statutes, but this is next to impossible, if only because Germany, which cannot forget its traumatic experiences with accelerating inflation from 1914 to 1923, would veto such a decision.

And even if the central bank wanted to produce inflation, it might not be able to do so because this would require reducing the central bank rate to stimulate investment demand. But the actual rates cannot be reduced further as they are already zero or close to zero. They cannot be pushed below zero because people would then prefer to hoard cash rather than invest their wealth in interest-bearing assets. Obviously, central banks have exhausted their options, because there is already excess liquidity in the economy.[57]

To understand the reason why the enormous increase in liquidity during the present crisis may not produce inflation, it is important to note that central banks were not actively thrusting liquidity into the economies, but merely reacting to an increased liquidity demand during the crisis. The bankruptcy of Lehman Brothers destroyed the mutual trust between banks and implied a collapse of the interbank market. This implied that the flow of savings that arrived at the commercial banks was hoarded and not transferred to investment banks. Moreover, the widespread increase in uncertainty induced many firms and households not to spend or lend their incomes. By pumping additional liquidity into the economy, the central banks simply tried to compensate for the shortage of credit, trying to replace some of the money that was withdrawn from the circular flow of liquidity via the goods and credit markets and was piling up in the pockets of market agents and their bank accounts. The central banks buffered the negative goods demand shock that hit the world economy, but they were unable to overcompensate this shock and avoid the recession. Hence, the additional liquidity was accompanied by deflationary rather than inflationary tendencies.

---

[57] The only possibility to produce inflation in such a situation is increasing the government debt to increase aggregate demand via Keynesian mechanisms. However, apart from doubts about the efficacy of such measures to stimulate aggregate demand, it seems hard to believe that the real value of public debt could be reduced by increasing the nominal stock of public debt because that would generate an inflation rate above the growth rate of the public debt. Sometimes it is argued that 'helicopter money' would do the job, but helicopter money is just a combination of debt-financed transfers combined with an expansionary monetary policy in which the central bank buys the public debt. It does not constitute an additional policy option.

That more liquidity can go along with deflationary as well as inflationary pressure is a trivial but important point that results from the theory of demand and supply. Just think of the market for computer chips. By simply observing an increase in the amount of chips sold, it is impossible to infer the direction in which the price of chips is changing. The price will be falling if the increase in quantity is the result of a growing supply. Via a falling price, supply is able to pull demand along. On the other hand, the price will be rising if the increase in quantity was induced by an increase in demand, as demand is able to pull supply along via a rising price.

In principle, it is the same with an increase in the stock of money. If this increase is the consequence of a higher supply of money that pulls the demand for money along in a normally functioning economy, the value of money will be falling, which means inflation. If it is the consequence of a higher demand for money that pulls the central bank supply of money along, the value of money will be rising, implying deflation (or a reduction in the rate of inflation when the trend rate of inflation is positive). A deflationary tendency is clearly the case during the current crisis, as the real economy suffers from the sudden increase in money hoarding. The reduction of spending and lending that resulted from the collapse of interbank transactions, the fear of stock price losses in the financial markets, and the fear of unemployment resulted in an increase in the demand for liquidity, and that came first, before the central banks reacted by increasing the supply of liquidity.

It is also important to note that a chronically deflationary economy has more money than a chronically inflationary economy because falling goods prices reward the postponing of consumption. When deflation is chronic and therefore anticipated, financial markets settle at a lower nominal rate of interest. This means that the opportunity cost of money holding is lower and that the stock of money balances relative to GDP is higher than in an inflationary economy.

During the crisis, rates of inflation were declining in the USA and Europe, as is shown in Figure 10.6. In the United States the annual inflation rate fell from +5.6 per cent in July 2008 to 0 per cent in January 2009 and −2.1 per cent in July 2009, but increased again to 2.7 per cent by the end of the year. The eurozone also slightly moved in the direction of deflation. The rate of inflation there declined from +4 per cent in July 2008 to −0.7 per cent in July 2009 and +0.9 per cent by the end of the year. While this

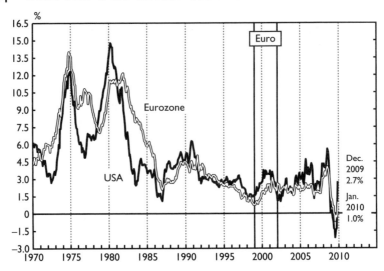

Fig. 10.6 The rate of inflation in the USA and the eurozone

Source: Eurostat, Online Database; US Bureau of Labor Statistics.

development is partly the result of temporarily falling oil prices and will therefore not last, the fear of inflation is clearly not justified by the data available at the time of writing. The crisis is definitely accompanied by lower rather than higher inflation rates.

If there is deflation on average, this does not, of course, mean that all prices decline. In fact, there is quite a substantial divergence in price changes behind the aggregate inflation rate reported in the statistics. This is shown in Figure 10.7, which applies to the eurozone countries in December 2009, when the average inflation rate was again in the positive range. Many goods and services, such as fuels and lubricants, electricity, and restaurant visits, had become more expensive over the previous twelve months, but others became cheaper. Besides natural gas, cheaper items included communications, fruit, milk, and, above all, computers. Obviously, the step to average deflation is not as discretionary as it might initially appear, because many prices are already deflating strongly. Transition to less inflation or more deflation on average just means that more items slide into negative territory.

Deflationary tendencies always signal a problem for the economy. However, the problem is not necessarily deflation as such but rather the resistance to deflation. In every country there are goods whose prices are downwardly sticky because suppliers refuse to sell at a lower price due to a combination

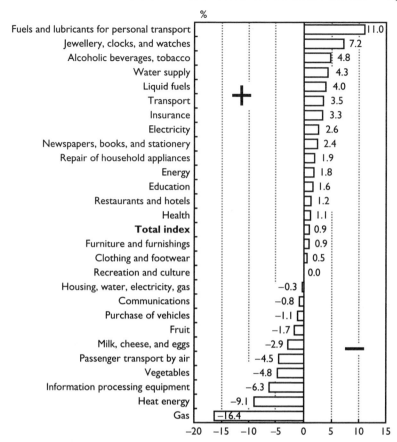

%

Fuels and lubricants for personal transport	11.0
Jewellery, clocks, and watches	7.2
Alcoholic beverages, tobacco	4.8
Water supply	4.3
Liquid fuels	4.0
Transport	3.5
Insurance	3.3
Electricity	2.6
Newspapers, books, and stationery	2.4
Repair of household appliances	1.9
Energy	1.8
Education	1.6
Restaurants and hotels	1.2
Health	1.1
Total index	0.9
Furniture and furnishings	0.9
Clothing and footwear	0.5
Recreation and culture	0.0
Housing, water, electricity, gas	−0.3
Communications	−0.8
Purchase of vehicles	−1.1
Fruit	−1.7
Milk, cheese, and eggs	−2.9
Passenger transport by air	−4.5
Vegetables	−4.8
Information processing equipment	−6.3
Heat energy	−9.1
Gas	−16.4

−20 −15 −10 −5   0   5   10   15

Fig. 10.7 Falling and rising prices: annual price changes of selected consumer prices for the eurozone (December 2009)

Source: Eurostat, Online Database, accessed on 10 February 2010.

of low productivity growth and a resistance to wage cuts, perhaps because of binding union contracts or because of minimum wage replacement incomes that the welfare state fixes in nominal terms.[58] For these goods the deflationary pressure translates into a reduction of quantity rather than in a decline of prices, exacerbating the crisis of the real economy.

But even if prices are, on average, downwardly flexible, there will be contractionary effects as the nominal interest rate cannot fall below zero (where it is in the USA at the time of writing) and as falling prices imply a

[58] T. Bewley, *Why Wages Don't Fall during a Recession* (Harvard University Press, Cambridge, Mass., 1999).

real interest rate that exceeds the nominal one by the deflation rate. If the nominal rate of interest is zero, the real rate of interest equals the deflation rate. But if this real rate is above the level where real investment demand is sufficiently large to absorb savings and capital imports, there is insufficient aggregate demand, and the economy remains in a chronic slump or recession with continued deflation. Harvard economist Alvin Hansen, a contemporary of Keynes, once coined the term 'secular stagnation' for such a situation.[59]

There is nevertheless an aspect that points to some future inflation, but it only applies to the USA. It is the huge US current account deficit, which cannot be financed any longer, given the collapse of the US mortgage securitization market (see Figure 6.4). As explained in Chapter 2, the elimination of the current account deficit will probably require a lasting dollar depreciation. A depreciation of the dollar makes US imports more expensive and increases foreign demand for US export goods, which both tend to be inflationary in the USA and deflationary in the rest of the world. This argument complements the observation that the limited independence of the US Federal Reserve could imply that the USA may actively try to pursue an inflationary policy in the future. Thus, there might be some risk of inflation for the USA.

In Europe, by contrast, the risk of unusual changes in price levels would be more on the deflationary side. Hopefully and probably Europe will exit the crisis undamaged. However, if things go wrong, it is much more likely that Europeans will follow the Japanese instead of the Italian example. Japan's horrible experiences over the last twenty years are the true danger that Europe should be wary of.

As is well known, Japan developed a real-estate price bubble in the 1980s. In 1989 Tokyo was worth about as much as Canada. So it was clear that there was a bubble. After the bubble burst in 1990, the Japanese economy began to tumble. Real estate property became overindebted, many owners could not service their debt, and banks lost substantial parts of their mortgage claims, which eroded their equity capital. They tried to muddle through by both concealing parts of the equity losses in their accounts and scaling down their balance sheets in proportion to the write-off losses they recognized to meet the regulatory equity requirements. The result was a credit crunch that reduced investment, curtailing aggregate demand and

---

[59] See A. Hansen, *Full Recovery or Stagnation* (Norton, New York, 1938).

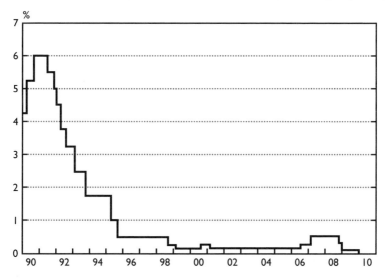

Fig. 10.8 The Japanese Central Bank lending rate

capacity growth.[60] Japan tumbled into a chronic stagnation with recessionary periods that has not ended at the time of writing. From 1990 to 2010 Japan's economy grew only 20 per cent, averaging just 0.9 per cent per year, the lowest growth rate of all OECD countries.[61]

Muddling through did not even work for the banks, because the strangulation of the real economy reduced their scope of business. Eventually, the banks had to come clean regarding their balance sheets, and in 1997 and 1998 many of them were driven into bankruptcy. About 40 per cent of the banks went bust in the crisis, among them important ones such as Hokkaido Takushoku Bank or the Long-Term Credit Bank of Japan.[62] As shown in Figure 10.8, the Japanese central bank had reduced its short-term lending

[60] See M. M. Hutchinson and F. Westermann (eds.), *Japan's Great Stagnation: Financial and Monetary Policy Lessons for Advanced Economies*, CESifo Seminar Series (MIT Press, Cambridge, Mass., 2006). See also F. Westermann, *From Credit-Boom to Credit-Crunch: Facts and Explanation of the Japanese Boom-Bust Cycle*, unpublished post-doctoral thesis (Ludwig Maximilian's University, Munich, Department of Economics, 2004).

[61] See International Monetary Fund, *World Economic Outlook Database*, October 2009, accessed on 12 February 2010 and International Monetary Fund, *Economic Outlook Update*, 26 January 2010.

[62] See Deutsch-Japanischer Wirtschaftskreis, *Japan Analysen Prognosen*, No. 200, December 2008, 7.

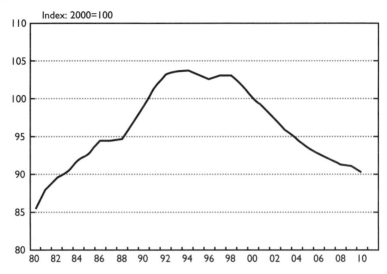

Fig. 10.9 The price index of Japanese GDP

Source: International Monetary Fund, *World Economic Outlook Database* (October 2009), accessed on 26 January 2010.

rate from 6 per cent to only 0.5 per cent over a period of five years to help the banks increase their margins and build up reserves, but this strategy came too late for many of them. The strategy was expensive for the taxpayers, who suffered from lower central bank profits being transferred to the government budget without being able to stop the credit squeeze early enough to prevent the Japanese economy from sliding into a protracted deflation.

As Figure 10.9 shows, at the time of writing, the domestic price level of goods produced in Japan is about as low as it was in 1984, a quarter of a century ago. After the central bank had reduced its lending rate to near zero in 1995, it lost its power to fight deflation by pumping even more money into the economy. Japan got stuck in a Keynesian liquidity trap from which it has not succeeded in escaping to this day. All the signs indicate that the country has experienced a secular stagnation as Hansen described.

One Japanese government after another has tried to overcome the crisis with Hansen's Keynesian recipes by introducing yet another deficit spending programme. As a result, the debt-to-GDP ratio has risen from 65 per cent in 1990 to nearly 190 per cent in 2009 (see Figure 10.1).[63] It has helped very little.

[63] See OECD, *OECD Economic Outlook Database*, Annual and quarterly data, vol. 2009, release 01.

The Japanese economy is still stagnating because the Keynesian policy consists of stimulating the heart by biting on a nitro capsule, which helps to prevent a collapse but is harmful in the long run and should not be taken on a continued basis.

All of this shows: inflation is a potential risk for the USA, but deflation could become a real threat for the rest of the western world, for Europe in particular. Americans may travel to Italy, and Europeans to Japan.

CHAPTER 11

Ways to a Better Banking System

Fire protection in the jungle

The US banking system is largely bankrupt and can no longer function without government aid. Its system of mortgage finance now has a strong socialist taste, with government agencies covering almost 95 per cent of the mortgage securitization market. Western Europe's banks are tarnished. Without government money, many of them would fail to meet the regulatory minimum equity ratios and would have to fear withdrawal of their banking licences. Some European banks are even running the risk of losing their entire equity. Even the Swiss banking system, for many the epitome of stability and solidity for decades, would have been doomed without government support. More and more European countries are tottering and must be saved by international support programmes. If national bankruptcies and related social unrest are to be averted, rescuing them cannot be avoided.

The disaster happened because the bacillus of limited liability, non-recourseness, and irresponsibility spread throughout the world, infecting the financial markets without the regulatory bodies doing anything to stop it. Banks, hedge funds, special purpose entities, investment funds, and real-estate financiers were able to do business almost without any equity. Those having no equity are not liable, and if not liable, they feel free to gamble. They will look for risk wherever it can be found, because they can privatize the profits and socialize the losses. By cutting off part of the loss distribution, they can conjure returns out of mere risk. Even if they finance projects that do not return true economic risk premiums, they still turn a tidy business profit. The dream returns that bankers generate in good times are to a large extent nothing but the mirror image of the losses to creditors and taxpayers who will have to foot the bill if catastrophe strikes.

Non-recourse financial products, from mortgage-backed securities (MBSs) to the multi-stage collateralized debt obligations (CDOs), all of them derivatives of the claims of the mortgage financiers against home-owners, or more precisely against their houses, were part of the roulette game that Wall Street played with the world. Again the business model was based on limited liability. The American banks sold credit claims to the world without having to take responsibility for those claims being honoured. The 1.9-trillion-dollar market for annual new private issues of MBSs and CDOs, produced by means short of alchemy, has vanished in the smoke of the crisis (see Chapter 6). The casino's main ballroom has had to close after being gutted by fire.

Even American homeowners became gamblers, on the back of the non-recourse mortgage loans extended to them. They dared to get involved in projects that they would not have touched under European liability law. Because they knew that they would be able to get off the hook in the event of house prices falling by sending jingle letters to the bank, they did not shy away from high house prices and so fuelled the American housing boom. Unscrupulous mortgage lending, forced upon the banks by the government to fight the so-called red lining, helped even poorer Americans dream Franklin Roosevelt's dream of general prosperity and widespread homeownership. When they awoke they found themselves in a burning jungle.

Whereas the Chicago or Manchester economics school has disgraced itself, more moderate and prudent interpretations of capitalism such as those proclaimed in Europe now appear much more reasonable. Neo- or ordoliberalism, as formulated by Alexander Rüstow, Wilhelm Röpke, or Walter Eucken, stands out. The central thesis of ordoliberalism was that markets can only unfold their beneficial effects if the government sets the rules of the game. There is no such thing as a self-regulation of markets, only self-ordering within a firm regulatory framework set by the state. The liability principle is one of the fundamental principles of the market order that Eucken wanted defined and enforced by the state.[1] The collapse of the financial capitalism edifice as a result of this constituting principle being undermined poignantly confirms his thesis.

The banking system can only regain stability if the principle of liability is once again given more recognition. Much stricter capital regulation and the limitation of non-recourse loans are among the essential barriers against gambling that politics must erect. These barriers will create new confidence in the markets for long-term credit contracts and allow capitalism to continue increasing the wealth of the masses. Eucken must go to America!

But before Eucken arrives there, Keynes must save the banks and the economy. Although the ordoliberal recipes serve to protect the jungle from an outbreak of fire, they are less effective in putting out fires that have already been ignited. There may possibly even be a contradiction between measures that create long-term stability and those aimed at battling acute threats, because expectations of government aid if a crisis should strike generate carelessness in dealing with risks. It may also be the other way around, however, that there is indeed a harmonious relationship between the short-term and long-term goals of economic policy. Clarification of this point is the objective of this final chapter.

Liquidity, solvency, and equity gifts

Many people see the biggest present danger for the international financial system in the illiquidity of the banks and in the breakdown of maturity transformation. The liquidity shortfalls of the banks, resulting from the collapse of the interbank market, were indeed the most urgent and initially most visible sign of the crisis. But the liquidity crisis was only the symptom of a much deeper solvency crisis, whose cause was the chronic undercapitalization of the banking system and the capital losses discussed in Chapters 7 and 8.

---

[1] W. Eucken, *Grundsätze der Wirtschaftspolitik*, 1st edn. (Francke und Mohr, Bern, 1952), here cited according to the 7th edn. (Mohr Siebeck, Tübingen, 2004, chapter 16: 'Die Politik der Wettbewerbsordnung—die konstituierenden Prinzipien', 254 n.) See also W. Röpke, *Civitas Humana: Grundfragen der Gesellschafts- und Wirtschaftsreform* (Eugen Rentsch Verlag, Zurich, 1944), 262 n. and 274 n.

By January 2010, the American banks had already lost more than half of the equity capital they had before the crisis, and they were likely to lose another one-fourth. Similarly, by mid-summer 2009 the Western European banks had already lost one-fifth of their equity capital and are likely to lose another 30 per cent. In total, 81 per cent of the 2007 equity capital of the US banking system and 50 per cent of the equity capital of the Western European banking system will have been wiped out by the end of 2010 through write-offs on toxic assets, not counting the subsequent public and private efforts to inject new equity.

Given that the regulatory system requires certain minimum equity levels in proportion to the business volume, the banks must react by scaling down their business and reducing their lending to firms. This problem cannot be solved by simply providing more liquidity. The central banks can pump as much money into the economy as they wish and even reduce their lending rates to zero, but they will still be unable to get credit flowing again.

Providing cheap central bank money while equity losses and bankruptcies limit the credit volume mitigates the solvency crisis only insofar as it drives up the banks' profit margins and generates exceptionally high rates of return on equity, out of which new equity can be formed (recall Figure 9.4). The reduced credit supply keeps the banks' lending rates up despite the fall in credit demand, and at the same time central banks allow banks to borrow as much as they wish at extremely low interest rates, in the eurozone at 1 per cent and in the USA even at 0 per cent during the crisis. Small wonder that investment banks like Goldman Sachs, Morgan Stanley, and Deutsche Bank were again reporting high profits in 2009. The high margins allow banks to gain weight, provided that they do not spend their windfall profits on dividends and bonus payments to their managers, and gradually recover, re-establishing their lending capacity.

This solution to the crisis is unsatisfactory as it takes an unnecessarily long time and slows down the recovery process of the real economy, carrying the risk of becoming infected by the Japanese disease, as discussed in Chapter 10. Moreover, it basically implies that firms and taxpayers are to re-establish the equity base of the banking system without getting anything in return. Firms, already stressed by the crisis of the real economy, pay higher interest rates, and taxpayers must bear the burden resulting from the reduced flow of interest earnings that the central bank normally transfers to the government budget.

In the presence of a shortage of private bank equity capital, a low-interest policy of central banks is little more than directly bailing out the banks with taxpayer money.

Bad banks and bad ideas

Bad banks are hardly a better means to hand public gifts to the banking system. It is true that the Geithner Plan (PPIP) used in the USA has the potential of re-establishing the equity base faster than mere interest rate policy would, in particular since it has a gigantic potential volume of up to $1 trillion. The plan contemplates the establishment of private–public limited liability partnerships that are highly leveraged with public or publicly guaranteed loans and that will, as discussed in Chapter 9, probably cause substantial losses for the government. The government losses mirror the likely private gains that the participating hedge funds and the banks selling the toxic assets will share. However, only some of the government's gifts end up as equity capital in the banks' balance sheets, and again, of course, taxpayers do not get anything in exchange for their good deeds.

Despite its advantages for the private sector, the plan currently does not really seem to be working, as it would require banks to recognize the write-offs on their toxic assets that they thus far have successfully kept concealed. The necessary scaling down of other operations to satisfy the regulatory equity requirements after the recognition of the write-offs scares many banks off and induces them to wait until the very last minute before they recognize such write-offs.

The German bad bank system suffers from the same problem, as many banks find it unbearable to recognize the required 10 per cent write-offs on the book values of assets to be sold to the bad bank. Unlike the American system, the German system does not involve gifts to banks, as all losses of a bad bank have to be covered with imputed interest from the dividends of the original bank. However, there are potential accounting advantages. For one, the toxic assets can be exchanged for government-guaranteed bonds issued by the bad banks that need no backing by regulatory equity capital. For another, the liability from being obliged to service the losses of the bad bank does not have to be shown on the balance sheet. Thus a surplus of regulatory equity capital is provided that banks can use to expand the credit flow to private business. However, in effect, this whole construct is nothing but a trick that helps private banks to undercut the regulatory minimum equity constraints of the Basel system, equivalent to measures that would cut the minimum equity requirements (see below). It will result in an even weaker banking system.

During its banking crisis of 1991 and 1992, Sweden showed what a successful strategy would be like and under what conditions a bad bank can be set up. Sweden's crisis started after the real-estate bubble of the 1980s had burst, the rate of inflation had risen sharply, and the exchange rate of the Swedish krona had come under pressure. The Swedish crisis was much more severe than the current crisis for the banks of the Western world, as its depreciation losses amounted to 12 per cent of gross domestic product at the time.[2] Today this value is only exceeded by Bermuda and Switzerland, as shown in Figure 8.2.

The Swedish government offered the troubled banks a partnership and a takeover of the toxic securities by government-financed bad banks. Two Swedish banks, Nordbanken and Götabanken, took advantage of this offer in 1991 and 1993, respectively. They had to accept the government as a co-owner, and only then were the toxic assets placed in bad banks. The government spent a total of 65 billion kronor for recapitalizing the banks, corresponding to 4 per cent of Sweden's gross domestic product.[3]

Having the government take over the banks did not mean that the banks lost their private legal status, but that the government became the dominant owner and then determined the business policy. The other banks procured additional capital in the market and had to write off their problem securities without being able to sell them to a government bad bank. Nordbanken and Götabanken were merged in 1993 and later, together with other northern European banks, merged into Nordea Bank. In the meantime the government has sold the majority of its shares and now holds only 19.9 per cent of the equity in the bank.

[2] European Economic Advisory Group at CESifo, *EEAG Report on the European Economy 2009* (CESifo, Munich, 2009), 95.

[3] 'Ich hätte nie gedacht, dass wir das nochmal machen müssen', interview with Bo Lundgren, Director General of the Swedish Finance Agency Riksgälden, *Frankfurter Allgemeine Zeitung*, 8 October 2008, online at www.faz.net, accessed on 13 April 2009.

Today Sweden again has a functioning private banking system. The crisis is long forgotten.

The bank hospital

Sweden basically hospitalized its troubled banks, performed surgery on them, and then released the recovered patients back to normal life. The Swedish experience could become a guideline for other countries, as it is neither acceptable that the governments and the central banks distribute gifts nor that the banks reduce their credit supply despite cheap central bank money and recapitalize their balance sheets via high interest margins. A bank hospitalization plan based on a potential co-ownership in a rescue fund could look like this: a minimum equity–asset ratio of 4 per cent (entailing a leverage ratio of 25) and a minimum Tier 1 ratio of 8 per cent (instead of the present 4 per cent in the Basel system) is introduced, subject to provisions to prevent scaling down the balance sheet as will be detailed below. If the bank cannot find enough private capital to satisfy this requirement, it must accept the fund stepping in with the missing capital and so becoming a temporary shareholder. When the crisis is over and the banks have recovered their health, they can leave the hospital. The fund sells its shares and the banks again stand on their own feet.

The fund should be financed by contributions of the banking system and have enough capital to help in case of crisis. If a crisis occurs before a sufficient amount of equity capital has been accumulated, the government must step in. It can lend the necessary capital to the fund at market conditions, and the fund would then have to repay the capital later.

The increase of the minimum equity requirements would help establish a better banking system with a larger equity buffer that enhances stability in case of a crisis, and it would foster a more prudent approach in the choice of business models, as shareholders will encounter higher potential losses if they demand risky investment strategies from their managers. Of course, there is a transition problem by requiring more equity even as the crisis has wiped out a substantial fraction of it. If banks cannot raise the necessary equity in the market, this problem has to be solved with equity provided by the rescue fund. The co-ownership of the fund would provide a quick way to solve an imminent crisis by re-establishing the lending capacity of the banking system, despite the necessity of increasing equity requirements. Unlike the low-interest policy of central banks or the Geithner Plan, the rescue fund would inject more equity into the banks without making gifts, because it would receive new shares in exchange for the capital it provides. The bank hospital rescues the banks, but not the banks' shareholders.

Some people may have misgivings about the possibility of the government being involved. But they ought to consider the severity of the crisis into which the banking system has slid, dragging down the world economy in the process. Before complaining of 'socialism' and becoming the victim of mere semantics, one should acknowledge that often there will only be two alternatives for the government: to provide repayable credit to the fund to save the banks, or to help nonetheless and get nothing in exchange. Equally impossible is to just ignore the huge write-offs that have already been performed and that will have wiped out more than half of the equity capital of the Western world's banking systems by 2010.

The fund's shareholding, after all, is not an expropriation, but a forced equity increase. There is little arguing against but a lot of arguing in favour of the private shareholders remaining on board. The bank must sell as many new shares to the fund at the going market price as are needed to achieve the required equity ratios. Private shareholders should not have the right to block this if they disagree with the terms. What their shares are worth is determined by the stock market, not the balance sheet.

Let us take the example of a bank that has $30 billion in its balance sheet but is valued at only $15 billion on the stock market. That is not an unrealistic case, as the stock market prices the expected future write-offs even before their booking is required by the accounting rules. Assuming that the bank needs a total of $60 billion to meet the minimum capital ratio, given the previous size of its balance sheet, the resuce fund would have to provide $30 billion for an equity increase. If it must pay the market price for the shares it receives in exchange for the capital provided, it will subsequently own two-thirds of the bank.

The fund now has the controlling interest, and that also has a market price. There are common procedures, applied by external consultants, for the determination of the necessary mark-up on the stock market price. The fund can present its offer on the basis of relevant expert analyses.

To ensure that the private shareholders are not cheated in this transaction, the bank should be allowed to offer the new shares at the agreed terms first on the stock market. If it gets a higher price than that offered by the rescue fund, it can sell its shares there. If not, it is the fund's turn to buy them.

The banks must not become a government agency. The government has money, but is a bad banker. It is imperative, therefore, that the private legal status be retained. It protects the minority shareholders and the economy from the government abusing its position of power. If it should use its power to force the bank into transactions that are supposedly in the common interest but reduce the bank's value, the minority shareholders have a right to compensation that they can enforce by legal action, if need be. The private legal status is also necessary because the rescue fund must sell its shares as soon as the crisis ends, at a profit if possible. The stay in the bank hospital should be as short as possible.

Too big to fail, too small for prudence to prevail

To prevent future banking crises, some economists, notably Mervyn King, the Governor of the Bank of England, advocate the old Chicago way of inducing prudence by threatening to let banks go under if they violate the minimum equity constraints.[4] These economists, of course, see the risk of another collapse of the financial system if the government does not rescue systemically relevant banks. However, they argue that one should dismember the big banks to create sufficiently small units that need not be rescued if they default. If banks are too big to fail, make them small enough so that they can fail without causing further problems!

While this idea does have intuitive appeal, at closer scrutiny it raises serious doubts. A world with small banks may not function well, and the government may have to rescue the small banks nevertheless in case of a systemic crisis.

The obvious argument against a system with many small banks is that it would destroy the network economies from which banks and the economy

---

[4] Address of Mervyn King to Scottish business organizations, Edinburgh, 20 October 2009, online at www.bankofengland.co.uk, accessed on 16 November 2009.

have benefited so much. Banks usually have huge networks of branch offices and subsidiaries, often even international ones, for their transactions. Cutting these networks into pieces will probably increase the transaction costs of the market economy and impede economic exchange, which is the basis of gains from specialization.

And, of course, dismembering the banks would not imply that the government could twiddle its thumbs in an epidemic like the current one. When many small banks fail simultaneously because of systemic or correlated investment risks, all of them will have to be rescued nonetheless. Smallness would make it possible to dispense with government help only if investment risks are uncorrelated, but this can hardly be turned into an argument for smallness, as big banks would not be destroyed by uncorrelated investment risks in the first place. The whole question of government help arises only in the case of correlated or systemic risks, and in this case small and big banks alike would have to be rescued.

And with uncorrelated investment risks smallness may even cause additional problems insofar as it increases the incentive to gamble, due to the operation of the Bloos Rule discussed in Chapter 4. This incentive would not result in a sudden systemic crisis, but could nevertheless create a chronically deficient economy that suffers from excessive risk-taking with high private but low social rates of return.

To clarify this point, let us compare a big bank with a number of small banks of the same aggregate size and assume the big bank consists of branches that resemble the small banks and finance the same type of investment projects. If the investment projects are safe, there is no difference between the big bank and the aggregate of small banks. But with risky investment projects whose maximum possible loss exceeds the liable equity capital, things are different. If risks are uncorrelated, losses normally do not occur simultaneously. Thus a big bank will in most cases simply subtract a loss occurring in a particular branch from another branch's profit. Only very rarely will the losses occur simultaneously, forcing the creditors to foot the bill. Things are different when the branches operate as separate small banks, because then they cannot net out losses and profits. Other things being equal, a small bank has a larger default probability and will therefore also have a higher probability of offloading its losses on its creditors, which implies a higher expected or average bank profit. Thus the incentive to gamble is larger for the small banks than for the big bank.[5] Midgets gamble more eagerly than giants.

As mentioned in Chapter 7, this is the reason why George Soros prefers to have many small legally separate hedge funds endowed with limited liability rather than a big one consolidating all the risks undertaken. Each hedge fund is a gamble in a stochastic environment. If the gamble is successful, the profit belongs to George Soros. If it fails, the excess of the loss over equity falls on the creditors. As at least some of the risks are stochastically independent, Soros is able to make more profit by keeping his hedge funds separate instead of combining them into one big conglomerate.

The Bloos Rule obviously implies diseconomies of scale, whereas the network effects mentioned above imply economies of scale. Policy-makers should not worry if the net effect of these diverging forces gives rise to big banks, because the economies of scale reflect social and private advantages, while the diseconomies of scale are only private, resulting from the reduction of a negative externality. Big banks are too big to fail, but small banks may be too small for prudence to prevail.

Building a common supervisory system

Rescuing the banks from their acute crisis does not necessarily require international harmonization. Every country is sufficiently interested in maintaining its banking system and implementing the necessary support measures.

---

[5] For the mathematically interested reader some statistical considerations may be helpful. Suppose the big bank consists of n similar branches with stochastically independent investment projects with identical probability distributions of end-of-period wealth (before limiting liability by imposing a lower wealth constraint at zero). The big bank is compared to n small banks, each of which acts as one of these branches. The end-of-period wealth distribution of the big bank has an expected value and a variance, each of which is n times the respective value of the small bank. This implies that the standard deviation of the big bank's end-of-period wealth is $\sqrt{n}$ times that of the small bank and that the coefficient of variation (the ratio of the standard deviation to the mean) for the big bank is $1/\sqrt{n}$ times that of the small bank. It follows from Chebycheff's inequality that, regardless of the shape of the probability distribution, the upper bound on the probability of default (wealth becoming negative) diminishes when n increases, approaching zero as n goes to infinity. For non-pathological probability distributions (including the normal one to which the big bank's distribution converges) the default probability itself (and not only its upper limit) diminishes throughout when n increases.

It suffices to create provisions that prohibit a government from excluding foreign banks from operating within its borders or foreign partners of domestic banks from the rescue measures.

It is important, however, to institute international harmonization of the long-term regulatory rules of the banking system in order to put paid to the competition in laxity that has crept in over the past decades (see Chapter 7). Toward this end, the governments of the world should agree on a Basel III framework that determines the details of banking regulation in terms of minimum standards for the quality of bank products. At the G-20 summits held during the crisis, initial efforts were made for such a harmonization of banking regulation.

In this endeavour, international institutions with corresponding competencies must be created. Entrusting the IMF, the UN, or the Bank for International Settlements (BIS) with the responsibilities of a super-ordinate regulatory body suggests itself. This cannot mean, of course, that this body should supervise the banks individually, but rather that it would stand at the apex of a hierarchy of supervisory agencies and give directives, if need be, that must be followed by the subordinate institutions.

The next level down could be occupied by the central banks or independent supervisory agencies designed in accordance with a uniform organizational plan. In Europe it is necessary in any case to create a common European agency, above the level of national regulatory bodies, endowed with the right to issue directives to the national agencies.

To be sure, in many areas the subsidiarity principle, anchored in the Maastricht Treaty, argues in favour of solutions at the national level. But such solutions are out of the question with respect to banking regulation, due to the destructive force of the competition in laxity.

The European Central Bank, with its subordinated national central banks and its political independence, offers a possible framework for the organization of supervision,[6] but it is not imperative that it assume this role. A new EU-wide supervisory agency could well enough be established, if desired.

---

[6] European Economic Advisory Group at CESifo, *EEAG Report on the European Economy 2003* (CESifo, Munich, 2003), chapter 4, 98 n.

It is obvious that national supervision in the individual European countries has outlived its purpose, given that hardly any of the big European banks restricts its activities to its home country. Almost all big banks are internationally active corporate groups today, so that national borders have lost significance. It is thoroughly impossible to have such corporations regulated in a meaningful way by national supervisors. But, of course, the content of regulation is even more important than the organizational structure of the supervisory bodies.

Basel III and the accounting rules

The crisis was caused by weaknesses of the US regulatory system and aggravated by deficiencies of the Basel I system used in Europe and many other countries. The new Basel II system, which became operative in 2008, did not do much better. The world now needs a Basel III system with much tougher regulatory constraints that reflect the lessons so painfully learnt during the crisis.

The new Basel system must be uniformly applied throughout the world, at least by the G-20 countries. The USA, in particular, would have to join in. Despite being one of the initiators of the Basel system, the country in the end did not subscribe to the system. This may have been one of the reasons why the US investment banks, freed from any equity regulation by the 2004 SEC decisions (see Chapter 7), turned into gambling casinos.

An important prerequisite for a worldwide application of a new Basel system is the harmonization of accounting rules. Currently there is a confusing variety of such rules. In Europe, for example, there are many national accounting systems that are only gradually being replaced by the common *IFRS* system endorsed by the EU Commission. The IFRS system is being defined and controlled by a London-based accounting institution, the *IASB*, which itself is a member of an organization based in Delaware, USA.[7] The USA, however, does not use the Delaware system, but the *US GAAP* as

---

[7] IASB stands for International Accounting Standards Board. It is an institution of the International Accounting Standards Committee Foundation (IASCF) that was founded in 2001 and is located in Delaware.

formulated and controlled by another accounting institution, the *FASB*.[8] US GAAP is not written in law, but it is binding insofar as the US supervisory authority SEC requires that it be followed in financial reporting by publicly traded companies. IFRS and US GAAP have the same origins and are largely based on the same basic principles, including the problematic mark-to-market principle. However, the IFRS has moved away from US GAAP in many respects, giving rise to substantial confusion. For example, as pointed out in Chapter 7, US GAAP allows banks to net out certain assets and liabilities, a practice that shortens the balance sheet relative to what the European accounting system would permit. How large the practical implications of this provision are was demonstrated by Deutsche Bank. It showed that its balance sheet would be cut in half if it switched from IFRS to US GAAP. In view of these differences, one of the most important tasks of the G-20 meeting is to agree on a procedure to establish a common worldwide accounting system.[9]

Other contents of a better regulatory system have already been discussed extensively elsewhere in this book. By far the most important rule consists of requiring substantially higher equity capital than today is the case. That is the key strategy for the recovery of the banking system. A high equity ratio provides a better buffer against shocks and, above all, encourages more prudence in dealing with risk because it increases the shareholders' liability.

The higher equity requirement also enjoys backing in Europe. For example, the Larosière Commission, established by the EU in February 2009, has argued emphatically for an increase in the minimum equity ratios as compared to Basel II.[10] On the other side of the Atlantic, however, tougher equity rules do not seem to meet with undivided agreement.

---

[8] US GAAP stands for United States Generally Accepted Accounting Principles, and FASB for Financial Accounting Standards Board. FASB is the highest US authority for the establishment of generally accepted accounting principles for public and private companies as well as non-profit entities. In 2008, the FASB issued the FASB Accounting Standards Codification that reorganized the thousands of US GAAP pronouncements into roughly 90 accounting topics.

[9] Some attempts in this direction have already been made. For example, in the *Norwalk Agreement* of 2002 FASB and IASB declared their commitment to a convergence of the accounting standards. However, in practice, little has happened.

[10] *The High-Level Group on Financial Supervision in the EU*, chaired by Jacques de Larosière, Report, Brussels, 25 February 2009, text to figure 59 and *passim*.

Thus, in the final protocol of the G-20 Summit in London in April 2009, this point was only mentioned briefly in connection with a limitation of leverage.[11]

Stating precise demands on the basis of general insights is, of course, not free from personal judgement. The figures mentioned above, 4 per cent for the equity asset ratio and 8 per cent for the Tier 1 ratio, could however serve as the basis for discussing a Basel III agreement. These ratios should not only apply during the crisis with the help of government equity, but also over the long term as minimum ratios to be adhered to by the banks of all countries. The difference from short-term crisis management is only that the ratios have to be achieved with private capital alone in the long term, as the government has to sell its shares once the crisis has been overcome.

While the two minimum equity ratios proposed should be adhered to quarter by quarter, it is important that an element of intertemporal smoothing be introduced to prevent banks from scaling down their operations during a crisis. An easy way to achieve this is to require that in each quarter the equity and Tier 1 capital available at the time satisfy the two ratios also with regard to a rolling average of the respective balance sheet items over the last three years. As banks know that they will not be able to accommodate equity losses with reduced lending, they will probably react to this provision by holding excess capital above the required minimum in order to minimize the risk of having to allow the government to step in, which is a useful reaction.

Basel III should also revise the system of risk weights used to calculate the sum of the risk positions. As explained, the Tier 1 ratio is at present calculated by dividing the capital, consisting of nominal capital, reserves, and dormant investment, by the sum of the risk positions. As the sum of the risk positions accounts for only a fraction of total assets, the Tier 1 ratio suggests a capital ratio that is sometimes up to five times the actual equity asset ratio. This confusing practice must stop. Basel III needs a fairer valuation of risk-weighted assets, on whose basis the sum of risk positions averaged over all banks can be brought much closer to the value of bank assets.

---

[11] See 'Leaders' Statement. The Global Plan for Recovery and Reform', paragraph 15, 2 April 2009, online at www.g20.org, accessed on 13 April 2009.

The system of risk weights should also be simplified. The sophistication of the Basel system was meant to bring about more clarity, but in fact it turned out to be one of the causes of the opaqueness of the banking system. It is impossible to really assess the soundness of a bank by looking at the Tier 1 ratio because the exact meaning of the sum of risk positions remains obscure as a result of the complexity of the calculations. Only insiders understand the system of risk weights, and all too often they cannot resist the temptation of using their superior knowledge to hide the inferior quality of some of their risky investments. This opaqueness also gives rating agencies a weightier role in the risk assessment process than they are able to play and creates huge moral hazard problems on their part. If bank-issued securities are lemon products it is because the sophistication of the system of risk weights has largely contributed to the opaqueness of financial products.

The new Basel system should prescribe much higher risk weights for investment in securities relative to company loans. In the current Basel system, for example, banks have to back loans they make to sound medium-sized firms of the real economy with substantially more equity than investments in mortgage-based US securities of the MBS or CDO type, whose market has meanwhile collapsed completely. This practice must be terminated. Loans made to individual borrowers who can be taken to court if they do not pay should generally be considered safer than anonymous securities that do not imply a title against the issuing institution but only against the collateral it provides. The risk weights must generally be increased and readjusted so as to recognize the high risks of structured financial products relative to claims against individuals or firms that are directly liable.

Theoretically, there could be bottlenecks in the short run when more equity is suddenly required, as the banks would first have to generate the needed equity. But, as explained, this problem will be solved by the government's equity injection according to the bank hospitalization plan. In the long term an economy may be organized with largely arbitrary capital ratios of banks, as the savings of the economy always suffice to finance the investment. In principle, it does not matter whether the savings flow to the firms as equity or debt. If higher capital ratios are demanded, a higher share of savings will be changed into bank equity via the purchase of newly issued bank shares or as retained bank profits while the proportion of savings that the banks receive as deposits or by the sale of bank bonds declines.

The representatives of the banks will not like these proposals, given that they imply capping the return on equity as a result of creditors and taxpayers not being as highly burdened if disaster strikes. The business model of the banks, described in Chapter 4, which consists of generating returns out of mere risk because the negative parts of the profit distribution are mostly pushed onto others, will lose its foundation. However, if a lesson may be learnt from this global crisis, it is that this business model must indeed be prohibited.

Credible regulation

A simple capital regulation prescribing the banks the equity ratios they must adhere to in good times will not knock down unsound business models, however. It is decisive for the success of regulation to determine what the government will do if the regulatory limits are breached. Without defining the penalties for a rule violation, the best regulatory law will be fairly toothless.

Therefore, it is important for the banks to be fully aware of the government's plans for the event of crisis. In today's crisis, the government's actual actions lay the foundation for determining the expectations of future government conduct. Two extreme cases of detrimental banks' expectations regarding government conduct spring to mind.

The first consists of the expectation that the government or the central banks will directly or indirectly bail out the banks with equity gifts such as appropriately constructed bad bank models, toxic asset purchase programmes, or low central bank interest rates. This case obviously means that the banks' equity will not be lost when things go wrong after excessive risk-taking, because the government or the central bank will act as lenders of last resort. It would be the same as if a thief caught *in flagrante* were paid compensation for surrendering the stolen goods. No wonder then if burglaries should increase.

The gambling described in Chapter 4 is even promoted in this case, because the liability of the owners is limited not to their entire capital but only to the capital that exceeds the regulatory minimum level. The part of the equity that is required by regulation is protected from any risk because the government or the central bank tops up the equity should it fall short of the required minimum. The shareowners' participation in the bank's profits and losses would then be even more asymmetric than in the case of limited liability alone, and an even greater portion of the losses would be socialized. As a result, in economically normal times the banks would take risks even more irresponsibly, thereby raising the probability of another crisis. This is the major reason for rejecting outright gifts to the banks like those implied by the Geithner Plan, and it even raises doubts about a central bank policy that simply reduces its interest rates while the supply of credit is constrained by insufficient bank equity.

The second case of detrimental expectations consists of the banks assuming that the prevailing regulatory law will be applied mercilessly: neither the government nor the central bank will help the banks but will, long before legal insolvency, cancel their banking licence if capital falls below the regulatory limit.

This case is not probable, as those banks that consider themselves systemically relevant do not believe in the effectiveness of this regulation. But let us assume for the moment that they do believe in it. The banks would still incur big risks whose possible losses could exceed the bank's equity capital, but in their normal business activity they would try to keep a good distance from the prescribed minimum capital ratios in order to avoid disclosure at smaller losses. They would reduce their loans and investments at the slightest sign of a potential crisis in order to avoid the risk of insufficient coverage. But this would depress the market value of the assets and would cause trouble for other banks and non-financial firms, thereby triggering and then aggravating the crisis. Related facts were discussed in Chapter 7 in the context of the pro-cyclical effect of the mark-to-market method and what Martin Hellwig called the 'regulation paradox'. Rigid capital regulation, which is intended to protect from a crisis, can accelerate the pace of the crisis if the government adheres strictly to the regulatory prescriptions and does not step in to help.

Both types of expectations are evidently detrimental. One leads to carelessness and increases the probability of a crisis. The other creates and aggravates the crisis once initial doubts spread. The solution to this dilemma is the bank hospitalization strategy described above that rescues the bank without rescuing the bank's owners. The rescue fund helps out when actual equity falls below the regulatory minimum and private capital cannot be found, but it requires shares of stock for whatever equity it provides. This strategy gives immediate relief in case of a crisis, avoiding a credit crunch, while at the same time setting the right incentives for more prudent bank behaviour in the future, reducing the incentives for excessive risk-taking, provided of course that regulations require sufficiently large capital ratios.[12]

Admittedly, banks will still have an incentive to scale down their operations if equity losses occur, to avoid the fund stepping in as a co-owner. However, they surely will be less afraid of the fund's help than of a loss of their banking licences and will therefore not resort to brutal deleveraging strategies. Moreover, the smoothing rule, according to which the minimum equity requirement is defined in relation to the average balance sheet items of the last three years, limits the possibilities for deleveraging strategies.

Another way of reducing the risk of deleveraging and the gambling incentives provided by government gifts is to temporarily soften the regulatory equity requirements in a crisis. This was argued by a group of German economic advisers,[13] and it is the road the EU followed with its decision of autumn 2008, discussed in Chapter 7, to permit the banks to move toxic assets retroactively from the trading book to the banking book of accounts.[14]

Indeed, softening the regulatory requirements also offers a way to subject a larger part of the capital stock to legal liability and to keep the banks operating despite the failure to meet the original regulatory capital limits.

---

[12] Martin Hellwig concludes his explanation of the regulation paradox by stating: 'To avoid such a vicious circle, one should not only demand more capital in the banks, but a *higher excess of capital over the required regulatory minimum amounts*. And yet we have no idea of how to deal with this paradox.' He then expresses his hope that I might supply a contribution to this. See M. Hellwig, foreword to H.-W. Sinn, *Risk Taking, Limited Liability, and the Banking Crisis* (Selected Reprints, Ifo Institute, Munich, 2009). My argument in favour of an automatic involvement of the government at fair terms in case the regulatory limits are not met is an attempt to fulfil Hellwig's hope.

[13] Scientific Advisory Council to the German Ministry of Economics, *Zur Bankenregulierung in der Finanzkrise*, letter to Minister Michael Glos of 23 January 2009, online at www.bmwi.de/BMWi.

[14] European Commission, Amendment to IAS 39 and IFRS 7 'Reclassification of Financial Assets', online at www.ec.europa.eu/internal_market/accounting

It thus avoids an aggravation of the crisis caused by the regulation paradox and does not provide any additional incentives to gamble beyond those already implied by the general limitation of liability to equity.

However, this strategy is incapable of increasing the capital base of the banks in a crisis and makes no contribution to strengthening the solidity of the banking system. It is, therefore, unable to restore the mutual confidence in interbank transactions and may actually contribute to the destruction of trust. Turning off a fire alarm during a fire may temporarily prevent panic, but it will reduce the efforts to fight the fire and could, in the end, fuel an even greater panic.

In addition, after the crisis it will be difficult to effect the political transition from a regulation that has become laxer, if only temporarily, to one that is stricter than before the crisis. How can one ever move from even lower regulatory equity requirements than those that allowed the storm of the crisis, to stricter requirements once the weather has cleared and the sun is shining again? Since memories are short and politicians are only elected for short terms of office, the banks' lobbies will be able to make sure that the business model that generates profits out of leverage, limited liability, and risk will not be touched. For political reasons, reforms of the banking system for the long term can best be implemented in the midst of the crisis. Politicians should take care not to let a serious crisis go to waste.

A credible hospitalization strategy for the case of insufficient equity consists of announcing the rescue fund's acquisition of an equity share in troubled banks and in demonstrating such a policy by the actions taken during the crisis. Capital regulation that threatens a penalty in the form of withdrawal of the banking licence is useless if the penalty is not imposed in case of crisis, on the grounds that no system-relevant bank can be allowed to collapse. And regulation that promises gifts in case of crisis fosters carelessness. But a regulation that announces and practises the bank hospitalization plan laid out above is credible, effective, and reasonable.

Executive pay

The prevailing public impression seems to be that the misconduct of the banks can be primarily ascribed to their managerial compensation systems. This criticism focuses on excessive bonuses that hinge on short-term success, inducing managers to gamble and neglect the long-term success of their bank. The greed of the manager caste is being thoroughly pilloried. All of this is understandable, as the managers stand in the limelight as puppets of the shareholders and are well suited to personifying the object of blame sought by the media and serve as scapegoats.

Indeed, the bank manager compensation systems are designed in such a way that they leave grounds for criticism: if managers are successful, they receive a juicy bonus, but in the event of failure there is no malus, or penalty. This asymmetry induces them to gamble. No wonder that even the G-20 countries are currently paying a lot of attention to manager compensation.[15]

However, as shown in Chapter 4, managerial compensation systems are not originally responsible for the misconduct, as they are derived from the shareholders' incentive systems. It is the shareholders who profit from the limited liability of the institution and push for risky business models with low capital input, in order to derive private profits from mere risk. Their own compensation system also knows only the bonus, but not the malus. In any case, the malus is limited to the little bit of capital that they inject into the banking business. The same asymmetry is reflected in the managerial compensation system. The shareholders are the principals, the managers only their agents. The shareholders look for managers who are able to juggle the risks of modern banking, and via the supervisory board they design the bonus systems in such a way that the managers fervently intensify their efforts in this respect. No management can survive its frequent 'road shows' in the face of the advice analysts give to shareholders, unless managers present a convincing business model that promises a sufficiently high rate of return on equity.

It is therefore fairly futile for the government to try to influence the design of the contracts between shareholders and managers in order to prompt the managers to pursue a sustainable, long-term business policy. The government will not succeed if it does not change the shareholders' compensation system. Only by forcing shareholders to provide more capital for the banking business and thus also to accept true penalties when business turns sour, will they design better incentive systems for their managers.

---

[15] See 'Leaders' Statement: The Global Plan for Recovery and Reform', Paragraph 15, 2 April 2009, online at www.g2o.org, accessed on 13 April 2009.

Besides, the compensation systems are much too complex and multifaceted for governments to even try to redesign them. The ideas to fine-tune policies to such an extent are absurd. No, the key to all of this is strict capital regulation with the goal of weaning shareholders from their gambling addiction, an addiction that, as explained in Chapter 4, is the result of evolutionary learning and imitation in good weather periods rather than a conscious or even conspiratorial optimization behind closed doors. If stricter capital regulation is introduced, market behaviour will gradually change and bring about more cautious and prudent business models implemented through appropriately incentivized bonus systems.

There is no disputing the fact that, from a legal point of view, reforms are needed to reformulate the responsibilities and the control function of banks' supervisory boards. Executives may have too much scope for procuring advantages from the shareholder representatives in an uncontrolled way.[16] But this is a completely different issue that has little to do with the crisis and the stabilization of the banking system. An improvement of manager control by shareholder representatives cannot limit gambling in any way and therefore cannot contribute to stabilizing the banking system. The opposite could well be the case. Despite all the public excitement over the managerial echelons, some executives do succeed in protecting the banks' capital from being looted by the shareholders. They may do more for the sustained development of the bank than is to the liking of shareholders, who prefer returns on capital of 25 per cent or more. To increase the power of banks' shareholders is certainly not the right strategy to induce executives to aim for greater sustainability.

The government has many responsibilities in the market economy. Intervening in the compensation systems of private businesses is surely not one of them. Prices and wages can only fulfil their control function if they are determined by market forces. They are signals of scarcity that optimally assign people and capital to alternative uses in an economy characterized by the division of labour. As important as it is to keep externalities under control by means of extensive regulation, it is wrong to try to change prices and wages through government intervention. It may not even be useful for

---

[16] See T. Baums (ed.), *Bericht der Regierungskommission Corporate Governance* (Verlag Dr Otto Schmidt, Cologne, 2001).

reasons of social justice, as distribution goals can be better achieved by the state's tax-and-transfer system. This is the basic tenet of economics that cannot be emphasized enough, even though this is not the place to present the economic foundations of this insight.[17]

Eliminating the pro-cyclicality of the supervisory system

More important than manager compensation are the accounting rules prescribed by the government, as they are partly to blame for the crisis. The mark-to-market method, which is specified by the globally valid IFRS accounting system, has intensified the crisis. It first overheated the bubble because it inflated book profits over and above the real value of the business, and then it exacerbated the downswing, as it forced the banks to write down assets and to scale down their business so as to satisfy the supervisory minimum equity constraints.

An option to overcome this deficiency could be to introduce Colbert's lowest-value principle. Creditor protection calls always for the most cautious valuation method to be chosen, instead of continuously adjusting the valuation of the assets to changing market prices. Accordingly, after comparing the market value and the acquisition cost, the lower of the two ought to be used. For long-lived assets it will normally be the acquisition cost, with the result that hidden reserves accumulate in the balance sheets.

The hidden reserves may serve as capital buffers in times of crisis to meet losses without having to change the balance sheet positions. The pro-cyclicality of the mark-to-market method, described in Chapter 7, would be avoided in this way. By following this proposal, the world would repeat the step taken by Germany after the bitter experience of the Big Panic (Gründerkrise) of 1873, with the reform of its commercial law in 1884 that reintroduced the lowest-value principle, as explained in Chapter 7.

Alternatively, or additionally, the supervisory capital ratios could be changed pro-cyclically. During a boom, when asset values increase and highly leveraged equity shoots up, the Tier 1 ratio could be increased, so as to force

---

[17] For an analysis of the disastrous effects of government intervention in wage systems in the welfare state see H.-W. Sinn, *Can Germany be Saved? The Malaise of the World's First Welfare State* (MIT Press, Cambridge, Mass., 2007).

the banks to build up an equity buffer; in recessions it could be reduced so as to prevent the banks from adjusting their lending pro-cyclically. Spain has already implemented such a system, with good success. The Larosière Commission also advocates it for a reformed Basel system.[18] An appropriate macro-prudential supervision framework for the respective central bank system could provide the guidelines for supervisory bodies to adjust the ratios.

Taming the special purpose vehicles and hedge funds

One can learn from Spain and Italy regarding another issue as well. As is well known, many European banks exploited a regulatory gap in the supervisory systems by running big risks outside their balance sheets via businesses carried out in special purpose vehicles and conduits residing in tax havens such as Ireland or Bermuda. Using their foreign shadow subsidiaries, they spun the big wheel of fortune without having to provide capital, as the transactions of the shadow banks were not carried on the domestic balance sheets and the countries hosting the shadow banks did not supervise such activities properly.

Regarding this issue, the Spanish and Italian supervisory agencies were smarter, as described in Chapter 7. They successfully banned shadow banking activities by forcing banks to carry all offshore transactions on their balance sheets, which automatically implied capital backing in accordance with Basel II.

The Spanish–Italian rule ought to be adopted by the new Basel III system. This would provide a buffer to cushion potential losses of the special purpose vehicles and, above all, would pull the rug from under this business model. Although this will be hard on Ireland and other countries as one of the motives for locating special purpose vehicles there would disappear, it is indispensable for the stability of the Western world's banking system.

Similar is the situation of hedge funds, the Anglo-Saxon counterparts to the special purpose entities more common in continental Europe. They undertake extremely risky transactions with huge leverage and minimum capital input, as they are not subject to any supervision. Their business no

---

[18] *The High-Level Group on Financial Supervision in the EU*, chaired by Jacques de Larosière, item 60.

longer has much to do with hedging capital markets, and much with gambling *par excellence* resulting from limited liability. As hedge funds are dying like flies during the current crisis, they can hardly be seen as exerting a stabilization function.

Should banks continue to be allowed to own hedge funds, such hedge funds must be fully carried on the balance sheets and subjected to Basel III regulation like the rest of the bank business, including special purpose companies. Those hedge funds not owned by banks should be regulated like independent entities and forced to back their transactions with capital. It is surprising that the Larosière Report is somewhat reluctant in this respect and that at the G-20 Summit it was only agreed to regulate the 'systemically relevant' hedge funds, whatever they may be.[19]

Reinstating the Glass–Steagall Act?

Initiated by former central bank president Paul Volcker, in autumn 2009, a new discussion began in the USA about reinstating a separation between commercial and investment banks. No less than President Obama suggested such a separation in a speech in January 2010.[20] He proclaimed the goal of separating the investment business from the deposit business to protect the savers and the federal deposit insurance agency FDIC against the risk incurred in the investment business. In particular, the President wanted to forbid commercial banks from participating in proprietary trade of financial products and from owning hedge funds and private equity firms.

The separation of investment and commercial banks has a long-standing tradition in the USA, dating back to the Glass–Steagall Act passed on 16 June 1933, a short time after the world depression's nadir. Commercial banks were allowed to use their depositors' money to lend to households, companies, and other banks, but were barred from acquiring securities or playing any role in their trading. The purchase of shares of stock was as prohibited as the acquisition of securitized financial products of any kind.

---

[19] See 'Leaders' Statement: The Global Plan for Recovery and Reform', paragraph 15.

[20] See the White House, *President Obama Calls for New Restrictions on Size and Scope of Financial Institutions to Rein in Excesses and Protect Taxpayers*, Office of the Press Secretary, 21 January 2010, online at www.whitehouse.gov, accessed on 26 January 2010.

Even the acquisition of company bonds or private debentures was reduced to a negligible minimum.[21]

After the Glass–Steagall Act was repealed in 1999, some commercial banks gingerly tried their hand at investment banking. This has fed the suspicion that this may have been one of the causes of the financial crisis. This is implausible, however, because the separation of the banking system into commercial and investment banks was in fact largely intact when the crisis hit. On the contrary, this separation itself may have exacerbated the crisis.

The crisis was triggered in 2008 when Lehman Brothers, against all expectations, was not bailed out by the government. This shattered the banks' mutual trust and caused the interbank market to seize up. The savers' funds could not be channelled on to investors anymore, accumulating instead in the commercial banks. This, in turn, brought about a collapse in the real economy. Had such banking separation not prevailed in the USA, the economy would have been less susceptible to a collapse of the interbank market, since the commercial banks would have been able to channel at least part of the savings directly to firms via the purchase of stocks, bonds, or debentures.

This makes one wonder what motivated Obama and Volcker. The answer probably lies in the metamorphosis that the investment banks Goldman Sachs and Morgan Stanley, the only ones among the large investment banks to survive the crisis, had undergone to turn into normal commercial banks on 22 September 2008 (see Chapter 3). Behind this transformation was the wish of both banks to gain access to cheap credit provided by the Fed and enjoy the protection afforded by the FDIC during the crisis. The government had actually intended to exclude investment banks from special help, but these banks outsmarted it by quickly changing their legal status. Now Obama wanted to settle the score.

---

[21] Commercial banks were allowed to hold investment securities (bonds, notes, or debentures) up to 10% of the stock of equity capital, which was close to nothing given that the stock of equity was small if not tiny relative to the balance sheet even at that time. See Banking Act of 1933 (Glass–Steagall Act), Pub. L. No. 73-66, esp. sections 16 and 21 and amendment of 1935. Cf. *The Provisions within the Sections of the Glass–Steagall Act*, online at www.cftech.com/ BrainBank/Specialreports/GlassSteagall, accessed 26 January 2010.

This is understandable, but for those parts of the world that have a universal banking system it is dangerous. This includes Europe, where the activities of investment and commercial banks have always been practised under the same roof. If Obama succeeds in pushing through such a banking separation system in its original form on an international basis during the G20 negotiations, it would amount to a dismantling of the European banking world, while the effects for the US banking system would be much more limited.

An across-the-board return to banking system separation in any case would not equate to crisis prevention. While it is correct that lowering the expectations of government help would spur investment banks to exercise greater caution in their business, the separation of banking functions would make the system more crisis-prone because it would give the interbank market an even more important role. Furthermore, there is room for doubt that such a separation would actually lower the expectations of government help. In a crisis, the government would have no option but to bail out large investment banks even if they hold no savings from depositors, unless it wanted to risk a repetition of the Lehman Brothers debacle. Lehman Brothers, it is worth noting, was not a commercial bank, and it was unable to impose a risk on its depositors because it had none.

As shown in this book, the banks' fondness for risk that led to the crisis stems from the overly lax equity requirements that made them play the Bloos gamble. As the banks' owners risked little of their wealth, they felt tempted to engage in overly risky activities, knowing that they would be able to keep all the profits and shift the potential losses onto other shoulders, regardless of whether the government came to the rescue or not. The Bloos gamble can only be banished by drastically increasing the regulatory equity requirements, which would have the added advantage of keeping the banks from keeling over when the wind picks up a bit. Strengthening the banks' equity capital is by far the most important requirement of any meaningful financial reform.

Still, the proposal of erecting a firewall between the normal banking business and extremely risky speculative activities could be useful, making such activities more transparent and preventing the banks' creditors from being made liable without their knowledge for the potential losses involved. This firewall, however, should not separate the entire investment banking business, as the Glass–Steagall Act did and Obama proposed, but instead be placed farther out, fencing out only the most risky business areas. This way, it would indeed make sense to ban banks from owning private equity firms, hedge funds, or special purpose vehicles. Investors could then decide in full knowledge to purchase stock in such highly risky companies. A more stringent equity capital rule, as proposed above, would in turn make it less easy even for these companies to gamble to the creditors' detriment. Commercial banks, however, should be allowed to conduct normal proprietary trading, in particular the purchase of shares of stock and bonds of companies in the real economy, in order to reduce the vulnerability of the banking system to a crisis in the interbank market.

Banning short sales

The need to rein in hedge funds and other financial institutions also results from the problematic effects of short sales, discussed in Chapter 7. Short sales not only toppled the pound sterling. They also played a major role in the collapse of Lehman Brothers and therefore are at the centre of the current crisis.

A short sale is speculation on a falling price, often a share price. The speculator borrows a large number of shares of a particular company and sells them. Because of its large volume, the sale significantly reduces the share price and raises the expectation of a further decline in this price. This induces a herd reaction with many shareholders trying to get rid of that particular share, which reduces the price further and triggers a downward spiral. When the pessimism is at a maximum and the price correspondingly low, the speculator repurchases the shares and returns them together with a fee to the original lender.

Speculating on falling prices is not a problem *per se*. Someone who sells a share forward is also speculating on a falling price. He promises today to sell the share at a particular point in time at a pre-agreed price and buys the share on the stock market when this time comes. He, too, profits only if the future share price (the spot price) falls after the contract is made, but unlike in the short-sale case he is unable to bring about this price drop through his own actions.

The fundamental difference between a forward sale and a short sale is that the prices are stabilized in the first case and destabilized in the second.

The forward seller stabilizes future share prices, as the transaction, which brings profits, drives the share price in the direction of the forward price. The more speculators engage in forward transactions, the stabler the stock market. Forward speculators destroy their own business through their activity, but that is the very reason why they stabilize the market.

The situation is different with respect to short sales. Initially the sale of the borrowed shares depresses the stock price, and then the repurchase increases it again. There is a downward and upward movement of the price that would not have existed in the absence of short sales. This is why short sales destabilize the market.

From the perspective of an individual speculator, at first glance the short sale offers no advantage over forward speculation. However, the crucial difference is that the short seller moves the market, because he trades with huge quantities of shares that he has borrowed. The sheer quantity gives him market power, enough to trigger a price decline that sets in motion the reinforcing herd reaction. By creating the conditions for a favourable repurchase of the shares, a short sale offers the speculator more chances for profit than a forward sale. But it is precisely this condition that raises doubts about such actions from an economic point of view.

Whenever an individual market participant can move the market price through his own actions, there is something wrong with the allocation of economic resources. A market economy functions well with atomistic competition where the participants are price takers, but not when they have enough power to change the nature of the market equilibrium. Market power usually leads to economic inefficiency and welfare losses. Since the private advantage of short sales exceeds the private advantage of forward sales only if market power is exerted, short sales do not offer any additional economic gain above forward sales. They ought to be limited, if not prohibited outright.[22]

---

[22] Moreover, higher risk weights imposing higher minimum equity constraints are appropriate for all sorts of short sales, because even a forward short sale can involve losses that far exceed the transaction volume, creating the incentive to exploit the Bloos Rule with excessive gambling. See H.-W. Sinn, *Economic Decisions under Uncertainty* (North Holland, Amsterdam, 1983), 288–94.

A new business model for the rating agencies

Chapter 6 showed how miserably the rating agencies failed in the current crisis. If, by way of a cascade of securitizations, housing loans with an average rating of B+ were converted into far more valuable instruments, 70 per cent of which were rated AAA, something must have gone wrong with the rating process. The same applies to the fact that Lehman Brothers was still rated A+ in the week preceding its demise. Given these facts, suspicion of opportunistic conduct on the part of rating agencies cannot be dismissed out of hand.

An obvious reason for the overly optimistic ratings given by the rating agencies to the investment banks and their CDOs is that they were paid by the banks whose products they rated. They even helped them to structure the CDOs in such a way as to yield as many desirable AAA ratings as possible. This is akin to the automobile club being not an association of car owners, but one that is paid by the automobile companies for help in designing the cars and subsequently testing and positively rating them.

The institutional conditions in the rating market are hair-raising and unacceptable from the point of view of bank customers and of the European competitors of American banks. To render the rating market operational again, four requirements should be met.

First, the rating agencies must no longer be involved in the structuring of the securities they are rating. As this was an important part of their business in the past, the corresponding business divisions must be spun off and managed as independent service companies.

Second, while the service companies can continue to be paid by the sellers of financial products, the rating agencies themselves should get their money from the buyers and/or from the government, due to the public goods nature of their services.

Third, the rating agencies must themselves be subjected to supervision, so that the criteria according to which they determine their rating categories will be completely transparent.[23] Basel III should draft a regulatory system for this.

---

[23] Greater transparency of the rating agencies is also demanded by the Issing Committee. See O. Issing (chairman) et al., *New Financial Order: Recommendations by the Issing Committee*, Center for Financial Studies, White Paper no. II (February 2009), 21–3.

Fourth, a European counterweight to the American rating agencies could be established so as to provide at least some international competition and break the problematic dominance of the US institutions. The EU could help in this endeavour, considering the public goods nature of the rating function.

Stop signs for non-recourse claims

The securitization process supported by the questionable ratings was itself a problem. Mortgage-backed securities were claims against non-recourse claims against homes that often were undercollateralized because of the common practice of cash-back sales and because of the inclusion of fees in the reported home value. CDOs based on MBSs, in turn, were even more dubious constructs, as their returns were further diminished by frequent fees and involved a chain of interwoven claims that often even the cleverest experts were unable to understand. The American market for mortgage-based financial products was a gigantic market for lemons that dwarfed the used-car market, on which Akerlof's theory had originally focused, both with respect to its volume and with respect to the lack of transparency regarding product characteristics. Small wonder that the market for annual issues of MBSs and CDOs has virtually disappeared in the crisis and that US mortgage finance had to be socialized. Drastic intervention by the regulatory agencies is needed in this market in order to create the transparency, accountability, and liability that are the precondition for buyers to regain their trust in such products.

Multi-stage securitization beyond simple CDOs should be prohibited entirely. Even at the first CDO stage, the buyer has a hard time finding out the probability of repayment in the various tranches and determining against whom he is acquiring claims. Multiple securitizations beyond that, sometimes six and even forty stages, are absurd and fulfil no economic function whatsoever. They are nothing but trickery to exploit the excessively lax and fragmentary rules of the supervisory systems. However, this is not enough to revitalize the US capital market. Three further measures are advisable.

First, non-recourse loans should be eliminated to ensure that the home-owners (and other debtors) remain responsible for the repayment of their loans with all their assets and cannot simply return their keys if house prices or the economy nosedive. The legal possibilities offered by private insolvency rules suffice entirely to protect homeowners from claims that would push them below the subsistence level. It is clear that this would trigger a minor revolution in the USA, but it is unavoidable if American mortgage-based securities should ever be sold again at substantial quantities in world markets.

Secondly, it should be stipulated in the Basel III system that every institution that securitizes claims must keep a certain fraction of them in its own books, say at least 20 per cent. If the American mortgage banks pool their credit claims in order to generate ABSs, they must keep at least 20 per cent of these securities. And if an investment bank constructs a hierarchy of structured claims out of such ABSs according to the waterfall principle, it must also keep at least 20 per cent of such securities and must do so out of each tranche that it creates. This rule will induce the participating bank to be much more circumspect in lending to the homeowner and also in selecting the mortgage claims it uses to construct the CDOs.

Thirdly, the investors in the financial markets could be encouraged to avoid non-recourse securitization entirely by developing an international market of covered mortgage bonds. As explained, covered mortgage bonds are not only secured by the collateralized properties (as securities are), but in the first place represent legal claims against the issuing banks. To develop such a market, a legal framework could be created in the Basel III system that would determine uniform minimum standards for covered mortgage bonds. As such bonds, thanks to being triply covered by bank, homeowner, and property, will presumably enjoy the highest creditworthiness of all privately issued securities, there will be no lack of demand for them.

Burying graveyard insurance

A final issue concerns credit default swaps (CDSs), guarantee-like credit insurance that has taken on a life of its own in a rather opaque way. This market is the most obscure of all, as it is not subject to any regulation, has taken on dubious forms, and has become so huge, with a volume of about $30 trillion most recently (see Figure 8.9), that the worst would have to be expected for the world economy if big collapses, with domino effects, were to occur. The fact that AIG specialized in CDS insurance because it was able to exploit a regulation gap and had to be nationalized in 2008 after incurring an annual loss of $100 billion, the highest loss of any private firm in history, speaks volumes (see Chapter 3).

Unfortunately, this book cannot clarify the many unsolved problems in the CDS area in any conclusive way. I can only point out the existence of a time bomb lurking in the dark that must still be defused. The reader may remember the disturbing details of the CDS market described in Chapter 8 that support this statement.

Of course, as explained in that chapter, CDS contracts also have benefits. By insuring banks against the default of their clients, they promote a more productive risk-taking and lending in the real economy that boosts economic growth and contributes to the prosperity of nations. So care is needed not to throw out the baby with the bathwater. However, in view of the huge negative externalities that CDS insurance potentially imposes on other parties, as shown by the AIG case, prudence-fostering regulation that keeps these externalities under control is indispensable. Certainly, high equity-asset ratios are also necessary for the CDS insurers to induce a more cautious business strategy and make sure that they can meet their payment obligations even in a systemic crisis.

Moreover, a rational strategy for eliminating unnecessary CDS risk includes the creation of an international supervisory body that registers and examines the various hedging contracts that exist today. The contract claims could then be offset against each other and simplified in part in order to sharply reduce the total volume of CDS contracts. Initial approaches in this direction, in the form of privately initiated clearing actions, are already under way in the United States.

It is paramount, however, to prohibit mere betting on the demise of firms or on other events that do not directly affect the contracting parties. Such gambles create risks rather than eliminate them. In their graveyard insurance guise they are even highly dangerous, as they may trigger mayhem in the financial markets. They were created by financial institutions having limited liability and working with minimum capital stocks, well-known features that lead to gambling at the expense of other market agents and the economy as a whole. To limit the misuse of CDS contracts, the contracting parties must be able to prove that the insurance buyer has an insurable interest in the sense that he would suffer a loss from the insured event that exceeds or equals the contracted indemnification payment. The prevalence of an insurable interest combined with the exclusion of overinsurance is a self-evident requirement for any normal insurance market, which, unfortunately, is rarely met in the CDS market. To ensure that such conditions are met, a reporting system for CDS contracts and an international register for such contracts should be established. This register should contain a convincing description of the insurable interest and a proof that overinsurance can be excluded.

Sometimes it is claimed that in CDS gambles the invisible hand was acting in a beneficial way that was just not yet understood by economists, sufficient reason for the markets to be left alone. In view of the obvious externalities resulting from limited liability, asymmetric information, and the expectation of government bail-out, I find this claim surprising. It reminds me of Voltaire's satire directed against Leibniz, *Candide, ou l'optimisme*, in which Dr Pangloss argues that everything that exists is good and has a purpose, which may be seen by looking at the nose, an appendage obviously shaped in the best possible way to support glasses.[24]

On the American life insurance market, graveyard insurance was prohibited back in the nineteenth century in order to prevent such problematic behavioural effects, and insurance contracts nowadays are only legal when they cover an insurable interest. Society is learning from its mistakes. The lesson to be learnt from the current crisis is that we cannot let people continue to play Wild West games on modern financial markets.

---

[24] ' "It is proved", said Dr. Pangloss, "that things cannot be other than they are, for since everything was made for a purpose, it follows that everything is made for the best purpose. Observe: our noses were made to carry spectacles, so we have spectacles..." ', cited from English edn.: Voltaire, *Candide: Or Optimism* (Penguin, London, 1947), 20.

Chronology of the Financial Crisis

Appendix

Market events	Date	Policy actions
	7 February 2007	US Senate Banking Committee holds hearing on predatory lending in subprime sector.
HSBC losses top $10.5 billion. Head of HSBC US mortgage-lending business is fired.	22 February 2007	
	7 March 2007	The Federal Deposit Insurance Corporation issues a cease-and-desist order to subprime lender, Fremont Investment & Loan, which had been 'operating without adequate subprime mortgage loan underwriting criteria'.
Donald Tommitz, the CEO of D. R. Horton, the largest US homebuilder, tells investors: 'I don't want to be too sophisticated here, but '07 is going to suck, all 12 months of the calendar year.'	8 March 2007	
Lenders to New Century Financial, a large subprime lender, cut off its credit lines. Trading in its shares is suspended by the New York Stock Exchange.	12 March 2007	
Subprime lender Accredited Home Lenders to sell, at a heavy discount, $2.7 billion of loans.	16 March 2007	The New York Attorney General announces an investigation into subprime lending.
New Century Financial files for bankruptcy.	2 April 2007	
The National Association of Realtors announces that existing home sales fell 8.4% during March, the largest drop in 18 years.	24 April 2007	
GMAC, the finance arm of General Motors, reports losses of $1 billion. UBS closes its US subprime business.	3 May 2007	First comprehensive plan to help homeowners avoid foreclosures presented in US Senate.

(cont.)

Appendix (Continued)

Market events	Date	Policy actions
	6 June 2007	The Bank of England reduces the overnight bank rate by 25 basis points to 5.5%.
Bear Stearns injects $3.2 billion into two of its hedge funds hurt by falling CDO prices.	22 June 2007	
	4 July 2007	UK authorities take action against five brokers selling subprime mortgages.
All three major credit-ratings agencies announce review of subprime bonds.	10 July 2007	
General Electric to sell WMC Mortgage, its subprime lending business.	13 July 2007	
US housing starts down 20% from the previous year.	18 July 2007	
	20 July 2007	Federal Reserve chairman Ben Bernanke gives a warning that the US subprime crisis could cost up to $100 billion.
The two Bear Stearns hedge funds that were under stress file for bankruptcy protection.	31 July 2007	
American Home Mortgage, one of the largest US home-loan providers, files for bankruptcy.	6 August 2007	
BNP Paribas suspends three investment funds hit by subprime crisis.	9 August 2007	
AIG warns that mortgage defaults are spreading beyond subprime sector.		

10 August 2007	The interest rate on 15-day triple-A asset-backed commercial paper hits 6.14% for a historic high. The ECB provides €61 billion of funds for banks. The Federal Reserve says it will provide the same amount of overnight money.
13 August 2007	Goldman Sachs to spend $3 billion to rescue a hedge fund. The ECB and the central banks in the United States and Japan continue supplying liquidity to markets.
16 August 2007	Countrywide draws down its $11.5 billion credit line.
17 August 2007	The Federal Reserve cuts the primary discount rate to 5.75%, warning that a credit crunch could be a risk to economic growth.
23 August 2007	Four large US banks announce coordinated borrowing of $2 billion from the Federal Reserve's discount window.
28 August 2007	Bank of America purchases 16% of Countrywide Financial for $2 billion. German regional bank Sachsen Landesbank faces collapse after investing in the subprime market. It is sold to larger rival Landesbank Baden-Württemberg. The S&P/Case-Shiller Home Price Index for the second quarter 2007 is down 3.2% from a year earlier, the largest drop in the 17-year history of the index.
31 August 2007	Subprime lender Ameriquest goes out of business.
3 September 2007	IKB, a German regional lender, records $1 billion loss due to US subprime market exposure.
4 September 2007	The interbank lending rate rises to its highest level since December 1998. Bank of China reveals $9 billion in subprime losses.

(cont.)

Appendix (Continued)

Date	Market events	Policy actions
6 September 2007	The delinquency rate on FHA mortgages on one- to four-family houses reaches 5.1% in the US, according to the Mortgage Bankers Association.	
13 September 2007	Global Alpha, a hedge fund managed by Goldman Sachs, reveals that it lost 22% during August.	British mortgage lender Northern Rock has asked for and been granted emergency financial support from the Bank of England.
14 September 2007	A run on the deposits of Northern Rock begins: depositors withdraw £1 billion in what is the biggest run on a British bank in more than a century.	British government steps in to guarantee depositor savings of Northern Rock to stop bank run.
18 September 2007		The Federal Reserve cuts the federal funds rate by 50 basis points to 4.75%. This is the first cut since 2003.
19 September 2007		After previously refusing to inject any funding into the markets, the Bank of England announces that it will auction £10 billion.
1 October 2007	UBS and Citigroup announce losses of $3.4 billion and $3.1 billion, respectively.	
9 October 2007	The Dow Jones Industrial Average closes at 14,164, its all-time high.	
10 October 2007		The US government teams up with mortgage servicers and investors to launch the HOPE NOW alliance, to encourage the voluntary modification of adjustable-rate mortgages to fixed rates.

14 October 2007	Citigroup, JPMorgan Chase & Co. and Bank of America, with the support of the Treasury Department, announce the formation of a joint fund of up to $80 billion in order to revive the market for asset-backed commercial paper.
15 October 2007	Citigroup and the Japanese bank Nomura announce subprime losses of $5.9 billion and $621 million, respectively.
16 October 2007	The National Association of Home Builders' confidence index hits 19, the lowest since the index began in 1985.
26 October 2007	Countrywide Financial reports a loss of $1.2 billion for third-quarter 2007. This is its first loss in 25 years.
30 October 2007	Merrill Lynch announces losses of $7.9 billion and the resignation of its CEO, Stan O'Neal.
31 October 2007	Deutsche Bank reveals a $2.2 billion loss.
1 November 2007	Credit Suisse discloses a $1 billion loss. Fed injects $41 billion.
5 November 2007	Citigroup announces that its $55 billion portfolio of subprime-related investments has declined in value between $8 billion and $11 billion. The CEO, Charles Prince, resigns.
8 November 2007	Morgan Stanley and BNP Paribas disclose mortgage losses of $3.7 billion and €197 million, respectively. AIG writes down $2 billion of mortgage investments.
	The Federal Reserve cuts the federal funds rate by 25 basis points to 4.5%.

(cont.)

Appendix (Continued)

Market events	Date	Policy actions
Wachovia announces $1.7 billion loss.	9 November 2007	
Bank of America announces $3 billion subprime loss.	13 November 2007	
Japan's second largest banking group, Mizuho, reports full-year operating profit fell 13%.	14 November 2007	
HSBC reports losses of $3.4 billion.		
Barclays reveals $2.7 billion loss.	15 November 2007	The US House of Representatives passes the Predatory Lending and Mortgage Protection Act.
Goldman Sachs forecasts financial losses due to subprime crises at $400 billion.	16 November 2007	
The reinsurance company, Swiss Re, to lose $1 billion on insurance of clients hit by subprime crises.	19 November 2007	
Freddie Mac reports a $2 billion loss.	20 November 2007	
Freddie Mac and Citigroup raise $6 billion and $7.5 billion of capital respectively.	27 November 2007	
US house prices record biggest quarterly drop in 21 years.		
The Bank of England reveals the number of mortgage approvals has fallen to a near three-year low.	29 November 2007	
	5 December 2007	The New York Attorney General sends subpoenas to major investment banks to investigate subprime mortgage securitization.
UBS and Lloyds TSB report $10 billion and £200 million losses respectively due to bad debts in the US housing market.	6 December 2007	US President George W. Bush outlines plans to help more than a million homeowners facing foreclosure.
		The Bank of England cuts interest rates by a quarter of one percentage point to 5.5%.

Washington Mutual subprime losses to reach $1.6 billion.	11 December 2007	The Federal Reserve lowers the federal funds rate by 25 basis points to 4.25%.
	12 December 2007	The Bank of Canada, the Bank of England, the European Central Bank, the Federal Reserve, and the Swiss National Bank announce measures designed to address elevated pressures in short-term funding markets. Actions taken by the Federal Reserve include the establishment of a temporary Term Auction Facility and the establishment of foreign exchange swap lines with the European Central Bank and the Swiss National Bank.
	13 December 2007	The Federal Reserve coordinates an unprecedented action by five leading central banks around the world to offer billions of dollars in loans to banks. The move succeeds in temporarily lowering interbank lending rates.
Citigroup takes $49 billion worth of SIV assets back on its balance sheet.	14 December 2007	
	17 December 2007	Federal Reserve makes $20 billion available to commercial banks.
	18 December 2007	The Federal Reserve Bank tightens rules on subprime lending.
		In a coordinated action of the Bank of Canada, the Bank of England, the ECB, the Federal Reserve, and the Swiss National Bank, the ECB lends European commercial banks €348 billion.
		The Bank of England makes £10 billion available to UK banks.

(cont.)

Appendix (Continued)

Market events	Date	Policy actions
As subprime losses reach $9.4 billion, Morgan Stanley sells 9.9% stake in the company.	19 December 2007	
Ratings agency Standard and Poor's downgrades its investment rating of a number of monoline insurers. There is concern that insurers will not be able to pay out, forcing banks to announce another big round of losses.		
The spread of 15-day AAA asset-backed commercial paper over equivalent duration AAA non-financial commercial paper hits 173 basis points as banks scramble for funding through the end of the year. The spread is usually less than 10 basis points.	21 December 2007	
The M-LEC plan to rescue struggling SIVs is abandoned by the sponsoring banks.	22 December 2007	
US job losses in residential construction and mortgage lending for the year 2007 estimated at 35,000.	4 January 2008	
Bear Stearns reveals subprime losses of $1.9 billion. The CEO, James Cayne, steps down.	9 January 2008	
The World Bank says that world economic growth will slow in 2008 due to subprime crisis credit crunch.		
Bank of America buys Countrywide for $4 billion after its shares plunge 48%.	11 January 2008	
Merrill Lynch doubles projection of subprime losses to $15 billion.		

15 January 2008	Citigroup reports a $9.8 billion loss for the fourth quarter, including $18 billion loss in mortgage portfolio.
17 January 2008	Lehman Brothers withdraws from wholesale mortgage lending and will cut 1,300 jobs.
18 January 2008	Crisis of monoline insurers: Fitch Ratings downgrades Ambac Financial Group's insurance financial strength rating to AA, Credit Watch Negative. Standard and Poor's place Ambac's AAA rating on Credit Watch Negative.
21 January 2008	Global stock markets suffer their biggest falls since 11 September 2001.
22 January 2008	The Federal Reserve cuts rates by three-quarters of a percentage point to 3.5%—its biggest cut in 25 years—to try and prevent the economy from slumping into recession. It is the first emergency cut in rates since 2001. The Norlaco Credit Union is sold to the Public Service Credit Union.
24 January 2008	The French bank Société Générale announces that it lost €4.9 billion due to the unauthorized activity of one of its traders. While the bank closed out the trades of this trader during a holiday weekend in the United States, stock markets plunged round the world.
25 January 2008	Douglass National Bank is sold to Liberty Bank and Trust Company.

(*cont.*)

Appendix (Continued)

Market events	Date	Policy actions
Regularly scheduled auctions for municipal debt of the state of Nevada and Georgetown University fail due to lack of bidders and uncertainty about monoline insurers. The debt issuers are forced to pay a penalty.	30 January 2008	The Federal Reserve cuts the federal funds rate by 50 basis points to 3.00%.
A major bond insurer, MBIA, announces a loss of $2.3 billion—its biggest to date for a three-month period—blaming its exposure to the US subprime mortgage crisis.	31 January 2008	
	7 February 2008	US Federal Reserve boss Ben Bernanke adds his voice to concerns about monoline insurers, saying he is closely monitoring developments 'given the adverse effects that problems of financial guarantors can have on financial markets and the economy'.
		The Bank of England cuts interest rates by a quarter of one per cent to 5.25%.
	10 February 2008	Leaders from the G7 group of industrialized nations say worldwide losses stemming from the collapse of the US subprime mortgage market could reach $400 billion.
	13 February 2008	President Bush signs the Economic Stimulus Act of 2008. The Act provides approximately $100 billion in tax rebates to be distributed in the summer of 2008 and $50 billion in investment incentives.
UBS announces fourth-quarter 2007 loss of CHF 12.4 billion ($12 billion).	14 February 2008	

15 February 2008	Problems in the auction-rate securities market continue to spread; over 1,000 auctions fail this week. Investment banks do not allow investors to withdraw funds invested in those securities.
17 February 2008	British government announces that struggling Northern Rock is to be nationalized for a temporary period.
28 February 2008	AIG announces fourth-quarter 2007 losses of $5.3 billion due to more than $11 billion of losses on its credit-default swap portfolio.
6 March 2008	The delinquency rate on family mortgages was 5.82% during the fourth quarter of 2007, up 87 basis points from a year earlier, according to MBA's National Delinquency Survey.
7 March 2008	Security Bank acquires Hume Bank. In its biggest intervention yet, the Federal Reserve makes $200 billion of funds available to banks and other institutions to try to improve liquidity in the markets.
11 March 2008	The Federal Reserve Bank of New York announces the creation of the term securities lending facility (TSLF), which lets primary dealers swap AAA-rated securities for Treasury securities. The Federal Reserve, the ECB and SNB increase the size of their dollar swap lines to $30 billion and $6 billion respectively.
14 March 2008	The investment firm, Carlyle Capital, defaults on $17 billion of debt. The fund is leveraged more than 30:1 and invests mostly in agency-backed residential mortgage-backed securities (RMBS).

(cont.)

Appendix (Continued)

Market events	Date	Policy actions
	16 March 2008	The Federal Reserve Bank of New York announces the creation of the primary dealer credit facility (PDCF), which essentially opens the discount window to primary dealers, including non-depository institutions.
Wall Street's fifth-largest bank, Bear Stearns, is acquired by larger rival JPMorgan Chase & Co. for $240 million in a deal backed by $30 billion of central bank loans. A year earlier, Bear Stearns had been worth £18 billion.	17 March 2008	The Federal Reserve Bank of New York agrees to guarantee $30 billion of Bear Stearns assets, mostly mortgage-related.
	18 March 2008	The Federal Reserve cuts the federal funds rate by 75 basis points to 2.25%.
	24 March 2008	The Fed announces that it will provide term financing to facilitate JPMorgan Chase & Co.'s acquisition of the Bear Sterns Companies, Inc.
LBBW acquires SachsenLB.	1 April 2008	
Washington Mutual, one of the largest US mortgage originators, raises $7 billion from TPG, a private equity firm.	8 April 2008	
The IMF's Global Financial Stability estimates that total credit losses will be $1 trillion.		
	10 April 2008	The Bank of England cuts interest rates by a quarter of one per cent to 5%.

15 April 2008	Alpha magazine reports that hedge-fund owner John Paulson was the highest-paid trader in 2007. His fund, Paulson & Co., rose more than $20 billion in value during the year by shorting the mortgage market.
18 April 2008	Confidence in the UK housing market falls to its lowest point in 30 years.
	Citigroup announces another $12 billion of losses related to subprime mortgages, leveraged loans, exposure to monoline insurers, auction-rate securities, and consumer credit.
21 April 2008	National City Corporation, a large regional US bank, announces a $7 billion capital infusion from Corsair Capital, a private-equity firm.
	The Bank of England announces details of an ambitious £50 billion plan designed to help credit-squeezed banks by allowing them to swap potentially risky mortgage debts for secure government bonds.
22 April 2008	Royal Bank of Scotland announces that it will raise about £16 billion from investors by selling assets.
30 April 2008	In the UK, the first annual fall in house prices in 12 years is recorded by Nationwide.
	The Federal Reserve lowers the federal funds rate by 25 basis points to 2.0%.
2 May 2008	The Fed expands Term Auction Facility (TAF) auctions from $50 billion to $75 billion.
3 May 2008	St Luke Baptist Federal Credit Union is closed.
6 May 2008	UBS announces CHF 11.5 billion ($11.1 billion) loss during first-quarter 2008.
9 May 2008	Pulaski Bank and Trust Company assumes control over ANB Financial of Arkansas.

(cont.)

Appendix (Continued)

Market events	Date	Policy actions
Monoline insurer MBIA announces a $2.4 billion loss during first-quarter 2008.	12 May 2008	
Father Burke Federal Credit Union placed into liquidation.		
UBS, one of the worst affected by the credit crunch, launches a $15.5 billion rights issue to cover some of the $37 billion it lost on assets linked to US mortgage debt.	22 May 2008	The Federal Reserve has auctioned $75 billion in loans to squeezed banks to help them overcome credit problems.
Standard and Poor's downgrades monoline bond insurers AMBAC and MBIA from AAA to AA.	5 June 2008	
The Catholic Building Society is sold to the Chelsea Building Society (UK).	6 June 2008	
	17 June 2008	The FBI arrests 406 people, including brokers and housing developers, as part of a crackdown on alleged mortgage frauds worth $1 billion. Separately, two former Bear Stearns workers face criminal charges related to the collapse of two hedge funds linked to subprime mortgages.
Barclays announces plans to raise £4.5 billion in a share issue to bolster its balance sheet. The Qatar Investment Authority, the state-owned investment arm of the Gulf state, will invest £1.7 billion in the British bank, giving it a 7.7% share in the business.	25 June 2008	
Countrywide Financial is sold to the Bank of America.	1 July 2008	
Cal State 9 Credit Union is bankrupt (USA).		
Sterlent Credit Union is bankrupt (USA).		

11 July 2008	US mortgage lender IndyMac collapses—the second-biggest financial institution in US history to fail. IndyMac is placed into the receivership of the FDIC.
13 July 2008	Financial authorities step in to assist America's two largest lenders, Fannie Mae and Freddie Mac. As owners or guarantors of $5 trillion worth of home loans, they are crucial to the US housing market and authorities agree they cannot be allowed to fail.
14 July 2008	Alliance & Leicester (UK) sold to Banco Santander (Spain).
15 July 2008	The Securities Exchange Commission (SEC) issues an emergency order temporarily prohibiting naked short selling in the securities of Fannie Mae, Freddie Mac, and primary dealers at commercial and investment banks.
16 July 2008	Meriden FA Federal Credit Union is bankrupt (USA).
25 July 2008	First National Bank of Nevada is acquired by the Mutual of Omaha Bank (USA).
28 July 2008	New London Security Federal Credit Union is bankrupt (USA).
30 July 2008	President Bush signs into law the Housing and Economic Recovery Act of 2008 (Public Law 110-289), which, among other provisions, authorizes the Treasury to purchase GSE obligations and reforms the regulatory supervision of the GSE under a new Federal Housing Finance Agency.

(cont.)

Appendix (Continued)

Market events	Date	Policy actions
UK house prices show their biggest annual fall since Nationwide began its housing survey in 1991, a decline of 8.1%.	31 July 2008	
Britain's biggest mortgage lender, HBOS, reveals that profits for the first half of the year sank 72% to £848 million, while bad debt rose 36% to £1.31 billion as customers failed to repay loans.		
First Priority Bank is sold to the SunTrust Bank (USA).	1 August 2008	
HSBC profits fall 28% as bad debt rises to £10 billion.	4 August 2008	
US inflation hits 27-year high.	6 August 2008	
Freddie Mac reports $821 million loss.	8 August 2008	European Central Bank cuts growth forecast for 2009 to 1.2% from 1.5%.
The Royal Bank of Scotland, RBS, reports a pre-tax loss of £692 million in the first half of 2008, after writing down £5.9 billion on investments hit by the credit crunch.		
Port Trust Federal Credit Union is sold to CPM Federal Credit Union (USA).		
	17 August 2008	Following an intermeeting conference call, the Fed's Federal Open Market Committee (FOMC) releases a statement about the current financial market turmoil, and notes that the 'downside risks to growth have increased appreciably'.
Lone Star (USA) acquires IKB (Germany).	21 August 2008	
Columbian Bank and Trust Company is sold to Citizens Bank and Trust (USA).	22 August 2008	

	Roskilde Bank is sold to the Danish National Bank.
26 August 2008	US unemployment rate rises to 6.1%.
5 September 2008	US government decides to take control of Fannie Mae and Freddie Mac.
7 September 2008	Fannie Mae and Freddie Mac announce outstanding liabilities of about $5.4 trillion. The Federal Reserve auctions another $25 billion in loans to squeezed banks to help them overcome credit problems.
9 September 2008	Lehman Brothers shares fall by more than 40 per cent because of worries about its ability to raise capital.
10 September 2008	Lehman Brothers posts a loss of $3.9 billion for the three months to August. Treasury Secretary Paulson claims that there will be no public funds involved in a possible rescue of Lehman Brothers.
	The stock market week ends with the biggest post-war loss. Extremely high cash withdrawals at banks in Western countries.
12 September 2008	Lehman Brothers seek rescue. Bank of America is a candidate for taking it over.
13 September 2008	Bank of America and Barclays head list of potential purchasers of Lehman Brothers.
14 September 2008	Lehman Brothers battles to avoid bankruptcy. Barclays pulls out of the bidding. Bank of America bids for Merrill Lynch. AIG seeks help for $10–20 billion. US authorities trying to put a rescue package together for insurance giant AIG agree a $20 billion lifeline.
15 September 2008	Merrill Lynch agrees to be taken over by Bank of America for $50 billion. Lehman Brothers files for bankruptcy. Shares in HBOS, Britain's biggest mortgage lender, crash 34% in early trading. On Wall Street the Dow Jones Industrial Average plunges 504 points to close at 10,917.51. US government takes control of AIG, after an injection of $85 billion.

(cont.)

Appendix (Continued)

Market events	Date	Policy actions
Goldman Sachs reports 70% drop in profits.	16 September 2008	The Federal Reserve Board authorizes the Federal Reserve Bank of New York to lend up to $85 billion to the American International Group (AIG) under Section 13(3) of the Federal Reserve Act.
Lloyds TSB announces it is to take over Britain's biggest mortgage lender, HBOS, in a £12 billion deal creating a banking giant holding close to one-third of the UK's savings and mortgage market. The deal follows a run on HBOS shares.	17 September 2008	Central banks around the world pump $180 billion into the system in a concerted effort to end the crisis.
HBOS is sold to Lloyds TBS.		The SEC announces a temporary emergency ban on short selling in the stocks of all companies in the financial sector.
Interfaith Credit Union is bankrupt.		Federal Reserve lends $85 billion to AIG to avoid bankruptcy.
Panic grips credit markets, causing huge flight to safety. US treasury yield at a minimum since 1941.		
Russian stock markets remain closed for a second day.	18 September 2008	US plan is announced. US government pledges $50 billion to guarantee money market mutual funds.
Nikkei drops 260 points to 11,489.		British government rushes through increase in guarantees for bank deposits to £50,000.
Wall Street closes 410 points higher as the US Federal Reserve starts briefing on an ambitious plan to create a federal 'bad bank'.		
Asia starts the recovery, with the Nikkei closing up 431 points at 11,920.	19 September 2008	The US treasury secretary, Henry Paulson, spends the weekend trying to thrash out his $700 billion 'bad bank' plan.
FTSE roars back, up 315 points in early trading to 5,195 thanks to the short-selling ban and the US 'bad bank' plan.		The Federal Reserve Board announces the creation of the Asset-Backed Commercial Paper Money Market Mutual Fund Liquidity Facility (AMLF) to extend

non-recourse loans at the primary credit rate to US depository institutions and bank holding companies to finance their purchase of high-quality asset-backed commercial paper from money market mutual funds. The US Treasury Department announces a temporary guarantee programme that will make available up to $50 billion from the Exchange Stabilization Fund to guarantee investments in participating money market mutual funds.

Russian stock markets bounce back after the government pledges 500 billion roubles to fight the crisis.

22 September 2008   Political opposition to the $700 billion bail-out plan grows in Washington.

Morgan Stanley and Goldman Sachs give up their status as investment banks and become traditional commercial banks.

23 September 2008   Henry Paulson bows to intense pressure to include limits on what Wall Street bankers can be paid in his $700 billion bail-out plan.

New figures show UK mortgage approvals hit a record low in August.

24 September 2008   Overnight the $700 billion bail-out plan in the USA appears to have stalled.

Warren Buffett invests $5 billion (£2.7 billion) in Goldman Sachs and warns that failure to agree a $700 billion bail-out could result in an 'economic Pearl Harbour'.

25 September 2008   Traders are worried about the possible failure of the $700 billion bail-out plan. The plan appears to be coming apart despite Paulson pleading for the deal to be passed.

Ireland becomes the first state in the eurozone to fall into recession.

Jobless figures are up and orders are down in the USA.

In the largest bank failure yet in the USA, Washington Mutual, the giant mortgage lender, which had assets valued at $307 billion, is closed down by regulators and sold to JPMorgan Chase & Co.

(cont.)

Appendix (Continued)

Market events	Date	Policy actions
	26 September 2008	The governments of Belgium, the Netherlands, and Luxembourg rescue insurance giant Fortis.
		In the USA, lawmakers announce they have reached a bipartisan agreement on a rescue plan for the American financial system.
		The package, to be approved by Congress, allows the Treasury to spend up to $700 billion buying bad debts from ailing banks. It will be the biggest intervention in the markets since the Great Depression of the 1930s.
Spain's Santander buys Bradford & Bingley's 200 branches and £22 billion savings book and the UK taxpayer gets lumbered with the mortgages.	28 September 2008	Congress rejects $700 billion plan: George Bush takes the podium to urge the House of Representatives to pass the $700 billion bail-out plan. His short speech falls on deaf ears and a few hours later the House of Representatives votes down the bail-out.
		Nationalization of Bradford and Bingley in the UK.
		Iceland takes control of Glitnir (country's third largest bank).
		Germany underwrites €35 billion bail-out of Hypo Real Estate.
		Citigroup saves Wachovia, with a $12 billion stake by the government.

29 September 2008	Ireland extends bank guarantees, covering an estimated €400 billion bank liabilities including deposits, covered bonds, senior debt, and dated subordinated debt for two years, de facto putting other countries at a disadvantage.
	Rescue of Dexia (€6.4 billion) by France, Belgium, and Luxembourg.
	Dominique Strauss-Kahn, the managing director of the IMF, believes a bail-out is the only option for the US economy.
	The Fed expands Term Auction Facility (TAF) auctions to a total of $150 billion.
	State rescue of Fortis by Belgium, Luxembourg, and the Netherlands.
	State rescue of Hypo Real Estate (Germany).
	Markets plunge around the world. Wall Street is in turmoil. The Dow Jones plunges 777 points, its biggest ever fall in points terms.
	As news of the Bradford & Bingley rescue sinks in, the London Stock Market plummets in what will end up being one of the FTSE 100 index's worst ever trading days.
	As a result of the intense fear among bankers about which institution will be next to fold, the interbank lending rate goes through the roof despite desperate attempts by central banks to pump cash into the system.
	The FDIC announces that Citigroup will purchase the banking operations of Wachovia Corporation.
	Integrity Bank is sold to Regions Bank (USA).
	Kaiperm Federal Credit Union is sold to Alliant Credit Union (USA).
	Wachovia is sold to Wells Fargo (USA).
	Problems in money market intensify.
30 September 2008	European leaders fail to agree on a joint rescue fund (€300 billion estimate).
	Asian stock markets nosedive in reaction to the news that the $700 billion Wall Street bail-out has failed.
	In the USA, July recorded the biggest ever fall in house prices.

(cont.)

Appendix (Continued)

Market events	Date	Policy actions
The banks themselves are finding it increasingly difficult to raise financing, with the cost of interbank borrowing experiencing its biggest ever one-day rise. New data shows British manufacturing shrinking at the fastest rate since records began nearly 17 years before. Warren Buffett decides to snap up $3 billion worth of General Electric as part of a $15 billion fund-raising effort by the industrial conglomerate.	1 October 2008	The US Senate votes in favour of the Wall Street bail-out. Greece extends guarantees on bank deposits. European leaders are considering their own bail-out, which could cost up to €300 billion. The French president, Nicolas Sarkozy, leads the push.
	2 October 2008	US Congress finally passes the $700 billion financial rescue package. UK raises deposit protection cap to £50,000. Dutch government announces that it will take over full control of Fortis. This is in effect a nationalization of ABN Amro.
Reaction in financial markets to the US rescue package is subdued. Wells Fargo announces a competing proposal to purchase Wachovia Corporation that does not require assistance from the FDIC.	3 October 2008	Emergency summit in Paris to discuss the crisis with French, German, British, and Italian leaders. Congress passes and President Bush signs into law the Emergency Economic Stabilization Act of 2008 (Public Law 110–343), which establishes the $700 billion Troubled Asset Relief Program (TARP).
The State of California is in need of $7 billion. TEXDOT—WF Credit Union is sold to Postel Family Credit Union (USA).		

Date		
US jobs data is worse than expected.	4 October 2008	Germany guarantees all private German bank accounts (up from €20,000). US Treasury Department working on details of the rescue plan.
Italian UniCredit raises capital by 6 billion.	5 October 2008	Germany announces a €50 billion plan to save Hypo Real Estate. Iceland announces part of a plan to shore up its troubled banking sector. The country's largest banks agree to sell some of their foreign assets. Fed ready to move into unsecured loans.
Currency and financial crises around the world. Very severe in Iceland, but also Korea, Pakistan, etc. The FTSE sees its largest one-day fall in points.	6 October 2008	UK unveils rescue plan for £35–50 billion, with the government injecting capital into the country's largest lenders. The Icelandic government takes control of Landsbanki, the country's second largest bank, which owns Icesave in the UK. Federal Reserve announces intervention in commercial paper markets. Spain follows US lead, offering to buy assets from banks. EU leaders agree on minimum deposit insurance.
Bank shares fall sharply.	7 October 2008	Historic coordinated rate cut by central banks around the world (Fed, ECB, BoE, BoC, SwissNB, Swedish Riksbank).

(cont.)

Appendix (Continued)

Market events	Date	Policy actions
The Icelandic internet bank Icesave prevents savers from withdrawing money.		People's Bank of China follows the rate cut without formal coordination. ECB changes its procedure, making unlimited funding available at the current interest rate (banks no longer have to bid for funds).
		Ireland extends guarantees to foreign-owned banks operating domestically.
		The UK government announces details of a rescue package for the banking system worth at least £50 billion. The government is also offering up to £200 billion in short-term lending support.
		The FDIC announces an increase in deposit insurance coverage to $250,000 per depositor.
		Landsbanki is nationalized (Iceland).
Large fall in commodities prices.	8 October 2008	The International Monetary Fund announces emergency plans to bail out governments affected by the financial crisis.
Russia, Ukraine, and Romania close down stock exchanges.		
Iceland also suspends all trading on stock exchanges.		Kaupthing Singer & Friedlander are nationalized (Iceland, UK).
Heritable Bank is sold to ING Direct (Iceland, UK).		Glitnir is nationalized (Iceland).
Kaupthing EDGE is sold to ING Direct (Iceland, UK).		The Fed cuts the primary credit rate from 2.25% to 1.75%.

House prices in UK fall at record rate during the year to the end of September, losing 13.3% of their value, Halifax reports.	9 October 2008	Kaupthing Bank is nationalized (Iceland).
The Dow falls to a five-year low, ending the day 7.3% lower at 8,579 points.		
Bank West is sold to Commonweal Bank of Australia.		
The end of a week of panic in which stock markets plunge by 20% around the world.	10 October 2008	Icesave is nationalized (Iceland, UK).
A global rout starts in Asia as recession fears deepen, with Japan's Nikkei index falling almost 10%, its biggest drop in 20 years.		
The Dow plunges nearly 700 points to 7,882 in the first few minutes of trading, a fall of 8%.		
The FTSE 100 plunges more than 10% to 3,847 points, falling under the 4,000 mark for the first time in five years. The sell-off wipes more than £100 billion off the value of Britain's biggest companies.		
Signs that panic is spreading to retail banking, pointing to the possibility of a run on deposits.		
Main Street Bank is sold to Monroe Bank and Trust (USA).		
Meridian Bank is sold to National Bank, Hillsboro, Illinois (USA).		
Yamato Seimei Hoken declares bankruptcy (Japan).		

(cont.)

Appendix (Continued)

Market events	Date	Policy actions
	11 October 2008	Meetings of the G-7 finance ministers and the IMF in Washington: the G-7 comes up with a five-point plan, which includes spending billions of taxpayers' money to rebuild the global banking system and reopen the flow of credit.
		ECB, the Swiss National Bank, and BoE announce unlimited funds at current rates.
		The British government announces it will pump £37 billion of emergency recapitalization into the Royal Bank of Scotland, HBOS, and Lloyds TSB.
	12 October 2008	EU summit in Paris. Governments present a rescue plan of €1,873 billion.
Global stocks rebound. Small positive effects in money markets.	13 October 2008	Historic bank rescue plan by the USA. $250 billion for recapitalization. $125 billion to be injected into 9 banks (Bank of America, JPMorgan Chase & Co, Wells Fargo, Citigroup, Merrill Lynch, Goldman Sachs, Morgan Stanley, Bank of New York Mellon, and State Street).
The Dow Jones closes up 11%, the largest daily jump in percentage terms since 1933.		
The Sovereign Bank is sold to Banco Santander (USA, Spain).	14 October 2008	Royal Bank of Scotland, HBOS, and Lloyds are nationalized (UK).
Cost of insurance against big US bank default drops sharply. However, interbank loan rates ease only modestly.		European leaders back call for a new Bretton Woods.

Shares in Asia and Europe rally for a second day.

The Icelandic Stock Exchange resumes trading for the first time since Wednesday the previous week, but six financial stocks remain suspended. The stock market plummets 76% after opening.

ECB announces plan to boost funding for commercial banks, extending the range of collateral and currency denomination.

Non-eurozone EU countries back bail-out plan.

15 October 2008

Recession fears drive down stocks around the world. The foreign exchange market 'almost ceases to function' amid row with UK over assets.

The Hungarian forint falls by 7% as the stock market plunges by 12%.

EU regulators accept emergency changes by the International Accounting Standards Board regarding reclassification of assets from trading to banking books.

Iceland rushes to stave off economic ruin by slashing interest rates by 3.5% and pursuing talks with Russia over the possibility of a multibillion euro loan.

US Treasury Department announces the Troubled Asset Relief Program (TARP) that will purchase capital in financial institutions ($250 billion).

European Central Bank provides €5 billion in facilities to help Hungary. This is the first time support is extended outside the eurozone.

Swiss National Bank provides $60 billion to take on most of the US toxic debt held by UBS (third capital raising by UBS in the year) after UBS suffered $50 billion in capital outflows in the third quarter of the year.

Run on Russian banks intensifies.

Dow Jones industrial average drops by 7.8%—its biggest percentage fall since 26 October 1987.

An EU summit ends in Brussels with a clear message that there is no time to lose in coming up with concerted action to tackle the financial emergency.

(*cont.*)

Appendix (Continued)

Market events	Date	Policy actions
Unemployment figures in the UK show the biggest rise since the country's last recession 17 years ago, up to 5.7%—1.79 million people.		OPEC calls an emergency meeting in Vienna as the oil price falls to less than half the $147 it traded at in July.
US banks JP Morgan Chase & Co. and Wells Fargo report big falls in profits.		
Figures for US retail sales in September show a fall of 1.2%, the biggest monthly decline in more than three years, with the drop in car sales hitting 3.8%.		
Japan's Nikkei Index suffers its worst fall since 1987.	16 October 2008	Iceland declares national insolvency.
In the US, Citigroup suffers its fourth consecutive quarterly loss.		
Sharp fall in US consumer confidence (sharpest monthly fall since 1978).	17 October 2008	Korea launches a $130 billion loan and liquidity rescue; tax cuts and spending increases announced.
French savings bank Caisse d'Épargne announces a loss of €600 million in a 'trading incident'.		Dutch savings bank ING accepts €10 billion capital injection to bring Tier 1 capital up to 8%.
	19 October 2008	Federal Reserve backs plan for second US stimulus package.
		Iceland to announce a $6 billion IMF rescue package.
		Sweden's government sets out its own bank rescue plan, with credit guarantees to banks and mortgage lenders up to a level of 1.5 trillion krona ($205 billion). The government says it will also set aside 15 billion krona as a bank stabilization fund.
		India's central bank unexpectedly cuts its short-term lending rates.

Small signs of relief in the money markets.

20 October 2008 — Federal Reserve ready to finance up to $540 billion to purchase short-term debt from money market mutual funds. The size of Fed balance increases from $900 billion in September to $2.2 trillion.

UK: mortgage lending slumped by 10% in September to its lowest level for more than three-and-a-half years.

China revises growth down to 9%.

21 October 2008 — IMF forecasts sharp squeeze in business credit. For the EU, growth forecasts are down from 1.7 to 0.6%.

Hungary raises rates 300 basis points to support currency.

Anticipation of Argentina's pension funds nationalization plan drives down Argentina's markets.

The stricken US bank Wachovia reports the biggest quarterly loss of any bank since the onset of the credit crunch, with a deficit of $24 billion.

22 October 2008 — Pakistan seeks emergency bail-out funds from the IMF. Former Fed chief Alan Greenspan admits he had been 'partially wrong' in his hands-off approach towards the banking industry. The credit crunch has left him in a state of 'shocked disbelief', he admitted before a congressional committee.

Barnsley Building Society is sold to the Yorkshire Building Society (UK).

23 October 2008 — In Denmark, the central bank raises its key interest rate by 0.5 percentage points to 5.5%.

Daimler issues its second profits warning this year.

24 October 2008 — IMF unveils a plan for $16.5 billion to support the Ukraine.

Large fall in share prices worldwide.

(cont.)

Appendix (Continued)

Market events	Date	Policy actions
Yen and dollar strengthen. Yen appreciation, attributed to a reversal of the 'yen carry trade', creates global concern.		
The UK is on the brink of a recession according to figures released by the Office for National Statistics. The economy shrank for the first time in 16 years between July and September, as economic growth fell by 0.5%.		
Commerce Bancorp is sold to the Toronto-Dominion Bank (USA, Canada).		
The National City Bank is sold to PNC Financial Services (USA).		
Alpha Bank and Trust is sold to Stearns Bank (USA).	25–6 October 2008	The spectre of a cascade of failing economies is raised as a $16.5 billion IMF bail-out for Ukraine is mired in political infighting and Hungary seeks its own $10 billion rescue package.
Swedish banks, relatively immune to the crisis, move to recapitalize.	27 October 2008	Iceland raises interest rates to 18%, in negotiations for a loan by the IMF ($2 billion) and other countries.
Autumn's market mayhem has left the world's financial institutions nursing losses of $2.8 trillion, according to the Bank of England.	28 October 2008	The International Monetary Fund, the European Union, and the World Bank announce a massive rescue package for Hungary.
	29 October 2008	

	The prospect of fresh cuts in interest rates on both sides of the Atlantic help propel Wall Street stocks to a dramatic rebound, with the Dow scoring its second-biggest points gain ever, just short of 900.
	Deutsche Bank reports steep falls in pre-tax and net profits and a further series of write-downs in the third quarter.
	The Federal Reserve cuts its key interest rate from 1.5% to 1%.
30 October 2008	The US Commerce Department issues figures showing the US economy shrank at an annualized rate of 0.3% between July and September.
	The Bank of Japan cuts interest rates for the first time in seven years in response to the global financial crisis. The bank cuts the key interest rate from 0.5% to 0.3%.
31 October 2008	Barclays said it will raise up to £7.3 billion, mainly from Middle East investors who could end up owning nearly a third of the UK's second largest bank.
	The International Monetary Fund (IMF) approves a $16.4 billion loan to the Ukraine.
6 November 2008	The Bank of England slashes interest rates from 4.5% to 3%—the lowest level since 1955. The European Central Bank lowers eurozone rates to 3.25% from 3.75%.
7 November 2008	Franklin Bank ends business and is sold to Prosperity Bank (USA). Security Pacific is sold to Pacific Western Bank (USA).
	China sets out a two-year $586 billion economic stimulus package to help boost the economy by investing in infrastructure and social projects, and by cutting corporate taxes.
8 November 2008	Parex Bank is nationalized (Latvia).

(cont.)

Appendix (Continued)

Market events	Date	Policy actions
	12 November 2008	US Treasury Secretary Henry Paulson formally announces that the government has abandoned plans to use some of the $700 billion bail-out money to buy up banks' bad debts and has decided instead to concentrate on improving the flow of credit for the US consumer.
		Leaders of the G-20 and emerging economies gather in Washington to discuss ways to contain the financial crisis and agree on longer-term reforms.
The eurozone officially slips into recession after EU figures show that the economy shrank by 0.2% in the third quarter.	14 November 2008	The International Monetary Fund (IMF) approves a $2.1 billion loan for Iceland, after the country's banking system collapsed in October. It is the first IMF loan for a Western European nation since 1976.
	20 November 2008	The US government announces a $20 billion rescue plan for troubled banking giant Citigroup after its shares plunge by more than 60% in a week.
Community Bank declares bankruptcy (USA). Downey Savings and Loan Association is bankrupt (USA). Downey Savings and Loan as well as PFF Bank and Trust are sold to US Bancorp (USA). Community Bank is sold to the Bank of Essex (USA).	21 November 2008	
	23 November 2008	The UK government announces a temporary cut in the rate of VAT—to 15% from 17.5%.

24 November 2008	The International Monetary Fund (IMF) approves a $7.6 billion loan for Pakistan so it can avoid defaulting on international debt.
	The US Federal Reserve announces it will inject another $800 billion into the economy. About $600 billion will be used to buy up mortgage-backed securities while $200 billion is being targeted at unfreezing the consumer credit market.
25 November 2008	The European Commission unveils an economic recovery plan worth 200 billion euros which it hopes will save millions of European jobs.
26 November 2008	The UK government becomes the majority owner of Royal Bank of Scotland with a stake of almost 60%.
1 December 2008	The Department of Labor reports that the USA lost 533,000 jobs in November, the biggest monthly loss since 1974. This raises the unemployment rate from 6.5% to 6.7%.
	US car-makers appeal to Congress for $34 billion in emergency loans.
3 December 2008	The European Central Bank announces a three-quarters of a percentage point cut in its main policy interest rate to 2.5%—its largest cut ever—just hours after Sweden's central bank surprised markets by reducing the country's official borrowing costs by a record 175 basis points. The Bank of England slashes its rates by another 1 percentage point to 2%, equal to the lowest rate since the central bank was founded in 1694.

(*cont.*)

Appendix (Continued)

Market events	Date	Policy actions
	4 December 2008	French President Nicolas Sarkozy unveils a 26 billion euro stimulus plan to help France fend off financial crisis.
	5 December 2008	The Bank of Canada lowers its key interest rate by 0.75% to 1.5%, the lowest it has been since 1958; at the same time the Bank officially announces that Canada's economy is in recession.
The West Hartford Credit Union is bankrupt (USA). The First Georgia Community Bank is sold to the United Bank (USA).		
Canada lost 70,600 jobs in the month of November, the most since 1982.	9 December 2008	The European Central Bank, as well as central banks in England, Sweden, and Denmark, slash interest rates again.
		Bernard Madoff, former Nasdaq chairman, is arrested after confessing to running a $50 billion Ponzi scheme.
Bank of America announces up to 35,000 job losses over three years following its takeover of Merrill Lynch in the new year.	11 December 2008	
The dollar slides to its lowest value in 13 years against the yen as the Senate fails to agree on a bail-out for the three US auto makers. The number of new workers filing claims for unemployment benefits jumps to a 26-year high.	12 December 2008	

Haven Trust Bank is sold to BB&T Company (USA).
Sanderson State Bank is sold to the Pecos County State Bank (USA).

16 December 2008	President George W. Bush says the US government will use up to $17.4 billion of the $700 billion meant for the banking sector to help the Big Three US car makers, General Motors, Ford, and Chrysler.
	Japan's central bank cuts rates from 0.3% to 0.1%. The government says the world's second largest economy will not grow in 2009.
	The US Federal Reserve slashes its key interest rate from 1% to a range of zero to 0.25%—the lowest since records began.
19 December 2008	The US Treasury unveils a $6 billion bail-out for GMAC, the car-loan arm of General Motors.
31 December 2008	The Federal Reserve Bank of New York begins purchasing fixed-rate mortgage-backed securities guaranteed by Fannie Mae, Freddie Mac, and Ginnie Mae under a programme first announced on 25 November 2008.
	The FTSE 100 closes the year down by 31.3%, which is the biggest annual fall in the 24 years since the index was started.
	The DAX in Frankfurt loses 40.4% for the year, while the CAC 40 in Paris drops 42.7%.
	UBS sells shares in the Bank of China for around $825 billion.
5 January 2009	The US recession is confirmed by the National Bureau of Economic Research, concluding that the US economy started to contract in January 2008.

(cont.)

Appendix (Continued)

Market events	Date	Policy actions
Eurostat publishes a sharp decline in the eurozone inflation rate from 2.1% in November to 1.6% in December.	6 January 2009	
The Congressional Budget Office projects an increase in the US budget deficit of more than $1 trillion due to the global recession.	7 January 2009	
	8 January 2009	The Bank of England cuts key interest rates to 1.5%, the lowest level in its 314-year history. The German government acquires a 35% equity share in Commerzbank.
	13 January 2009	German Chancellor Angela Merkel announces plans for a second economic recovery package worth €50 billion.
Deutsche Bank issues a profit warning after losing €4.8 billion in the fourth quarter.	14 January 2009	
Stock prices on Asian markets drop markedly. The Nikkei 225 in Tokyo loses 4.9%. In the course of the afternoon the Hang Seng in Hong Kong loses 5%, the Kospi in South Korea 6%. The major indices in Singapore and Taiwan fall by 3.2% and 4.4%, respectively.	15 January 2009	The ECB cuts its interest rate by 0.5 points to 2%. The Irish government announces the nationalization of Anglo Irish Bank.
Citigroup has a quarterly loss of $8.29 billion and announces intentions to split the company in two.	16 January 2009	The US government helps Bank of America with $20 billion.

19 January 2009	The Royal Bank of Scotland reports record losses, causing its stocks to fall by 67%.
	The German DAX loses 0.9%, and the French CAC 40 0.7%.
20 January 2009	The UK inflation rate falls to 3.1%.
21 January 2009	The Italian car-maker Fiat acquires 35% of Chrysler. Two of the biggest British co-op banks, Co-op and Britannia, merge.
26 January 2009	The Dutch banking group ING announces the cut of 7,000 jobs, after having asked for support funds of €1 billion.
	Profits of American Express fell by 79% in the fourth quarter 2008.
27 January 2009	The German government agrees the biggest rescue package in Europe worth €50 billion.
28 January 2009	Iceland's coalition government breaks apart.
30 January 2009	The IMF forecasts global economic growth of only 0.5% in 2009.
5 February 2009	The European Commission prepares for an application of membership by Iceland to save the country from collapse.
10 February 2009	The Bank of England cuts key rates by 0.5 points to 1%.
11 February 2009	UBS reports record losses of CHF 20 billion and further lay-offs of 200 people.
	Credit Suisse reports a record annual loss of CHF 8.2 billion, caused by CHF 14.2 billion in investment banking.

(cont.)

Appendix (Continued)

Date	Market events	Policy actions
13 February 2009	Following a profit warning, stocks of the Lloyds Banking Group lose 32%.	The US Congress passes President Obama's rescue package.
17 February 2009		President Obama signs the American Recovery and Reinvestment Act of 2009 in the amount of $787 billion.
		The British government limits the bonuses of Royal Bank of Scotland (RBS) managers.
18 February 2009	US car makers GM and Chrysler ask Congress for $21.6 billion in support, in addition to the $17.4 billion already received.	The German government decides on a €50 billion second economic recovery programme.
19 February 2009		The German government announces a law on the temporary nationalization of distressed banks.
		The European Commission criticizes France, Ireland, Spain, Greece, Latvia, and Malta for their large budget deficits, highlighting these countries' limited ability to spend their way out of recession.
20 February 2009	UBS pays $780 million in a tax settlement to US authorities. It also agrees to hand over customer data to US authorities and openly admits to guilt.	The German Upper House (Bundesrat) passes the Economic Recovery Package II and the supplementary budget with additional federal debt of €36.8 billion.
24 February 2009	UBS share price falls to CHF 9.85, the lowest in ten years.	

26 February 2009	The partially nationalized banking group RBS reports massive losses of $34.6 billion for 2008. Fannie Mae reports a quarterly loss of $25.2 billion and an annual loss of $58.7 billion. UBS CEO Marcel Rohmer is replaced by Oswald Grübel, former CEO of Credit Suisse.
27 February 2009	The US government raises its stake from 8% to 36% in Citigroup, once the biggest bank in the world. The US government provides additional support in the amount of $30 billion.
2 March 2009	AIG reports record losses of $61.7 billion for the fourth quarter of 2008. As a result the annual losses for 2008 add up to $99.3 billion. This is the highest annual loss of any company ever.
5 March 2009	The ECB cuts the key interest rate to 1.5%. The Bank of England cuts its interest rate to a new low of 0.5%.
9 March 2009	The last of the big Icelandic banks is closed by the authorities.
11 March 2009	Freddie Mac reports a net quarterly loss of $23.9 billion and an annual loss for 2008 of $50.1 billion. The Bank of England starts purchasing long-term British government bonds in a volume of £75 billion.
12 March 2009	Profits of the German car maker BMW fall by 90%.
13 March 2009	The German government renews its guarantee pledge to the mortgage bank Hypo Real Estate, which has already been supported with €100 billion.
17 March 2009	The US government wants to force the insurer AIG to compensate the taxpayers for millions in bonuses to its employees.
18 March 2009	The financial crisis pushes the German HypoVereinsbank into the red. Its parent, the UniCredit Group, looks into applying for state support in the amount of up to €4 billion.

(cont.)

Appendix (Continued)

Market events	Date	Policy actions
BMW cuts production by another 40,000 cars.		The Fed begins purchasing long-term government bonds for $300 billion. The government intends to more than double its stake in Fannie Mae and Freddy Mac to $1,450 billion.
The dollar temporarily loses more than 3% against the euro.	19 March 2009	
The IMF considers a shrinking of the world economy by 1% in 2009 a possibility.		
UBS may have to write off another €1.5 billion due to raised risk premiums and CLO securities.	30 March 2009	
The IMF raises its forecast of depreciation losses on US-based securities from $2.2 billion to $2.7 billion. It publishes, for the first time, an estimate of total losses in the USA, Europe, and Japan in the amount of $4 trillion.	21 April 2009	
The GDP of Lithuania shrinks by 12.6% year-on-year in the first quarter of 2009.		
The German government revises its economic growth forecast for 2009 from −2.25% to −6%.	24 April 2009	
Estimate: US economic growth in the first quarter −6.1% year-on-year.		
Unemployment in the 27 EU member states rises to 20 million.	28 April 2009	
Japanese industrial production rises in March for the first time in six months.		

29 April 2009	US President Obama announces that US auto maker Chrysler has filed for Chapter 11 bankruptcy protection and will be acquired by Fiat.	The Fed leaves the key interest rate in a range of 0% to 0.25% and indicates a weakening of the recession.
	March figures in Japan show that the country is again in deflation.	
	The British 'Insolvency Service' reports that the number of insolvent citizens in England and Wales has reached a new high.	
	The biggest Japanese bank, Mitsubishi UFJ, corrects its profit forecast of ¥50 billion and now reports a balance sheet loss for 2009 of ¥256.9 billion (approx. $2.7 billion).	
30 April 2009	The European Commission forecasts a decline of economic grow in the eurozone by 4% in 2009.	
1 May 2009	Due to the old-car scrappage scheme the number of registered new cars in Germany rises by 19% over the previous year.	
	UBS reports a loss of CHF 2 billion for the first quarter of 2009.	
4 May 2009	The stress tests for banks conducted in the USA find shortfalls of $34 billion at Bank of America.	US President Obama announces plans to crack down on overseas tax shelters.
	Profits of the entertainment group Walt Disney fall by 46%.	
5 May 2009	GM reports losses of $6 billion for the first quarter of 2009.	

(cont.)

Appendix (Continued)

Market events	Date	Policy actions
Barclays Bank notes a strong rise in profits for the first quarter of 2009.	6 May 2009	
Car sales in the UK fall by 24% year-on-year in April.		
Wells Fargo must raise its reserves and intends to sell new stocks to the amount of $7.5 billion.		
Commerzbank reports additional losses.		
In the USA the decline in the number of jobs is lower, at 539,000, than in prior months.		
Oil prices rise to above $58 per barrel. This corresponds to a 10% rise over the preceding week.		
Warren Buffet's investment firm reports losses for the first time in eight years.	7 May 2009	US President Obama urges Congress to save $17 billion in 2010 by cutting programmes.
10 US banks fail to pass the stress tests initiated by the US government. According to the US Treasury, these banks must raise their reserves by a total of $75 billion, of which $33.9 billion is accounted for by Bank of America alone.		The ECB lowers its key interest rate from 1.25% to 1%.
US Bankcorp., Capital One, BB&T, and Keycorp announce plans for a capital increase amounting to a total of $6 billion, to increase repayments to the government rescue plan.	11 May 2009	The Bank of England leaves the key interest rate at 0.5% and announces that it will provide another £50 billion to British business from the Asset Purchase Programme.

Date		
	In China prices fall in April for the third consecutive month.	
	The CEO of GM says that the company's insolvency was probable.	
	French and Italian industrial production falls more in March than had been projected.	
12 May 2009	China's exports drop by 22.6% in April compared to the previous month. This is the sixth consecutive monthly decline.	The International Monetary Fund calls for stress tests for European banks like those done for US banks.
	The number of unemployed in the UK rose by 244,000 to 2.22 million in the first three months of 2009.	
	Spain's Prime Minister Zapatero announces economic recovery measures including subsidies for new car purchases.	
13 May 2009	Pessimistic forecasts of the Bank of England.	The German government passes a 'bad bank' bill.
	Growth of Chinese industrial production slows down.	
	Japan's current account surplus declined by 50.2% or $127 billion from the beginning of the year to the end of March.	
14 May 2009	US retail sales come in 0.4% lower in April than in March.	
	Sony reports its first annual loss in 14 years.	
	In the first quarter of 2009 the Spanish economy suffers the biggest decline in 50 years.	

(cont.)

Appendix (Continued)

Market events	Date	Policy actions
BT reports an annual loss of £134 million and announces a cut of 15,000 jobs, primarily in the UK. US producer prices rise faster than expected in April. Chrysler tells the bankruptcy court that it will close about one-quarter of its dealerships.		
Eurostat reports that the economies of the eurozone shrank by a total of 2.5% year-on-year in the first quarter.	15 May 2009	Due to its negative growth forecast, the Norwegian government plans to raise government spending.
According to a government forecast, economic output in Norway will fall by 1.9% in 2009.	17 May 2009	EBRD will invest a record sum of €7 billion to counter the recession.
GM reveals additional cost-saving measures, according to which up to 1,100 dealerships in the USA will be closed.		
Lloyds Banking Corporation cuts 625 jobs in the UK. New car sales in the USA fall to a record low in April. Japan's biggest bank, Mitsubishi UFJ, reports an annual loss due to write-downs on bad loans.	19 May 2009	
American Express will cut 4,000 jobs to save $800 million in 2009. This corresponds to about 6% of the company's worldwide workforce.		
The Japanese economy shrinks by 12.7% year-on-year in the first quarter of 2009. This is the fastest decline ever. Bank of America plans to raise capital by $13.5 billion. The Fed says that the US recession is gradually easing.	20 May 2009	

The US Treasury announces that American banks next year will repay $25 billion of the funds made available for equity by the government rescue fund.

The Mexican economy shrinks by 8.2% year-on-year in the first quarter of 2009.

21 May 2009

China plans the expansion of a programme subsidizing the purchase of new cars and household equipment.

The US Treasury grants another $7.5 billion in government aid to the financial group GMAC so that GMAC can grant loans to car buyers.

British Airways reports its biggest loss since its privatization in 1987.

22 May 2009

The Japanese central bank revises its economic forecast upwards.

UK industrial production declines by 1.9% in the first quarter of 2009 over the unrevised fourth quarter of 2008. This amounts to a year-on-year decline of 4.1%.

The Emirates Group, the Middle East's biggest airline, reports a 72% fall in profits for the 2008/9 accounting year.

25 May 2009

In Germany, the Ifo Business Climate index continues to improve.

26 May 2009

The economy of South Africa reports a recession for the first time since 1992.

Japanese exports show first signs of a recovery.

27 May 2009

The British pound jumps the mark of $1.60 for the first time since November.

The number of distressed US banks rises by 40% during the first three months of 2009 to a 15-year annual high.

(cont.)

Appendix (Continued)

Market events	Date	Policy actions
The US economy shrinks more slowly in the first quarter of 2009 than originally assumed by the Commerce Department.	29 May 2009	
GM files for Chapter 11 bankruptcy protection. This is the biggest bankruptcy of a manufacturer in US history.	1 June 2009	
According to Eurostat, unemployment in the eurozone rises in April to its highest level in almost ten years.	2 June 2009	
The recession spreads to Switzerland. Official figures confirm that the country's economy shrank by 0.8% in the first quarter of 2009 over the preceding quarter, in which GDP had already fallen by 0.3% over the preceding quarter.		
The stock price of Barclays Bank falls by 13.5% after one of the biggest investors from the Middle East sells $3.5 billion worth of stocks.		
The Australian economy grows by 0.4% in the first quarter of 2009 over the preceding quarter.	3 June 2009	
French unemployment rises to a two-year high.	4 June 2009	The Bank of England continues its programme of purchasing securities to a total of £125 billion.
The OECD reports that the recession of the world's biggest economies is slowing down.	8 June 2009	
The recession arrives in Brazil. The country's economy shrinks by 0.8% in the first quarter of 2009 over the preceding quarter.	9 June 2009	

9 June 2009	The IMF forecasts a faster recovery of the US economy than originally assumed.
12 June 2009	Latvia's prime minister announces that his government has saved the country from national bankruptcy.
16 June 2009	Chinese President Hu Jintao announces that China will grant loans totalling more than $10 billion to Russia and four Central Asian countries.
	The Bank of Japan reports that the state of the Japanese economy has not continued to worsen and leaves the key interest rate at 0.1%.
17 June 2009	American banks start repayments of government financial aid that they received from the Troubled Asset Relief Program (TARP).
	The US government announces extensive reforms of bank regulation to prevent future financial crises.
18 June 2009	The bankruptcy of three other banks is announced: Southern Community Bank, Cooperative Bank, and First National Bank of Anthony.
	UK Treasury Secretary Alistair Darling rejects fundamental structural reforms of financial institution regulation.
	The US Treasury defends its extensive reform recommendations for the banking system and asks Congress to pass these legal changes soon.
	The Swiss Financial Supervisory Authority considers emergency rules to break up distressed banks.
21 June 2009	India experiences deflation for the first time in 30 years.
	ECB President Trichet says that the governments that went deep into debt in their fight against the economic crisis ought not to take up additional loans.

(cont.)

Appendix (Continued)

Market events	Date	Policy actions
The World Bank forecasts economic growth of the developing countries at 1.2% this year, compared to 5.9% in 2008 and 8.1% in 2007.	22 June 2009	The Japanese government is willing to grant an emergency loan to Japan Airlines, the country's biggest airline.
	23 June 2009	Ministers of 18 countries support a plan that entails sanctions against countries that fail to take strict action against tax evasion.
The OECD announces that the international economy is beginning to bottom out from the worst post-war recession.	24 June 2009	
In France the number of jobless rises by 36,400 in May. Most affected are young jobseekers.	25 June 2009	
The American economy shrinks by an annualized 5.5% in the first quarter of 2009 over the preceding quarter.		
In June US consumer sentiment rises to its highest level since February 2008.	26 June 2009	The Chinese central bank repeats its demand for a new foreign reserve currency to replace the dollar.
Japanese industrial production rises in May by 5.9% from the preceding month. This is the third consecutive increase.	29 June 2009	
UK GDP declines by 2.4% in the first quarter of 2009 from the preceding quarter.	30 June 2009	
Prices in the eurozone fall compared to the preceding year for the first time since the introduction of the euro in 1999.		

(cont.)

Appendix (Continued)

Market events	Date	Policy actions
Deflation in Japan is stronger than ever before.	9 July 2009	A €2.8 billion Chinese government bond auction fails.
German exports grow by 0.3% in May over the preceding month.		
US car sales rise by 48% year-on-year in June thanks to subsidy programmes.		
Australian unemployment rises in June to a six-year high of 5.8%.		
British Airways reports a pre-tax loss of $245 million in the second quarter of 2009.		
Barclays reports profit growth of 8% year-on-year in the first half of 2009, driven primarily by investment banking.	10 July 2009	
Pre-tax profits of the HSBC Banking Group halved to $5 billion in the first half of 2009 compared to the first half of 2008.		
US consumption rises in June for the second consecutive month.	31 July 2009	
Despite a loss of £4 billion in the first half of 2009, stocks of the Lloyds Banking Group rise by 11%.	3 August 2009	
German exports rise by 7% in June over the preceding month.	5 August 2009	
In the USA, another 247,000 jobs are lost in July.		
Russian GDP shrinks by 10.9% year-on-year in the first quarter of 2009.	6 August 2009	The Bank of England decides to pump another £50 billion into the economy as part of its quantitative easing strategy.

The number of approved mortgages to British homeowners increases by 23% over the preceding month.	7 August 2009	
UK unemployment reaches its highest level since 1995.		
Japanese wholesale prices fall by 8.5% year-on-year in June.		
Industrial production in the eurozone declines in June.		
The Scandinavian airline SAS cuts another 1,000–1,500 jobs.		
The French and the German economies grow by 0.3% each in the second quarter of 2009 compared to the first quarter.	11 August 2009	The Bank of Japan remains pessimistic regarding economic growth.
The number of repossessed homes in the UK fell by 10% in the second quarter of 2009 over the first quarter.	12 August 2009	The Bank of England emphasizes that the British economy will need some time to recover from the financial crisis.
		New rules of the UK Financial Services Authority stipulate that salaries of bankers must be tied more closely to the long-term business development of the banks.
The Japanese economy grows by 0.9% in the second quarter of 2009 over the preceding quarter.	13 August 2009	
The South African economy shrinks in the second quarter for the third consecutive quarter.	14 August 2009	
The OECD reports that the economies of the member states stabilized in the last quarter.	17 August 2009	
British retail sales rise by 0.3% over the preceding month.	18 August 2009	China reduces its holdings of US government bonds by the biggest amount in nine years.
The number of US mortgages continues to rise.		

(*cont.*)

Appendix (Continued)

Market events	Date	Policy actions
Mexico's economy shrinks by 10.3% year-on-year in the first quarter or by 1.1% over the preceding quarter.	19 August 2009	Mervyn King, the Governor of the Bank of England, pleads for more financial support for British business, but his proposal is voted down.
Positive comments by Fed Chairman Ben Bernanke lead to price increases on international stock exchanges.		
Following negotiations, accusations of the US Justice Department against UBS are dropped.	20 August 2009	
The Purchasing Managers Index in the eurozone rises in June.	24 August 2009	
New home sales and consumer goods sales in the USA rise in July.	25 August 2009	The White House and the American Congress warn of a possible budget deficit of $2.6 trillion in 2009.
Unemployment in Japan climbs to 5.7% in July. The price level continues to decline.		
The airline Iberia reports losses of €165.4 million in the first half of 2009.		
The investment of Japanese industry fell by 23% between April and June.	28 August 2009	
Lloyds Banking Group rejects government funds, preferring instead to raise money through a rights issue.	30 August 2009	In Japan the conservative party, which had governed almost without interruption since 1955, is voted out. Winner is the Democratic Party of Japan.
Daimler Chairman Dieter Zetsche predicts that the sales crisis of the automobile industry will continue in 2010.		

3 September 2009	Jürgen Stark, member of the ECB Directorate, estimates that the losses of eurozone banks due to the financial crisis will amount to about $600 billion.
4 September 2009	Commerzbank head Martin Blessing warns that the self-regulation of banks will not work.
7 September 2009	Central banks demand stricter regulation of financial institutions. UBS raises its equity by CHF 16 billion with a successful capital increase. Barclay's recommends investors to sell 'rich, off-the-run' Greek government bonds, because the next administration is likely to issue more of them to fund the 2010 budget deficit. Off-the-run bonds are those of which there is a more recent issue of the same maturity in circulation.
8 September 2009	According to estimates by Goldman Sachs, the European Central Bank has made additional profits of about €1 billion from emergency loans during the crisis.
10 September 2009	The Bank of England maintains the bank rate at 0.5% and continues with its £175 billion Asset Purchase Programme. One year after the collapse of Lehman Brothers, the US banks still in operation report high profits again.
12 September 2009	Greece's main opposition party promises to boost public investment and increase wages faster than inflation to spur consumer confidence and revive growth if it wins the national elections on October 4.
14 September 2009	Fed Chairman Bernanke declares 'recession is very likely over'.
15 September 2009	Initial applications for unemployment compensation in the USA fall in September.

(cont.)

Appendix (Continued)

Market events	Date	Policy actions
Philadelphia Fed Index surprisingly strong in September. German producer prices rise marginally in August.	16 September 2009	British regulatory authorities want to oblige banks to present advance plans according to which potential insolvencies are to be processed.
The eurozone exhibits a monthly current account surplus for the first time in more than a year. Greek Economy and Finance Minister Ioannis Papathanasiou says that due to a contracting economy and shrinking revenues, the Greek budget deficit will increase to 6% of GDP.	17 September 2009	At the international financial summit the EU increases pressure on the USA. The Swiss National Bank sticks to its expansionary monetary policy.
Expiration of the Fed's MBS Purchase Program as well as mortgage lending is likely to lead to a renewed decline in US home sales. In Spain there are 3 million properties on the market that are not finding any buyers.	18 September 2009	Ireland pays €54 billion to five banks for property-related loans which have a face value of about €77 billion, as part of its rescue package. California's Attorney General wants to have rating agencies investigated. Peer Steinbrück, German Finance Minister, advocates uniform equity rules at the G-20 Meeting. The new Japanese government wants to support the yen as part of its economic policy. The SEC wants to prohibit flash orders and agrees to new transparency rules.

German exports fall markedly by a nominal 23.5% to €391.2 billion from January to June 2009. This corresponds to a year-on-year decline of 18.2%.

| 22 September 2009 | The IMF warns governments of enforcing excessively strict equity rules for banks in order not to risk the recovery of the security markets. |
| | Axel Weber, President of the German Bundesbank, says that the ECB should maintain its loose monetary policy. |

China forecasts about 13 million car sales for 2009.
The German construction industry reports a marked decline in orders in July.

| 23 September 2009 | |

In Germany a new, conservative-liberal government is elected.

| 24 September 2009 | |

In Portugal the socialist government is confirmed but loses its absolute majority.

| 25 September 2009 | |

In Germany the GfK Consumer Sentiment Index rises for the sixth consecutive month, moving above the zero mark for the first time since 2008.
France's biggest bank, BNP Paribas, issues new shares worth €4.3 billion in order to pay back the government bail-out it received.

| 27 September 2009 | The G-20 leaders fail to agree on uniform rules on limiting the bonuses of top managers. |

According to US government plans, the reserves of the Federal Deposit Insurance Corporation, which were depleted by the 95 bank collapses in the USA, are to be replenished by new injections of funds by the commercial banks.

(cont.)

Appendix (Continued)

Market events	Date	Policy actions
Moody's downgrades Lithuania's credit rating from A3 to Baa1.		
	28 September 2009	ECB President Trichet emphasizes the importance of a strong dollar for the stability of the world economy.
	29 September 2009	ECB President Trichet speaks out against a rapid exit strategy from the central bank's liquidity provision.
		The Board of Directors of the US Federal Deposit Insurance Corporation (FDIC) adopts a Notice of Proposed Rulemaking (NPR) that would require insured institutions to prepay their estimated quarterly risk-based assessments for the fourth quarter of 2009 and for all of 2010, 2011, and 2012.
	4 October 2009	George Papandreou is elected new Greek president.
	14 October 2009	The European Commission says that worsening budget deficits in the UK, Spain, Ireland, Greece, and Latvia pose a 'serious concern'.
Fitch cuts the rating for Greece to A– with a negative outlook.	22 October 2009	The new Greek government discloses that the 2009 budget deficit will be 12.7%.
The Dow Jones closes above 10,000 for the first time since 3 October 2008.		The US Federal Reserve Board issues a proposal for the incentive compensation policies of banking organizations.
		The Special Master for TARP Executive Compensation releases information on the top 25 most highly paid

executives at the seven firms that received exceptional TARP assistance (AIG, Citigroup, Bank of America, Chrysler, Chrysler Financial, GM, and GMAC).

29 October 2009	Moody's reduces the outlook on Portugal's Aa2 credit rating from stable to negative. The spread between 10-year German and Portuguese bonds widens to 57 basis points.
1 November 2009	CIT Group files for bankruptcy protection under Chapter 11 of the bankruptcy code. The US Government had purchased $2.3 billion of CIT preferred stock in December 2008 under the Troubled Asset Relief Program (TARP).
3 November 2009	The European Commission says that Greece would make little progress in reducing its shortfall, estimating a deficit of 12.2% in 2010 and 12.8% in 2011 on a 'no-policy-change' basis.
5 November 2009	The Acting Director of the Federal Housing Finance Agency submits a request for $15 billion from the US Treasury to cover Fannie Mae's deficit.
	Fannie Mae reports a net loss of $18.9 billion in the third quarter of 2009, compared with a loss of $14.8 billion in the second quarter of 2009. Fannie Mae has lost a total of $111 billion since September 2008, when the firm was placed under government conservatorship.
9 November 2009	The Federal Reserve Board announces that 9 of the 10 bank holding companies that were determined to need additional capital by the Supervisory Capital Assessment Program earlier this year have increased their capital sufficiently to meet or exceed their required capital buffers.
	GMAC has not raised enough capital to meet its required capital buffer.

(cont.)

Appendix (Continued)

Market events	Date	Policy actions
The difference in yield between 10-year Greek securities and benchmark German Bunds widens to 156 basis points, the highest value since 16 July.	16 November 2009	
	17 November 2009	Citing continued improvement in financial market conditions, the Federal Reserve Board approves a reduction in the maximum maturity of primary credit loans at the discount window for depository institutions to 28 days from 90 days, effective 14 January 2010.
EU forecasts on Greece for 2010 project the deficit at 12.2% of GDP and national debt rising to 124.9% of GDP.	20 November 2009	Greece promises to cut its budget deficit to 9.1% of GDP in 2010.
AIG announces that it has closed two transactions with the Federal Reserve Bank of New York. This agreement reduces the debt AIG owes the Federal Reserve Bank of New York by $25 billion in exchange for preferred equity interests in newly formed subsidiaries.	1 December 2009	
Bank of America announces that it will repurchase the entire $45 billion of cumulative preferred stock issued to the US Treasury under the Troubled Asset Relief Program (TARP) after the completion of a securities offering.	2 December 2009	
Standard & Poor's puts Greece's A− sovereign rating on negative watch.	7 December 2009	

8 December 2009	Fitch lowers Greek debt to BBB+ with a negative outlook. For the first time in 10 years a ratings agency has put Greece below the A investment grade.
	A two-day rally pushes yields on 10-year Greek bonds down to 5.31%.
	Moody's says that mounting sovereign debt may 'test the AAA boundaries' of the debt ratings of the USA and the UK.
9 December 2009	US Treasury Secretary Geithner announces that TARP will be extended to 3 October 2010.
	Standard & Poor's lowers the outlook from stable to negative on Spain's debt grade.
	The yield on 10-year Spanish government bonds rises 8 basis points to 3.83%.
10 December 2009	The extra yield investors demand on 10-year Greek bonds instead of similar-maturity German bonds widens by 21 basis points to 229 basis points. Credit default swaps on Greek government debt rise 15 basis points to 215.
11 December 2009	The US House of Representatives approves legislation that would create a Financial Stability Council to identify, overview, and regulate financial firms that pose systemic risk.
	The dollar advances to a two-month high against the euro as a bigger-than-forecast increases in retail sales and consumer sentiment indicate the US economic recovery may be gaining momentum.

(cont.)

Appendix (Continued)

Market events	Date	Policy actions
Ten-year Greek bonds decline and two-year notes slide for the seventh time in eight days. The euro rallies after Abu Dhabi pledges to bail out Dubai, easing concern that Europe's biggest banks will suffer write-downs on loans to the Gulf emirate. Citigroup announces that it has reached an agreement with the US government to repay the remaining $20 billion in TARP trust preferred securities issued to the US Treasury. Citi will issue $20.5 billion in capital and debt, and the US Treasury will sell up to $5 billion of the common stock it holds in a concurrent secondary offering. Wells Fargo announces that it will redeem the $25 billion of preferred stock issued to the US Treasury under TARP upon successful completion of a $10.4-billion common stock offering.	14 December 2009	Greek President Papandreou announces a 10% cut in social security spending in 2010. He says that he will abolish bonuses at state banks and slap a 90% tax on private bankers' bonuses. He also announces a drastic overhaul of the pension system in six months and a new tax system that will make the wealthier bear more of the burden.
The dollar climbs to a two-month high against the euro as a report shows US industrial output rose in November more than economists had forecast.	15 December 2009	
Standard & Poor's cuts Greece's rating by one notch to BBB– from A–.	16 December 2009	Greece sells €2 billion of floating-rate notes privately to banks. The Fed reiterates that it will keep its target rate at virtually zero for an 'extended period'.
The cost of insuring sovereign debt against default rises in Europe after Greece's downgrade by Standard &	17 December 2009	

	Poor's fuels the concern that countries with deteriorating public finances may struggle to fund their commitments.
	Credit-default swaps on Portugal's debt jump 6.5 basis points to 80. Those on Hungary's climb 13 basis points to 243, on Spain's 5 basis points to 98, and on Germany's 1 basis point to 23.
19 December 2009	Yield spreads between Greek and benchmark German 10-year Bunds widen to an average 272 basis points, the widest in more than 8 months.
22 December 2009	Moody's cuts Greek debt to A2 from A1 over soaring deficits. The spread between 10-year Greek and German Bunds tightens after the downgrade.
24 December 2009	The US Treasury Department announces the removal of caps on the amount of preferred stock that the Treasury may purchase in Fannie Mae and Freddie Mac to ensure that each firm maintains a positive net worth. Previously, such purchases had been capped at $200 billion for each firm.
30 December 2009	Germany's Finance Minister, Wolfgang Schäuble, rules out help for Greece.
31 December 2009	Iceland's parliament approves plans to repay £3.4 billion lost by savers in Britain and the Netherlands when the country's banking system collapsed.
6 January 2010	Fitch downgrades Iceland's sovereign debt to junk status.

(cont.)

Appendix (Continued)

Market events	Date	Policy actions
	7 January 2010	EU officials arrive in Athens to ask Greece for more specifics of its three-year plan to shore up its finances.
The Federal Reserve Board announces preliminary unaudited results indicating that the Reserve Banks transferred approximately $46.1 billion of their estimated 2009 net income of $52.1 billion to the US Treasury. This represents a $14.4 billion increase over the 2008 results. The increase was primarily due to increased earnings on securities holdings during 2009.	12 January 2010	
	14 January 2010	Greece unveils a stability programme stating it will aim to cut its budget deficit to 2.8% of GDP in 2012 from 12.7%.
	18 January 2010	Greek unions protest against the austerity plan, and announce strikes for February. The European Central Bank says the Estonian government must ensure that national statistics are collected independently before the country may be allowed to enter the eurozone.
	19 January 2010	The New York Fed extends credit to Maiden Lane III to purchase multi-sector collateralized debt obligations from certain counterparties of AIG Financial Products.
The euro weakens to a five-month low against the dollar.	21 January 2010	US President Obama backs ex-Fed chairman Paul Volcker's proposal to return to a separation of commercial and investment banks, arguing that the

Date		
	Eurozone industrial orders increase 1.6% from October.	former should be prohibited from owning or sponsoring hedge funds and private equity funds and from engaging in proprietary trading.
25 January 2010	Moody's says it may upgrade the rating outlooks for Hungary, Latvia, Lithuania, Estonia, and Montenegro from negative to stable by next July.	Bank of Japan policy-makers are prepared to consider expanding an emergency-loan programme for banks and increasing purchases of government debt should the recovery falter.
26 January 2010	The Ifo business confidence index for Germany rises to an 18-month high in January.	
28 January 2010	European executive and consumer sentiment rises to 95.7 from a revised 94.1 in December.	
29 January 2010		Iceland's President, Olafur R. Grimsson, blocks the UK and Dutch depositor bill and sends the legislation to a referendum.
1 February 2010	The Commercial Paper Funding Facility, Asset-Backed Commercial Paper Money, Market Mutual, Fund Liquidity Facility, Primary Dealer Credit Facility, and Term Securities Lending Facility programmes expire.	
2 February 2010	UK manufacturing activity increases in January at the fastest pace in 15 years. House prices have risen for sixth months.	Greek president Papandreou says that the government will extend a public-sector wage freeze to those earning less than 2,000 euros a month for 2010, excluding seniority pay hikes.

(cont.)

Appendix (Continued)

Market events	Date	Policy actions
	3 February 2010	The European Commission will issue recommendations for Greece to correct its excessive deficit and set a deadline for reducing it below 3%.
	4 February 2010	The ECB cautiously backs the Greek austerity plan. The Bank of England pauses its £200 billion bond-purchase programme.
Latvian economic output falls a preliminary 17.7% in the fourth quarter, the smallest decline of the year, though more than economists forecast.	9 February 2010	
Greek bond yields fall the most since the creation of the euro after media coverage on German Finance Minister Wolfgang Schäuble's alleged rescue plans for Greece.	10 February 2010	The Greek socialist government imposes a wage freeze for civil servants earning more than 2,000 euros a month and various cuts that will amount to a 2–3% drop in real wages. Greek public-sector employees union ADEDY calls a 24-hour nationwide strike to protest against the government's austerity measures.
Standard & Poor's lifts Estonia's outlook on its A– rating from negative to stable.	11 February 2010	A special European Union summit on the economy will make recommendations on Greece's recently submitted fiscal plan, which targets a 4% deficit reduction this year to 8.7% of GDP and a return to the EU's 3% cap by 2012.
Traders drive relative yields on Fannie Mae and Freddie Mac mortgage bonds to the lowest in 17 years, speculating that the cash the companies use to buy delinquent loans will be recycled back into the securities.	12 February 2010	The accord by leaders of the EU 27-nation bloc amounts to an implicit assurance to help Athens if it has problems refinancing debt in April and May.

French GDP increases 0.6% in the three months through December, from a revised 0.2% expansion in the third quarter.

Stock markets in Europe and Asia rise as earnings improve.

European Commissioner Rehn says Europe will put its member states under increased scrutiny after the Greek debacle.

15 February 2010

ECB President Trichet considers European government action on Greece sufficient.

The Greek government wants to delay any austerity measures until mid-March, when the EU and IMF review is complete.

Luxembourg Prime Minister Jean-Claude Juncker reiterates Europe's support for Greece.

Sources: ARD Deutschland, www.boerse.ard.de
Bank of England, www.bankofengland.co.uk
BBC online, www.bbc.co.uk
Bloomberg, www.bloomberg.com
European Economic Advisory Group at CESifo, *The EEAG Report on the European Economy 2009*, CESifo, Munich 2009
Federal Reserve Bank of St Louis, http://timeline.stlouisfed.org
Financial Times Online, www.ft.com
Finanznachrichten, www.finanznachrichten.de
Finanztreff, www.finanztreff.de
Frankfurter Allgemeine Zeitung Online, www.faz.net
New York Times Online, www.nytimes.com
Redaktion Tagesschau, www.tagesschau.de
Reuters Deutschland, http://de.reuters.com
Reuters UK, http://uk.reuters.com
The Global and Economic Financial Crisis: A Timeline, http://lauder.wharton.upenn.edu

SUBJECT INDEX

PERSON AND COMPANY INDEX

AUTHOR INDEX